Bertrand Russell : The Colours of Pacifism

Claudio Giulio Anta

Bertrand Russell
The Colours of Pacifism

PETER LANG
Lausanne – Berlin – Bruxelles – Chennai – New York – Oxford

Library of Congress Cataloging-in-Publication Control Number: 2023005556

Bibliographic information published by the **Deutsche Nationalbibliothek**.
The German National Library lists this publication in the German
National Bibliography; detailed bibliographic data is available
on the Internet at http://dnb.d-nb.de.

Cover design by Peter Lang Group AG

ISBN 9781636672533 (hardback)
ISBN 9781636672540 (ebook)
ISBN 9781636672557 (epub)
DOI 10.3726/b20668

© 2023 Peter Lang Group AG, Lausanne
Published by Peter Lang Publishing Inc., New York, USA
info@peterlang.com - www.peterlang.com

All rights reserved.
All parts of this publication are protected by copyright.
Any utilization outside the strict limits of the copyright law, without the permission of the
publisher, is forbidden and liable to prosecution.
This applies in particular to reproductions, translations, microfilming, and storage and
processing in electronic retrieval systems.

This publication has been peer reviewed.

To the memory of my dear Mother

Table of Contents

Chapter One: Ideas and Models of Modern Pacifism 1
    The Evolution of the Concept of Pacifism in the 19th and 20th Centuries 1
    Between Anthropologism, Internationalism, and Irrationalism 9
    The New Theorized European Order Between the World Wars 17
    Nonviolent Methods Towards the End of the Second Millennium 25

Chapter Two: Bertrand Russell Witness for Peace 35
    A Renaissance Intellectual of the 20th Century 35
    The Great War as Watershed of His Pacifist Commitment 46
    The Debate on the Russian Revolution Beyond the English Channel 57
    Between Scientific Psychology and the International Political Scenario 67
    British Neutrality and Collective Security in the 1930s 78

Chapter Three: Between Fear and Hope in the Atomic Age 91
    The Hypothesis of a Preventive Nuclear Conflict 91
    The Futility of War and the Need for a World Government 102
    The Disarmament Policy and Beyond 112
    From the Committee of 100 to the International War Crimes Tribunal 122
    A Pragmatic and Active Pacifism in Various Shades 133

Bibliography 143
Index 205

CHAPTER ONE

Ideas and Models of Modern Pacifism

The Evolution of the Concept of Pacifism in the 19th and 20th Centuries

The concept of pacifism refers to a doctrine, or even a set of ideas or attitudes, and their corresponding movements. At least two meanings denote all this: firstly, the condemnation of war as an appropriate means of resolving international disputes; secondly, the consideration of permanent – or perpetual – peace among states as a possible and desirable goal. Therefore, pacifism includes the sum of all endeavours and programmes for the realization of lasting or, if possible, perpetual peace among peoples who believe that this goal is of positive value and can be achieved in the foreseeable future; this is a broader definition, of course, which refers to movements in favour of the total abolition of war. Pacifism has existed in all higher cultures and in different historical epochs as a more or less distinct and vivid idea; indeed, in its broadest sense, it dates back to classical antiquity – for example, we can find invocations for peace in Xenophon and Isocrates – and in the religious conceptions of the main Biblical prophets and the first Evangelical Irenicism, which were handed down in certain Protestant sects such as the Quakers. This concept acquired authority in the theorizations of the "peace of submission", from the *Pax Romana* of the Augustan era to the *Pax Universalis* supported by Dante Alighieri in *De Monarchia* (1312–1313) as a function of the Byzantine Empire. In the 19th century, a period of relative peace in Europe and in the world was identified with the *Pax Britannica*, which lasted as long as the British Empire retained its dominant position.

For the purpose of this introduction, it is useful to recall some reflections drawn from authoritative contemporary intellectuals. In his *Profilo ideologico del '900*, the Italian philosopher Norberto Bobbio (1909–2004), Emeritus Professor of Political Philosophy at the University of Turin, wrote that in the 19th century there were two main and antithetic conceptions of war (and peace): "the positivist and evolutionist one", whereby the Industrial Revolution would transform military societies based on war "to the point that peace would be inevitable"; and "the romantic one", which, based on a dramatic and dialectic conception of history, considered war as "not only inevitable but also beneficial"[1]. However, as Bobbio pointed out, the end of the 19th century witnessed the emergence of antagonism between the great powers, which fought each other in order to conquer new colonies and markets. Thus "passive" and "fatalistic" pacifism – a sign of the positivistic age – gave way to "active" pacifism as a result of man's "intelligent and organised effort"[2]. Bobbio also noted that "active pacifism" could move in three directions depending on whether it acted on means, institutions or men. In the first case, he spoke of "instrumental pacifism", whose action was aimed at drastically limiting the instruments of war (doctrine and disarmament policy) or at replacing violent means with nonviolent ones (the theory of nonviolence, such as Gandhi's doctrine of *Satyagraha*). Instead, "institutional pacifism" directed its criticism at the institution of the state through a twofold analysis: the first referred to "juridical pacifism", which, through law enforcement, aimed to establish a universal state that would be able to resolve conflicts between sovereign countries; the second related to "social pacifism", according to which war was an event that depended on a certain notion of the state characterized by the class struggle between the bourgeoisie and the proletariat (in internal relationships), and by imperialist expansion (in external relationships), the remedy being a transition from a capitalist society to a socialist one. Finally, he outlined the concept of "finalist pacifism": peace could be achieved through an understanding of humans either from an ethical-religious standpoint or from a purely biological one. The real reason for war was to be found, respectively, in man's moral defects (Leo Tolstoy) or in the primitive impulses of human

---

1 See N. Bobbio, *Profilo ideologico del '900*, Milano, Garzanti, 1990, p. 117 (translation from the Italian by C.G. Anta).
2 Id., "Pacifismo", in *Dizionario di Politica*, edited by Norberto Bobbio, Nicola Matteucci, Gianfranco Pasquino, II ed., Torino, Utet, 1983, pp. 745–747 (for the quotation, see p. 746).

nature (Sigmund Freud): in this respect, Bobbio used the expressions "ethical-religious pacifism" and "scientific pacifism", respectively[3].

In the entry *Pacifism* published by the *Enciclopedia del Novecento* (*Encyclopedia of the Twentieth Century*) Mulford Quickert Sibley (1912–1989), Professor of Political Science at the University of Minnesota, underscored the typical 20th-century difference between "political pacifism" and "non-political pacifism"[4]. The former emphasized nonviolent political action, including parliamentary activity, and was called "pacifism of the transformation"; the latter argued that peace movements were not to engage directly in the renewal of political and social institutions. For this reason, it was befitting to limit the economic needs of the citizens in order to avoid this involvement, proposing that they live in communities separated from industrial and commercial centres, and urban life; in essence, non-political pacifism implied "an ethic of isolation and simplicity", as Sibley pointed out. For example, Tolstoy incorporated it in his thought; in fact, in the last period of his life, he became a pacifist-anarchist, focusing his attention on the values of simplicity, the necessity of hard manual labour, and a refusal to obey the state when it demanded tributes and compulsory military service.

We must also note the entry "Pacifism and Nonviolent Movements" published in *The New Encyclopædia Britannica* and written by Wilhelm Emil Mühlmann (1904–1988), Emeritus Professor of Sociology and Anthropology at the Rupert Charles University of Heidelberg. Mühlmann claimed that pacifism was based on three key points: the postulate of tolerance; religious and philosophical demands for the abandonment of violence; and programmes aimed at the improvement of relations between nations, limitation of armaments, moderation and rational discussion of conflicts, and the institution of neutral courts of arbitration. As a rule, the basis for such programmes lay in the conception of an ethical and harmonious human society. Mühlmann identified different conceptions of pacifism: firstly, an "integral pacifism" that condemned violence as a means of settling conflicts in any circumstances and rejected war unconditionally; secondly, a less severe "semi-pacifism" that permitted wars under certain conditions, for instance when they were "just", or were decidedly wars of "defence", or wars against "unbelievers" or "rebels"[5].

---

3   See N. Bobbio, *Il problema della guerra e le vie della pace*, Bologna, Il Mulino, 1984, pp. 75 ff.
4   See M.Q. Sibley, "Pacifismo", in *Enciclopedia del Novecento*, vol. V, Roma, Giovanni Treccani, 1980, pp. 35–47.
5   See W.E. Mühlmann, "Pacifism and Nonviolent Movements", in *The New Encyclopædia Britannica*, 15th edition, Chicago, Benton Foundation and Encyclopædia Britannica Inc., 1974–1984, vol. 13, pp. 845–853.

From this point of view, it is possible to examine the distinction between "absolute" and "non-absolute pacifism". The former expressed an uncompromising condemnation and rejection of violence; one of its most recent supporters was the American philosopher Michael Allen Fox, who argued that war was inconsistent with morality: "Even military action aimed at protecting people against acute and systematic human-rights violations [could] not be justified"[6]. Along these lines, the US scholar and peace activist David Cortright used the concept of "realistic pacifism" to claim the essential and vital need to avoid war in the nuclear age, although in other kinds of conflicts "the use of force, constrained by rigorous ethical standards, [might] be necessary at times for self-defense and the protection of the innocent"[7]. This reflection adequately introduces us to the concept of "non-absolute pacifism", also called "contingent pacifism" or "just war pacifism"[8], for it accepted the permissibility or even the necessity of war in some cases, and rejected it in others. For example, in his famous work *A Theory of Justice* (1971), John Rawls (1921–2002) asserted that "the possibility of a just war [was] conceded", while also considering the danger of nuclear weapons but "not under present circumstances"[9].

With reference to the distinction between absolute and contingent pacifism, we can note the difference between "particular" and "universal pacifism". Particular pacifists articulated their position as merely personal and did not condemn the war system *a priori*; in contrast, universal pacifists condemned war unconditionally. Eric Reitan, Professor of Philosophy at Oklahoma State University, supported a sort of "personal pacifism" that need not be universally applied; he defined it as "a purely personal commitment to nonviolence, one that is not adopted on the basis of a perceived general obligation to refrain from violence and [...] not intended to express the belief that all persons ought to oppose violence under every circumstance"[10]. In more recent times, some intellectuals – Johan Galtung and David

---

6 See M.A. Fox, *Understanding Peace: A Comprehensive Introduction*, New York-London, Routledge, 2014, p. 126.
7 See D. Cortright, *Peace: A History of Movements and Ideas*, Cambridge, Cambridge University Press, 2008, p. 334.
8 The US philosophers James Sterba and Larry May used the just war theory to develop the concept of "contingent pacifism" or "just war pacifism". In principle, just war pacifism meant that modern conflicts were not fought according to the main criteria of the just war theory (*jus ad bellum* and *jus in bello*) because they made use, for example, of aerial bombardment that did not distinguish between civilians and military. See J. Sterba, *Justice for Here and Now*, Cambridge, Cambridge University Press, 1998; L. May, *Contingent Pacifism: Revisiting Just War Theory*, Oxford, Oxford University Press, 2015.
9 See J. Rawls, *A Theory of Justice*, Cambridge, Harvard University Press, 1971, p. 382.
10 See E. Reitan, "Personally Committed to Nonviolence: Towards a Vindication of Personal Pacifism", in *The Acorn*, 2000, vol. 10, no. 2, pp. 30–41 (for the quotation, see p. 30).

Boersma among them – have especially emphasized the distinction between "negative" and "positive" pacifism: the former described the mere absence of violence or war, the latter involved the construction and consolidation of harmonious relations between states[11]. This difference had already been underlined by Baruch Spinoza (1632–1677), who, in his *A Political Treatise* (1677), identified peace through the presence of justice, law and order: "Peace is not just the absence of war, but a virtue which comes from strength of mind"[12].

The reflections of Bobbio, Sibley, Mühlmann, Fox, Cortright, Rawls, Reitan, Galtung, and Boersma give us fundamental insights to understand the evolution of modern pacifism. The latter was born in the form of a philosophical-legal doctrine at the beginning of the 18th century with the famous work of Charles-Irénée Castel, abbot of Saint-Pierre (1658–1743), *Projet pour rendre la paix perpétuelle en Europe* (*Project for Making Peace Perpetual in Europe*, 1713); he published his book in Cologne while he was engaged in the Congress of Utrecht as the secretary of Cardinal Melchior de Polignac. In his work, he emphasised that only lasting peace between European states would represent the necessary condition to ensure the welfare and progress of France and the Old Continent. Saint-Pierre was among the most farsighted supporters of the ideal of perpetual peace perceived as fundamental for the coexistence of the European peoples and of a renewed *jus gentium*. He described the relationships between European sovereigns according to natural-law models; as ordained by nature to rule, princes enjoyed absolute sovereignty and were competing against each other to satisfy their aspirations. Therefore, states were in a condition of perpetual struggle: neither treaties nor the balance of the European powers would be enough to preserve the continent from the misfortunes of war, he wrote. A free contract among equal countries was to be approved in order to overcome this natural conflict, possibly signed by all European sovereigns to create a "permanent society" that could enforce what was promised, namely the laws imposed by the rulers with their treaties[13]. Despite its limitations, Saint-Pierre's work was of primary importance for the history of European unity. In fact, for the first time in the philosophical-legal and political sphere, it theorized the existence of a structural connection between the value of "perpetual peace" and the

---

11   See J. Galtung, "Violence, Peace, and Peace Research", in *The Journal of Peace Research*, 1969, vol. 6, no. 3, pp. 167–191; D. Boersma, "Positive and Negative Peace", in A. Fiala (ed.), *The Routledge Handbook of Pacifism and Nonviolence*, New York, Routledge, 2017, chapter 10.

12   See B. Spinoza, *A Political Treatise* (1677), in Id., *Complete Works*, edited by Michael L. Morgan, Indianapolis-Cambridge, Hackett Publishing Company, 2002, p. 699. With the formula *Pax enim non belli privatio*, Spinoza marked a fundamental paradigm shift in political theory.

13   See C.I. Saint-Pierre (Castel de), *Projet pour rendre la paix perpétuelle en Europe*, 2 vols., Utrecht, Schouten, 1713.

European federative pact, and at the same time, between the rules governing the "permanent society" – deriving from this pact – and the reform of international law. Hence the need to replace traditional diplomacy and the state of armed peace with a permanent seat of arbitration for the definitive removal of the state of war.

The discourse on "perpetual peace" was revived through a federal interpretation and examined in depth from the philosophical-legal point of view by Immanuel Kant (1724–1804). The philosopher drew inspiration from the Peace of Basel signed by Prussia and revolutionary France for his most famous political text, *Zum ewigen Frieden* (*Perpetual Peace*, 1795). In the footsteps of the abbot of Saint-Pierre, Kant transferred the model of the state of nature from the interpersonal level to the level of relations between states; in the condition of "wild freedom", men lived in perpetual antagonism generated by their "unsocial sociability". This contradictory trait would lead them to unite by reaching a condition of legality represented by the rule of law; however, legal certainty within the single state did not keep mankind safe from destructive conflicts between states. Faced with such a scenario, Kant offered the following solution: as the transition to civilian constitution allowed for the regulation and the resolution of inter-individual conflicts and guaranteed civil peace even through coercion, so a legal constitution among states decided their disputes, ensuring perpetual peace through a universal cosmopolitan order, namely a situation diametrically opposed to the Hobbesian state of nature (*bellum omnium contra omnes*). Kant offered a series of precepts concerning the preconditions for the establishment of peace such as the disappearance of standing armies and good faith in the observance of treaties. The central part of his essay was devoted to three "definitive articles" proposed as the basis of the future legal community with a supranational and universal character. Firstly, "the civil constitution of each state shall be republican"; in this respect, he did not oppose the term "republican" to "monarchical" but to "despotic" – in fact, according to Kant's political lexicon, republics were also monarchies. Secondly, "the law of nations shall be founded on a federation of free states". Thirdly, "the rights of men, as citizens of the world, shall be limited to the conditions of universal hospitality"[14].

Criticising the natural-law model in his *Grundlinien der Philosophie des Rechts* (*Elements of the Philosophy of Right*, 1821), Georg Wilhelm Friedrich Hegel (1770–1831) argued that states were not a mere sum of individuals; more precisely, "States [were] not private persons but completely independent totalities in themselves", so that "the relations between them [were] not the same as purely moral relations

---

14   See I. Kant, *Perpetual Peace: A Philosophical Essay* (1795), translated with introduction and notes by Mary Campbell Smith, with a preface by Robert Latta, London, Swan Sonnenschein & Co., 1903, pp. 120 ff.

or relations of private right"[15]. Therefore, war was an inevitable phenomenon because, among sovereign subjects such as states, it was impossible to imagine any impartial authority capable of resolving conflicts. According to Hegel, however, war had also a moral value; as a matter of fact, through it "the moral health of peoples [was] preserved"[16]. While supporting the inevitability and ethicality of such a dramatic event, Hegel did not exclude that interstate relations could be regulated from a legal point of view. He had already clarified this issue in the *Enzyklopädie der philosophischen Wissenschaften im Grundrisse* (*Encyclopaedia of the Philosophical Sciences*, 1817): if, on the one hand, the exclusive sovereignty of states caused a potential condition of war, on the other hand, peace was necessary for their mutual recognition; hence the need to establish an international law in order to ensure a peaceful situation among people[17]. In short, despite the temporary inevitability of war, Hegel found a solution to international disputes.

In the 19th century, particular projects linked to individual figures were gradually replaced by newly established peace associations. Firstly, these had a religious character; examples are offered by the New York Peace Society founded by the Presbyterian David Low Dodge (1815), the American Peace Society created by William Ladd (1828) and the Society of Peace set up by Count Jean-Jacques of Sellon in Geneva (1830). Secondly, the peace associations drew inspiration from the economic doctrine of free trade, of which Richard Cobden (1804–1865) was one of the leading exponents; they organised the first international conferences for peace (London, 1843; Brussels, 1848; Paris, 1849). It was during the Peace Congress of Paris, held on Cobden's initiative, that Victor Hugo (1802–1885) delivered one of his most significant speeches, which can be regarded as "the pinnacle of French pacifist literature"[18]. On 21 August 1849, Hugo supported a form of universal peace of a religious nature: "The law which rules the world cannot be different from the law of God [...] which is not war, [but] peace"[19]. Moreover, he

---

15 See G.W.F. Hegel, *Elements of the Philosophy of Right* (1821), edited by Allen Wood and translated by Barry Nisbet, Cambridge, Cambridge University Press, 1991, p. 366.

16 Id., *Natural Law: The Scientific Ways of Treating Natural Law, Its Place in Moral Philosophy, and Its Relation to the Positive Sciences of Law* (1802–1803), translated by T.M. Knox with a foreword by John R. Silber, Philadelphia, University of Pennsylvania Press, 1975, pp. 53 ff.

17 Id., *Encyclopedia of the Philosophical Sciences in Outline and Critical Writings* (1817), edited by Ernst Behler and translated by Steven A. Taubeneck, New York, Continuum Publishing Company, 1990.

18 See T. Ruyssen, *Les sources doctrinales de l'internationalisme*, 3 vols., Paris, Puf, 1961, vol. III, p. 399 (translation from the French by C.G. Anta).

19 See V. Hugo, "Discours d'ouverture du Congrès de la Paix – 21 août 1849", in Id., *Œuvres complètes de Victor Hugo Actes et Paroles, I, Avant l'exil*, Paris, Hetzel-Quantin, 1882, pp. 475–486 (translation from the French by C.G. Anta).

explicitly used the expression "United States of Europe"[20]; this idea represented a peaceful alternative to despotic regimes and was identified in a Europe of Peoples in opposition to a Europe of Kings. Hugo was one of the forerunners of this project, together with Carlo Cattaneo (1801–1869) and Giuseppe Mazzini (1805–1872)[21]. Thirdly, peace organisations were inspired by democratic and radical groups seeking to promote peace through the triumph of the principle of nationality, the dissolution of the old empires, and the establishment of governments based on popular sovereignty. Soon after the 1848 Revolution had generated a different policy framework from that of the Restoration, Mazzini proposed his political programme in contrast to the *Realpolitik* of the self-styled Concert of Europe formulated by Napoleon III, Cavour and Bismarck; it rallied democratic and revolutionary forces from various countries to liberate the oppressed nationalities and contribute to the establishment of a European confederation[22]. From this perspective, the Geneva Congress (1867) was organized by the International League of Permanent Peace of Frederick Passy, with the participation of Giuseppe Garibaldi; subsequently, the congresses of Bern (1868) and Lausanne (1869) were organized.

On the initiative of Tsar Nicholas II of Russia, Russian Foreign Minister Michail Nikolayevich Muravyov urged European governments to find concrete measures to reduce armaments; in 1899, an international conference attended by representatives of 26 states was held in The Hague with the aim of achieving "a real and lasting peace, and above all, of limiting the progressive development of existing armaments". The participating states did not reach an agreement on disarmament; however, they signed three conventions, two of which concerned the

---

20 Hugo was not the first author to advance the idea of the unity of the Old Continent in France. On the eve of the Congress of Vienna, Claude Henri de Saint-Simon (1760–1825) and Augustin Thierry (1795–1856) published in Paris the book *On the Reorganization of European Society*; they proposed to regenerate political life after the collapse of the Napoleonic empire through a project for the organization of the United States of Europe based on people's need and not on dynastic purposes. See C.-H. Saint-Simon (de), A. Thierry, *De la réorganisation de la société européenne* (1814), Lausanne, Centre de recherches européennes, 1967.
21 From April 1834, Mazzini appealed to Swiss patriots during his exile in Bern; he argued that a "Young Europe of Peoples" would prevail over the "Old Europe of Kings". From this perspective, he urged individual nations to fraternize so that the construction of a European confederation would represent the crowning of their process of democratic emancipation. See G. Mazzini, "Appello ai patrioti svizzeri", in M. Scioscioli, M. Billi, G. Torlontano (eds.), *Europeismo repubblicano*, Prefazione di Giovanni Spadolini, Roma, Archivio trimestrale, 1984, p. 9.
22 Mazzini shared these reflections in an article published in *L'Italia del popolo* on 15 June 1848. In this regard, see A. Colombo, "Il federalismo europeo in tre tempi", in G. Angelini, A. Colombo, V.P. Gastaldi, *Poteri e libertà. Autonomie e federalismo nel pensiero politico democratico italiano*, Milano, FrancoAngeli, 2001, pp. 131–153 (see p. 133).

regulation of land and sea war, and the third – and most important – provided for the peaceful resolution of international disputes. In this regard, the Permanent Court of Arbitration based in The Hague was created, namely an international organization that encouraged the resolution of disputes involving states, intergovernmental organizations and private parties by assisting in the establishment of arbitration tribunals. In 1907, a second conference took place in The Hague with representatives from 44 states – this time there were also Latin American states. Despite the failure of the proposals to limit armaments, on this occasion 13 conventions were signed, including one on the Limitation of the Employment of Force for Recovery of Contract Debts and the Opening of Hostilities[23].

Between Anthropologism, Internationalism, and Irrationalism

War was also considered intrinsic to the human condition; its anthropological analysis was inspired by Charles Darwin's revolutionary ideas. In his *On the Origin of Species* (1859), Darwin developed an evolutionary theory characterized by three main peculiarities: the "natural selection" of the best and most adaptable species, made on the basis of innumerable microvariations accumulated by nature over millions of years; the "struggle for existence", namely the spring capable of activating the mechanism of natural selection and, at the same time, its environmental context; the drawing of a "tree" of the species that visually rendered the concept of their infinite biological ramifications from a single infinitely distant root. Darwinian theories determined an epochal revolution not only in the scientific field but also in the cultural sphere. In fact, the struggle for existence could be used by those who claimed their racial superiority, thus justifying their aggressiveness. An example is offered by the French diplomat Arthur de Gobineau (1816–1882), who enunciated the superiority of the white man and, in particular, the purity of the Aryan race; his *Essai sur l'inégalité des races humaines* (*An Essay on the*

---

23 Regarding the two Hague Conferences, see T.J. Lawrence, *International Problems and Hague Conferences*, London, Dent & Co., 1908; P.A. Higgins, *The Hague Peace Conferences and other International Conferences Concerning the Laws and Usages of War*, Cambridge, University Press, 1909; J.H. Choate, *The Two Hague Conferences*, Princeton-London-Oxford, Princeton University Press-Frowde-Oxford University Press, 1913; W. Schucking, *The International Union of the Hague Conferences*, translated from the German by Charles G. Fenwik, Oxford, Clarendon Press, 1918; W.I. Hull, *The Two Hague Conferences and Their Contributions to International Law*, New York, Kraus, 1970.

Inequality of the Human Races, 1853–1855)[24] represented the first full-bodied document of doctrinal legitimation of European imperialism. In a forward-looking way, Darwin outlined not only the incessant struggle between animal and plant species but also the aggressiveness that emerged within the same species; indeed, in this case, the behaviours were extremely violent. He believed that the struggle for survival was particularly hard among individuals of the same species, for they frequented the same places, required the same food, and were exposed to the same dangers. In the third chapter of *On The Origin of Species*, "Struggle for Existence", he wrote: "As species of the same genus have usually, though by no means invariably, some similarity in habits and constitution, and always in structure, the struggle will generally be more severe between species of the same genus, when they come into competition with each other, than between species of distinct genera"[25].

In the mid-19th century, pacifism distinguished itself from internationalism, which proclaimed the unity of supranational individuals belonging to the same social group, class or party in order to strengthen solidarity and cooperation among peoples by not always peaceful means. An example was offered by the proletarian internationalism inspired by the solidarity of the working classes, which considered the overthrow of class division dictated by capitalist society as a necessary condition to foil national antagonisms. Moreover, pacifism was antithetical to imperialism as a concept interpreted based on the "reason of state" doctrine, with particular reference to the German doctrine of the power-state; it highlighted the primacy of foreign politics over domestic politics, which was rather a distinguishing feature of internationalism. While not excluding peace *a priori*, imperialism pursued it through the political, economic and military hegemony of the stronger countries over the weaker ones; from this perspective, it developed as a kind of new colonialism between 1870 and 1914. Finally, pacifism was the flip side of bellicism, represented by the political position of those states willing to resolve international disputes through armed conflicts; bellicism was a doctrine often inspired by the irrational thought that exalted war as a factor of moral or social progress, especially from the late 19th to the early 20th century.

Within the various socialist theories, war was considered not so much as a product of a particular type of political regime as a particular form of production, namely the capitalist one. Karl Marx (1818–1883) and Friedrich Engels (1820–1895) formulated their war theory; it was based essentially on its structural

---

24 See A. Goubineau (de), *Essai sur l'inégalité des races humaines*, Paris, Firmin-Didot frères & Rumpler, 1853–1855.
25 See C. Darwin, *On the Origin of Species by Means of Natural Selection, or the Preservation of Favoured Races in the Struggle for Life*, London, John Murray, 1859, p. 76.

causes, which were inherent in the nature of social relations. Only by abolishing the struggle between the working class and the capitalist class would conflicts be stopped, both within countries and internationally. In fact, wars were none other than a direct result of the antagonisms between the bourgeoisies of the various countries that were competing for control of markets, hoarding of resources and domination over other states. Moreover, in the essay *Die deutsche Ideologie* (*The German Ideology*, 1845–1846), the internationalist thought of the two German intellectuals emerged when they wrote that "the relations of different nations among themselves depend upon the extent to which each has developed its productive forces, the division of labour and internal intercourse"[26]. Furthermore, since industrial growth occurred unevenly in different countries, international relations were necessarily based on a relationship of inequality. Marx entrusted an ambitious mission to the International Working Men's Association – better known as the First International – founded in London in 1864; it was outlined in the last lines of his inaugural address: "The working classes [have] the duty to master themselves the mysteries of international politics; to watch the diplomatic acts of their respective governments; to counteract them, if necessary, by all means in their power [...] and to vindicate the simple laws or morals and justice, which ought to govern the relations of private individuals, as the rules paramount of the intercourse of nations. The fight for such a foreign policy forms part of the general struggle for the emancipation of working classes"[27].

The First International argued in one of its clearest stances on the problems of war and peace in a collective address adopted at the Geneva Peace Congress on 9–12 September 1867. On this occasion, it asserted that "war weighs chiefly on the working class, in that it not only deprives it of the means of existence, but also constrains it to shed the workers' blood"; furthermore, "peace, first condition of general well-being, needs in its turn to be consolidated by a new order of things that will no longer know in society two classes, the one of which is exploited by the other"[28]. This ideological approach constituted not only the basis on which the labour movement initially oriented its action despite various contradictions, but also the reference point for the subsequent development of Marx and Engels's thoughts on the causes of war, namely Lenin's theory of imperialism. This involved a review

---

26 See K. Marx, F. Engels, *The German Ideology – Part One* (1845–1846), edited and with an introduction by Christopher John Arthur, New Work, International Publisher, 1977, p. 43.
27 See K. Marx, "Inaugural Address of the International Working Men's Association", in Id., *The First International and After: Political Writings*, edited and with an introduction by David Fernbach, London-Harmondsworth, Penguin Books with New Left Review, 1974, pp. 73–81.
28 See G.D.H. Cole, *A History of Socialist Thought*, 4 vols., London-New York, MacMillan-St. Martin's Press, 1953–1968, vol. II, *Socialist Thought: Marxism and Anarchism 1850–1890*, p. 115.

of the internationalist strategy, which manifested itself mainly through the total aversion to war generated by the system of bourgeois states. Faced with a massacre that was likely to involve the proletariat, the workers' cause – ideally united by a common feeling of solidarity – could be pursued through strong support for peace; therefore, working classes around the world would have to work jointly to achieve this aim. The outbreak of the First World War caused the failure of internationalism. The affirmation of national solidarity over class solidarity proved that a "foreign policy" of the working class could not be identified solely through the fight against war. Internationalism did not determine a limitation of sovereignty within the system of nation-states because it conceived the nation-state as the highest form of political organisation. This situation generated the collapse of the Second International (1914), the alignment of most socialist parties to the interventionist choices of their respective countries in the name of nations' "sacred union" and defence of the motherland.

The diffusion of the capitalist model strongly influenced relations among states between the 19th and the 20th century; the growing economic and social interdependence led industrialized countries to seek new markets. The most relevant consequence of this phenomenon was represented by the advancement of imperialism; this was analysed from the early 20th century by the English economist John Atkinson Hobson (1858–1940). In his essay *Imperialism* (1902), he confuted the thesis that wars were generated by man's aggressive natural tendencies; in short, they were not the product of "blind passions of races or of mixed folly and ambition of politicians"[29]. Instead, he argued that wars were caused by the most economically developed countries, which sought new investment opportunities outside the national borders after reaching the saturation threshold of their profits. In light of these considerations, the foreign policy of Great Britain – which inspired Hobson's work – was primarily embodied in "a struggle for profitable markets"; this also concerned France, Germany, the United States and, more generally, all those countries in which "modern capitalism [had] placed large surplus savings in the hands of a plutocracy or of a thrifty middle-class"[30].

Vladimir Ilyich Lenin (1870–1924) described this phenomenon in his famous work *Imperializm, kak novejsij etap kapitalizma* (*Imperialism, the Highest Stage of Capitalism*, 1916) within a different historical context, namely the Russian Revolution. In his view, the system of bourgeois states had involved the proletariat in the world war because it was unable to resolve its contradictions without resorting to armed conflict. Lenin's analysis did not differ radically from Hobson's;

---

29 See J.A. Hobson, *Imperialism: A Study*, New York, James Pott & Company, 1902, p. 52.
30 Ibid., pp. 60–61.

his thought was innovative because he identified imperialism with "the highest stage of capitalism". More precisely, imperialism emerged "at a definite and very high stage of its development", namely "when the features of the epoch of transition from capitalism to a higher social and economic system had taken shape and revealed themselves in all spheres"[31]. At the end of this evolution, imperialism was "moribund capitalism, capitalism in transition to socialism"[32]; it could only be overcome in a violent way. According to this interpretation of history, summarized by the theories of the imperialist phase of capitalism, international peace could not be achieved except through the elimination of capitalism. Already two years before the formulation of Lenin's theories, the Manifesto adopted by the Zimmerwald International Conference of the Socialist Parties on 5–8 September 1915 had explicitly stated that war was "the product of imperialism"; it represented the attempt on the part of the capitalist classes of every nation to "feed their greed for profit by the exploitation of human labour and of the natural resources of the entire globe"[33]. This view was confirmed at the following Kienthal Conference held in April 1916, which reaffirmed that "the modern development of bourgeois property relations gave rise to imperialist antagonism. The present World War is one of the consequences of these antagonisms in the interest of which unsolved national problems, dynastic aspirations, and all the historical relics of feudalism are being utilized"[34].

The affirmation of imperialist policy was one of the most debated topics within the *Sozialdemokratische Partei Deutschlands* (*Social Democratic Party of Germany*, SPD); it is sufficient to remember the theses formulated by Karl Liebknecht (1871–1919) in *Militarismus und Antimilitarismus* (*Militarism and Anti-militarism*, 1907)[35]. On 2 December 1914, Liebknecht was the only representative of the Social

---

31 See V.I. Lenin, *Imperialism, the Highest Stage of Capitalism* (1916), Chippendale, Resistance Books, 1999, p. 91.

32 Ibid., p. 125.

33 In the Manifesto written by Leo Trotsky at the Zimmerwald Conference, there was a declaration against the "sacred union" and the "sacred egoism" of nations, and conversely in favour of "freedom of the peoples". See H. Lademacher (hrsg.), *Die Zimmerwalder Bewegung. Protokolle und Korrespondenz*, Paris, The Hague, 1967; G. Arfé, *Storia del socialismo italiano*, Torino, Einaudi, 1965, p. 226.

34 "The Attitude of the Proletariat Toward the Question of Peace (Resolution of the Kienthal Conference)", in O. Hess Gankin, H.H. Fisher, *The Bolsheviks and the World War. The Origins of the Third International*, Stanford, Stanford University Press, 1940, pp. 421 ff. (for the quotation, see p. 421).

35 See K. Liebknecht, *Militarismus und Antimilitarismus. Unter besonderer Berücksichtigung der internationalen Jugendbewegung*, München, Kommunistische Partei Deutschlands, 1907. On Liebknecht, see M. Adler, *Karl Liebknecht und Rosa Luxemburg*, Wien, Wiener Volksbuchhandlung

Democratic Party who voted against the renewal of war credits in the Reichstag. At the outbreak of the First World War, he hoped for the awakening of the Socialist International; in this view, the peace movements in all belligerent countries had to be simultaneously strengthened – the only way of calling a "halt to the bloody slaughter". However, only the international solidarity of the working class could create the conditions to achieve secure and lasting peace. Therefore, as Liebknecht pointed out, it was the task of the proletariat "to carry out common socialist work in every country for peace"[36]. He claimed that the armed conflict had not broken out to advance the interests of the people; instead, it represented "an imperialist war to dominate the capitalist world market" hatched by the "pro-war forces" of the Central Powers in "the obscurity of semi-absolutism and secret diplomacy". As Liebknecht pithily asserted, it was a "Bonapartist venture to demoralize and destroy the rising workers' movement"[37]. Referring to the concept of Bonapartism, he dissociated himself even more from the expansionist policy of the Wilhelmine Empire because it aimed at enhancing the prestige and power of the ruling classes to the detriment of internal adversaries, first and foremost the proletariat, making their claims appear as factors in weakening the state.

The main ideas of pacifism were seriously put to the test by irrationalism, which exalted war as an example of social progress and moral integrity. Irrationalism was not only the expression of a crisis of values but also the favourite ground of those who accepted reality without having to worry about explaining it. This supine attitude spurred a mystical exaltation of war and therefore absolute obedience to the omnipotence of the state; man was not to understand, judge or criticise but to obey because the purposes of history were inscrutable. Given this preliminary remark, it was not difficult to recognize the warning signs of the birth of a culture that in some countries, such as Germany and Italy, would show the triumph of violence. If the origins of this cultural crisis could be traced back to Social Darwinism, Friedrich

---

Ig. Brand & C., 1919; H. Schumann, *Karl Liebknecht. Ein unpolitisches Bild seiner Persönlichkeit*, Dresden, Reiszner, 1919; K. Meyer, *Karl Liebknecht: Man without a Country*, Washington, Public Affairs Press, 1957; W. Kerff, *Karl Liebknecht: 1914–1916. Fragment einer Biographie*, Berlin, Dietz Verlag, 1967; W. Bartel, *Karl Liebknecht*, Leipzig, VEB Bibiliographisches Institut, 1971; H. Wohlgemuth, *Karl Liebknecht. Eine Biographie*, Berlin, Dietz Verlag, 1973; Id., *Karl Liebknecht. Stationen seines Lebens*, Berlin, VEB Deutscher Verlag der Wissenschaften, 1977; H. Trotnow, *Karl Liebknecht; eine politische Biographie*, Köln, Kiepenheuer & Witsch, 1980; A. Laschitza, *Karl Liebknecht. Eine Biographie in Dokumenten*, Berlin, Dietz Verlag, 1982; O.K. Flechtheim, *Karl Liebknecht zur Einführung*, Hamburg, Junius, 1985.

36 See K. Liebknecht, "Il risveglio dell'Internazionale socialista", in *Coenobium*, 1914, vol. VIII, no. 11–12, pp. 87–88, translation from the Italian by C.G. Anta (for the citation, see p. 88).

37 Ibid., p. 87.

Nietzsche (1844–1900) was the author who best embodied the values – or rather the *dis*values. Nietzsche revalued man and his "will to live", denying the values of positivistic civilisation and outlining the concept of the Dionysian that was contrary to metaphysics, theology, the social system and the triviality of everyday life. It followed the nihilistic vision contained in *Menschliches, Allzumenschliches* (*Human, All Too Human*, 1878), which overturned the prospects of the bourgeois world and the myth of human "redemption" described in *Jenseits von Gut und Böse* (*Beyond Good and Evil*, 1886) with the figure of the Superman solely conditioned by his Will to Power[38]. In *Morgenröte – Gedanken über die moralischen Vorurteile* (*The Dawn of Day: Thoughts on the Prejudices of Morality*, 1881), Nietzsche foretold an era of absolute anarchy for men: "Whatever may be the influence in high politics of utilitarianism and the vanity of individuals and nations, the sharpest spur which urges them onwards is their need for the feeling of power – a need which rises not only in the souls of princes and rulers, but also gushes forth from time to time from inexhaustible sources in the people. The time comes again and again when masses are ready to stake their lives and their fortunes, their consciences and their virtue, in order that they may secure that highest of all enjoyments and rule as a victorious, tyrannical, and arbitrary nation over other nations"[39]. Nietzsche's theory was soon accepted by the German academic world, as evidenced by the posthumous publication of one of the most famous works by Heinrich von Treitschke (1834–1896), *Politik* (*Politics*, 1897–1898), which brought together his lectures at the University of Berlin. Supporting the idea of Pan-Germanism through the doctrine of the power-state, he wrote: "Without war no State could be. All those we know of arose through war, and the protection of their members by armed force

---

38 Regarding the Nietzschean concepts of the "Superior Man" (Übermensch) and "Will to Power" (Wille zur Macht), see H.-L. Miéville, *Nietzsche et la Volonté de puissance ou l'aventure nietzschénne et le temps présent*, Lausanne, Payot & Cie, 1934; L. Giesz, *Nietzsche: Existenzialismus und Wille zur Macht*, Stuttgart, Deutsche Verlags-Anstalt, 1950; F. Decher, *Wille zum Leben – Wille zur Macht. Eine Untersuchung zu Schopenhauer und Nietzsche*, Würzburg-Amsterdam, Königshausen & Neumann-Rodopi, 1984; G.G. Grau, *Ideologie und Wille zur Macht. Zeitgemässe Betrachtungen über Nietzsche*, Berlin-New York, Walter de Gruyter, 1984; A. Pieper, *"Ein Seil geknüpft zwischen Tier und Übermensch": Philosophische Erläuterungen zu Nietzsches erstem "Zarathustra"*, Stuttgart, Klett-Cotta, 1990; N. Reichel, *Der Traum vom höheren Leben: Nietzsches Übermensch und die Conditio humana europäischer Intellektueller von 1890 bis 1945*, Darmstadt, Wissenschaftliche Buchgesellschaft, 1994; D.W. Conway, P.S. Groff (eds.), *Nietzsche: Critical Assessments*, 4 vols., London, Routledge, 1998; G. Haberkamp, *Triebgeschehen und Wille zur Macht: Nietzsche – zwischen Philosophie und Psychologie*, Wurzburg, Königshausen & Neumann, 2000; P. Montebello, *Nietzsche: la volonté de puissance*, Paris, Puf, 2001.

39 See F. Nietzsche, *The Dawn of Day* (1881), translated by John M. Kennedy, New York, The Macmillan Company, 1911, pp. 159–160.

remains their primary and essential task. War, therefore, will endure to the end of history, as long as there is multiplicity of States"[40].

Among the intellectuals who openly supported the war, we should remember Henri Bergson (1859–1941)[41], the Parisian writer of Jewish origin who endorsed French nationalism and was the author of works such as *Matière et mémoire* (*Matter and Memory*, 1896), *Le Rire* (*Laughter*, 1900) and *L'Évolution créatrice* (*Creative Evolution*, 1907)[42]. In March 1915, Bergson delivered a speech on the evolution of German imperialism at the Académie des Sciences Morales et Politiques entitled "La Signification de la Guerre" (The Meaning of the War)[43]; on this occasion, he interpreted the World War that had just begun by identifying France – the creative and spiritual power – as the "vital momentum", and Prussian Germany as "the continuous clang of militarism and industrialism, of machinery and mechanism, of debased moral materialism"[44]. In his opinion, Prussia was the homeland of rigidity and automatism; therefore, it was imprisoned in its armour according to the will of the "evil genius", as he called Bismarck.

At the beginning of the 20th century, Filippo Tommaso Marinetti (1876–1944) expressed a somewhat provocative thesis in his *Manifesto del Futurismo* (*Manifesto of Futurism*, 1909)[45]; article 9 of this document stated that war was the

40 See H. Treitschke (von), *Politics* (1897–1898), 2 vols., translated by Blanche Dugdale and Torben de Bille, New York, The Macmillan Company, 1916, vol. I, p. 65.
41 On Bergson's philosophy see R. Gillouin, *La philosophie de M. Henri Bergson*, Paris, Grasset, 1911; E. Le Roy, *Une philosophie nouvelle: Henri Bergson*, Paris, Alcan, 1912; F. Grandjean, *Une révolution dans la philosophie: la doctrine de M. Henri Bergson*, Genève-Paris, Atar-Alcan, 1913; E. Otto, *Henri Bergson der Philosoph moderner Religion*, Leipzig-Berlin, Teubner, 1914; V. Jankélévitch, *Henri Bergson*, Paris, Puf, 1959; M. Barlow, *Henri Bergson*, Paris, Editions Universitaires, 1966; I.J. Gallagher, *Morality in Evolution: The Moral Philosophy of Henri Bergson*, The Hague, Nijhoff, 1970; C. Migliaccio, *Invito al pensiero di Henri Bergson*, Milano, Mursia, 1994; P. Rodrigo, *La pensée et le mouvant: Henri Bergson*, Paris, Ellipses, 1998; C. Stancati, D. Chirico, F. Vercillo (eds.), *Henri Bergson: esprit et langage*, Sprimont, Mardaga, 2001; S. Guerlac, *Thinking in Time: An Introduction to Henri Bergson*, Ithaca-London, Cornell University Press, 2006; F. Frangella, *Henri Bergson: l'evoluzione creatrice*, Soveria Mannelli, Calabria Letteraria, 2009.
42 See H. Bergson, *Matière et mémoire*, Paris, Alcan, 1896; Id., *Le Rire*, Paris, Alcan, 1900; Id., *L'Évolution créatrice*, Paris, Alcan, 1907.
43 Id., *The Meaning of the War: Life and Matter in Conflict*, with an introduction by Herbert Wildon Carr, New York, The Macmillan Company, 1915.
44 Ibid., p. 33.
45 The *Manifesto of Futurism* was published in the following Italian newspapers: *Giornale dell'Emilia*, Bologna, 5 February 1909; *Il Pungolo*, Naples, 6 February; *Gazzetta di Mantova*, 8 February; *L'Arena*, Verona, 9 February; *Il Piccolo*, Trieste, 10 February; *Il Giorno*, Rome, 16 February. On 20 February, it was also published in French on the front page of *Le Figaro* in Paris, thus achieving international fame.

"only hygiene of the world". Therefore, it was identified as a kind of purification of the human spirit, the privileged place for a radical renewal of mankind and the fertile ground to give birth to a new man, even at the cost of many lives sacrificed in the name of a palingenetic idea. These reflections would inspire the different forms of totalitarianism developed in the following years in Germany, Italy and Russia. In turn, Oswald Spengler (1880–1936), in his masterpiece *Der Untergang des Abendlandes* (*The Decline of the West*, 1918–1923)[46] left neither possibility nor hope for a future redemption of Western civilization. His voice did not remain isolated; in fact, there were some who even hypothesized a sort of imminent "end of the world". For example, in the 1930s the Swiss writer and historian Louis Gonzague de Reynold (1880–1970) described the disturbing spectacle of a continent, once ambitiously civilizing, that had now lost its undisputed prestige and showed many signs of decay; he presented a very gloomy picture of a "tragic Europe"[47].

The New Theorized European Order Between the World Wars

Due to the outbreak of the Great War, it was no longer possible to cultivate the idea – widespread in the previous century through positivist and evolutionary philosophy – that war could disappear with the growth of industrial societies. The efforts and interventions of prestigious figures proved fruitless; see the case of the English journalist Norman Angell (1872–1967)[48], who was especially remembered for his 1909 pamphlet *Europe's Optical Illusion*[49], expanded and published two years

---

46   See O. Spengler, *Der Untergang des Abendlandes. Umrisse einer Morphologie der Weltgeschichte*, 2 vols., Wien-Münich, Braunmüller-Beck, 1918–1923.
47   See L. Gonzague de Reynold, *L'Europe tragique*, Paris, Spes, 1934.
48   On the intellectual path of Norman Angell, see V.W. Germains, *The Struggle for Bread: A Reply to "The Great Illusion" and Enquiry into Economic Tendencies*, London, Lane, 1913; J.H. Jones, *The Economic of War and Conquest: An Examination of Mr. Norman Angell's Economic Doctrines*, London, King and Son, 1915; G.G. Coulton, *The Main Illusions of Pacifism: A Criticism of Mr. Norman Angell and of the Union of Democratic Control*, Cambridge, Bowes & Bowes, 1916; A.M. Trucco, *La mobilitazione della ricchezza: risposta di un italiano a Norman Angell*, Roma, Hallesint edizioni, 1920; A. Marrin, *Sir Norman Angell*, Boston, Twayne Publishers, 1979; J.D.B. Miller, *Norman Angell and the Futility of War: Peace and Public Mind*, London, Macmillan, 1986; M. Ceadel, *Living the Great Illusion: Sir Norman Angell, 1872–1967*, Oxford, Oxford University Press, 2009.
49   See N. Angell, *Europe's Optical Illusion*, London, Simpkin-Marshall-Kent & Co., 1909.

later under the title *The Great Illusion*[50]. In this essay, Angell proposed the model of uneconomic war: in a world increasingly influenced by the "economic interdependence of civilized nations", conflicts that strengthened political supremacy had become futile and anachronistic. He feared the risks of a conflict, even more likely if the states had succumbed to the "great illusion" of the traditional policies of imperialism, nationalism and colonialism. Wars for conquest between established industrial states such as Great Britain and Germany – relations between the two countries worsened with the Moroccan crises of 1906 and 1911, and with rivalry in naval construction – were futile because the international economic system involved a high degree of interdependence between such states, so enmeshed in one another that none could benefit significantly at the expense of the other.

Major industrial states were unable to capture one another's trade either through wars or through annexing one another's colonies. This would be a "logical fallacy and an optical illusion [...], because when a province or State is annexed, the populations, who are the real and only owners of the wealth therein, are also annexed, and the conqueror gets nothing"[51]. It followed that even a victorious war did not result in any financial gain and, at the same time, did not serve people's general interest; indeed, the ideologies and institutions of war would clearly hamper the development of the idea of progress. Angell described these concepts in the context of a possible war between Great Britain and Germany; however, he was conscious that the other European states might be similarly compared with these two countries. His theses were rooted in English liberal thought, which, based on a utilitarian logic, assigned the harmonious and integrated development of relations between states to market potential, reaching the optimistic prediction that trade would eliminate the wars as costly and futile[52]. This idea had already been advocated by Charles-Louis de Secondat de Montesquieu (1689–1755) in *De l'esprit des lois* (*The Spirit of the Laws*) in the mid-18th century. In this regard, Montesquieu observed: "Peace is the natural effect of trade. Two nations that differ from each other become reciprocally dependent; if one has an interest in buying, the other has an interest in selling; thus their union is founded on their mutual

---

50 Id., *The Great Illusion: A Study of the Relation of Military Power in Nations to Their Economic and Social Advantage*, New York-London, Putnam's Sons, 1911.
51 Ibid., pp. 36–37.
52 A few years before the French Revolution, Jeremy Bentham (1748–1832) published *A Plan for a Universal and Perpetual Peace* (1786–89); consistently with his utilitarian thought, Bentham stated that the war was not only in conflict with people's happiness but was also harmful from an economic and commercial point of view. See J. Bentham, *A Plan for a Universal and Perpetual Peace* (1786–1789), London, Peace Book Co., 1939.

necessities"[53]. This reflection would find concrete expression a century later when John Stuart Mill wrote in the *Principles of Political Economy*: "It is commerce which is rapidly rendering war obsolete, by strengthening and multiplying the personal interests which are in natural opposition to it"[54].

In contrast, Romain Rolland (1866–1944) evoked a highly idealistic and humanitarian form of pacifism[55]; in his extensive literary production, he promulgated a creed of peace and brotherhood, drawing inspiration from the Russian Revolution and Eastern philosophy (Tolstoy, Gandhi, Gorky). When he took shelter in Switzerland during the First World War, Rolland became a point of reference for the international peace movement; his tireless efforts earned him the Nobel Prize for Literature (1915). Moreover, in Switzerland he wrote "Au-dessus de la mêlée" (*Above the Fray*, 1915), published in the *Journal de Genève* on 22-23 September 1914. Despite his strong aspiration to place himself "above the fray" in order to maintain true impartiality towards the belligerent countries, Rolland also expressed deep empathy and moral indignation in the face of the huge tragedy. He believed that war did not represent a fatality, and therefore an inevitable phenomenon – a thesis supported by Hegel, for example – but was the result of people's weakness and folly. More precisely, in an incisive and metaphorical language, he defined the armed conflict that had just begun as a "sacrilegious melee offering the spectacle of a crazy Europe on the stake like Hercules

---

53 See C.L. Montesquieu (Secondat de), *The Spirit of Laws* (1748), 2 vols., London, Bell, 1914, vol. I, p. 341.

54 See J.S. Mill, *Principles of Political Economy* (1848), London, Macmillan, 1929, p. 582. Angell's thesis also represented the logical extension of Richard Cobden's thought; like Cobden, Angell was a free trader whose economic ideas were firmly based on those found in Adam Smith's *The Wealth of Nations* (1776). If we recognize an affinity between the two intellectuals, we must distinguish their methods of approach. Cobden's economic objections to war were based on the effects of the imposition of abnormal taxation on trade; however, he could not be aware of the international interdependence generated by the world economy that Angell so strongly emphasised.

55 On Rolland's pacifism, see S. Zweig, *Romain Rolland: el hombre y su obra*, Buenos Aires, Claridad, 1942; M. Doisy, *Romain Rolland: 1866–1944*, Bruxelles, La Boétie, 1945; A.R. Levy, *L'idéalisme de Romain Rolland*, Paris, Nizet, 1946; M. Descotes, *Romain Rolland*, Paris, Éditions du Temps Présent, 1948; W.T. Starr, *A Critical Bibliography of the Published Writings of Romain Rolland*, Evanston, Northwestern University Press, 1950; J.-B. Barrère, *Romain Rolland par lui-même*, Paris, Seuil, 1962; R. Cheval, *Romain Rolland. L'Allemagne et la guerre*, Paris, Puf, 1963; J. Perus, *Romain Rolland et Maxime Gorki*, Paris, Les Éditeurs Français Réunis, 1968; W.T. Starr, *Romain Rolland: One against All. A Biography*, Paris, The Hague, 1971; P. Sipriot, *Guerre et paix autour de Romain Rolland: le désastre de l'Europe, 1914–1918*, Paris, Bartillat, 1997; B. Duchatelet, *Romain Rolland tel qu'en lui-même*, Paris, Albin Michel, 2002.

mangling his own body with his own hands"[56]. Faced with the tragedy of a war on such a large scale unleashed by the "three rapacious eagles" – the German, Austro-Hungarian and Russian empires – it was necessary to promote the creation of a High Moral Court, namely a kind of Tribunal of Consciences that could judge the crimes perpetrated. As proof of the noble humanitarian ideal of peace and brotherhood that distinguished his thought, he wrote that there was a need to elevate the human spirit "above the storms", removing "the clouds that can obscure it". In almost utopian undertones, he finally hoped for the construction of an "[ideal] city where the fraternal and free souls will gather from all over the world"[57] to defeat national hatred and injustice.

After the end of the conflict, Rolland drew up a *Déclaration d'Indépendance de l'Esprit* (*The International of Intellect*); it was an original proposal for the establishment of a sort of International of Thought conceived in response to an International of Labour. Already in the *Journal des années de guerre* (*Journal of the War Years*), a voluminous diary written between 1914 and 1919[58], Rolland had hoped that intellectuals would assume the task of defeating expressions of fanaticism, nationalism and imperialism, becoming a moral guide for humanity. In this context, he advanced the idea of creating an International of Thought composed of those who shared the ideals of peace and brotherhood among peoples, beginning from prestigious personalities such as Albert Einstein, Hermann Hesse and Bertrand Russell. This idea was characterized by the humanitarian and idealistic inspiration typical of Rolland's pacifism: "Amongst so many other disastrous effects of this war, one of the most dangerous for the future is the severance which has made itself felt, and which is daily increasing between the intellectuals and the world of Labour. […]. Nothing could be more calamitous for the world than this divorce between the higher thought and the workers. The former […] would become even as a dusty relic of libraries or museums. The latter, deprived of guiding light, would fling themselves forward in disordered conflict […]. Let us then, workers and thinkers, unite – all those of us who believe in the possibility of a freer, worthier and happier world, in which the forces of production and of creation would associate in harmony – instead of mutually annihilating and destroying one another as we do to-day by our absurd and criminal opposition"[59]. Thus, Rolland's reflections on peace were based on quite different ideological assumptions compared to Angell;

56   See R. Rolland, "Au-dessus de la mêlée", in *Journal de Genève*, 22 September 1914, p. 5 (translation from the French by C.G. Anta).
57   Ibid.
58   See R. Rolland, *Journal des années de guerre: 1914–1919*, Paris, Albin Michel, 1952.
59   Id., "The International of Intellect. An Appeal", in *Maoriland Worker*, 8 October 1919, vol. 10, no. 448, p. 6.

as a matter of fact, Rolland's pacifism, like Tolstoy's, was ethical and pedagogical enough to take on the features of a secular religion. In contrast, Angell's pacifism was utilitarian: he did not care whether war was right or wrong, moral or immoral; more pragmatically, he considered it unnecessary and anachronistic.

The building of a new European order – as a solution to overcome the perennial state of belligerence – became an important leitmotiv in the European political debate after the First World War. Some intellectuals reproposed and further explored the ideas of those who, over the centuries, had interpreted international relations beginning from the analogy that states could be considered as citizens belonging to the same community. Hence the need to transfer the traditional model of natural law from the individual level to the interstate one, as individual countries would still be in a sort of belligerent state of nature and thus potentially unsafe; from Thomas Hobbes, this ideological approach had been complemented by the cosmopolitan vision of Immanuel Kant. Across the Atlantic, Nicholas Murray Butler (1862–1947)[60] put forward a concrete proposal aimed at overcoming the anarchy of international relations. In his article "The United States of Europe"[61], Butler hoped that Europe could draw inspiration from the federalist model of the United States to construct its future order, in the same way in which North America had secured pacific relations between different races and cultures for nearly 150 years. Thus, the future peace treaty should not simply restore the *status quo* but would remove the causes of the perpetual belligerence in the Old Continent that derived from the dogma of absolute state sovereignty; in his view, the United States of America could represent a farsighted example for Europe's most practical and authoritative minds. In this way, Butler referred to Alexander Hamilton's thought in *The Federalist* (1788)[62], which, by allowing for a clear distinction between federation and confederation, prevents confusion between the phenomenon of mere interstate cooperation and forms of unification.

---

60 In 1890, Nicholas Murray Butler became professor of philosophy and education at Columbia University, and in 1902, the president of this academic institution. Active in the Republican Party for a long time, he went on to seek Republican presidential nomination for himself in 1920 and 1928. He helped in establishing the Carnegie Endowment for International Peace, of which he later became the president (1925–1945). His efforts won him considerable prestige; so much so that in 1931 he shared the Nobel Peace Prize with Jane Addams. On Butler see M.H. Thomas, *Bibliography of Nicholas Murray Butler 1872–1932*, New York, Columbia University Press, 1934; R. Whittemore, *Nicholas Murray Butler and Public Education 1862–1911*, New York, Teachers College Press, 1970.

61 See N.M. Butler, "The United States of Europe", in *The New York Times*, 18 October 1914. Regarding this article, see also *The United States of Europe*, an interview with Nicolas Murray Butler by Edward Marshall, Washington, Columbus Memorial Library, 1915.

62 See A. Hamilton, J. Jay, J. Madison, *The Federalist Papers*, New York, MacLean's Edition, 1788.

The new European structure outlined by the Treaty of Versailles led to the widespread conviction that overcoming international anarchy represented the *conditio sine qua non* to achieve lasting peace. The discussion of the future of the continental order was concomitant to the epochal crisis of the system of nation-states of the early 20th century, which led to the birth of the League of Nations; the latter was the subject of a lively European debate in the 1920s. In this regard, Richard Nikolaus Coudenhove-Kalergi (1894–1972), the author of *Pan-Europa* (1923) and the founder of the eponymous movement, defined the League of Nations as an "inorganic structure"[63] because it did not group states according to their historical, economic and cultural affinities but "in a mechanical way". Drawing on the doctrine outlined by James Monroe in "America for the Americans", Coudenhove-Kalergi argued with equal strength for the concept of a "Europe for Europeans" – a confederate alliance extending from Portugal to Poland, clearly separated from other world powers such as Communist Russia and the British Commonwealth. Using the words *Föderation* (Federation) and *Staatenbund* (League of States) synonymously, he did not assign to them the same meaning as in Hamilton's federal understanding; in contrast, Luigi Einaudi (1874–1961) hoped for a "second sort of League of Nations" in the form of a superstate that exerted direct sovereignty on citizens, with power to impose taxes, and to create and maintain its own army. Einaudi made a clear distinction between the principles of a Federation, which derived from the example of the American Constitution, and a Confederation, which was the expression of a consolidated European tradition. He argued that the structure conceived by Thomas W. Wilson referred to the latter concept because it constituted a sort of Alliance or League, unsuitable for ensuring everlasting peace[64]. He believed that only by weakening the absolute sovereignty of the European states – in the form of a federal union – would it be possible to overcome international anarchy and then avoid new conflicts. Einaudi's criticisms were not isolated either, for they were supported by both Giovanni Agnelli and Attilio Cabiati, who declared to be in favour of the model of the British Commonwealth, founded on the principles of "self-government" and "rule of law". Furthermore, they underlined the inefficiency of the League of Nations, claiming that no international organization, even one entrusted with peacekeeping, would be able

---

63 See R.N. Coudenhove-Kalergi, *Pan-Europe* (1923), Paris, Puf, 1988, p. 68; see also A. Agnelli, "Da Coudenhove-Kalergi al piano Briand", in S. Pistone (ed.), *L'idea dell'unificazione europea dalla prima alla seconda guerra mondiale*, Torino, Fondazione Einaudi, 1975, pp. 39–57.

64 See L. Einaudi, *La guerra e l'unità europea*, Milano, Comunità, 1948, pp. 122–123.

to impose their decisions, in the absence of popular legitimation, over another country's finances and army[65].

The Treaty of Versailles did not promote a real reconciliation between the victors and the vanquished; on the contrary, it stirred up new antagonisms, derived mainly from a desire to keep Germany in a state of economic and moral inferiority. In Great Britain, severe criticism of this situation came from the English economist John Maynard Keynes (1883–1946), who criticized the "Carthaginian Peace" of Versailles in his work *The Economic Consequences of the Peace*[66]. According to Keynes, who personally participated in the Paris Peace Conference, this punitive policy towards Germany would lay the foundations for a new war. The second half of the 1920s was very significant from the point of view of international relations: the Treaty of Locarno was signed in October 1925; in 1926, Germany was admitted to the Wilsonian Institution; on 27 August 1928, the Briand-Kellogg Pact was signed in Paris; and in 1929, Great Britain resumed diplomatic relations with the Soviet Union. This policy of detente ultimately proved ineffective, however: in October 1935, Mussolini invaded Abyssinia; in March 1936, Hitler occupied the Rhineland in violation of the clauses of the Pact of Locarno; and in June, the Spanish Civil War broke out. These events determined the end of the so-called spirit of Locarno and the failure of the Geneva institution.

This new political scenario induced two British liberals, Lord Lothian (1882–1940) and Lionel Robbins (1898–1984), to further their federalist hypotheses. In 1935, Lord Lothian (Philip Kerr) published *Pacifism is not Enough, nor Patriotism Either*; this essay carried a special message for the British peace movement because, in his opinion, it had not as yet understood the real causes of the war. In this work, Lothian considered peace not merely as a "negative condition" in which war was not being waged, but as a "positive thing" or more precisely that "state of society" in which political, economic, and social issues were "settled by constitutional means"[67]. He established three propositions: firstly, war was "inherent" in a world of sovereign states; secondly, the League of Nations and the Briand-Kellogg Pact could not preserve "civilisation or peace"; finally, peace could only be established by bringing the "whole world under the reign of law"[68]. He also refuted

---

65 See G. Agnelli, A. Cabiati, *Federazione europea o Lega delle Nazioni?* (1918), edited by M. Monti, Pordenone, Studio Tesi, 1995, pp. 45–93; see also V. Castronovo, "Alle origini dell'europeismo in Piemonte. La proposta di Agnelli e Cabiati e la cultura industriale", in *Piemonteuropa*, 1992, vol. XVII, no. 2–3, pp. 19–21.
66 See J.M. Keynes, *The Economic Consequence of the Peace*, London, Macmillan, 1920, p. 56.
67 See Lord Lothian, *Pacifism Is Not Enough, Nor Patriotism Either. Being the Burge Memorial Lecture for the Year*, Oxford, The Clarendon Press, 1935, p. 7.
68 Ibid., p. 10.

the thesis that capitalism and nationalism were the main causes of wars: on the one hand, capitalism was an "international force" since businessmen had few racial or national prejudices; on the other hand, nationalism was a "creative force" because it engendered a feeling of "common citizenship and common loyalty to the state" rather than of differences in race, language, culture or religion[69]. In Lothian's thought, pacifism and world patriotism among nations were virtues that were necessary but not in themselves sufficient for building a lasting peace: only a federation capable of embracing not Europe alone but the whole world could create the right foundation to overcome international anarchy. In 1937, Lionel Robbins wrote *Economic Planning and International Order*, in which he drew from the problems concerning economic growth and social independence stemming from the Industrial Revolution. He argued that the market could not operate unless there was a structure in place to ensure the necessary rules for peaceful coexistence. Hence the need for "national states to surrender certain rights to an international authority […]. There must be neither alliance nor complete unification, but Federation"[70]. John Atkinson Hobson (1858–1940) did not share these ideas; in *Thoughts on Our Present Discontents* (1938)[71], he considered war as the result of capitalist imperialism. For him, peace could be built through the establishment of a planned economy involving the redistribution of national wealth and the creation of a large market to eliminate the reasons for expansionist imperialism.

The idea of a European federation was supported not only by the English school[72] but also by the Italian school headed by Luigi Einaudi and Altiero Spinelli. In the 1940s, the federalist method found its main reference points in the *Manifesto di Ventotene* – written in 1941 by Altiero Spinelli (1907–1986) and Ernesto Rossi (1897–1967) during their political confinement on the Tyrrhenian Island and published in 1944 by Eugenio Colorni (1909–1944). The central idea

69 Ibid., pp. 13–16.
70 See L. Robbins, *Economic Planning and International Order*, London, Macmillan, 1937, p. 245.
71 See J.A. Hobson, "Thoughts on Our Present Discontents", in *The Political Quarterly*, January–March 1938, vol. 9, no. 1, pp. 47–57.
72 On the English federalist school and the causes of the war, see Lord Lothian, *Pacifism Is Not Enough, Nor Patriotism Either*; Robbins, *Economic Planning and International Order*; Lord Lothian, *The Ending of Armageddon*, London, Federal Union, 1939; L. Robbins, *The Economic Causes of War*, London, Cape, 1939; Id., *Economic Aspects of Federation*, London, Macmillan, 1941; F. Rossolillo, "La scuola federalista inglese", in Pistone (ed.), *L'idea dell'unificazione europea dalla prima alla seconda guerra mondiale*, pp. 59–76; A. Bosco, "National Sovereignty and Peace: Lord Lothian's Federalist Thought", in J. Turner (ed.), *The Larger Idea: Lord Lothian and the Problem of National Sovereignty*, London, THP, 1988, pp. 108–123; M. Burgess, *The British Tradition of Federalism*, London, Leicester University Press, 1995; C.G. Anta (ed.), *Lord Lothian: The Paths of Federalism*, Brussels, Peter Lang, 2014.

of this work was based on a reflection already found in Kant and in subsequent pacifist authors: the main cause of the wars that afflicted contemporary society was represented by the existence of absolute sovereign states that considered the other states as competitors and potential enemies. In this view, the European federation was designated as the priority target of a political programme that aimed at meeting the historical challenge of the time. According to Rossi and Spinelli, the criterion for the division between progressive and reactionary forces was no longer identifiable with the "formal line of major or minor democracy, of the superior or inferior socialism to be established", but rather with the line that discriminated between "those who conceive the old goal, that is to say the conquest of the national political power, as the essential aim of the struggle [...], and those who will see the creation of a solid international state as a central task"[73].

So, British and Italian federalists were inspired by Hamilton's thought in *The Federalist*; they implicitly compared the two American Constitutions of 1781 and 1787, and underscored the superiority of the federal model over the confederal one, highlighting the failure of the former and the success of the latter. In this context, the European Federation could be considered as a model to legalize the relationships among national states.

Nonviolent Methods Towards the End of the Second Millennium

In the 20th century, Bertrand Russell (1872–1970) was one of the main reference points for world pacifism for over 50 years. Beginning from the First World War, he strongly supported pacifist propaganda; in 1916, he was dismissed from Trinity College for following his convictions and, two years later, sentenced to six months' imprisonment for his defence of conscientious objection in opposition to the British war policy. In *Justice in War-Time* (1916), Russell described the poverty of economic and social conditions caused by the conflict, the feelings of hatred and injustice, and he outlined the theory of non-resistance already developed by the Quakers and Leo Tolstoy (1828–1910)[74]. In his subsequent essay *Why Men Fight* (1917), Russell asserted that "all human activity [sprang] from two sources: impulse and desire"[75]. Impulses, which were at the basis of our life much

---

73 See A. Spinelli, E. Rossi, *Il Manifesto di Ventotene* (1944), Napoli, Guida, 1982, p. 37 (translation from the Italian by C.G. Anta).
74 See B. Russell, *Justice in War-Time*, Chicago, Open Court Publishing Company, 1916.
75 Id., *Why Men Fight. A Method of Abolishing the International Duel*, New York, The Century Company, 1917, p. 7.

more than desires, could be divided into those related to life and death: the former had created art and science, the latter were embodied in war. Besides, he supported the idea that passions and instincts of war had to be prevented and controlled by the three forces of love, constructiveness and joy; in short, he argued that war was intrinsic to human nature rather than being a historical social construct.

Therefore, he implicitly shared Sigmund Freud's theses; in two 1915 writings, "Triebe und Triebschicksale" (*Instincts and Their Vicissitudes*)[76] and "Zeitgemäßes über Krieg und Tod" (*Thoughts for the Times on War and Death*)[77], Freud in essence identified aggression as an inherent impulse of man. It was only in the essay "Jenseits des Lustprinzips" (*Beyond the Pleasure Principle*, 1920), however, that he outlined this new orientation; human nature could be explained through the antagonistic action of two opposing instincts, namely Eros and death: "The expressions of Eros were obvious and noisy enough", while "the death drive worked silently" within the organism towards the external world, appearing as a means for aggression and destruction[78]. In the paper "Das Ich und das Es" (*The Ego and the Id*, 1923), Freud confirmed the existence of the "sexual" and "death" instincts, emphasising that "the precarious balance of life" derived from the "fusion of the two classes"[79]. In the essay entitled "Das Unbehagen in der Kultur" (*Civilization and Its Discontents*, 1929), he further highlighted the link between individual aggressiveness and war: "*Homo homini lupus*; who has the courage to dispute it in the face of all the evidence in his own life and in history?"[80]. As Freud wrote, it was enough to remember the numerous atrocities that had marked human history: from the invasions of the Huns or of the Mongols under Genghis

---

76 See S. Freud, "Instincts and Their Vicissitudes", in Id., *The Standard Edition of the Complete Psychological Works of Sigmund Freud. On the History of the Psycho-Analytic Movements, Papers on Metapsychology and Other Works*, vol. XIV (1914–1916), translated and edited by James Strachey in collaboration with Anna Freud, London, The Hogarth Press-The Institute of Psycho-analysis, 1957, pp. 117–140.

77 Id., "Thoughts for the Times on War and Death", ib., pp. 275–300.

78 See S. Freud, "Beyond the Pleasure Principle", in Id., *The Standard Edition of the Complete Psychological Works of Sigmund Freud. Beyond the Pleasure Principle, Group Psychology and Other Works*, vol. XVIII (1920–1922), translated and edited by James Strachey in collaboration with Anna Freud, London, The Hogarth Press-The Institute of Psycho-analysis, 1955, pp. 1–63.

79 See S. Freud, "The Ego and the Id", in Id., *The Standard Edition of the Complete Psychological Works of Sigmund Freud. The Ego and the Id and Other Works*, vol. XIX (1923–1925), translated and edited by James Strachey in collaboration with Anna Freud, London, The Hogarth Press-The Institute of Psycho-analysis, 1961, pp. 1–66 (for the quotations, see pp. 39–40).

80 Id., *Civilization and Its Discontents* (1929), translated by Joan Riviere, London, The Hogarth Press, 1930, p. 85.

Khan and Tamerlane to the horrors of the Great War, passing through the capture of Jerusalem by the Crusaders.

The diffusion of ideas and methods that were originally alien to the Western democratic tradition, but integrated themselves within it, marked the first half of the 20th century; this occurred because of the influence of religious-cultural systems and ideologies typical of East Indian and Buddhist rationality. An example is offered by the theory of nonviolence derived from the teachings of Mohandas Karamchand Gandhi (1869–1948)[81], the Great Soul and the symbol of Indian independence from the British Empire. Gandhi had links with Western socialist and utopian thought; he was inspired by authors such as Henry David Thoreau (1817–1862) and Leo Tolstoy. In a particular way, Tolstoy's pacifist ethic[82] influenced the moral conversion to nonviolence of the then-young lawyer Gandhi; in his *Autobiography*, he pointed out: "It was [...] when I was passing through a severe crisis of scepticism and doubt that I came across Tolstoy's book, *The Kingdom of God Is Within You*, and was deeply impressed by it. I was at that time a believer in violence. Its reading cured me of my scepticism and made me a firm believer in *ahimsa* (nonviolence)"[83]. However, the Gandhian doctrine of nonviolence had its

---

81 On Gandhi's doctrine of nonviolence, see S.C. Gangal, *The Gandhian Way to World Peace*, Bombay, Vora & Co. Publishers, 1960; T. Merton (ed.), *Gandhi on Non-Violence*, New York, New Directions, 1965; R.N. Iyer, *The Moral and Political Thought of Mahatma Gandhi*, New York, Oxford University Press, 1973; A. Naess, *Gandhi and Group Conflict: An Exploration of Satyagraha, Theoretical Background*, Oslo, Universitetsforlaget, 1974; M. Chatterjee, *Gandhi's Religious Thought*, Notre Dame, University of Notre Dame Press, 1983; S.H. Rudolph, L.I. Rudolph, *Gandhi: The Traditional Roots of Charisma*, Chicago, University of Chicago Press, 1983; R.-S. Puri, *Gandhi on War and Peace*, New York-London, Praeger, 1987; P. Bandyopadhyay, *Mahatma Gandhi: The Prophet of Peace*, Calcutta, Anglia Books, 1988; B.C. Parekh, *Gandhi's Political Philosophy: A Critical Examination*, Basingstoke, Macmillan, 1989; D. Dalton, *Mahatma Gandhi: Nonviolent Power in Action*, New York, Columbia University Press, 1993; C. Clément, *Gandhi: The Power of Pacifism*, New York, H.N. Abrams, 1996; T. Weber, *Gandhi's Peace Army: The Shanti Sena and Unarmed Peacekeeping*, Syracuse, Syracuse University Press, 1996; E. Easwaran, *Gandhi the Man: The Story of His Transformation*, Tomales, Nilgiri Press, 1997; M. King, *Mahatma Gandhi and Martin Luther King Jr.: The Power of Nonviolent Action*, Paris, Unesco Publishing, 1999.

82 Regarding Tolstoy's ethical pacifism, see E.B. Greenwood, *Tolstoy: The Comprehensive Vision*, New York, St. Martin's Press, 1975; P. Brock, *The Roots of War Resistance: Pacifism from the Early Church to Tolstoy*, New York, The Fellowship of Reconciliation, 1981; R.F. Gustafson, *Leo Tolstoy, Resident and Stranger: A Study in Fiction and Theology*, Princeton, Princeton University Press, 1986; J.A. Sokolow, P.R. Roosevelt, *Leo Tolstoy's Christian Pacifism: The American Contribution*, Pittsburgh, University of Pittsburgh Center for Russian and East European Studies, 1987; A.N. Wilson, *Tolstoy*, New York, Norton, 1988; D. Redfearn, *Tolstoy: Principles for a New World Order*, London, Shepheard-Walwyn, 1992.

83 See M.K. Gandhi, *An Autobiography: The Story of My Experiments with Truth*, Ahmedabad, Navajivan Publishing House, 1969, p. 102. On the relationship between Gandhi and Tolstoy,

deep roots mainly in Hindu mysticism and in the interweaving of his two principles: *ahimsa* and *satyagraha*. The concept of *ahimsa* established not to kill and to keep a friendly attitude towards all human beings; *satyagraha* (passive resistance) implied an agreement of one's own being with the truth, a practice of moral and sober conduct, governed by the principle of non-possession and frugality. In his view, the attempt to conform to these precepts would entail an inner human effort aimed at seeking to solve every problem of existence with nonviolent methods, primarily nonviolent resistance. Gandhi offered a precise and idealized justification for nonviolence; he gathered the most significant experiences of practical successes and failures, and designed a systematization of nonviolent campaigns in which the methods of non-cooperation and civil disobedience were conceptually and practically differentiated and graded. Gandhi sought to act in an exemplary manner as a charismatic leader. His many visible symbolic actions, including numerous hunger strikes "unto death", were demonstrative actions aimed at raising public awareness. The fascinating effect he had on his disciples and the worldwide public lay in his presentation of a doctrine that was at the same time a demand for action, and in its connection with mysticism and activism.

The period following the Second World War was characterized by the establishment of the United Nations (UN), following the failure of the League of Nations, with the aim of promoting peaceful settlement of international disputes and respect for human rights. In other words, the UN represented an attempt to democratize the international system by transferring the fundamental principles of the democratic state in relations among sovereign states. The birth of the UN determined the coexistence of the so-called Westphalian model and the United Nations Charter model within the international legal order. The former had emerged in Europe after the end of the Thirty Years' War; the subjects of international law were exclusively the nation-states whose absolute sovereignty was an unconditional principle that allowed them the right to resort to war in order to achieve their hegemonic goals. Through the latter, a new international legal order forced the nation-states to respect the dignity and fundamental rights of man; the recourse to war was limited to their self-defence, and sanctioning of the use of force was entrusted to the UN Security Council. Nevertheless, this new model, based on a weak globalist approach, ran the risk of achieving very limited success; from this perspective, it was necessary to advocate the primacy of international law and the progressive removal of the sovereign prerogatives of individual states preserved inside the Security Council. In 1948, the Committee

---

see above all M.B. Green, *Tolstoy and Gandhi, Men of Peace: A Biography*, New York, Basic Books, 1983; P.C. Bori, G. Sofri, *Gandhi e Tolstoj. Un carteggio e dintorni*, Bologna, Il Mulino, 1985.

to Frame a World Constitution – composed of 11 university professors, among them six of the University of Chicago[84] – produced *The Preliminary Draft of a World Constitution*. In its preamble we read: "The age of nations must end, and the era of humanity begin"; the individual countries had to surrender "their separate sovereignties" to a world government whose main aim was "the maintenance of peace"[85]. It was an idea closely related to the fear of a nuclear conflict, as we read in *The Preliminary Draft*.

A real transition from international anarchy to a peaceful and stable political system entailed that the individual nation-states subscribe to both a *pactum societatis* and a *pactum subjectionis*. The former involved a preliminary agreement of nonaggression among states through a common set of rules for the resolution of disputes; the latter implied the subjection of the individual countries under a common power that would be able to enforce the signed pact and coercively regulate their relationships. However, the UN – like the League of Nations – was the result of a *pactum societatis* but not of a *pactum subjectionis*; indeed, through their right of veto exercised within the Security Council, its member states had maintained their sovereignty by not transferring the monopoly of force to a higher authority. It was not by chance that some leading figures of the international world pacifism, beginning from Einstein and Russell, were staunch supporters of the idea of a world government with the right to resolve disputes and impose its resolutions; this aim became a necessity rather than an ideal due to the manufacture of the atomic weapon. A world government with at least the legitimate monopoly of international force could guarantee a lasting peace through the abolition of the absolute sovereignty of individual states; all this called to mind Hobbes's contractualism in the Kantian sense, giving it a cosmopolitan value.

Growing mutual suspicion between the two superpowers caused the escalation of the Cold War; the discovery of the hydrogen bomb, tested almost simultaneously by the United States and the Soviet Union[86], increasingly induced fear in the international community. The Russell-Einstein Manifesto of July 1955 can

---

84 This Committee consisted of six professors from the University of Chicago (Chancellor Robert Maynard Hutchins, Dean of the Law School Wilber Griffith Katz, Giuseppe Antonio Borgese, Mortimer Adler, Robert Redfield and Rexford Guy Tugwell); four professors from other American universities (Stringfellow Barr, former President of St. John's College; Albert Léon Guérard, Stanford University; Erich Kahler, Cornell University; and Charles H. McIlwain, Harvard University); finally, Professor Harold Innis from the University of Toronto.
85 See Committee to Frame a World Constitution, *The Preliminary Draft of a World Constitution*, Chicago, The University of Chicago Press, 1948, p. 5.
86 The first US hydrogen bomb was tested on 1 November 1952; the Soviet Union tested it for the first time on 12 August 1953.

be placed in this context; it sought to raise public awareness of the perils deriving from the new weapon of mass destruction and to discuss a peaceful resolution, not as members of this or that nation, continent or creed, but as human beings.

In the 1950s, the national sections of the International Fellowship of Reconciliation (IFOR) and the War Resisters' International (WRI) resumed their pacifist and antimilitarist propaganda; in 1958, the Campaign for Nuclear Disarmament (CND) was launched in Great Britain, focusing its activities against nuclear testing. The pacifist themes converged in the programmes and activities of groups linked to the new Left, to feminist and environmentalist organizations; in many western-European countries, we witnessed a mobilization against the Vietnam War. In this climate, there was the establishment of the International War Crimes Tribunal; this was a private body founded in November 1966 by Russell and Jean-Paul Sartre (1905–1980), which began to investigate crimes committed by the US Army in Vietnam[87]. In the United States, there were the civil-rights campaigns of Martin Luther King (1929–1968)[88] inspired by the non-violent action of Mahatma Gandhi. As a theologian, King described his own "pilgrimage to nonviolence" beginning from his *Stride Toward Freedom* (1958): "True pacifism" or "nonviolent resistance" was "a courageous confrontation of evil by the power of love"[89]. Two years later, he asserted that the Christian doctrine of love

---

87   The Russell-Sartre Tribunal was composed of 25 prestigious figures from 18 countries, primarily from peace organizations; it was conducted in two sessions in 1967 (Stockholm and Roskilde).
88   Among the most recent essays on Martin Luther King and his battle for the civil rights, see especially J.J. Ansbro, *Martin Luther King, Jr.: Nonviolent Strategies and Tactics for Social Change*, Lanham-New York-Oxford, Madison Books, 2000; C. Carson (ed.), *The Autobiography of Martin Luther King, Jr.*, New York, Abacus, 2000; M.E. Dyson, *I May Not Get There with You: The True Martin Luther King, Jr.*, New York, Free Press, 2000; A. Claybourne, *Martin Luther King, Jr.: Civil Rights Hero*, London, Hodder Wayland, 2001; M.-C. Combesque, G. Deleury, *Gandhi et Martin Luther King*, Paris, Autrement, 2002; P. Ling, *Martin Luther King, Jr.*, London-New York, Routledge, 2002; D.D. Hansen, *The Dream: Martin Luther King, Jr., and the Speech that Inspired a Nation*, New York, Ecco, 2003; J.A. Kirk, *Martin Luther King, Jr.*, Harlow, Pearson Longman, 2005; T.F. Jackson, *From Civil Rights to Human Rights: Martin Luther King, Jr., and the Struggle for Economic Justice*, Philadelphia, University of Pennsylvania Press, 2007; J.A. Kirk (ed.), *Martin Luther King, Jr., and the Civil Rights Movement: Controversies and Debates*, Basingstoke, Palgrave Macmillan, 2007; A.C. McLean, *Martin Luther King*, Oxford, Oxford University Press, 2008; S. Molla, *Les idées noires de Martin Luther King*, Genève, Labor et Fides, 2008; R.W. Wills, *Martin Luther King, Jr., and the Image of God*, New York, Oxford University Press, 2009; L.V. Baldwin, *The Voice of Conscience: The Church in the Mind of Martin Luther King, Jr.*, New York, Oxford University Press, 2010; H. Buchele, *Spiritualität und politischer Kampf aus dem Geist der Bergpredigt: Mahatma Gandhi und Martin Luther King*, Innsbruck, Innsbruck University Press, 2013; S. Molla, *Martin Luther King, prophète*, Genève, Labor et Fides, 2018.
89   See M.L. King, *Stride Toward Freedom: The Montgomery Story*, New York, Harper, 1958, p. 80.

operating through the Gandhian method of nonviolence was "one of the most potent weapons available to oppressed people in their struggle for freedom"[90]. King experienced directly the power of nonviolent action during the Montgomery bus boycott in 1955; on this occasion, he understood that nonviolence could become a way of life, applicable to all situations. A trip to India in 1959 helped him to connect more intimately with Gandhi's spiritual legacy; as a matter of fact, he called the principle of nonviolent resistance the "guiding light" of his political and religious activism. More precisely, "Christ [had] furnished the spirit and motivation, while Gandhi […] the method"; at the same time, King began to advocate nonviolence not just in a national sphere but internationally as well, since the potential destructiveness of nuclear weapons convinced him that "the choice" was no longer between violence and nonviolence, but between "nonviolence or nonexistence"[91]. In one of his last writings, he stated that in his life he had rarely developed "a conviction so precious and meaningful as nonviolence"[92].

One of the most important aspects of the 1980s was the affirmation of a deep-rooted feminist pacifism at the international level[93]; it was inspired by the themes of nonviolence, criticism of the male models of aggression and oppression on women, the forms of power borrowed from the model of war, and the victory of the strong over the weak. The concrete involvement of women in the pacifist cause harks back to 1915, when Jane Addams, Marian Cripps, and Margaret E. Dungan established the Women's International League for Peace and Freedom (WILPF).

---

90 Id., "Pilgrimage to Nonviolence", 13 April 1960, in Id., *The Papers of Martin Luther King, Jr.*, vol. 5, edited by Clayborne Carson, Tenisha Armstrong, Susan Carson, Adrienne Clay, and Kieran Taylor, Barkeley, University of California Press, 2005, pp. 419–425 (for the quotation, see p. 422).
91 Ibid., pp. 423–424.
92 See M.L. King, *Where Do We Go from Here: Chaos or Community?*, New York, Harper, 1967, pp. 63–64.
93 On the relationship between pacifism and feminism, see J. Addams, *Peace and Bread in Time of War*, New York, Macmillan, 1922; C. Bouglé, *De la sociologie à l'action sociale: pacifisme, féminisme, coopération*, Paris, Puf, 1923; H. Schenk, *Frauen kommen ohne Waffen: Feminismus und Pazifismus*, München, Beck, 1983; A. Chemello (ed.), *Per un futuro nonviolento: lotta delle donne, nonviolenza, pacifismo*, Torino, Satyagraha, 1984; D. Bricquir (Le), O. Thibault, *Féminisme et pacifisme, même combat*, Paris, Lettres Libres, 1985; R.J. Evans, *Comrades and Sisters: Feminism, Socialism and Pacifism in Europe, 1870–1945*, Brighton-New York, Wheatsheaf-St. Martin's Press, 1987; S. Lynn, *Progressive Women in Conservative Times: Racial Justice, Peace, and Feminism, 1945 to the 1960s*, New Brunswick, Rutgers University Press, 1992; L.J. Peach, "An Alternative to Pacifism? Feminism and Just-War Theory", in *Hypatia*, 1994, vol. 9, no. 2, pp. 152–172; L.K. Schott, *Reconstructing Women's Thoughts. The Women's International League for Peace and Freedom before World War II*, Stanford, Stanford University Press, 1997; A. Wilmers, *Pazifismus in der internationalen Frauenbewegung (1914–1920). Handlungsspielräume, politische Konzeptionen und gesellschaftliche Auseinandersetzungen*, Essen, Klartex Verlag, 2008.

Its main aim was to bring together women of different political, philosophical and religious views "to study and make known the causes of war and work for a permanent peace". After the First World War, the famous British suffragist and spiritual leader Maude Royden (1876–1956) rested her hopes for a peaceful future on the women's movement. Her suffrage campaign was based on the assertion that moral force must be the foundation stone of political power, and she believed that feminists could not deny that war was women's worst enemy. Furthermore, women's previous exclusion from international affairs could also mean that they did not have the political myopia that made it difficult for men to achieve and maintain peace. Therefore, Royden hoped that women's common sense and relative freedom from the constraints and conventions of national pride could transform the fledgling League of Nations into a viable and effective agent for a lasting peace[94].

Following the Second World War and the conflicts of the mid and late 20th century, there was an evident development of feminist pacifism which emphasized the need for women to act against male destructiveness and in support of their sense of motherhood. Feminism and pacifism were considered as both theoretically and pragmatically relevant to each other; this was demonstrated by the success of the two World Conferences on Women (1975–1980)[95]. Feminism played an important role in anti-war movements; its critique of militarism as a patriarchal instrument made the rejection of women's participation in state-armies understandable, although feminists generally did not distinguish between statist, colonialist, and imperialist militarism. The traditional association of violence with masculinity and the systematic exclusion of women from politics, economy, war, and peace, reproduced patriarchy through a gender-based division of roles in the field of power. The feminist critique of violence was also based on the reasoning of a gender-based morality, which could reproduce the portrayals of women as inherently apolitical, and in need of protection.

The end of bipolarity in international relations caused by the fall of the Berlin Wall (1989) led to an overall rethinking of strategy within the peace movement; in fact, it addressed primarily the issue of national and ethnic wars, the question of a new international order with a democratic government, the policies against new

---

94 See M. Royden, "War and the Women's Movement", in C.R. Buxton (ed.), *Towards a Lasting Settlement*, New York, The Macmillan Co., 1916, pp. 131–146.

95 The First World Conference on Women took place in 1975 in Mexico City and was held by the United Nations to eliminate discrimination against women viewed as part of the process to develop and implement policy. The Second World Conference on Women took place in Copenhagen in 1980; it was the mid-decade assessment of progress and failure in implementing the goals established five years before.

forms of despotism, and the prevention and resolution of conflicts. It is therefore no exaggeration to say that the future of peace is closely linked to the future of democracy and respect for human rights. The relationship between democracy and peace shows the importance of homogeneity among the political systems which could give rise to a future cosmopolitan order – based on a world government, for example. Kant had already perceived this need in 1795, when, with extraordinary political farsightedness, he argued that the form of government of the states associated in a peaceful league had to be republican.

CHAPTER TWO

Bertrand Russell Witness for Peace

A Renaissance Intellectual of the 20th Century

In his *Autobiography*, Bertrand Arthur William Russell (1872–1970) highlighted the three passions – "simple but overwhelmingly strong" – that had governed his life: "The longing for love, the search for knowledge, and unbearable pity for the suffering of mankind. These passions, like great winds, have blown me hither and thither, in a wayward course, over a deep ocean of anguish reaching to the very verge of despair"[1]. These words effectively introduce us to his multifaceted personality: a brilliant mathematician, logician, and philosopher, Russell was engaged in the cause of civilization, progress, and human rights for almost a century. He was born on 18 May 1872 in Trellech, Monmouthshire, Wales. His grandfather John Russell, a famous Whig politician, had been prime minister twice[2], and in 1861 Queen Victoria elevated him to the peerage as the 1st Earl Russell. The first years of Russell's life were marked by bereavements; by the time he was six years of age, his sister, his parents, and his grandfather had all died, and he and his elder

---

1 See B. Russell, *The Autobiography of Bertrand Russell*, 3 vols., London, Allen & Unwin, 1967–1969, vol. I, p. 3.
2 Lord John Russell (1792–1878) had been prime minister from 1846 to 1852 and from 1865 to 1866.

brother Frank were left in the care of their grandmother. He was soon absorbed in learning Euclidean geometry; in 1890, he entered Trinity College, University of Cambridge, where he studied mathematics and philosophy. At the end of 1895, Russell and his first wife, the American-born Quaker Alys Pearsall Smith, visited Berlin to observe the German socialist movement; they met the leaders of the "Sozialdemokratische Partei Deutschlands" (SPD) August Bebel and Wilhelm Liebknecht. After his trip, Russell wrote his first book, *German Social Democracy* (1896), in which he underscored Ferdinand Lassalle's ideological inspiration for the establishment of the SPD by highlighting its reformist aims and criticized the tyrannical methods of the Kaiser's government against its opponents. In his opinion, democratic socialists who were not bound by dogmatic Marxist theory had to demonstrate a "friendliness to the working class" or rather a "common humanity", so that the detestable notion of the inevitability of a class war could "find less acceptance, and less ground in the conduct of rulers"[3]. It was not by chance that in 1897 he joined the Fabian Society, which included Sidney and Beatrice Webb, George Bernard Shaw, Herbert George Wells and Graham Wallas; the Fabians devoted themselves to spreading democratic socialist ideas rather than inciting revolution.

At this time, Russell's philosophy was influenced by the metaphysical idealism that he had adopted as a student at Cambridge alongside his Kantian methodology; idealism dominated English philosophy in the last decades of the 19th century, and this represented a break in an almost continuous tradition of empiricism – John Locke, George Berkeley, David Hume, and John Stuart Mill. Russell was guided by the thoughts of John Ellis McTaggart, professor of philosophy at Trinity College, contained in his *Studies in the Hegelian Dialectic* (1896)[4]; in this regard, he affirmed: "As presented to me by its adherents, especially McTaggart […], Hegel's philosophy had seemed both charming and demonstrable"[5]. However, he abandoned his metaphysical idealism and adopted the view that logical analysis, rather than synthesis, was the surest method of philosophy. George Edward Moore was the main critic of metaphysical and anti-empiricist idealism; in his *The Nature of*

---

3   See B. Russell, *German Social Democracy: Six Lectures*, London-New York-Bombay, Longman-Green and Company, 1896, p. 171. In the autumn of 1896, Russell visited the United States for the first time; he delivered a series of lectures based on "An Essay on the Foundations of Geometry" (1897) at Bryn Mawr College and at Johns Hopkins University.

4   See J.E. McTaggart, *Studies in the Hegelian Dialectic*, Cambridge, Cambridge University Press, 1896.

5   See B. Russell, "Why I Took to Philosophy", in Id., *The Basic Writings of Bertrand Russell: 1903–1959*, edited by Robert E. Egner and Lester E. Denonn, London, Allen & Unwin, 1961, pp. 28–31 (for the quotation, see p. 31).

Judgment (1899), Moore affirmed that a "proposition" was a unity that could be broken up into its constituent parts called "concepts", including a "specific relation between them"[6]. As Russell would state a few years later, "It was towards the end of 1898 that [...] I rebelled against both Kant and Hegel. Moore led the way, but I followed closely in his footsteps"[7].

The notion of class became fundamental in Russell's thought. The relationship between a class and its members was similar to the relationship between a whole and its parts; unlike a "whole", however, a class could be understood independently from that relationship. This allowed him to overcome his doubts about Georg Cantor's theory of the infinite, since he could now think of infinite classes without worrying about the problems of infinite "wholes". Russell believed that mathematics could be reduced to logic[8]; this led him to the discovery of the paradox bearing his name. The contradiction arose from the idea that some sets were members of themselves (e.g., the class of all classes), and some were not (e.g., the class of all men). It was possible to define R as the set of all sets that were not members of themselves; if R was not a member of itself, then its definition dictated that it must contain itself, and if it contained itself, then it contradicted its own definition as the set of all sets that were not members of themselves. The seeds of Russell's paradox were contained in his 1901 article "Recent Work on the Principles of Mathematics"[9], written at the time of his initial enthusiasm for Peano's logic, and later in *The Principles of Mathematics* (1903)[10]. The response to the paradox came with the development of his theory of types; it was introduced in the 1908 article "Mathematical Logic as Based on the Theory of Types"[11] and in the three-volume work he co-authored with Alfred North Whitehead, *Principia Mathematica* (1910–1913)[12]. In his opinion, it was possible to arrange all sentences into a hierarchy, beginning with sentences about individuals at the lowest level,

---

6   See G.E. Moore, "The Nature of Judgment", in *Mind*, April 1899, vol. 8, no. 2, pp. 176–193 (for the quotation, see p. 180).
7   See B. Russell, *My Philosophical Development*, London, Allen & Unwin, 1959, p. 54.
8   Like the German philosopher and logician Gottlob Frege, Russell's basic idea for supporting logicism was that numbers could be identified with classes of classes.
9   See B. Russell, "Recent Work on the Principles of Mathematics", in *International Monthly*, 1901, vol. 4, pp. 83–101.
10 Id., *The Principles of Mathematics*, Cambridge, Cambridge University Press, 1903.
11 Id., "Mathematical Logic as Based on the Theory of Types", in *American Journal of Mathematics*, July 1908, vol. 30, no. 3, pp. 222–262.
12 See A.N. Whitehead, B. Russell, *Principia Mathematica*, 3 vols., Cambridge, Cambridge University Press, 1910–1913.

sentences about sets of individuals at the next lowest level, sentences about sets of sets of individuals at the next lowest level, and so on.

Russell used logic to clarify issues concerning the foundations not only of mathematics but also of philosophy. He believed that accepted statements were open to doubt because they referred to entities that might be known only through inference; therefore – he explained in *Our Knowledge of the External World* (1914)[13] – it was not possible to think that our beliefs were reliable. In this regard, Russell's response was twofold. From a metaphysical point of view, he developed his famous theory of logical atomism, whereby the world was considered as a complex of logical atoms with their properties and relations; they formed the atomic facts that, in turn, combined to form logically complex objects. From an epistemological point of view, he argued that each questionable entity might be defined in terms of another entity – or entities – whose existence was more certain.

He made advances in philosophical analysis also in his article "On Denoting" (1905)[14]; more precisely, "denoting" was the concept used for the purely logical – rather than linguistic – relation between a concept and that to which it referred. For example, the description "the next prime after seven" denoted the number eleven, "the positive square root of four" denoted the number two, and so on. Denoting phrases were central to mathematics, especially in Russell's "logistic" theory, in which they were crucial in identifying classes – "the class of all moral beings", "the class of natural numbers". Another of Russell's relevant contribution was his defence of "neutral monism", the view that the world consisted of just one type of substance that was neither exclusively mental nor exclusively physical. In this sense, it rejected dualism – the view that distinct mental and physical substances existed. He began to develop this theory while working on his *Theory of Knowledge* (1913) and his article "On the Nature of Acquaintance" (1914)[15]; he conceived "neutral monism" as "the theory that the things commonly regarded as mental and the things commonly regarded as physical [did] not differ in respect of any intrinsic property possessed […], but differ[ed] only in respect of arrangement and context"[16]. In 1910, Russell was appointed lecturer at Trinity College. Before the war, he met Ludwig Wittgenstein, a brilliant young Austrian who was

---

13 See B. Russell, *Our Knowledge of the External World as a Field for Scientific Method in Philosophy*, Chicago-London, Open Court Publishing, 1914. This work was composed of lectures delivered as Lowell Lectures in Boston in March and April 1914.
14 Id., "On Denoting", in *Mind*, October 1905, vol. 14, no. 56, pp. 479–493.
15 Id., "On the Nature of Acquaintance", in *Monist*, January 1914, vol. 24, no. 1, pp. 1–16; ib., April 1914, vol. 24, no. 2, pp. 161–187; ib., July 1914, vol. 24, no. 3, pp. 435–452.
16 Id., *The Collected Papers of Bertrand Russell. Theory of Knowledge. The 1913 Manuscript*, vol. 7, edited by Elizabeth Ramsden Eames, London, Routledge, 1984, p. 15.

studying logic at Trinity College; from 1911 to 1914, he collaborated with Russell, who soon considered Wittgenstein as a real example of genius. In a series of articles entitled *The Philosophy of Logical Atomism*, Russell acknowledged his debt to Wittgenstein in the development of analytic philosophy: on the logical structure of language, the atomic propositions were the simplest statements; more complex molecular propositions were composed of atomic propositions through the logical connectives[17]. However, the following – and only – book by Wittgenstein, published as *Logisch-philosophische Abhandlung*, would undermine the approach to logic that had inspired Russell's contributions[18].

Alongside his brilliant studies in mathematics, philosophy and logic, Russell began to develop an intense civil and political commitment. In 1907, he unsuccessfully ran for Parliament; although he stood as an independent, he endorsed the Liberal platform. He advocated extending women's suffrage, provided that such a radical political change be introduced by constitutional means; three years later, he published the work *Anti-Suffragist Anxieties*[19]. In the first half of 1914, Russell was a lecturer in logic at Harvard University; in this capacity, he visited several East Coast universities. In those months, he hoped for the survival of the Liberal government headed by Herbert Henry Asquith, since he thought that a Conservative government would wage war against Germany, but his faith vanished when also the Liberal Party decided to fight the Second Reich. With the outbreak of the First World War, Russell became involved in campaigning for peace and against conscription; the British authorities regarded him as a political agitator. In November 1914, Fenner Brockway and Clifford Allen established the No-Conscription Fellowship, a British pacifist movement that included Robert Smillie, Philip Snowden, John Clifford, Bruce Glaiser, and Russell himself.

In 1916, as the chairman of the No-Conscription Fellowship, he was fined 100 pounds for authoring a pamphlet in defence of Ernest Everett, a young pacifist teacher who had refused to perform military service. Due to his anti-war conviction, he was dismissed from Trinity College, following the "Defence of the Realm Act"[20]. Two years later, he was once again convicted for his lecturing against

17 Id., "The Philosophy of Logical Atomism (Lectures 1–2)", in *The Monist*, October 1918, vol. 28, no. 4, pp. 495–527; Id., "The Philosophy of Logical Atomism (Lectures 3–4)", ib., January 1919, vol. 29, no. 1, pp. 32–63; Id., "The Philosophy of Logical Atomism (Lectures 5–6)", ib., April 1919, vol. 29, no. 2, pp. 190–222; Id., "The Philosophy of Logical Atomism (Lectures 7–8)", ib., July 1919, vol. 29, no. 3, pp. 345–380.
18 See L. Wittgenstein, "Logisch-Philosophische Abhandlung", in *Annalen der Naturphilosophie*, 1921, vol. XIV, pp. 185–262 (published in English as *Tractatus Logico-Philosophicus*, Introduction by Bertrand Russell, London, Kegan Paul, 1922).
19 See B. Russell, *Anti-Suffragist Anxieties*, London, People's Suffrage Federation, 1910.
20 See G.H. Hardy, *Bertrand Russell and Trinity*, London, Cambridge University Press, 1942.

inviting the United States to enter the war on the United Kingdom's side; the result was six months' imprisonment in Brixton Prison. During the Great War, Russell began to support the pacifist cause also in his books. *Justice in War-Time* (1916) contained a collection of his articles on the war; in these essays, he traced the theory of non-resistance and imagined what might happen if Great Britain used it with the invaders as a means of defence[21]. In *Political Ideals* (1917), he discussed the need for an "international government" to overcome the anarchy between states endowed with "legislative" and "judicial" functions, and one "only army and navy"[22]. In *Why Men Fight* (1917), he developed some ideas related to the Freudian theories. Indeed, he stated that "all human activity" sprang from two sources: "impulse and desire"[23]. Impulses, which were at the basis of our life much more than desires, could be "divided into those that [made] for life and those that [made] for death"[24]: the former created art and science, and the latter were embodied in the war. In *Proposed Roads to Freedom* (1918), he highlighted the capitalistic factors that promoted war, first of all the desire of the financial world to exploit the resources of undeveloped countries; however, he did not recommend abolishing capitalism as a means of achieving peace[25].

At the end of the Great War, his political views gradually changed; he abandoned his inherited liberalism to approach a liberal and humanitarian socialism. He was initially sympathetic to the 1917 Russian Revolution; after the abdication of Tsar Nicholas II, the Provisional Government declared its commitment to civil and political liberties, and its intention to end war on the basis of "no annexations and no reparations". All this appeared to Russell as a useful combination of liberalism and socialism. However, the subsequent brutal suppression of the Bolshevik Government, as well as his visit to the Soviet Union in 1920 with a British Labour Party delegation, left him with a deep loathing for Soviet communism, which he expressed in his book *The Practice and Theory of Bolshevism* (1920)[26]. On his return from Russia, he received an invitation from the Chinese Lecture Association to spend a year at the University of Peking as a visiting lecturer.

In 1921, Russell married his second wife, Dora Black, a young graduate of Girton College, Cambridge, with whom he had two children, John and Kate.

---

21 See Russell, *Justice in War-Time*.
22 Id., *Political Ideals*, New York, The Century, 1917, p. 155 and p. 157.
23 Id., *Why Men Fight. A Method of Abolishing the International Duel*, p. 7.
24 Ibid., p. 18. Already in the *Principles of Social Reconstructions* Russell had affirmed that "all human activity [sprang] from two sources: impulse and desire". See B. Russell, *Principles of Social Reconstructions*, London, Allen & Unwin, 1916, p. 12.
25 Id., *Roads to Freedom: Socialism, Anarchism, and Syndicalism*, London, Allen & Unwin, 1918.
26 Id., *The Practice and Theory of Bolshevism*, London, Allen & Unwin, 1920.

Between 1922 and 1923, he ran twice more for Parliament, once again unsuccessfully; in these years, he wrote books relating to developments in modern science such as *The ABC of Atoms* (1923) and *The ABC of Relativity* (1925)[27]. In the second half of the 1920s, Russell's writings on ethics and politics made him internationally a charismatic and controversial figure for his pursuit of educational reform, his anticlericalism, and his provocative challenge to conventional sexual morality. In his book *On Education* (1926), he highlighted "the conception of gradual chequered progress, perpetually hampered by the savagery which we inherited[ed] from the brutes" favoured by the "mastery of ourselves through knowledge"; to this end, human race as a whole had to fight "against chaos and darkness" through "the little tiny lamp of reason"[28]. In his public lecture *Why I Am Not a Christian* (1927), delivered at the Battersea Town Hall in London, Russell sought to explain why he did not believe in a personal God and in immortality while expressing doubts over the morality of Christian religion as predominantly based on fear[29]. In *Marriage and Morals* (1929), he overcame the Victorian notions of morality regarding sex and marriage; he conceived love as "the principal means of escape from the loneliness which afflict[ed] most men and women"[30]. *The Conquest of Happiness* (1930) was a detailed practical application of Russell's ethic; the debt to Spinoza appeared explicit: "The man capable of greatness of soul will open wide the windows of his mind, letting the winds blow freely upon it from every portion of the universe"[31]. The happy man was one who had expanded his interests in life beyond the merely personal; thus, Russell adhered to utilitarianism but despised the mechanical approach of the "felicific calculus".

However, it was Spinoza who primarily influenced his religious view[32]; Russell did not support the traditional religion of Christianity because it was independent of dogmatic theology and any particular knowledge or revelation, and of so-called natural theology, which held to the conception of God as a person[33]. In this regard, he defined Spinoza as "the noblest and most loveable of the great philosophers" and "ethically supreme", and added that "he was born a Jew, but the

---

27 Id., *The ABC of Atoms*, New York, Dutton & Company, 1923; Id., *The ABC of Relativity*, New York, Harper & Brothers, 1925.
28 Id., *On Education, Especially in Early Childhood*, London, Allen & Unwin, 1926, pp. 208–209.
29 Id., *Why I Am Not a Christian*, London, Rationalist Press, 1927.
30 Id., *Marriage and Morals*, London, Allen & Unwin, 1929, p. 99.
31 Id., *The Conquest of Happiness*, London, Allen & Unwin, 1930, p. 226.
32 Russell was influenced by English jurist Frederick Pollock's book *Spinoza: His Life and Philosophy* (London, Paul Kegan & Co., 1880).
33 Regarding Spinoza's influence on Russell's works, see K. Blackwell, *The Spinozistic Ethics of Bertrand Russell*, London, Allen & Unwin, 1985.

Jews excommunicated him. Christians abhorred him equally; although his whole philosophy [was] dominated by the idea of God, the orthodox accused him of atheism"[34].

From 1931, Russell sat in the House of Lords as he became the 3rd Earl Russell upon the death of his brother. Between the two World Wars, he wrote the book *Which Way to Peace?* (1936)[35], in which he once again supported the establishment of an international government with an armed force to prevent conflicts; he did not imagine that Hitler, Mussolini, or Stalin would voluntarily renounce their national and dictatorial power. In 1936, Russell married his third wife, Patricia Spence, a young University of Oxford undergraduate with whom he had a son, Conrad[36]. In highlighting a realistic *modus pensandi*, he did not fail to epitomize the liaison between empiricism and liberalism; he portrayed himself as a "British Whig, with a British love of compromise and moderation"[37]. In *Power: A New Social Analysis* (1938), he emphasized the liberal dilemma. He demonstrated how to preserve liberty without falling into anarchy and how to use power without falling into domination, since "every community [was] faced with two dangers, anarchy and despotism"[38]; the antithesis of these seemed to be built into liberal theory, giving it instability. Consistently with the Freudian theories, politics issued out of the needs of individual passions. Animal desires were specific and satiable, whereas human desires were "essentially boundless and incapable of complete satisfaction"; for mankind's "infinite desires" came "the need of compromise and government [...] and the need of morality to restrain anarchic self-assertion"[39]. Therefore, he conceived liberalism as a middle ground between anarchy and despotism. From 1938 to 1944, Russell lived in the United States, where he taught at Chicago and Los Angeles Universities. In 1940, he was appointed philosophy professor at the City College of New York, but the appointment was revoked following a judicial decision based on his atheism and advocacy of open marriages. In the same year, he was offered a fellowship at the Barnes Foundation in Philadelphia; he was able to integrate the lectures he delivered in Philadelphia between 1941 and 1942 into

---

34 See B. Russell, *A History of Western Philosophy and Its Connection with Political and Social Circumstances from the Earliest Times to the Present Day*, London, Allen & Unwin, 1945, p. 592.
35 Id., *Which Way to Peace?*, London, Michael Joseph, 1936.
36 His private life remained turbulent; in 1952 he married his fourth wife, Edith Finch.
37 See B. Russell, *Sceptical Essays*, London, Allen & Unwin, 1928, p. 11.
38 Id., *Power: A New Social Analysis*, London, Allen & Unwin, 1938, p. 211.
39 Ibid., pp. 7–9.

the book *A History of Western Philosophy* (1945)[40], which analysed a wide range of philosophers from the Pre-Socratics to John Dewey.

In 1944, Russell returned to Trinity College, where he lectured on the ideas that formed his last major contribution to philosophy, *Human Knowledge: Its Scope and Limits* (1948). After the Second World War, he was awarded the Order of Merit in 1949, and on 11 December 1950, he received the Nobel Prize for Literature "In recognition of his varied and significant writings in which he champions humanitarian ideals and freedom of thought". These words showed his intense and farsighted commitment to peace and human rights. From 1950 until his death, he continued to be a leading figure in the international peace movement because of his campaigns for nuclear disarmament and human rights, and against the Vietnam War[41]. The Bikini test of the H-bomb in March 1954 made it clear that this weapon was about a thousand times more powerful than the A-bomb. He once again considered world government as the only alternative to the disaster of nuclear war between the Americans and the Soviets. Thus, he recommended that some neutral countries form a commission of experts to report on the destructive effects of the hydrogen bomb and to submit it to the great powers. He subsequently drafted a statement for scientists to sign, which he sent to Albert Einstein. The 1955 Russell-Einstein Manifesto highlighted the dangers posed by nuclear weapons and called for world leaders to seek peaceful resolutions to international conflicts; it was signed by 11 of the most prominent nuclear physicists and intellectuals of the time. In 1958, Russell became the founding president of the Campaign for Nuclear Disarmament[42] and, two years later, Honorary President of the "Committee of 100"[43]. In 1961, he was once again imprisoned, this time for a week in connection with antinuclear protests. He made his authoritative voice heard also in the last years of his life. In October and November 1962, he

---

40 Id., *A History of Western Philosophy and Its Connection with Political and Social Circumstances from the Earliest Times to the Present Day*.

41 On Russell's view on nuclear disarmament and the Vietnam war, see *New Hopes for a Changing World*, London, Allen & Unwin, 1951; *Common Sense and Nuclear Warfare*, London, Allen & Unwin, 1959; *Has Man a Future?*, New York, Simon & Schuster, 1961; *War Crimes in Vietnam*, London, Allen & Unwin, 1967; *Russell's Peace Appeals*, edited by Tsutomu Makino and Kazuteru Hitaka, Tokio, Eichosha's New Current Books, 1967.

42 The Campaign for Nuclear Disarmament was set up in November 1957 due to widespread fear of nuclear conflict and the effects of nuclear tests; in the mid-1950s, Britain had become the third atomic power after the United States and the USSR had just tested an H-bomb.

43 The "Committee of 100" was a British antiwar group. It was created in 1960 with a hundred public signatories that included Bertrand Russell, Ralph Schoenman and Michael Scott. Its supporters used civil disobedience and mass nonviolent resistance as a means of achieving their aims.

intervened as a peacemaker in two delicate international situations: the Cuban Missile Crisis, which represented the most critical moment of the Cold War, and the dispute between China and India in Kashmir. From 1963, the Bertrand Russell Peace Foundation supported his work for human rights and social justice with a specific attention to the dangers of nuclear war; with the US military intervention in Vietnam, he founded, with Jean-Paul Sartre, the Russell Tribunal against war crimes. He also called for Israel's withdrawal from the territories occupied in June 1967.

The bibliography of publications on Russell appears to be very consistent. His first biography by Alan Wood (1957)[44] was written with the cooperation of Russell himself; however, Wood had no access to his unpublished manuscripts. The following three biographies by Ronald William Clark (1975)[45] and Caroline Moorehead (1992)[46] focused more on Russell's private life than on his philosophical work; John Greer Slater (1994)[47] further explored his life and influence. A philosophical approach can be found in Peter Hylton's (1990) and Nicholas Griffin's works (1991)[48]; other biographical sources included Ray Monk's two volumes (1996, 2001)[49] and Andrew David Irvine's four volumes (1999)[50]. The books by Nicholas Griffin (1992, 2001)[51] and Bernard Linsky (2011)[52] have helped in making archival material available to the public; furthermore, it is worth mentioning some more recent works by Michael K. Potter (2006), Gregory Landini (2011), Rosalind Carey and John Ongley (2013), Samuel Lebens (2017)[53]. In addition, the amount of writing produced by Russell was extraordinary; he published more than 70

---

44   See A. Wood, *Bertrand Russell: The Passionate Sceptic*, London, Allen & Unwin, 1957.
45   See R.W. Clark, *The Life of Bertrand Russell*, London, Jonathan Cape-Weidenfeld & Nicolson, 1975.
46   See C. Moorehead, *Bertrand Russell: A Life*, London, Sinclair-Stevenson, 1992.
47   See J.G. Slater, *Bertrand Russell*, Preface by Ray Monk, Bristol, Thoemmes Press, 1994.
48   See P. Hylton, *Russell, Idealism and the Emergence of Analytic Philosophy*, Oxford, Clarendon Press, 1990; N. Griffin, *Russell's Idealist Apprenticeship*, Oxford, Clarendon Press, 1991.
49   See R. Monk, *Bertrand Russell: 1872–1920. The Spirit of Solitude*, London, Jonathan Cape, 1996; Id., *Bertrand Russell 1921–1970: The Ghost of Madness*, London, Jonathan Cape, 2000.
50   See A.D. Irvine (ed.), *Bertrand Russell: Critical Assessments*, 4 vols., London, Routledge, 1999.
51   See B. Russell, *The Selected Letters of Bertrand Russell*, edited by Nicholas Griffin, 2 vols., London, Allen Lane-The Penguin Press, 1992–2001.
52   See B. Linsky, *The Evolution of Principia Mathematica: Bertrand Russell's Manuscripts for the Second Edition*, Cambridge, Cambridge University Press, 2011.
53   See M.K. Potter, *Bertrand Russell's Ethics*, London-New York, Continuum, 2006; G. Landini, *Russell*, London-New York, Routledge, 2011; R. Carey, J. Ongley, *Russell*, London, Bloomsbury, 2013; S. Lebens, *Bertrand Russell and the Nature of Propositions: A History and Defence of the Multiple Relation Theory of Judgment*, New York-London, Routledge, 2017.

books, and his bibliography numbers more than 3,000 publications; the Bertrand Russell Archives at McMaster University in Hamilton, Ontario, estimated to hold over 40,000 of his papers[54]. Since 1983, the Bertrand Russell Editorial Project has begun to release his *Collected Papers*; this collection, which is almost completed, will be published in more than 35 volumes.

Russell has been described in both realistic and picturesque ways. The Oxford logician Alfred Jules Ayer (1910–1989) argued that Russell more than any other philosopher of his time "combine[d] universal learning with the direction of human conduct"[55]. The English historian and philosopher Charlie Dunbar Broad (1887–1971) lamented that Russell "produc[ed] a different system of philosophy every few years"[56]; moreover, a man who lived for almost 100 years could potentially change his views several times. Alan Wood (1914–1957), Russell's first biographer, wrote that his philosophy was "an attempt to eliminate the *a priori* and to accentuate the empirical"; this was "perfectly legitimate in a world [...] where changing circumstances continually change[d] the balance of arguments"[57]. Another significant reflection came from the Harvard philosopher Willard Van Orman Quine (1908–2000), who asserted that Russell's books expressed "wit and a sense of newfound clarity with respect to central traits of reality"[58]. In contrast, the British philosopher Ray Monk highlighted Wittgenstein's original thought according to which Russell's books could be identified in two colours, namely "those dealing with mathematical logic in red – and all students of philosophy should read them; those dealing with ethics and politics in blue – and no one should be allowed to read them"[59]. Scholars have generally celebrated Russell's panoptic intelligence by focusing especially on his formidable contributions to mathematics, logic, and epistemology. This book aims to primarily analyse his pacifism; this is a less known dimension to his Renaissance personality, but it serves to help better understand the troubled path of the 20th century.

---

54 The "Bertrand Russell Archive" is contained in over a thousand boxes, each of which holds between 250 and 750 sheets.
55 See A.J. Ayer, "Bertrand Russell as a Philosopher", in *Proceedings of the British Academy*, 1972, vol. 58, pp. 127–151 (for the quotation, see p. 127).
56 Cited by A.J. Ayer, *Russell and Moore: The Analytic Heritage*, London, Allen & Unwin, 1971, p. 9.
57 See A. Wood, *Bertrand Russell: The Passionate Sceptic*, London, Allen & Unwin, 1957, p. 64.
58 See W.V.O. Quine, "Russell's Ontological Development", in *The Journal of Philosophy*, 1966, vol. 63, no. 21, pp. 657–667 (for the quotation, see p. 657).
59 See Monk, *Bertrand Russell 1921–1970: The Ghost of Madness*, p. 278.

The Great War as Watershed of His Pacifist Commitment

In the essay "Experiences of a Pacifist in the First World War" in *Portraits from Memory and Other Essays* (1956), Russell highlighted the real watershed of his pacifist commitment; indeed, he wrote that his life had been "sharply divided into two periods", one before and one after the outbreak of the First World War[60]. On 3 August 1914, the Foreign Secretary Edward Grey delivered a speech at the House of Commons in which he condemned the German invasion of Belgium, highlighting the risks of British non-intervention: "I do not believe [...] that at the end of this war, even if we stood aside we should be in a position [...] to use our force" to "undo what had happened in the course of the war" and above all "to prevent the whole of the west of Europe opposite to us falling under the domination of a single power"[61]. He received the Parliament's support, and on 4 August, Great Britain declared war on Germany. On the same day, Russell wrote a letter for *The Nation*, the house journal of the liberal intelligentsia; he expressed his sense of disillusionment and criticized both Asquith's government and the Liberal Party. Identifying with the "friends of progress", he pointed out that they had been "betrayed" by their "chosen leaders", who had suddenly plunged the country into the war; therefore, "no man whose liberalism [was] genuine [could] hereafter support the members of the present Cabinet"[62]. *The Nation*, which until then had upheld the cause of neutrality, refused to publish this letter; the editor Harold John Massingham accepted to publish the more temperate article "The Rights of War". In this paper, he wrote that those who saw the London crowds on the nights leading to the Declaration of War observed "a whole population, hitherto peaceable and humane, precipitated in a few days down the steep slope to primitive

---

60   See B. Russell, "Experiences of a Pacifist in the First World War", in Id., *Portraits from Memory and Other Essays*, New York, Simon and Schuster, 1956, pp. 26–31 (for the quotation, see p. 26). In reality, Russell's pacifism dated back to 1901 – he was 28 years of age – and appeared as a kind of spiritual conversion: "Ever since my marriage [...] I had forgotten all the deeper issues, and had been content with flippant cleverness"; but suddenly "the ground seemed to give way beneath me", so much so that "I had become a completely different person": a sort of "mystic illumination possessed me" and despite having been "an imperialist I became [...] a pro-Boer and a pacifist"; Id., *The Autobiography of Bertrand Russell 1872–1914*, vol. I, pp. 220–221.

61   Sir Edward Grey's Speech Before Parliament, 3 August 1914, Parliamentary Debates, Commons, Fifth Series, vol. LXV, 1914, cols. 1809–1834.

62   See B. Russell, "Friends of Progress Betrayed", 4 August 1914, in Id., *The Collected Papers of Bertrand Russell. Prophecy and Dissent, 1914–16*, vol. 13, edited by Richard A. Rempel, London, Routledge, 1988, pp. 3–5.

barbarism"; however, the real target of his polemic was the "secret diplomacy" of the Foreign Office, which had caused "all this madness, all this rage, all this flaming death of our civilisation and our hopes"[63].

Russell believed that authoritarian government measures, notably the Defence of the Realm Act already approved on 8 August, could inflict a mortal blow to the Victorian values of tolerance and internationalism by closing an era of progressive enlargement of democratic institutions and personal liberties. In this regard, Leonard Woolf pointed out: "In the decade before the 1914 war [...] it seemed as though human beings might really be on the brink of becoming civilized"; the enemies of progress brought about the war, however, and thus "postponed the danger of becoming civilized for at least a hundred years"[64]. After Philip Morrell's brave speech in the House of Commons on 3 August 1914[65], a group of politicians and writers opposed to the war – including Labour leader Ramsay MacDonald, Quaker Joseph Rowntree, "Neutrality League" founder Norman Angell, journalist Edmund Dene Morel, and Liberal MP Charles Trevelyan – converged into the Union of Democratic Control (UDC), a British pressure group formed in September 1914 to advocate a less aggressive foreign policy[66]. Their British Foreign Policy, Anti-War Party Manifesto shared many of Russell's views: a foreign policy under a democratic parliamentary control, no punitive measures or humiliations imposed upon the defeated countries, the need to re-establish civilized and harmonious relations between the European powers; thus, he joined the UDC. In his

---

63 Id., "The Rights of War", in *The Nation*, 15 August, 1914. This article can also be found in Id., *The Collected Papers of Bertrand Russell. Prophecy and Dissent, 1914–16*, vol. 13, pp. 6–9 (for the quotations, see p. 7).

64 See L. Woolf, *Beginning Again: An Autobiography of the Years 1911–1918*, London, The Hogarth Press, 1964, pp. 36–37.

65 At the House of Commons, Philip Morrell was among the prominent Liberal MPs who expressed their horror on the eve of war. On 3 August, he stressed that Germany had never refused to negotiate and had guaranteed Belgian integrity: "We are going to war now because of fear and jealousy fostered by large sections of the press [...] the fear and jealousy of German ambition, that is the real reason". Edmund Harvey – Liberal MPs, Quaker and pacifist – claimed that war had been caused "by men in high places, by diplomatists working in secret, by bureaucrats who [were] out of touch with the peoples of the world". Germany and Belgium, Hansard, House of Commons, Adjournment Debate, 3 August 1914, vol. 65, cc1839.

66 On the UDC, see G.G. Coulton, *The Main Illusion of Pacifism: A Criticism of Mr. Norman Angell and of the Union of Democratic Control*, Cambridge, Bowes & Bowes, 1916; H.M. Swanwick, *Builders of Peace, Being Ten Years' History of the Union of Democratic Control*, London, The Swarthmore Press, 1924; M. Swartz, *The Union of Democratic Control in British Politics during the First World War*, Oxford, Clarendon, 1971; S. Harris, *Out of Control: British Foreign Policy and the Union of Democratic Control, 1914–1918*, Elloughton, The University of Hull Press, 1996.

UDC pamphlet entitled *War, the Offspring of Fear* (1914), he conceived the ongoing war in racial terms: it was like the barbarian invasion of the Roman Empire, or the medieval wars of Christians and Muslims, a "great race-conflict", more precisely a "conflict of Teuton[s] and Slav[s], in which certain other nations, England, France and Belgium, ha[d] been led into cooperation with the Slav[s]"[67]. In addition, he once again criticized the deceptive plots of diplomacy through which the government had received the House of Commons' consent for the British intervention without informing the public: "Secret diplomacy must cease"[68].

In the paper "Why Nations Love War" written for Norman Angell's monthly journal *War and Peace*, Russell began to highlight the psychological causes of armed conflicts: due to primitive instincts – such as distrust of foreigners; lust for excitement; desire for triumph, honour and power; a passionate devotion to one's own nation – the impulse to war could not be eradicated, hence he argued that "a stable peace [could] only be attained by a process of popular education"[69]. Angell represented a relevant point of reference for Russell; according to Angell, war was not justifiable due to its destructiveness, which almost always outweighed any potential benefits, rather than from a belief that it was immoral. In this view, Russell also supported a kind of utilitarian pacifism; it was not by chance that he shared Richard Cobden's conviction that peace and British interests were most effectively protected through the international diffusion of free trade and the practice of non-interference in European affairs. Moreover, the basic assumption of both Tory and Whig diplomacy, from George Canning in the 1820s to Edward Grey in 1914, was that British continental and imperial interests were best served by maintaining a balance of power among the major European states.

In January 1915, Russell published the article "Ethics of War" in *The International Journal of Ethics*[70], in which he argued that contrary to widespread

---

67 See B. Russell, "War the Offspring of Fear", London, Union of Democratic Control, 1914. This article has been reprinted as paper 4 in Id., *The Collected Papers of Bertrand Russell. Prophecy and Dissent, 1914–16*, vol. 13, pp. 39–47 (for the quotation, see p. 40).
68 Ibid., p. 46.
69 See B. Russell, "Why Nations Love War", in *War and Peace*, November 1914, pp. 20–21, reprinted as paper 9 in Id., *The Collected Papers of Bertrand Russell. Prophecy and Dissent, 1914–16*, vol. 13, pp. 32–36 (for the quotation, see p. 36).
70 See B. Russell, "The Ethics of War", in *The International Journal of Ethics*, January 1915, pp. 127–142. Russell classified wars of "colonization", "principle", "self-defence" and "prestige". The first kind of war, for example the conflicts between the Europeans and American Indians, could be justified because there was "a very great and undeniable difference between the civilization of the colonizers and that of the dispossessed natives". He justified the English and the American Civil Wars as wars of principle, where "the progress of mankind depend[ed] upon the adoption of certain beliefs or institutions, which, through blindness or natural depravity, the other side

opinion, treaties were only observed when "it [was] convenient to do so". The "rules of diplomatic games" had nothing to do with the question of whether participating in a war was or was not for the good of mankind; it was "this question which ha[d] to be decided in considering whether a war is justified or not"[71]. He also pointed out that "the principle of non-resistance contain[ed] an immense measure of wisdom" if men had the courage to carry it out; more precisely, it was not only a "distant religious ideal" but also "the course of practical wisdom" between "civilized nations"[72]. The US philosopher Ralph Barton Perry did not share Russell's opinions; in April 1915, he wrote the paper "Non-Resistance and the Present War: A Reply to Mr. Russell", in which he defined the war as an "unmitigated calamity" and regarded England as a country capable of taking international treaties and conventions seriously, and of strongly condemning "a nation that violate[d] them"[73]. He also criticized Russell for being "willing to contemplate, as preferable to warlike resistance, even the loss of political independence", proposing to "combine with non-resistance [...] the English constitutionalism"[74]. Russell's reply came in October 1915 in his article "The War and Non-Resistance: A Rejoinder to Professor Perry". On this occasion, he recognized that "treaty-breaking [was] a crime", for respecting treaties could lead to the diffusion of the idea of "law between nations". At the same time, however, he realistically pointed out that it was not necessary to "embark upon a universal crusade against other nations which fail[ed] to observe them"[75]. As for Perry's theses against non-resistance, he argued that his

[did] not regard as reasonable". He believed that the war of self-defence could be "almost universally admitted" but presented the risk of being "very convenient"; from this perspective, every state could claim that "the true defence [was] offence" and that its own overwhelming strength was "the only possible guarantee of the world's peace". The fourth kind of war could be traced back to the current goal of Balkan hegemony, which was "entirely a question of prestige"; in this case, men desired "the sense of triumph" and feared "the sense of humiliation": such evils could be considered "worthy of a great nation, showing fidelity to ancestral traditions". In short, Russell justified a war against an inferior civilization – those of colonization, principle, self-defence – but no a war of prestige. Ibid., pp. 133–140.

71 Ibid., pp. 129–130.
72 Ibid., pp. 139–140.
73 See R.B. Perry, "Non-Resistance and the Present War: A Reply to Mr. Russell", in *The International Journal of Ethics*, April 1915, vol. 25, no. 3, pp. 307–316 (for the quotations, see p. 308 ff.).
74 Ibid., pp. 312–313.
75 See B. Russell, "The War and Non-Resistance: A Rejoinder to Professor Perry", in *The International Journal of Ethics*, October 1915, vol. 26, no. 1, pp. 23–30 (for the quotations, see pp. 25–26).

interlocutor ignored the limitations that he himself had already suggested: "The doctrine of non-resistance [was] only applicable to wars between civilized states"[76].

Russell also formulated a motivated indictment against those who had betrayed their mission as intellectuals, their illuminating function and cultural commitment as educators and reformers of consciences, their duty to defend eternal values such as rationality, peace, and democracy. In the article "An Appeal to the Intellectuals of Europe" (1915), he criticized the "complete lack of detachment" shown by most of the intellectual world on the occasion of the outbreak of the Great War. Due to allegiance to their own country, their "thought ha[d] become the slave of instinct, not its master"; so much so that "the guardians of the temple of Truth […] [had] been the first to promote the idolatrous worship"[77]. Suffice to say that the Germans spoke of England's brutal national egotism and represented themselves as fighting to maintain a great ideal of civilization against an envious world; the English stressed the ruthless militarism of the Second Reich and considered themselves as defenders of the sacredness of treaties and the rights of small nations. Russell's theses were criticized by Gilbert Murray, Regius Professor of Greek at Oxford University, in his essay "The Foreign Policy of Edward Grey 1906–1915". With implicit reference to Russell, Murray pointed out that it was a characteristic of British politics that even in times of crisis there were men who criticized severely their country's action and expounded sympathetically the case for their enemies. So, "the central enemy of the human race" was Edward Grey, together with the British Cabinet; furthermore, "the Kaiser [was] to them a prisoner in the dock"[78]. However, the most informed people considered the German attack on Belgium as one of the most obvious events that had caused the war. Already in December 1915, Russell published the pamphlet *The Policy of the Entente, 1904–1914: A Reply to Professor Gilbert Murray*, in which he argued that the "central enemy of the human race" appeared as a "melodramatic conception", and therefore, it was "more profitable to be conscious of our own faults than of the faults of our enemies" so as not to further foment hatred on both sides; furthermore, he "consistently regarded him [the Kaiser] as one of the sources of evil in the world". If Murray were correct

---

76 Ibid., p. 27.
77 See B. Russell, "An Appeal to the Intellectuals of Europe", in *International Review*, 1915, vol. 1, no. 4–5, pp. 145–151 and pp. 223–230. This article was also published in Id., *Justice in War-Time*, pp. 1–19 (for the quotation, see pp. 2–3).
78 See G. Murray, *The Foreign Policy of Sir Edward Grey 1906–1915*, Oxford, Clarendon Press, 1915, p. 6.

in his argument, however, he would perceive that "the Kaiser's guilt [could not] alone suffice to establish the immaculate sinlessness of our Foreign Office"[79].

A harsh criticism of Russell's pacifism came also from David Herbert Lawrence. Russell had begun a correspondence with, and a series of visits to, Lawrence, which seemed to promise a productive cultural relationship[80]; in June 1915, they discussed giving a series of public lectures together in response to the war. Russell sent Lawrence a copy of his article "The Danger to Civilisation" of 4 September 1915, in which he emphasized the catastrophic effect of the war on the tradition of European civilization. If the conflict did not come to an end soon, "the mental calibre of the next generation [was] almost certain to be considerably lower than that of generations educated before the war", and with "the end of a great epoch [...] the future of Europe [would] not be on a level with its past"[81]. The essay expressed a well-founded series of moral and social concerns; therefore, it is difficult to explain Lawrence's reflections contained in a 14 September letter in which he accused Russell of harbouring the desire for war in repressed forms: "You [were] really the super-war-spirit" and "what you want[ed was] to jab and strike, like the soldier with the bayonet", and he added: "You [were] simply full of repressed desires, which ha[d] become savage and anti-social"[82]. In contrast, Russell received the support of the Bloomsbury Group, which included English writers, philosophers, economists, critics and artists such as Virginia and Leonard Woolf, John Maynard Keynes, Edward Morgan Forster, Roger Fry, and Lytton Strachey. As Professor of English Literature at Oxford University Hermione Lee notes, this group reacted against "the bourgeois habits [...] and the conventions of Victorian life"[83], with its

---

79 See B. Russell, *The Policy of the Entente, 1904–1914: A Reply to Professor Gilbert Murray*, Manchester, The National Labour Press, 1915. This essay was also published in Id., *Justice in War-Time*, pp. 123–215 (for the quotations, see p. 126).

80 As for the relationship between Lawrence and Russell, see above all R. Monk, "The Tiger and the Machine: D.H. Lawrence and Bertrand Russell", in *Philosophy of the Social Science*, June 1996, vol. XXVI, no. 2, pp. 205–246.

81 See B. Russell, "The Danger to Civilisation", in *The Times*, 4 September, 1915. This article was later published in Id., *Justice in War-Time*, pp. 105–122 (for the quotations, see pp. 115–116 and p. 121).

82 Letter from David Herbert Lawrence to Bertrand Russell, 14 September 1915, in Bertrand Russell Archives (henceforth BRA), Class no. 710, Box no. 5.27, Document no. 052048N, McMaster University Library, Hamilton. See also D.H. Lawrence, *The Letters of D.H. Lawrence*, edited by James T. Boulton et al., 8 vols., Cambridge, Cambridge University Press, 1979–2000, vol. II, p. 392. The British philosopher Ray Monk justified this kind of response because "Russell seem[ed] to argue precisely for the repression [of bodily life in favour of mental life] that Lawrence takes to be the cause of the trouble". See Monk, *Bertrand Russell: 1872–1920. The Spirit of Solitude*, p. 425.

83 See H. Lee, *Virginia Woolf*, London, Chatto & Windus, 1996, p. 54.

emphasis on public achievement in favour of a more informal and private focus on personal relationships and individual pleasure; politically, it embraced mainly left-liberal positions – for example in the fields of feminism, pacifism, sexuality. Keynes had admired Russell's discoveries in symbolic logic[84]; Leonard Woolf stated that Russell had the quickest mind of anyone he had ever known[85]. In 1907, the Bloomsbury Group supported him when he ran as a candidate in favour of women's suffrage and shared his pacifism.

After the downfall of Asquith's Liberal government on 25 May 1915 and its replacement by a coalition government headed by the same Asquith that included the Conservative and Labour Parties, Russell did not fail to criticize the section of the British press that supported the United Kingdom's entry into the war. He sarcastically congratulated the newspapers magnate Alfred Charles William Northcliffe because of his alleged advocacy in an article published in *The Labour Leader*[86]; between 1915 and 1916, Northcliffe's newspapers also called for the establishment of a Minister of Munitions chaired by David Lloyd George[87]. In the article "War and Non-Resistance" published in *The Atlantic Monthly* in August 1915, Russell began to examine in depth – as evidenced by the title – one of the themes most in line with his pacifism. The principle of non-resistance applied in "its extreme form by Quakers and by Tolstoy"[88] could achieve "a far more perfect protection […] than armies and navies", but such progress was hardly to be expected because "the imaginative effort required [was] too great". It was much more likely that it would come through the establishment of a "central government of the world" capable of securing "obedience by force", since the great majority of men would recognize that "obedience [was] better than the present international anarchy"[89]. It was exactly the issue of international anarchy that Russell addressed in two 1915 articles; more precisely, he focused his attention on Anglo-German

---

84 See J.M. Keynes, "My Early Beliefs", in Id., *The Collected Writings of John Maynard Keynes*, 30 vols., London, Macmillan-St. Martin's Press for the Royal Economic Society, 1972, vol. X, pp. 438–439.

85 See L. Woolf, *Sowing: An Autobiography of the Years 1880–1904*, London, The Hogarth Press, 1960, p. 134.

86 See B. Russell, "Lord Northcliffe's Triumph", in *The Labour Leader*, 27 May 1915, vol. 12, no. 21, p. 1.

87 Northcliffe's ownership of *The Times*, the *Daily Mail* and other newspapers meant that he dominated the British press "as it never [had] been before or since by one man", as US historian David Fromkin pointed out. See D. Fromkin, *A Peace to End All Peace: Creating the Modern Middle East 1914–1922*, London, André Deutsch, 1989, p. 233.

88 See B. Russell, "War and Non-Resistance", in *The Atlantic Monthly*, August 1915, pp. 266–274 (for the quotation, see p. 266).

89 Ibid., p. 274.

rivalry. In February, he published "Can England and Germany Be Reconciled After the War?"[90], in which he blamed the naval rivalry between the two countries by proposing, after the war, the establishment of an international neutral navy capable of policing and protecting the waters of both countries. "The Future of Anglo-German Rivalry" can be considered on the same wavelength: the destiny of civilization could be guarantee through "an international army and navy for police purposes", he argued. Within all the great powers, however, "pride [was] stronger than self-interest", so much so that men feared to lose "the opportunity for bullying which [was] afforded by [their] army and navy"[91].

One of Russell's most significant pacifist writings of this period was the pamphlet *The Philosophy of Pacifism* (1916), which was read at the "Conference of the Pacifist Philosophy of Life" held at Caxton Hall, London, on 8 and 9 July 1915. In it, he divided "the moral arguments against war" into "three classes". As to "the intrinsic evils of war", it was incomprehensible how men could tolerate them; this could only be justified through "the blindness of war-time": hatred, cruelty, injustice, and violence were all recognized as "vices" in peacetime, but as soon as war broke out, they were "universally praised and stimulated"[92]. Secondly, he emphasised the "ethical uselessness of punishing a nation": the conception of national punishment had a "psychological source", namely the vindictive desire to cause suffering to the enemy country, but "it [was] impossible for a punishment to be reformatory"[93]. Thirdly, it needed to consider "the practical impossibility of destroying by force" what was of "real value in a nation's life"; the countries that opposed force by "a merely passive resistance" could better discourage the use of force in international relations by instilling "a sense of shame in the aggressive nation"[94].

At the beginning of 1916, Russell criticized the Military Service Act approved by the second Asquith Government, which came into force on 2 March; this act introduced conscription for all single men from 18 to 41 years of age who were liable to be called up for service in the army unless they were married or widowed with children. The Military Service Act also included the so-called conscience

---

90 See B. Russell, "Can England and Germany Be Reconciled after the War?", in *The Cambridge Review*, 10 February 1915.
91 Id., "The Future of Anglo-German Rivalry", in *The Atlantic Monthly*, July 1915, vol. 116, pp. 127–133 (for the quotation, see p. 133). This essay was also published in Id., *Justice in War-Time*, pp. 67–82.
92 Id., *The Philosophy of Pacifism*, London, League of Peace and Freedom, 1915. For this essay see also Id., *The Collected Papers of Bertrand Russell. Prophecy and Dissent, 1914–16*, vol. 13, pp. 147–158 (for the quotation, see p. 147).
93 Ibid., p. 149.
94 Ibid., p. 152.

clause, which established three levels of exemption: firstly, absolute exemption, which was usually reserved for those who were deemed medically unfit for service; secondly, exemption from combatant service, which entailed being conscripted into the Non-Combatant Corps and sent to France to serve behind the lines, digging trenches; thirdly, exemption on condition of taking up work of national importance, such as on farms or in factories. On this theme, his lecture on "The State" – contained in *Principles of Social Reconstructions* (1916) – was very emblematic; he described compulsory military service as "perhaps the extreme example of the power of State". In this regard, he wrote that "it [was] amazing" that "the vast majority of men [had to] tolerate a system which compel[led] them to submit to all the horrors of the battlefield at any moment when their Government compel[led] them to do so"[95].

Principles of Social Reconstructions, which was composed of a series of eight lectures delivered at Caxton Hall, London, between 18 January and 7 March 1916, constituted one of the most original contributions of Russell's political and social thought. As he wrote in the preface, a central theme of these lectures was the distinction between "creative" and "possessive" impulses, together with the conviction that "liberation of creativeness ought to be the principle of reform both in politics and economics"[96]. People were often moved to act by blind and unconscious impulses, as well as by conscious and directed desires; it was necessary not to repress the impulses leading to war but to redirect the energy and the vigour that would otherwise be put into killing people. Russell further analysed the psychological causes of war in the essay *Political Ideas* (1917), in which he highlighted two different types of impulses: the "possessive" ones, which satisfied the acquisition of private goods not always available because they were limited – they could be attributed to the desire for property – and the "creative" or "constructive" ones, which helped in acquiring knowledge and therefore could always be satisfied. The best society was the one in which "the creative impulses play[ed] the largest part and the possessive impulses the smallest"[97]. Unfortunately, institutions rested upon "property and power", and even those that nature had endowed with "great creative gifts" were "infected with the poison of competition", Russell argued[98]. Political institutions had to increase "the opportunities for the creative impulses" by shaping

---

95 See B. Russell, "The State", in Id., *Principles of Social Reconstructions*, pp. 44–76 (for the quotations, see p. 48).
96 Ibid., p. 6.
97 See Russell, *Political Ideas*, p. 8.
98 Ibid., pp. 16, 18.

education and to diminish "the outlets for the possessive instincts" as synonyms for force and domination[99].

In March 1916, Russell joined the No-Conscription Fellowship (NCF), the British pacifist organization founded by Fenner Brockway and Clifford Allen on 27 November 1914. He made strenuous efforts to convert traditional liberal opinion to the NCF's cause. In an impassioned letter to *The Nation*, he described this pacifist organization as "a spontaneous association of those who believe[d] in the sacredness of human life and the brotherhood of man", whose delegates wished to "build Jerusalem in England's green and pleasant land"[100]. In a letter dated 17 April 1916 to Gilbert Murray, Russell hoped for an inquiry into the action of the tribunals and the suspension of the proceedings against those who declared themselves CO: "The objection [was] a matter of conscience", and almost all the COs had "a much greater sense of public duty than the average man" because they were "intensely desirous of serving the community"; given these premises, "we [were] opposed to the Act", since "men who disapproved of war" could not be "in favour of conscription"[101]. His battle against conscription intensified in May, when the government introduced a new Conscription Act that made married men liable as well as single men[102]; in the same month, Russell published an article emblematically entitled "War as an Institution", in which he essentially embraced the idea of a "world federation". He laconically stated that "war [was] one of the permanent institutions of most free communities, just as Parliament [was] one of our permanent institutions". Furthermore, it was a fulfilment of one side of our nature, so it was difficult to suppress the war because it "[sprang] from an impulse rather than from a calculation of the advantages to be derived from it"[103]. Therefore, a lasting peace could be assured only through the establishment of a "world-federation", for as long as there were many sovereign states, each with its own army, there would be war. At the same time, he was realistically aware that this idea was remote, so he argued that "devotion to the nation" was perhaps "the deepest and most widespread religion of the present age"[104].

During a tour of South Wales sponsored by NCF in summer 1916, Russell made propaganda speeches that urged immediate peace negotiations. The case was

---

99 Ibid., p. 34.
100 See B. Russell, "A Clash of Consciences", in *The Nation*, 15 April 1916.
101 Letter from Bertrand Russell to Gilbert Murray, 17 April 1916, in BRA, Class no. 710, Box no. 5.33, Document no. 053519, McMaster University Library, Hamilton.
102 In 1918, a subsequent Act extended the upper age limit to fifty-one.
103 See B. Russell, "War as an Institution", in *The Atlantic Monthly*, May 1916, vol. 117, pp. 603–613 (for the quotation, see p. 603).
104 Ibid., p. 610 and p. 613.

scheduled to be heard at the Mansion House before the Lord Mayor. The court found him guilty, and a fine was imposed of 100 pounds or two months in prison; he was deprived of his Fellowship at Trinity College[105] and forbidden to travel to Harvard University because he was denied his passport. A resolution of the Committee of the League of Peace and Freedom thanked him for his sacrifice in the cause of peace and freedom. It expressed "its strongest indignation at the persecution to which Mr. Russell has been subjected by the Government" while congratulating him for "the homage thus unintentionally paid to his influence and integrity"[106]. Unable to win the support of his countrymen and persuade them to call for their government to begin peace negotiations, Russell looked to the United States as the country that embodied European democratic ideals and was powerful enough to impose a just settlement upon the belligerents. On 4 December, he wrote an "Open Letter to President Wilson" published in *Survey*, in which he affirmed that, after more than two years since the beginning of the conflict, "terror and savagery [had] become the very air we breathe"; if nothing was done to defeat the "fury of national passion", European civilization could "perish as completely as it perished when Rome fell before the Barbarians"[107]. Since "the desire for peace [was] almost universal", the deadlock that prevented the end of the war could only be overcome through the mediation of an external power, and the US Government had the power to "making itself the guarantor of the peace"[108].

Already during the first years of the Great War, Russell developed different forms of pacifism that did not contradict each other. If we consider the classifications made in the first paragraph of this essay, more precisely Norberto Bobbio's thought, Russell supported an "instrumental pacifism" whose action was aimed at limiting the means of war as its disarmament policy – see his strenuous battle against compulsory military service within the CNF – and a "scientific pacifism" whereby the real reason for war was to be found in the primitive

---

105 His five-year lectureship at Trinity ended in summer 1915; the college had offered him a more prestigious Research Fellowship when he received a telegram from Harvard University inviting him to visit once again.
106 Letter from the League of Peace and Freedom to Bertrand Russell, 1916, in BRA, Class no. 710, Box no. 5.28, Document no. 052069, McMaster University Library, Hamilton.
107 See B. Russell, "An Open Letter to President Wilson" (4 December 1916), in *Survey*, 1916, vol. 37, pp. 372–373; this letter was also published in Id., *The Autobiography of Bertrand Russell 1914–1944*, vol. II, pp. 22–25 (for the quotations, see p. 23–24).
108 Ibid., p. 24. Russell had already expressed his confidence in the US president in a letter written to the American poet Gretchen Warren on 18 September 1914: "I admire President Wilson and I hope that he will play a prominent role when peace comes to be discussed". Letter from Bertrand Russell to Gretchen Warren, 18 September 1918, in BRA, Collection code RA3, Recent acquisition no. 1628, McMaster University Library, Hamilton.

impulses of human nature, above all in "creative" or "possessive" ones (*Principles of Social Reconstructions* and *Political Ideas*); in this regard, he shared Sigmund Freud's theories. Instead, if we rely on Wilhelm Emil Mühlmann's reflections, we can affirm that Russell developed a "semi-pacifism" that justified wars under certain conditions, for instance when they were wars of "defence" or against "rebels"; in the article "The Ethics of War", he justified war against inferior civilizations. If we consider Mulford Quickert Sibley's remarks, Russell supported a "political pacifism" that emphasized the need for nonviolent political action based on parliamentary activity: he condemned the secret plots of the British diplomacy headed by Foreign Secretary Edward Grey, which had led to the Great War and the need to respect the treaties – as demonstrated, for example, by his discussions with Ralph Barton Perry and Gilbert Murray. Lastly, if we refer to the opinions of Johan Galtung and David Boersma, we can assert that Russell embraced a "positive pacifism" that involved the establishment of harmonious relations among states, hoping for the overcoming of international anarchy to guarantee a durable peace: in the May 1916 article "War as an Institution", he supported for the first time the idea of a "world federation".

The Debate on the Russian Revolution Beyond the English Channel

In the articles "The Momentum of War" and "Why the War Continues" published between 1916 and 1917, Russell once again explored in depth the theme of human impulses – with special reference to the destructive ones – as causes of war. As he pointed out in the first article, it was necessary to make men and women aware of the "twin passions of fear and hatred"; if the hatred fomented by the militarists was not overcome, "no stable peace [could] be secured"[109]. In the second article, he underlined the growing demand for revenge coming from British public opinion: the "desire for punishment" towards Germany was "merely a form of pride", and it "increase[d] ferocity"; the man in the street believed that peace could be achieved only after "victory" because it seemed "a state of affairs" that "enable[d] him to feel the satisfaction of castigating sin"[110]. In the same vein it is possible to consider the 1917 article "Is Nationalism Moribund?" that Russell wrote on request of the American literary critic Van Wyck Brooks for the US monthly *The Seven Arts*. On this occasion, he analysed the "obscure roots of human nature";

---

109   See B. Russell, "The Momentum of War", in *The Tribunal*, 14 December 1916, no. 39, pp. 1, 3.
110   Id., "Why the War Continues", in *The U.D.C.*, February 1917, no. 2, pp. 41–42.

he argued that the British, the French and the Germans considered themselves as, respectively, the "champions" of parliamentary institutions, the intellectual enlightenment spread by the 1789 Revolution, and the *Kultur* as a synonym for knowledge. However, the belief whereby the nation was "the special guardian of some important idea" was nothing more than a "delusion" fostered by "pride and self-interest". Indeed, beneath "the illusory beliefs of nationalism", there was "a substructure of the herd instinct" that was part of the fundamental structure of human nature. Nevertheless, Russell doubted that nationalism would be "the dominant form of herd instinct" in the next hundred years; an example was offered by the United States, of which he appreciated the federal organization as a guarantee for a peaceful coexistence[111]. He found further confirmation of the darker side of human nature in Freudian psychology; emphasizing his ideological affinity, he wrote: "I am reading Freud [...]. The psychology of [...] political opinion, is an almost untouched field and there is room for really great work in it. In am quite excited about it"[112].

On 22 January 1917, US President Wilson delivered to the Senate his famous "peace without victory" speech calling for a world order in which there would exist "not a balance of power, but a community of power"[113], consistently with the Monroe Doctrine. Germany's announcement of full-scale U-boat warfare came on 31 January; the United States broke off diplomatic relations with the Second Reich, and on 6 April, they declared war. In the months leading up to the United States' entry into the war, Russell observed that part of the US public opinion was denying its support for the League to Enforce Peace (LEP)[114] due to the possible exclusion of the Central Powers. He harboured this reservation because he was afraid of the creation of an authoritarian world order based primarily on the use of force and composed only of the US Allies. In the article "Two Ideals of Pacifism" published in the magazine *War and Peace*, he took issue with Goldsworthy Lowes Dickinson, who believed that this kind of coercion was the best that could be expected in the near future. Russell retorted that although the League to Enforce

---

111 Id., "Is Nationalism Moribund?", in *The Seven Arts*, October 1917, vol. 2, no. 12, pp. 673–687.
112 For this quotation, see Monk, *Bertrand Russell: 1872–1920. The Spirit of Solitude*, pp. 495–496.
113 See T.W. Wilson, "Address to the United States Senate, 22 January 1917", in Id., *The Papers of Woodrow Wilson*, vol. 40, Princeton, Princeton University Press, 1982, pp. 536–537.
114 The League to Enforce Peace was an organization established in Philadelphia in 1915 to promote the formation of an international body for world peace after the outbreak of the Second World War; it was headed by former US President William Howard Taft. LEP proposed an international agreement between participating nations to "jointly use their economic and military force against any one of their number that [went] to war or commit[ed] acts of hostility against another".

Peace could prevent wars for a long time, it was "intolerable" because it would create a scenario similar to that of the Holy Alliance. Therefore, he contemplated the idea of a "neutral authority" to solve the international disputes, but at the same time, he believed that goal could be achieved "without the sanction of force", which was the most dangerous aspect "in the whole scheme" of the LEP[115].

News of the Russian Revolution reached England in early March 1917; the official message of the House of Commons welcomed the overthrow of the oppressive tsarist regime and of "an autocratic militarism which threaten[ed] the liberty of Europe"[116]. The statement of principles of the Russian Provisional Government, initially chaired by Prince Georgy Lvov and then by Alexander Kerensky, provided for a general amnesty for all political and religious offences, freedom of speech and press, and freedom to form labour unions and to strike. Exploiting this opportunity, Russell, along with British campaigner against conscription Catherine Marshall, set up the Committee for Anglo-Russian Co-operation; this committee intended to draw inspiration from Russia's Charter of Freedom issued by the revolutionaries. A British Charter of Freedom was drawn up; it provided for the release of Irish prisoners and of conscientious objectors, the cessation of prosecutions under the Defence of Realm Act, Home Rule and, finally, the request for adult suffrage[117].

On 31 March 1917, anti-war Labour leaders organized a mass meeting in the Royal Albert Hall; this convention was to urge the Lloyd George Coalition to emulate the Russian programme of civil liberties and to exert pressure on the government to negotiate by setting up Workers' and Soldiers' Councils. A resolution was passed sending "joyful congratulations to Russia" and calling upon the British Government "to follow the Russian example by establishing the same freedoms"[118]. Little was heard of the Charter of Freedom campaign after the Albert Hall meeting; however, the British Government was concerned about the great strikes in the engineering industry that took place in May. Lloyd George was alarmed by the "highly-organised labour movement", which showed the danger of "being exploited by violent anarchists"[119]. Lord Milner, one of the members of the War Cabinet, feared that an alliance between pacifists and workers was

---

115 See B. Russell, "Two Ideals of Pacifism", in *War and Peace*, January 1917, no. 40, pp. 58–60.
116 See S.R. Graubard, *British Labour and the Russian Revolution*, Cambridge, Harvard University Press, 1956, pp. 17–18. See also Parliamentary Debates (Commons), 22 March 1917, fifth Series, vol. XCI, col. 2085.
117 See "Britain's Charter of Freedom", 17 March 1917, Catherine Marshall Papers, Box no. 9 4/38, Cumbria County Record Office, Carlisle.
118 See G. Lansbury et al., *Russia Free! Ten Speeches Delivered at the Royal Albert Hall London on 31 March 1917: Authorized Report*, London, The Herald Office, 1917, pp. 20–21.
119 Cabinet Papers, 6 April 1917, 23/2/115[9], Public Record Office, London.

imminent[120]; in fact, he urged Lloyd George to "counteract the very systematic and active propaganda of the pacifists, and to prevent their capturing [...] the working classes"[121].

Russell's faith in the Russian Provisional Government increased in May 1917 because it urged a "peace without annexations or indemnities, on the basis of the self-determination of peoples" (Petrograd formula); this commitment was exactly what the British pacifists were urging[122]. The main activity of the Labour movement's left wing was the calling of the Leeds Convention of 3 June[123]; Francis Johnson of the Independent Labour Party (ILP) and Albert Inkpin of the British Socialist Party (BSP) were responsible for making the arrangements[124]. This event was attended by over 3,000 socialist delegates from the ILP and BSP, united in their pacifist beliefs; speakers included Ernest Bevin, Charlotte Despard, Willie Gallacher, Ramsay MacDonald, Tom Mann, Dora Montefiore, Sylvia Pankhurst, Bertrand Russell, and Philip Snowden. The British sociologist Ralph Miliband described the event as "perhaps the most remarkable gathering of the period"[125]. The Leeds Convention welcomed the Russian Revolution and its attempt to defend civil liberties; it called for an end to the First World War and voted for the establishment throughout the country of Soviet-style Councils of Workmen's and Soldiers' Delegates to work for peace and "the complete political and economic emancipation of international labour"[126]. In Leeds, Russell expressed his belief that the Russian Revolution would involve a complete change in the political, social and economic field at the international level by removing the causes of war. In addition to his weekly editorials for *The Tribune*, the weekly NCF paper, he began his collaboration with *The Herald*, and on 23 June 1917, the latter published a

---

120   See J.O. Stubbs, "Lord Milner and Patriotic Labour, 1914–1918", in *English Historical Review*, October 1972, vol. 87, no. 345, pp. 717–754 (for the quotation, see pp. 738–741).
121   David Lloyd George Papers, 26 May 1917, F/38/2/5 (marked confidential), House of Lords Record Office, London.
122   See B. Russell, "Russia and Peace", in *The Tribunal*, 24 May 1917, no. 60, p. 2.
123   On the 1917 Leeds Convention, see Various Authors, *What Happened at Leeds. Report Published by the Council of Workmen's and Soldiers' Delegates*, London, Adelphi, 1917; S. White, "Soviets in Britain: The Leeds Convention of 1917", in *International Review of Social History*, 1974, vol. 19, no. 2, pp. 165–193; J. Douglas, C. Høgsbjerg (eds.), *British Labour and the Russian Revolution. The Leeds Convention of 1917*, Nottingham, Spokesman Books, 2017.
124   See K. Coates, *British Labour and the Russian Revolution*, Nottingham, Bertrand Russell Peace Foundation, 1974.
125   See R. Miliband, *Parliamentary Socialism: A Study of the Politics of Labour*, London, Allen & Unwin, 1961, p. 55.
126   Various Authors, *What Happened at Leeds. Report Published by the Council of Workmen's and Soldiers' Delegates*, pp. 9–10.

Manifesto; Russell contributed to this document, which, among other measures, called for equality of income and a "complete democracy" in which all titles would be abolished. He wrote to the British philosopher Herbert Wildon Carr that since the Russian Revolution, "every hope of a real international spirit" was spreading across Europe, "combined with a far more humane economic system"[127]. From this perspective, by the time of the Leeds Convention, Russell had already "largely shifted the emphasis from psychological to socio-economic considerations in accounting for war"[128], as the British historian Royden Harrison pointed out. After the Leeds Convention, some local Councils or Soviets were formed; the government was alarmed, and in June, it planned the establishment of the National War Aims Committee (NWAC) to combat pacifist appeals to soldiers and workers alike. The War Cabinet decided that the time had come to undertake "an active campaign to counteract the pacifist movement"[129]; on 15 July, Secretary of State for War Lord Derby warned Lloyd George that there were "signs of Soldier and Workmen Committees being formed"[130].

Influenced by the so-called spirit of Leeds, on 10 July Russell decided to join the ILP; this marked his separation from the Liberals, the party that his grandfather, Earl Russell, had led twice as prime minister. During the summer, he examined in depth the relationship between pacifism, and economic and political revolution in three articles published in *The Tribune*: "Pacifism and Economic Revolution", "A Pacifist Revolution?" and "Pacifism and Revolution". In the first article, he stated that although the movement inaugurated at Leeds was still in "its infancy", the principle of the "brotherhood of man" would lead to "a more just economic system"; more precisely, it was impossible to doubt that "the abolition of capitalism would be a tremendous step towards the abolition of war", as opposed to the British Government's policy engaged in its "war to end war"[131]. In the second article, he wrote that "it [was] through the revolutionary spirit that peace [was] being brought nearer"; so much so that the present economic system had placed "a terrible power in the hands of the landowner and the capitalist" and therefore had condemned the great majority of the population to "a life which ha[d] few possibilities of free development"[132]. In the third article, Russell mainly

---

127 Letter from Bertrand Russell to Herbert Wildon Carr, 27 June 1917, in BRA, Class no. 710, Box no. 5.07, Document no. 048071, McMaster University Library, Hamilton.
128 See R. Harrison, "Bertrand Russell: From Liberalism to Socialism?", in *Russell: The Journal of Bertrand Russell Studies*, 1986, vol. 6, no. 1, pp. 5–38 (for the quotation, see pp. 16–17).
129 Cabinet Papers, 5 June 1917, 23/3/154[22], Public Record Office, London.
130 David Lloyd George Papers, 15 July 1917, F/714/4/59, House of Lords Record Office, London.
131 See B. Russell, "Pacifism and Economic Revolution", in *The Tribunal*, 5 July 1917, no. 65, p. 2.
132 Id., "A Pacifist Revolution?", in *The Tribunal*, 19 July 1917, no. 67, p. 2.

analysed the possible coexistence of pacifism and revolution: "The greatest force on the side of peace" had become "the international revolutionary spirit"; violence and bloodshed were not the essence of revolution, whose success always depended "upon the power of the new ideas over men's minds". Indeed, through the Russian Revolution, "the victims of the old system" had begun to see that "liberty, equality and fraternity" were better than "slavery, injustice, and competition"[133]. In these three articles, we can identify a kind of dualism in Russell's attitude: intellectually, he was now an international socialist who hoped for the abolition of capitalism and the redistribution of economic power, together with the destruction of militarism and bureaucracy; emotionally and methodologically, however, he was still a liberal, believing in ideas, in maximum of personal liberty, and in the power of ideas and reason. His involvement in revolutionary politics did not last long; on 28 July 1917, a meeting was organized at the Brotherhood Church in Southgate Road (London) to elect a Workers' Council on the lines of those proposed at Leeds. Some 1,000 rioters, many of them soldiers and sailors, assaulted the approximately 250 delegates and the meeting was broken up; on this occasion, Russell wrote to the English aristocrat Ottoline Morrell: "I realized vividly how ghastly the spirit of violence is [...]. The mob is a terrible thing when it wants blood"[134].

Compulsory conscription was one of Russell's most debated subjects in 1917. In his first address to the Commons as Prime Minister, David Lloyd George expressed the hope that industrial conscription would mobilise the entire domestic workforce. This legislative threat reaffirmed the convictions of the "absolutists" whereby any acceptance by the conscientious objectors of an alternative service would show connivance in the war effort; the Quakers were among the most convinced supporters of absolutist theses through their American Friends Service Committee[135]. Russell's advocacy of a larger political role for the NCF led him to develop a lively debate within *The Tribunal*[136]; he discussed the prospects of the No-Conscription Fellowship, supporting especially the absolutists who did not

---

133 Id., "Pacifism and Revolution", in *The Tribunal*, 19 July 1917, no. 67, pp. 2–3.
134 Letter from Bertrand Russell to Ottoline Morrell, 28 July 1917, in BRA, Class no. 710, Box no. 2.67, Document no. 001468, McMaster University Library, Hamilton. This letter can also be found in Russell, *The Selected Letters of Bertrand Russell*, edited by Nicholas Griffin, vol. II, pp. 116–117.
135 The American Friends Service Committee (AFSC) was a Quaker organization established in the United States in 1917; it worked for peace and social justice, and to assist civilian victims of the First World War.
136 In January 1917, Russell took over from Clifford Allen as the chairman of the organization, and Catherine Marshall took over from Fenner Brockway as secretary; new sections were established across the country, and from March 1916 the NCF began to publish *The Tribunal*.

accept alternative service under the Home Office Scheme[137]. Russell was aware that their position had a fundamental weakness: their claim to be unable to accept any form of compulsory service was not susceptible to objective proof, and therefore it could be subject to abuse. However, the authorities had to realise that the request for absolute exemption was "a genuine conscientious claim"; therefore, they did not have to punish these men for "a proved and tested conscientious conviction"[138].

In this regard, on 19 March Russell wrote to the editor of *The Manchester Guardian*; he criticized Peter Green, a.k.a. Artifex[139], who had objected to the real motivations of the conscientious objector in the 15 March issue, describing him as a man who was "consciously or unconsciously, an extreme individualist with little sense of solidarity of mankind"[140]. In contrast, Russell countered that the conscientious objector did not believe that "violence [could] cure violence" or that "militarism [could] exorcise the spirit of militarism", for he shared just that "sense of solidarity" with "those called enemies"[141]. Because of his support of the "absolutists", like the leading member of the Independent Party Clifford Allen who had refused to take part in the scheme, Russell was criticized by the "alternativists" – the so-called Home Office men who were prepared to undertake alternative civilian work instead of prison life. On 18 May, he wrote a letter of resignation as Acting Chairman of the NCF; nevertheless, he remained with it for another eight months because he continued to harbour hopes that the organization could play a role in pushing the government to negotiate peace.

The War Cabinet observed the pacifist movements with suspicion; an opportunity to discredit them was provided by the treason trial in France of Bolo Pasha, a newspaper owner who stood accused of being in the pay of the Germans. From about mid-October, the government accepted the allegations that the pacifist defeatists were linked to the British "Bolos"; on 22 October, in a speech

---

137 The Home Office Scheme consisted of work camps set up by the government in 1916 after the Central Tribunal had decided that prisoners were genuine objectors; some COs believed that all this was an act of indirect support for the war, and therefore they remained in prison.

138 See B. Russell, "The Government and Absolute Exemption", in *The Tribunal*, 8 February 1917, no. 46, p. 2.

139 "Artifex" was the pseudonym used by Peter Green (1871–1961), Rector of St. Philips in Salford and Residentiary Canon of Manchester.

140 See B. Russell, "Conscientious Objectors", in *The Manchester Guardian*, 19 March 1917, p. 8.

141 Ibid. Russell supported the cause of the absolutists also in the pamphlet *I Appeal unto Caesar* (1917), emphasizing their respectability and the harshness of the treatment meted out to them in prison. This article can be found in Id., *The Collected Papers of Bertrand Russell. Prophecy and Dissent, 1914–1916*, vol. 13, pp. 206–211.

delivered at the Albert Hall to launch the new war economy campaign, Lloyd George invited his countrymen to condemn "Boloism in all its shapes and forms" because "it [was] the latest and most formidable weapon in the Germany armoury"[142]. At the same time, the First Lord of the Admiralty Edward Carson persuaded the War Cabinet to sanction pacifist organizations such as the UDC, the NCF, the National Council of Civil Liberties (NCCL), and the Fellowship of Reconciliation (FOR); in mid-November 1917 in the Commons, Carson alleged that "the amount of subterranean (pacifist) influence of a pernicious and pestilential character [...] [went] far beyond anything that ha[d] been described in this House"[143]. According to the War Office, the "absolutists" were no different from "agitators", and their release would therefore give them the opportunity to work with organizations such as the NCF, which were "unpatriotic and dangerous"[144]. Lloyd George's views had already been outlined by his private secretary, Lord Lothian (Philip Kerr); Lothian believed that they were "passive resisters" who refused to perform even the civilian service "lawfully imposed by the community", furthermore "at a time of grave national danger"[145]. At the end of 1917, Russell once again criticized compulsory military service in the article "Will Conscription Continue After the War?". He was inspired by the Second Note of Pope Benedict XV to the belligerent powers, which suggested, as one of the Terms of Peace, the universal abolition of conscription through an international agreement. A further source of inspiration was Ottokar Czernin's speech of 2 October 1917, in which the Foreign Minister of Austria-Hungary appeared ready to extricate himself from German policy by sharing the lines of the Petrograd formula. As long as conscription persisted, Russell argued, it was almost impossible for the "neighbouring nations [...] to be on genuinely friendly terms", since each was "continually obsessed by the fear of what its neighbour's conscript army might do"[146].

The British government showed its determination to reject the peace initiatives throughout 1917. In this regard, the case of Arthur Henderson was emblematic; in June, the leader of the Labour Party travelled to Petrograd on behalf of the

---

142 See D. Lloyd George, "The Destruction of a False Ideal", in Id., *The Great Crusade. Extracts from Speeches Delivered During the War*, New York, George Doran Company, 1918, pp. 193–198 (for the quotation, see p. 198). In this regard, see also *The Times*, 23 October 1917, p. 6.
143 *Representation of the People Bill*, Parliamentary Debates (Commons), 21 November 1917, 5th ser., 99, cols. 1209–1325.
144 Cabinet Papers, 22 May 1917, 22/3/142[14], Public Record Office, London.
145 Letter from Kerr to Lloyd George, 16 July 1917, Lord Lothian Papers 40/17/219.f5, National Records of Scotland, Edinburgh.
146 See B. Russell, "Will Conscription Continue After the War?", in *The Tribunal*, 8 November 1917, no. 82, p. 2.

War Cabinet, of which he was a member, to convince the Russian delegates that the peace conference convened at Stockholm would be harmful. On his return, however, he hoped that the proposed conference could start peace negotiations along the lines of the Petrograd formula; this action infuriated the War Cabinet, and Lloyd George forced Henderson to resign on 11 August. On 3 December, German and Russian delegates opened peace negotiations at Brest-Litovsk; in this renewed political scenario, Russell hoped for British participation in the peace negotiations. He was heartened when a special conference of delegates from both the Labour Party and the Trades Union Congress passed a Memorandum on War Aims, which endorsed the foreign policy platform of the UDC: after the war, it was necessary to make the world safe for the development of democracy, define the territorial questions, regulate the economic relations, restore the devastated areas, and hold an international conference of Labour organizations[147]. No less emblematic was the article "International Opinion During 1917", in which Russell highlighted the two outstanding facts of the year: the US entry into the war and the Russian Revolution. Through a kind of self-criticism – see his December 1916 Open Letter to President Wilson – he affirmed that if the United States had remained neutral, "peace would have come during the summer, as a gift of the Russian democracy". He added that after defeating tsarism, Russia imagined that "the Western champions of democracy" would welcome the victory of their revolutionary principles in what had been "the home of autocracy"[148].

In January 1918, Russell became Vice-President of the NCCL, and this commitment coincided with his increasing involvement in the UDC, especially with its executive committee; by working with both organizations, he would reach a larger political audience. The new Military Service Act of March 1918 raised the age limit to 51; this upper limit included Russell himself, who had supported the absolutist positions. The events that led to Russell's imprisonment can be found in an editorial for *The Tribunal*, "The German Peace Offer"; on this occasion, he asserted that any legitimate reason for war was now irrelevant because the Second Reich was ready to negotiate with the Bolsheviks on the basis of "no annexation, no indemnities". If, on the one hand, he urged the Labour Party to use its influence to convince the British Government to accept the Germans' offer of a general peace, on the lines suggested by the Russians, on the other hand, he feared that Western governments were reluctant to respond to the German offer to avoid a triumph of "the hated Bolsheviks" and a lesson on "the way to treat with capitalists, imperialists and war-mongers"[149]. This issue of *The Tribunal* arrived at the Home Office; the

147   Id., "Freedom or Victory?", in *The Pioneer*, 15 December 1917, no. 352, p. 2.
148   Id., "International Opinion During 1917", in *The Tribunal*, 27 December 1917, no. 89, p. 1, 3.
149   Id., "The German Peace Offer", in *The Tribunal*, 3 January 1918, no. 90, p. 1.

authorities criticized Russell's reflections as well as his remarks concerning the American garrison being used to intimidate strikers against war. He was sentenced to six months in Brixton Prison. Furthermore, his hopes that Germany would lead the West by concluding a generous peace with Russia collapsed rapidly; Lenin and Trotsky gave in to German demands concerning the annexation of large portions of the old tsarist empire and the indemnities; all this was formalized through the punitive treaty of Brest-Litovsk of 3 March.

The Russian Revolution led Russell to examine in depth the doctrine of Guild Socialism as the ideology that combined the last authoritarian aspects of socialism – transcending the idea of the dictatorship of the proletariat – with the libertarian characteristic of liberalism. The National Guilds League had been founded in April 1916 by socialists dissatisfied with the collectivism and pro-war policies of the Fabian Society. Russell had read the works of the dominant theorist of Guild Socialism George Douglas Howard Cole, namely *World of Labour* (1913) and *Self-government in Industry* (1917)[150]. In his article "Why I am a Guildsman" (1919), Russell described Guild Socialism as a "necessary compromise" between the tyranny of state socialism and the chaos of anarchism. If state socialism was to be feared because it could become "rigid and Byzantine", anarchism, which aimed to avoid these evils, could soon end in "a military tyranny". To overcome these dangers, "Guild Socialism seem[ed] to me [...] capable, not only of putting an end to poverty and economic injustice, but of securing the greatest sum of liberty and initiative"[151]. As British historian Royden Harrison wrote, "Rightly discerning the impossibilities of anarchism as well as its attractions, he [Russell] needed to show how the state might exercise its function unobtrusively, indirectly and moderately"[152].

Until the end of the First World War, Russell regarded the March Revolution as the greatest missed opportunity during the war because Europe had been on the verge of realising the brotherhood of men. In *Roads to Freedom*, he argued that if the Russian Revolution had been accompanied by a simultaneous revolution in Germany, "the dramatic suddenness of the change might have shaken Europe" and "the idea of fraternity might have seemed, in the twinkling of an eye, to have entered the world of practical politics"; while those who "reject[ed]

---

150   See G.D.H. Cole, *The World of Labour*, London, Bell & Sons, 1913; Id., *Self-Government in Industry*, London, Bell & Sons, 1917.
151   See B. Russell B., "Why I Am a Guildsman", in *The Guildsman: A Journal of Social and Industrial Freedom*, September 1919, no. 33, p. 3; in this regard, see also K. Blackwell, H. Ruja (henceforth B&R), *A Bibliography of Bertrand Russell*, 3 vols., London, Routledge, 1994, C19.31.
152   See Harrison, "Bertrand Russell: From Liberalism to Socialism?", pp. 5–38 (for the quotation, see p. 19).

revolution as a method, and prais[ed] the gradual piecemeal development", as was common in the English-speaking world, overlooked "the effect of dramatic events in changing the mood and the beliefs of whole populations"[153]. In the same essay, Russell highlighted the theme of the uselessness of war that derived from Angell's thought. Before the Great War, Angell had proposed the model of uneconomic war: due to the "economic interdependence of civilized nations", wars of conquest between industrial countries were futile because no state could benefit at the expense of the other. In this regard, Russell emblematically wrote: "As time goes on, the destructiveness of war grows greater and its profits grow less: the rational argument against war acquires more and more force"[154].

On 26 September 1918, the US Army launched one of the biggest offensives of the First World War, namely the Meuse-Argonne Campaign; this battle lasted until Armistice Day on 11 November. In his *Autobiography*, Russell pointed out that his political actions during the Great War had been futile: "When the War was over, I saw that [...] I had not saved a single life or shortened the War by a minute"[155]. This was too harsh a self-appraisal, for he had been instrumental in preserving the NCF, ensuring that the plight of the "absolutists" was kept before the authorities; moreover, a few years later, Prime Minister Neville Chamberlain would share Russell's condemnation of their imprisonments. On 4 May 1939, Chamberlain declared to the Commons that the rights of conscientious objectors would not be violated; referring to the "absolutists", he pointed out that during the Great War "we learned that it was [...] an exasperating waste of time and effort to force such people to act in a manner which was contrary to their principles"[156].

Between Scientific Psychology and the International Political Scenario

The October 1917 Revolution caused Lenin's dissolution of the Constituent Assembly and the Bolshevik Government's brutal suppression of all forms of dissent; despite this, Russell's faith in Socialist Russia had not yet been shattered. In spring 1920, he emphasized the historical importance of the new Russian Revolution: "The Bolsheviks [...] had at any rate proved that Socialism [was]

---

153 See Russell, *Roads to Freedom: Socialism, Anarchism, and Syndicalism*, p. 159.
154 Ibid., p. 157.
155 Id., *The Autobiography of Bertrand Russell 1914–1944*, vol. II, p. 40.
156 *Military Training Bill*, Parliamentary Debates (Commons), 4 May 1939, 5th ser., vol. 346, cols. 2095–2099 (for the quotation, see 2097–2098).

compatible with vigorous and successful State" and what they were doing was of "even greater importance for the future of the world than what [had been] accomplished in France by the Jacobins" because their operations were "on a wider scale" and their theory was "a more fundamental novel"[157]. In May 1920, Russell accompanied the British Labour Delegation as an observer to concretely assess the Bolshevik experiment[158]; he interviewed Gorky in Petrograd, and Kamenev, Trotsky and Lenin in Moscow. After his 19 May interview with Lenin, his disillusionment grew; he described the Bolshevik leader: "He is dictatorial, calm, incapable of fear, extraordinarily devoid of self-seeking, an embodied theory. The materialist conception of history, one feels, is his life-blood"[159]. However, Russell sought to escape official scrutiny: indeed, the anarchist Emma Goldman recalled that "from the very first he refused to be officially chaperoned. [...]. But then what can you expect of a *bourgeois*?"[160]. And the American foreign correspondent Marguerite Harrison noted that Russell was "profoundly shocked by what he regarded as a tendency to Communist imperialism"[161]. In his *Autobiography*, he criticized the rigid orthodoxy and control of the Bolshevik Government: "The time I spent in Russia was one of continually increasing nightmare. [...]. Cruelty, poverty, suspicion, persecution, formed the very air we breathed"[162].

Russell shared his reflections in a series of articles that were later included in *The Practice and Theory of Bolshevism* (1920). In this book, he emblematically considered Bolshevism as "a social phenomenon" that was to be "reckoned as a religion, not as an ordinary political movement", and added that people who accepted it became "impervious to scientific evidence" and committed "intellectual suicide". Among the main religions, Bolshevism could be compared with Mohammedanism rather than with Christianity and Buddhism: the latter were primarily "personal religions, with mystical doctrines and a love of contemplation", whereas Mohammedanism and Bolshevism were "practical, social, unspiritual,

---

157 See B. Russell, "Socialism and Liberal Ideals", in *The English Review*, May–June 1920, vol. 30, pp. 449–455 and pp. 499–508 (for the quotations, see p. 454); see also B&R C20.14.
158 The eleven members were led by trade unionist Ben Turner as chairman, former Liberal Charles Roden Buxton, and physician Leslie Haden-Guest as joint secretaries. Ethel Snowden, Tom Slaw and Robert Williams represented the Labour Party; Margaret Bondfield, Albert Arthur Purcell and Herbert Skinner represented the Trades Union Congress (TUC); Clifford Allen and Richard Collingham Wallhead represented the Independent Labour Party.
159 See Russell, *The Practice and Theory of Bolshevism*, p. 37.
160 See E. Goldman, *Living My Life*, 2 vols., New York, Alfred Knopf, 1931, vol. II, p. 794.
161 See M. Harrison, *Marooned in Moscow. The Story of an American Woman Imprisoned in Russia*, London, Thornton Butterworth, 1921, p. 179.
162 See Russell, *The Autobiography of Bertrand Russell 1914–1944*, vol. II, p. 102.

concerned to win the empire of this world"[163]. Some left-wing members shared his critique of Bolshevism; the future General Secretary of the Independent Labour Party Fenner Brockway acknowledged him as a significant voice of caution: "it was the writing of Russell which bought back me and many others to the value of personal liberty"[164]. In his memoirs, the American writer Max Eastman highlighted that "Russell's adverse report on the 'Great Experiment'" testified to what "the rest of us wasted so much time in summoning the mental force or humanity to say"[165]. And the Kremlinologist Edward Crankshaw affirmed that the value of *The Practice and Theory of Bolshevism* lay "precisely in the fact that it was written nearly thirty years ago and not today"[166].

Despite his growing criticism of Bolshevism, Russell believed that the Great War had signalled the end of traditional European liberalism and made clear the need to replace capitalism, with its inherent competition and strife, with some form of international socialism; meanwhile, he had moved towards the Labour Party, which had supported the peace negotiations. Labour was ideally divided in two groups: a radical militant wing that shared the methods and the aims of the Bolshevik revolutionaries, and a larger moderate wing led by the main members of the Labour Party – Ramsay MacDonald, Arthur Henderson and Philip Snowden, among others – experienced parliamentarians who achieved their political aims through traditional constitutional means. The majority of the Independent Labour Party instead advocated joining the Third International.

Russell demonstrated his continuing support of international socialism in the article "La Civilisation et la lutte des classes" (*Civilization and the Class Struggle*) published in February 1920 in *Clarté*, the journal of the eponymous movement[167]. On this occasion, he argued that it was hardly possible to imagine that Bolshevism and capitalism could live side by side: if the class struggle had continued for some years, "the intellectual and artistic level of the living world [would] decline

---

163   Id., *The Practice and Theory of Bolshevism*, pp. 113–114.
164   See F. Brockway, *Towards Tomorrow. The Autobiography of Fenner Brockway*, London, Hart-Davis – MacGibbon, 1977, p. 168.
165   See M. Eastman, *Great Companions: Critical Memoirs of Some Famous Friends*, New York, Farrar-Straus & Cudahy, 1959, p. 200.
166   See E. Crankshaw, "How Russell Saw Russia", in *The Observer*, 3 April 1949, p. 4.
167   On 10 May 1919, *L'Humanité* published an article in which Henry Barbusse announced the creation of *Clarté*. It was to be a sort of International of the Mind; its founders – Henry Barbusse, Raymond Lefebvre and Paul Vaillant-Couturier – took as their guiding principle the idea of an intellectual vanguard that would take a leading role in fashioning a new social and international order. See H. Barbusse, "Le Groupe 'Clarté'" in *L'Humanité*, 10 May 1919, p. 1. In August 1919, British journalist and pacifist Edmund Dene Morel shared Russell's and Barbusse's plan for a UK section; in November, the movement was officially launched in London.

fatally". In turn, however, the capitalist regime had become "what the church in the Renaissance period [had been], a real instrument of spiritual oppression"; if intellectuals really understood their mission, they would be the natural allies of socialism, for it was only in "a regenerated and free world that this function could be freely and healthily exercised"[168]. He also implicitly motivated his ideological approach to internationalist socialism in the article "Socialism and Liberal Ideals" (1920): "I have passed over from Liberalism to Socialism, not because I have ceased to admire many of the Liberal ideals", which had suffered an "eclipse" due to the war. He argued that "so long as it [had] fought against feudalism", capitalism had been associated with the liberal ideas of freedom, democracy and peace. Now, however, in their struggle against socialism, capitalist regimes stood not for freedom but for oppression, as demonstrated by the suppression of Communist opinion by the US government and of nationalist movements in Ireland and India by the British. In addition, the idea that capitalism was associated with peace had been utterly destroyed by the war, as a result of which every thoughtful person had to realise that the "continuance of the capitalist system [was] incompatible with the continuance of civilization"[169].

Russell had already analysed the role of intellectuals on the occasion of the "Déclaration d'Indépendance de l'Esprit" (*The International of Intellect*) drawn up by Romain Rolland at the end of the Great War, namely a proposal for the establishment of a sort of International of Thought in response to an International of Labour; a year earlier, however, his reflections on this topic had appeared more idealistic than materialistic. When Rolland asked Russell to be among the English signatories in a letter dated 29 March 1919 ("a project for which we would like to achieve your adhesion"[170]) that included a copy of the manuscript, Russell agreed to sign the document while expressing some reservations about the second paragraph. On 4 May, he replied to Rolland, formulating his indictment against the intellectuals; Russell proffered a motivated *j'accuse* against those who, during the Great War, had betrayed their mission as educators and reformers of consciences because they had been at the service of worldly passions – patriotism, nationalism, and imperialism – instead of defending the universal values of peace and democracy. He wrote that as long as the war lasted, many intellectuals harboured "the hatred that dug the abyss" between the various states involved in the conflict in

---

168 See B. Russell, "La Civilisation et la lutte des classes", in *Clarté*, 21 February 1920, no. 11, p. 1. see also B&R C20.05. This article was translated from the French by John G. Slater.
169 Id., *Socialism and Liberal Ideals*, pp. 449–450 (for the quotation, see p. 452).
170 Letter from Romain Rolland to Bertrand Russell, 29 March 1919, in BRA, Class no. 710, Box no. 5.40, Document no. 054895F2, McMaster University Library, Hamilton (translation from the French by C.G. Anta).

order "to contribute to victory of their country". Since the war was over, "the essential task of intelligence" was not "to denounce" but "to understand without bias, by recognizing the ineluctable potentiality of the human spirit". He added that the time had come for "intellectual love" to preserve what remained of "science and art, of civilized life, and of the hope of a less brutal, freer and happier world"[171]. In his 5 June reply, Rolland thanked him for his "repugnance" to condemn the intellectuals during the war, expressed with "great nobility"[172].

After his return from Russia, Russell received an invitation to spend a year at the University of Peking as a visiting lecturer; he stayed in China from October 1920 to June 1921. He arrived at the height of the May Fourth Movement, an anti-imperialist and cultural movement that grew out of student protest advocating the transformation from a preindustrial society to a modern state. The Chinese historian Zhou Ce zong asserted that Russell's arrival livened up the debate on whether capitalism or socialism was the right road to modernization[173]. In his speeches in Shanghai and Peking, Russell observed that the dissemination of mass education was more important for China than the immediate establishment of socialism; thus, the main problem concerned the leadership. In a November 1920 interview, he argued that what China needed was "ten thousand resolute men, inspired by an ideal and willing to risk their lives"; these men had to combine "the altruism and wisdom of Plato's guardians" with "the patriotic and military qualities of Garibaldi's thousand"[174]. Mao Zedong, then a 26-year-old student, probably attended at least one his lectures in Changsha; he criticised especially Russell's idea of first winning popular support through education. Mao argued that the capitalists who controlled the press and education would not favour the diffusion of literacy; therefore, he dismissed Russell's proposal because it was "all very well as a theory, but it [was] unfeasible in practice"[175]. In the book *The Problem of China* (1922), Russell noted that the Chinese had a great love of literature, art and music,

---

171 Letter from Bertrand Russell to Romain Rolland, 4 May 1919, in BRA, Class no. 710, Box no. 5.40, Document no. 054919, McMaster University Library, Hamilton (translation from the French by C.G. Anta).

172 Letter from Romain Rolland to Bertrand Russell, 5 June 1919, in BRA, Class no. 710, Box no. 5.40, Document no. 054899, McMaster University Library, Hamilton (translation from the French by C.G. Anta).

173 See T.-T. Chow, *The May Fourth Movement: Intellectual Revolution in Modern China*, Cambridge, Harvard University Press, 1960, p. 232.

174 Interview with Mister Russell, in *Eastern Miscellany*, 25 November 1920, vol. 17, no. 22, pp. 9–17.

175 See S.R. Schram, *The Political Thought of Mao Tse-tung*, New York-London, Praeger, 1963, p. 214.

and a healthy attitude to religion; what they lacked was science, technology and industry. But this country also had to evaluate the possible benefits of the modernization process, since it could import the aggressive militarism that characterized the Western nations[176]. As Emeritus Professor of History at McMaster University Richard A. Rempel wrote, his experiences in the Far East provided another dimension to his pacifism; indeed, "his vision for peace, henceforth, would be global rather than Eurocentric"[177].

In February 1921, the No More War Movement (NMWM) was formed in London; this socialist-pacifist organization sought to spread the principles of the now-disbanded No-Conscription Fellowship. The editor of the eponymous journal was Fenner Brockway, who had promoted the establishment of the NCF. The mandate of the NMWM was to affiliate with people in other countries to create an international movement devoted to work for disarmament and peace. In the article "The Prevention of War" published in June 1922 in *No More War*, Russell seemed to embrace more and more a scientific pacifism rather than a utilitarian pacifism: "War spr[ang] mainly from the passions of hatred, envy and greed"; if, on the one hand, "greed as a motive for war" could be eliminated by "the arguments which Norman Angell ha[d] made familiar", and which the outcome of the great war had confirmed, on the other hand, "hatred and envy" required to be treated with "different methods". In this view, mankind had acquired, through science, "a control over the forces of nature [...] used in order to kill each other"[178]. In other words, he believed that Bentham's principle of utility, whereby the purpose of all conscious acts was the attainment of individual pleasure and the avoidance of pain, was based on a limited view of human nature.

During the 1922 election, Russell was offered the candidature in his home constituency of Chelsea, one of the safest Tory seats in the country. He had no chance of winning against the sitting MP Samuel Hoare, the scion of a famous Norfolk banking family, but accepted the candidacy all the same. Russell would support the Labour Party primarily through his journalism while remaining distant from its policy-making decisions. After all, as he would write some years later to his Cambridge friend, the political philosopher Maurice Amos, "an Englishman

---

176   See B. Russell, *The Problem of China*, London, Allen & Unwin, 1922, pp. 13–14.
177   Id., *The Collected Papers of Bertrand Russell. Uncertain Paths to Freedom: Russia and China, 1919–22*, vol. 15, edited by Richard A. Rempel and Beryl Haslam, London-New York, Routledge, 2000, p. lxxiii.
178   See B. Russell, "The Prevention of War", in *No More War*, June 1922, vol. 1, no. 5, p. 5; see also B&R C22.15.

has to have a Party just as he has to have trousers, and of the three Parties I find [Labour] the least painful"[179].

The establishment of the League of Nations generated a lively debate in Great Britain. The strong success achieved by Keynes's book *The Economic Consequences of Peace* (1919)[180] contributed to the diffusion of a strong aversion to the Versailles Treaty within a section of British public opinion; according to Keynes, the attempt to keep Germany in a state of economic inferiority compared to France and Great Britain would prevent a homogenous economic development in Europe and create the premises for a new war. In the first half of the 1920s, some of the most authoritative leftist intellectuals supported an ever-greater integration among states, including Leonard Trelawny Hobhouse and Harold Joseph Laski. In *Social Development. Its Nature and Its Conditions* (1924), Hobhouse emphasized the need to extend the rule of law to an international level in order to put an end to authoritarian and militaristic tendencies. He believed that the League of Nations could not be effective due to the exclusion of three great powers and its mandate to keep a manifestly unjust order alive based on a modern state with absolute sovereignty. It was necessary to pass from a league with limited functions of interstate coordination to a true federation due to the increasing interdependence of states from the economic and social point of view[181]. In his book *A Grammar of Politics* (1925), Laski put forward similar theses. Since political and economic interests were strongly interconnected on a global level, no state could be left free to pursue its own aims without the control of a superior international authority. In this regard, the League of Nations was not the optimal solution: it "is not likely to become a State in the normal sense of the word. [...]. It will, therefore, be a source of principle rather than an agent of action"[182].

Despite these criticisms, the Labour Government led by Ramsay MacDonald – the first Labour Government in British history – expressed confidence in the League of Nations; it believed that the tensions generated by the war could be resolved with dialogue between the most important European powers such as Great Britain, Germany and France. From this perspective, the British Prime Minister sought to enhance the role of the League of Nations by both participating in its

---

179 Letter from Bertrand Russell to Maurice Amos, 16 June 1930, in BRA, Class no. 710, Box no. 5.01, Document no. 046918, McMaster University Library, Hamilton. This letter can also be found in Russell, *The Autobiography of Bertrand Russell 1914–1944*, vol. II, pp. 279–280 (for the quotation, see p. 280).
180 See Keynes, *The Economic Consequence of the Peace*.
181 See L.T. Hobhouse, *Social Development. Its Nature and its Conditions* (1924), London-New York, Routledge, 1996, pp. 292–293.
182 See H.J. Laski, *A Grammar of Politics*, London, Allen & Unwin, 1925, p. 589.

assemblies and pressing to transform it from an instrument of the victorious countries into an organization for the peaceful resolution of international disputes. As proof of the MacDonald Government's commitment to peace, the report of the 1924 Labour Party conference stated: "Peace is not an interlude of apparent quiet in a germinating war policy. Peace has its own natural policy and organisation, its own method of handling questions, its own mentality, its own standards of justice"[183].

Russell made his authoritative voice heard on the League of Nations on several occasions. The opinions he expressed can be ascribed to both juridical-institutional and scientific pacifism. Already before the end of the war, he had predicted the risks deriving from the establishment of an international confederal body such as the League of Nations. In the article "National Independence and Internationalism" published in *The Atlantic Monthly*, he strongly criticized the concept of "absolute [national] sovereignty", namely the main cause of international anarchy; it implied that every state tended to look at every problem from the point of view of its own interests instead of the instruments of international law. He confirmed the ideas of those who, beginning with Thomas Hobbes, had interpreted international relations on the premise that states could be considered as citizens belonging to the same community. Hence the need to transfer the traditional model of natural law from the individual level to the interstate one through the establishment of an international government, as individual countries would still be in a sort of belligerent state of nature. Russell wrote that "the claim to absolute sovereignty" involved that "all external affairs" were to be regulated "purely by force", and this was nothing but "the war of all against all which Hobbes [had] asserted to be the original state of mankind". There could not be secure peace in the world until states were willing to part with "their absolute sovereignty as regards their external relations" and to leave their decisions to an "international government" – an idea already proposed in *Political Ideals* – which had to be "legislative as well as judicial"[184].

The latter concept reappeared in the article "Bring Us Peace" published in October 1922 in the US journal *The New Student*. On this occasion, he wrote almost provocatively: "Only some kind of international government, perhaps informal and unavowed, [could] avert war", and added: "Even if it were unjust and oppressive, it would be better than the existing anarchy"[185]. In *The Prospects of*

183   The Labour Party, *Report of the 24th Annual Conference held in the Queen's Hall, London, on 7th, 8th, 9th, and 10th 1924*, London, Labour Party, w.d., p. 108.
184   See B. Russell, "National Independence and Internationalism", in *The Atlantic Monthly*, May 1917, vol. 119, pp. 622–628 (for the quotation, see p. 624).
185   Id., "Bring Us Peace: An Appeal to American Students", in *The New Student*, 7 October 1922, vol. 2, no. 1, pp. 1–2; see also B&R C22.28.

Industrial Civilization (1923), Russell went beyond the idea of an "international government" while consolidating the bases of his institutional and juridical pacifism. He asserted that international socialism could favour the establishment of a "world government" through which to pursue two fundamental aims: "the prevention of war" and "the securing of economic justice between different nations and different populations"[186]. In this way, he overcame the Kantian prejudice towards the world state, proposing it as the most appropriate political order to ensure lasting peace. If within an international body – with reference to the League of Nations – each member represented a nation, it was likely to reproduce "the diplomatic tug of war between the nations" in its debates. The existence of a "genuinely international spirit" implied that "the members should represent, not nations, but international organizations such as the financiers or the miners"[187]. Russell referred once again to this topic – though from a different point of view – in the United States, where he held a series of lectures between April and May 1924[188]; on 3 April at the League for Industrial Democracy in New York, he stated that a "world government" could be formed not by a "voluntary federation" but through "an extension of the US financial empire" over the American Continent, the whole of Western Europe as well as the Near East, but this would be "illiberal and cruel", thereby crushing trade unionism[189]. A synthesis between the last two articles can be found in four essays published in *The Jewish Daily Forward* in summer 1927, collectively entitled "The Future"; on this occasion, he stressed once again the need to establish a "central authority to control the whole world", an aim initially achievable through the power of American finance and then the ideals of socialism. Once world unity was realized, socialism would become inevitable, for the alternative was the destruction of mankind: "If our civilisation continues for much longer to pursue the interests of the rich, it is doomed"; and he argued further: "I do not desire the collapse of civilisation, because I am socialist"[190].

Russell also criticized the League of Nations in some reflections that could be ascribed to scientific pacifism; in the 1920s, he furthered his interest in scientific psychology, a fundamental means to understand the aggressive and possessive instinctual drives that caused social and economic injustices. Starting from these

---

186 Id., *The Prospects of Industrial Civilization*, in collaboration with Dora Russell, London, Allen & Unwin, 1923, p. 84.
187 Ibid., p. 231.
188 On the Russell lectures held in the United States, see B. Feinberg, R. Kasrils, *Bertrand Russell's America: His Transatlantic Travels and Writings*, 2 vols., London, Allen & Unwin, 1973–1984.
189 The 3 April 1924 lecture to the League for Industrial Democracy was published in *The New York Times* with the title "What is Wrong with Western Civilization?".
190 See B. Russell, "The Future", in *Jewish Daily Forward*, 26 June–3, 10, 17 July 1927.

assumptions, it was necessary to conceive a society based on democratic socialism and to restore the real values of Western civilization such as tolerance, freedom of conscience and civil liberties. He implicitly opposed social Darwinism and discussed the psychological and biological basis of human bellicosity; man's real struggle was not against his fellow men, but to subdue his aggressive impulses, sharing in this sense the Freudian theories – see the 1915 essays "Instincts and Their Vicissitudes" and "Thoughts for the Times on War and Death", in which Freud had considered aggression as an inherent impulse of man. In the article "The Triumph of Common Sense" (1919), Russell wrote that as "wars [were] rooted in human nature, the League of Nations could not prevent them"[191]. In addition to "Socialism and Liberal Ideals" mentioned earlier, he argued that inside the new states created by the Treaty of Versailles, "nationalism appear[ed] to be absolutely dominant"; this "attitude of mind" was "instinctive" and, at the same time, "the result of education and propaganda"[192]. Therefore, the League of Nations, with "its legacy of war hatreds", was unable to guarantee a lasting peace; only international socialism alone could "alter the mentality of bellicose populations"[193]. In October 1923, the Fabian Society organized a series of public lectures under the title "Is Civilisation Decaying?"; these debates were animated by prestigious intellectuals such as Sidney Webb, George Bernard Shaw, Harold Laski, Richard Henry Tawney and Russell, whose lecture "The effect of Science on Social Institutions" was published in four parts in the *Daily Herald* under the title "Science and Civilisation". Russell argued that the future of civilization rested upon the triumph of "kindly impulses" over "aggressive and rivalrous" ones; therefore, it was necessary to use scientific psychology to "train the instincts" and move to "the gradual formation of an orderly economic and political world-government"[194]. On the same wavelength we can consider the lecture "Psychology and Politics" of 16 October 1925, held for the 1917 Club in London; Russell analysed the reasons generating the wickedness of political leaders, arguing that those who ruled the world were often sexually and emotionally frustrated because they had not studied scientific psychology: "Most modern politics, while nominally based on economics", was negatively conditioned

---

191   Id., "The Triumph of Common Sense", in *The Athenaeum*, 11 July 1919, no. 4654, p. 589 (Review of Jones, *Patriotism and Popular Education*); see also B&R C19.22.

192   Id., "Socialism and Liberal Ideals", in *The English Review*, May–June 1920, vol. 30, pp. 449–455 and pp. 499–508 (for the quotations, see pp. 502–503).

193   Ibid., p. 503.

194   See B. Russell, "Science and Civilisation", in *Daily Herald*, 16, 19, 20, 21 November 1923, p. 4.

by a "lack of instinctive satisfaction" and this was largely due to "a false popular psychology"[195].

A few years later, Freud confirmed these theses in *Civilization and Its Discontents* (1929). Freud deemed any attempt to impose an economic modification of social life an "untenable illusion"[196], looking instead for the psychic symptoms produced by the discontent of civilization. Referring to economic factors was not enough, he argued, but it was necessary to investigate the deep and unconscious roots of man's behaviour in his repressed sexuality. Dissatisfaction of pleasure instincts caused a neurosis to spread from the individual to the collectivity; sexual repression was the premise for the individual to commit himself to the optimal perspective from a productive point of view in social life. A scientific pacifism emerged in Russell's lecture "The Danger of Creed Wars" held in autumn 1926 at the Fabian Society. The ideological dispute between the capitalism of the United States and the Communism of the Soviet Union was excessively based on economic reflections to the detriment of biological ones, he argued; indeed, the "fundamental delusion of our time" was "the excessive emphasis upon the economic aspects of life". The strife between these two economic systems could cease only if public opinion recognised that "both [were] inadequate through their failure to recognise biological needs"[197]. Russell's reflections on scientific psychology can also be considered as a sort of gradual development of behaviourism; on this, he had been inspired by John Broadus Watson, whose influence had emerged in *The Analysis of Mind* [198].

In the mid-1920s, Russell confirmed his firm criticism of Bolshevism. Although he had defended the UK Government's 2 February 1924 decision to recognize the Soviet Union, he reassured public opinion – as on the occasion of his US visit in spring 1924 – that the Labour Party was not revolutionary, insisting that MacDonald's plans for social reform were moderate. When MacDonald announced his decision to grant the Soviets a loan to help their economic reforms, however, opposition MPs supported the slogan "no money for Bolshevik murderers". Therefore, the October 1924 campaign was dominated by fear of communism, which both the Liberals and the Conservatives used to discredit the Labour Government. The result of the election was a huge victory

---

195   Id., "Psychology and Politics", in *The Dial*, March 1926, vol. 80, no. 3, pp. 179–188; this article was also published in Id., *Sceptical Essays*, London, Allen & Unwin, 1928, pp. 202–214 (for the quotation, see p. 209).
196   See Freud, *Civilization and Its Discontents*, p. 88.
197   See B. Russell, "The Danger of Creed Wars", in *The Socialist Review*, May 1927, no. 16, pp. 7–19. This article was also published in Id., *Sceptical Essays*, pp. 215–233 (for the quotations, see p. 231).
198   Id., *The Analysis of Mind*, London-New York, Allen & Unwin-Macmillan, 1921.

for the Conservatives; in November 1924, Stanley Baldwin became once again British Prime Minister. Regarding Russell's analysis of the perspectives of British socialism, it is worth remembering his 1926 controversy with Trotsky. In a review of Trotsky's *Where Is Britain Going?*, Russell criticized his advocacy of a communist revolution that would sweep aside the British Labour Government, leading to civil war and to the "revolutionary dictatorship" of the proletariat. This was "a programme that could only be advocated by an enemy or a fool"; however, Trotsky "[was] not a fool", and British socialists were not so unwise in taking "a course of action that was intolerable to the United States"[199]. In his reply, Trotsky sarcastically called Russell "a dilettante of socialism"[200].

The second half of the 1920s was very significant from the point of view of international relations. The Treaty of Locarno was signed in October 1925; in 1926, Germany was admitted to the League of Nations; on 27 August 1928, the Kellogg-Briand Pact was signed in Paris; and in 1929, Great Britain resumed diplomatic relations with the Soviet Union. These events determined the affirmation of the so-called spirit of Locarno, characterized by a climate of détente among the main European powers. As Keynes argued, it was as though, once the last remnants of the "Carthaginian Peace" of Versailles were left behind, Europe and the world could pave the way for peace under the aegis of the League of Nation.

British Neutrality and Collective Security in the 1930s

In the second half of the 1920s, the struggle for disarmament and against compulsory military service became a growing leitmotif in Russell's thought. In 1926, he signed the Manifesto against Conscription and the Military System; in this document, we read that "in the name of humanity", it encouraged all people to emancipate themselves from "the military system and, therefore, apply methods of non-violent resistance on the lines of Mahatma Gandhi and Martin Luther King", namely "conscientious objection [...], civil disobedience, war tax resistance, non-cooperation with military research, military production and arms trade"[201].

---

199 Id., "Trotsky on Our Sins", in *The New Leader*, 26 February 1926, vol. 13, no. 22, pp. 3–4 (Review of Trotsky, *Where Is Britain Going?*).
200 See L. Trotsky, "A reply to *The New Leader*", 26 February 1926, "Trotsky On Our Sins by Bertrand Russell", in Id., Leon Trotsky's Writings on Britain, London, Chappell-Clinton, 1975, vol. 2, Ch. 3, Part, 4.
201 The Manifesto against Conscription and the Military System was signed, among others, by Henri Barbusse, Annie Besant, Martin Buber, Edward Carpenter, Georges Duhamel, Albert Einstein, Auguste Forel, Mohandas Karamchand Gandhi, Kurt Hiller, Toyohiko

In October 1930, Russell also signed the Manifesto against Conscription and the Military Training of Youth[202]; it was issued by the Joint Peace Council, a coalition of international peace organizations that included the Quakers, the War Resisters' International and the Women's International League for Peace and Freedom. Their signatories appealed to the states that had subscribed to the Kellogg-Briand Pact (1928) to end the "slavery" of compulsory military service once and for all. Einstein, too, supported the struggle for disarmament and against compulsory military service; in this regard, he delivered one of his most famous pacifist speeches at the Ritz-Carlton Hotel in New York for the "New History Society" on 14 December 1930. Einstein proposed "uncompromising war resistance" and "refusal to do military service under any circumstances"; he also emblematically stated that "even if only two percent of those supposed to perform military service should declare themselves war resisters [...] governments would be powerless – [since] they could not put such masses into jail"[203].

The Japanese invasion of Manchuria in September 1931 was the earliest sign of the international community's inability to counter and deter aggression. It was also a test for the League of Nations Union (LNU)[204], which had reached out to absolute pacifists attracted by its disarmament message and those who shared the liberal internationalism of its leaders, namely Lord Cecil and Gilbert Murray; the LNU provided an anti-war alternative to the more unbending pacifism of the Quakers' Society of Friends or the socialist No More War Movement. At the beginning of 1932, the Geneva Disarmament Conference was inaugurated[205];

Kagawa, George Lansbury, Paul Löbe, Arthur Ponsonby, Emanuel Rádl, Leonhard Ragaz, Romain Rolland, Rabindranath Tagore, Miguel de Unamuno, Fritz von Unruh, and Herbert George Wells.

202 The Manifesto against Conscription and the Military Training of Youth was signed, among others, by Jane Addams, Valentin Bulgakov, John Dewey, Albert Einstein, Auguste Forel, Sigmund Freud, Arvid Järnefelt, Toyohiko Kagawa, Selma Lagerlöf, Judah Leon Magnes, Thomas Mann, Ludwig Quidde, Emanuel Rádl, Leonhard Ragaz, Henriette Roland Holst, Romain Rolland, Upton Sinclair, Rabindranath Tagore, Herbert George Wells, and Stefan Zweig.

203 See A. Einstein, "Militant Pacifism", in Id., *A Flight Against War*, edited by Alfred Lief, New York, The John Day Company, 1933, pp. 34–37 (for the quotation, see pp. 35–36).

204 The League of Nations Union was established in October 1918 through the merger of the League of Free Nations Association and the League of Nations Society, which were already working for world peace through disarmament and universal collective security. In this regard, see D.S. Birn, *The League of Nation Union: 1918–1945*, Oxford, Clarendon Press, 1981.

205 The Geneva Disarmament Conference (February 1932–November 1934) was organized by the member states of the League of Nations with the participation of the United States and Russia; it involved the representatives of 60 countries.

on this occasion, more precisely on 16 March 1933, the UK Government presented a British Draft Convention – known as MacDonald Plan – which was a detailed scheme of aerial disarmament.

The Labour Government had to face the financial crisis that followed the Wall Street Crash of 1929. Prime Minister Ramsay MacDonald and Chancellor of the Exchequer Philip Snowden felt that cuts in public spending were essential to the survival of the British economy; they would not allow any deficit spending, despite the urgings of Oswald Mosley, David Lloyd George and John Maynard Keynes. Because of this internal split within the Labour Party, on 24 August 1931 MacDonald resigned and then, urged by King George V, agreed to form a National Government with the Conservatives and the Liberals. The 27 October general election determined a large victory for the National Government, largely supported by the Conservative Party – it obtained 55 percent of the votes. British policy was now controlled primarily by Conservatives: Stanley Baldwin and Neville Chamberlain became, respectively, Lord President and Chancellor of the Exchequer. Deep cuts in defence spending had been made by MacDonald's second government and during his first year as leader of the National Government; Britain's defence requirements continued to be trumped by budgetary constraints that reflected Chamberlain's conviction that a stable economy was the vital "fourth arm" of defence. Two prestigious pacifists, George Lansbury and Arthur Ponsonby, were ensconced as leaders of the parliamentary Labour Party in the Commons and Lords. As late as October 1933, the Labour Party's annual conference affirmed that it would "take no part in war"; in the following year's conference, however, Labour dispensed with this war-resistance line to firm up its commitments to the League of Nations and the collective system[206].

In July 1934, Hitler demonstrated his ruthlessness against political opponents on the Night of the Long Knives; in August, he became Chancellor following the death of Paul von Hindenburg, and at the Nuremberg rally in September, he announced his vision of a glorious millennial Reich. In his 28 November speech at the House of Commons, Winston Churchill invited the British Government to increase military expenditure and urged it to take seriously the threat to Britain's defence posed by Hitler's armed forces, highlighting "the kind of danger which reasonably [had] to be taken into consideration" if a "breakdown in European peace occur[ed]"[207]. The Italian invasion of Abyssinia in October 1935, Nazi Germany's

---

206 See H.R. Winkler, *British Labour Seeks a Foreign Policy, 1900–1940*, London, New Brunswick, 2005, pp. 98–104.
207 See W. Churchill, Parliamentary Debates (Commons), 28 November 1934, vol. 295, cols. 857–983 (for the quotation, see col. 860).

occupation of the Rhineland in March 1936, and the outbreak of the Spanish Civil War in July determined the failure of the spirit of Locarno. The rapid rise of authoritarian and totalitarian regimes caused dramatic international tension; some prestigious intellectuals made their voices heard because Europe needed a boost to its pride in order to counter the new hegemonic demands. As Thomas Mann publicly stated, "we could not help but denounce" the disturbing fate that was looming on the horizon; he was over 60 years of age when he decided to issue a lucid and scathing imperative: "Achtung, Europa!" (*Europe, Beware!*, 1935)[208]. Mann still harboured hopes that his literature, which voiced the need for love, humanity and tolerance, might be a force of resistance against the forces of irrationality and anti-humanism in the Third Reich. He never mentioned German National Socialism or Hitler, but his assessment of the primitive mass movements, irrationalism, and anti-intellectualism was received as a critique of the Nazi regime. His explicit purpose was to shake, or at least put on guard, those who persisted in ignoring what was happening in the Old Continent. He pointed at the decline of European culture, highlighting "the enormous wave of egocentric barbarity and of trivial primitive democratic-plebeian vulgarity that crosses the world"[209]. In Mann's opinion, responsibilities were also to be identified in the increasing spread of the "mass man" phenomenon analysed by José Ortega y Gasset only a few years before[210]. Nevertheless, the Spanish philosopher did not believe in irresolvable crises because "the common European stock"[211] had always overcome the limitations of individual nations and their residual differences as there might be between, for example, the French, the Spanish, and the English. Johan Huizinga added his voice to this debate; during the years characterized by the affirmation of the Nietzschean idea of the Superman (*Übermensch*) and the concomitant rise of Nazism, Huizinga described the tragic perspective that loomed over Europe and outside its borders. More precisely, he looked at the future with a critical mind and pessimism, using

---

208 "Achtung, Europa!" was a speech that Mann had planned to present in Nice in April 1935; instead, he asked that it be read in his absence in France because he did not want to compromise his German publisher or endanger the publication of his works in Germany. Regarding the text of this speech, see T. Mann, *Order of the Day: Political Essays and Speeches of Two Decades*, translated by Helen T. Lowe-Porter, Agnes E. Meyer and Eric Sutton, New York, Alfred Knopf, 1937, pp. 69–82.
209 Ibid.
210 See J. Ortega y Gasset, *La rebelión de las masas*, Madrid, Revista de Occidente, 1930 (English version: *The Revolt of the Masses*, New York, Norton, 1964).
211 Id., *The Revolt of the Masses*, p. 180.

some significant expressions such as the "Autumn of the Middle Ages" and the "crisis of civilization"[212].

Russell considered the exaltation of irrationalism as one of the main reasons for the affirmation of totalitarianisms; in October 1934, he delivered the Fabian lecture "The Revolt against Reason"[213], in which he charted the rise of a kind of philosophy that exalted intuition and the pursuit of power while disdaining the concern for rationality and truth typical of the philosophers of the Enlightenment. Johann Fichte, Thomas Carlyle, Giuseppe Mazzini and Friedrich Nietzsche were mentioned as the "ancestors" of fascism, whose intellectual root was identified in the denial of objective standards of truth and the adoption of the view that "there [was] an English truth, a French truth, a German truth". Faced with these different "truths", nations could solve the international disputes "by means of war and rivalry in propagandist insanity"; in contrast, "reason, being impersonal, made strife inevitable"[214].

On 21 May 1935, Hitler presented a 13-point programme for peace to the Reichstag; this speech followed the increased diplomatic isolation of Nazi Germany after his provocative 16 March announcement to enlarge the Wermacht to 36 divisions, namely a military force five and a half times bigger than was sanctioned by the Treaty of Versailles. According to Russell, this speech afforded the opportunity for negotiation "in a spirit of conciliation" and "not at the point of the bayonet". In line with British appeasement, Russell wrote that Hitler could be "justified" because he had stated that Germany could not return to the League of Nations until it ceased to be bound up with the Treaty of Versailles[215]. As the League of Nation had turned out to be "an instrument for preserving to the victors the gains of the War", this had to cease if it was to serve its purpose of "preserving peace and securing justice"[216]. Russell made his voice heard once again in his 18 August 1935 article "How to Keep the Peace" published in *The Sunday Referee*, in which he severely criticized the main British political parties, which had not condemned the idea of a new war. He advocated neutralism, which differed from both the isolationism of the Tory-imperialist right and collective security as conceived by

---

212 See J. Huizinga, *In de schaduwen van morgen: een diagnose van het geestelijk lijden van onzen tijd*, Haarlem, Tjeenk Willink & Zoon, 1935 (English version: *In the Shadow of Tomorrow: A Diagnosis of the Spiritual Distemper of Our Time*, London, Heinemann, 1936).
213 It was later reprinted with the title "The Ancestry of Fascism" in B. Russell, *In Praise of Idleness and Other Essays*, London, Allen & Unwin, 1935, pp. 82–108.
214 Ibid., p. 107.
215 See B. Russell, "Hitler's Thirteen Points", in *Sunday Referee*, 26 May 1935, p. 12; see also B&R C35.19.
216 Ibid.

the Labour Party and the supporters of the League of Nations. The Great War had taught politicians little; despite "preserving democracy and destroying militarism", he argued, "we have given the Germans Hitler instead of the Kaiser" due to "the injustices of Versailles"[217]. So, he welcomed the Unites States' decision on neutrality – it was the title of the 27 August article published in the *New York Post* – whereby the US Congress suspended the exports of arms to all belligerent countries, while a National Munitions Control Board was created to license the production of war material. He wrote that America was "wise in determining on neutrality"; since at this stage of the world's history war was likely to destroy the European powers, this decision was "imperative to the interest of civilization"[218].

The growing political-institutional weakness of the League of Nations had not solved the problem of international anarchy; in his 1 September 1935 article "Keep Out of War!", Russell affirmed that the League of Nations as conceived by President Wilson had been a "potentially beneficent idea", but its "lack of universality" had made it "unable to ensure peace" – see the non-membership of the United States and of the Soviet Union, which became a member only in 1934. In this context, the Italian invasion of Abyssinia was only the last in a series of failures; therefore, he emphasized that the pursuit of "collective security" under the League of Nations' auspices was producing instead a destabilizing form of "collective insecurity"[219]. No less significant was the 29 September 1935 article "'The Dangers of Bluff' Between Britain and Italy"; a few days before, on 11 September, after Mussolini had rebuffed all attempts at mediation on the Abyssinian question, Foreign Secretary Samuel Hoare had promised that Britain would stand squarely with the league "for steady and collective resistance to all acts of unprovoked aggression"[220]. In this article, Russell argued that the use of economic sanctions by the British Government against fascist Italy could generate "a gigantic game of bluff" in which all parties to the dispute, including Mussolini, were participating. He accused the "devotees of the League" – with implicit reference to Labour Party leaders who professed a sort of devotion to the League of Nations even greater

---

217   See B. Russell, "How to Keep the Peace", in *Sunday Referee*, 18 August 1935, p. 12; see also B&R C35.32.
218   Id., "Bertrand Russell Applauds U.S. Neutrality Decision", in *New York Post*, 27 August 1935, p. 4.
219   Id., "Keep Out of War!", in *Sunday Referee*, 1 September 1935, p. 10.
220   See R.A.C. Parker, *Chamberlain and Appeasement: British Policy and the Coming of the Second World War*, New York, St. Martin's Press, 1993, p. 50.

than that towards the National Government – of naivety in failing to acknowledge that the application of sanctions could lead to war[221].

In November 1935, Baldwin, who a few months earlier had replaced MacDonald as Prime Minister of the National Government, called a general election. During the election campaign, both Labour and Conservative Parties kept invoking the "collective security" supported by the League of Nations as a means of dealing with the threat of Nazism and Fascism. Before the election, the Labour Party had replaced Lansbury as its leader with Clement Atlee after the tumultuous annual conference at Brighton from 30 September to 4 October 1935: on this occasion, the dissident Labour leftist Richard Stafford Cripps defined the League of Nations as an "International Burglars Union"[222]. During the LP conference, Lansbury affirmed that Britain should continue unilaterally with a programme of disarmament despite the massive rearmament taking place in Germany, but he was defeated because the LP adopted Attlee's tougher line. Russell shared Lansbury's thesis; this can be seen in the essay "The Case for Socialism", which appeared before the general election. In it, Russell argued: "The world" was "in the condition of a drunkard" surrounded by "kind friends offering him drinks". The "drunks" were those intoxicated by concepts of "patriotism and national honour" who wanted to wage war against their neighbours; the "kind friends" were the capitalist – principally steel magnates – who wanted to encourage the consumption of these "dangerous intoxicants" in order to make huge profits[223]. Thus, if capitalism were to be defeated, people would then realize "the absurdity of war". From this perspective, international socialism was the best means of preventing war, but "nationalization" in each of the leading industrial countries would equally suffice "to remove the pressing danger of war"; for example, if Britain nationalized its steel industry, peace with Germany would become a much more likely prospect[224].

No less significant was Russell's book *Which Way to Peace?* published in October 1936. Faced with the increasingly threatening international situation, he dismissed isolationism, collective security and all policy of expedients as a misguided strategy for Britain, for the only rational response was a "national pacifism". He wanted strict neutrality to be observed in conjunction with the unilateral measures of disarmament; he emblematically affirmed: "Suppose England and

221   See B. Russell, "'The Dangers of Bluff' Between Britain and Italy", in *Sunday Referee*, 29 September 1935, p. 10.
222   See P. Clarke, *The Cripps Version: The Life of Sir Stafford Cripps, 1889–1952*, London, Allen Lane-The Penguin Press, 2002, p. 64.
223   See B. Russell, "The Case for Socialism", in Id., *In Praise of Idleness and Other Essays*, pp. 121–156 (for the quotations, see p. 149).
224   Ibid., pp. 149–150.

France were both to disarm"; in this case, if the Nazis continued their military parades and their glorification of war, "they would cease to look heroic and would become ridiculous". Therefore, non-resistance would challenge Nazi militarism more effectively than "even the most victorious war"[225]. His absolute pacifism was not a dogmatic declaration of principle, however; Russell considered it strictly limited "to the present time", while "in other circumstances" he should be prepared "to concede that war might be worthwhile"[226]. We can consider his 5 December 1936 article "No Continental Entanglements" published in *The Yorkshire Post* on the same wavelength. He wrote that in the next war "the only real victors will be the neutrals", while the "belligerents" – both victors and vanquished – "will be ruined". If Britain were to remain neutral, it would use its "strength sanely" to build a "less brutal world"; but if it were to take part in the war, it would become "more vindictive than in 1918", promoting an "even more disastrous peace than that of Versailles"[227]. After the publication of *Which Way to Peace?* Russell signed Hugh Richard Lawrie Sheppard's famous Peace Pledge Union (PPU)[228]; he was invited to become an executive committee member, and from autumn 1936, he addressed some public meetings held by this new organization. In these years, some prominent pacifists, including George Lansbury, John Middleton Murry and Reverend Sheppard, were opposed to war on religious grounds. For example, Murry wrote that to commit oneself to pacifism was "to pass out of the realm of rationality into that of religion faith"[229]. Despite his membership in the PPU, Russell did not share this view; in fact, he defended his absolute pacifist view not based on a categorical principle but rather as the outcome of an entirely rational calculation of foreseeable consequences.

Russell supported an absolute pacifist position right up to the outbreak of the Second World War, whereas Einstein had already changed his opinion on war resistance and compulsory military service, thus embracing a relative pacifism. In his January 1935 article "A Re-examination of Pacifism" published in the US

---

225 See Russell, *Which Way to Peace?*, pp. 137, 141, 142.
226 Ibid., pp. 151–152.
227 Id., "No Continental Entanglements", in *The Yorkshire Post*, 5 December 1936, p. 8.
228 The PPU was established in 1934 thanks to the initiative by Reverend Sheppard, canon of St. Paul's Cathedral. Its members were signatories to the following pledge: "War is a crime against humanity. I renounce war, and am therefore determined not to support any kind of war. I am also determined to work for the removal of all causes of war". The PPU formed the British section of War Resisters' International. Regarding the PPU, see S. Morrison, *I Renounce War: The Story of the Peace Pledge Union*, London, Sheppard Press, 1962; W. Hetherington, *Swimming Against the Tide: The Peace Pledge Union Story, 1934–2014*, London, Peace Pledge Union, 2015.
229 See J.M. Murry, *The Pledge of Peace*, London, Joseph, 1938, p. 9.

magazine *Polity*, Einstein stressed that some dictatorial regimes were becoming a menace to the rest of the world. The refusal to perform military service would involve the weakening of the "power of resistance of the remaining sane portions" within these states, if not "the martyrdom and death for those [who had] courage enough to object". Therefore, a realist pacifist should pursue a "plan of action different" from that of "more peaceful times" to lessen the warlike programmes of totalitarian regimes founded on violence and terror[230].

In the December 1936 article "The Paralysis of England" published in the Chicago-based political monthly *Coronet*, Russell underlined the ineffectiveness of UK foreign policy caused by "a sense of insecurity" due to its imperial decay and by "the co-existence of incompatible desires" within the main political parties. As to the former point, the British Empire had established itself as sea power but no longer had this supremacy because submarines and aircraft of enemy countries would prevent the importation of food required to keep the population alive and raw materials required to fight; therefore, it could not conduct a successful war. As to the second point, the Conservatives believed that cooperation with the League of Nations was "constitutionally repugnant" because it meant submitting to "collective decisions" instead of coming to "decisions dictated solely by British interests". However, among socialists "the conflict of desires [was] deeper"; ever since the Russian Revolution, they had been "gravely embarrassed by the war" on two fronts, namely against capitalism and communism. Those who were pacifist as well as socialists disagreed with communists, since they hoped "to minimize the use of violence in establishing a new economic order"[231].

Russell also criticized the principle of "collective security" in his 13 February 1937 article published in the pacifist weekly *Peace News*, the official voice of the Peace Pledge Union. This concept meant that if any one power in the League of Nations was involved in war, all the others would be as well. However, he argued, in this way the League of Nation showed "fatal defects as a means of preserving peace". Thus, "collective security" had ceased to be "a method of preventing wars" because it had become "a method of making sure that any conflict [could] become a first-class great war"[232]. In this way, Russell modified the famous slogan of Soviet Foreign Minister Maxim Litvinov whereby "peace [was] indivisible" as a symbol of a new-found Soviet enthusiasm for the League of Nations; in fact, he argued that war – and not peace – was "indivisible". On 24 February, he made

---

230 See A. Einstein, "A Re-examination of Pacifism", in *Polity*, vol. 3, no. 1, January 1935, pp. 4–5.
231 See B. Russell, "Paralysis of England", in *Coronet*, December 1936, vol. 1, no. 2, pp. 3–8.
232 Id., "Collective 'Security'", in *Peace News*, 13 February 1937, no. 35, p. 6; see also B&R C37.05.

neutralism the theme of his maiden speech in the House of Lords[233]. The LP pacifists who spoke on that day disagreed with the dominant Labour thinking concerning the policy on rearmament, seconding the neutralist course proposed by Lord Arnold[234]. On this occasion, Russell directed his critical comments at the massive rearmament plans of the National Government proposed in the Defence White Paper for 1937, since he regarded disarmament as a corollary of neutrality. He asserted that modern warfare was "a mad atrocity" for both the victors and the vanquished; therefore, he added: "Whatever cost there may be to be paid, we will be neutral"[235]. When the debate was resumed a week later, Ponsonby endorsed the pacifist thrust of Russell's argument; in turn, League of Nations Union President Lord Cecil responded to attacks on collective security inside the Houses of Parliament and criticized Russell's "complete pacifism"[236]. One of Russell's most relevant engagements in 1937 was the debate with Norman Angell staged by the Oxford University Liberal Club on 1 June; he had been among those who had nominated Angell for the Nobel Peace Prize (1933), but in the meantime, the two intellectuals had developed different views on foreign policy. Angell believed that it was possible for pacifists to vote for "a system of collective security by means of arms" without sacrificing their principle; he suggested that the policy of national pacifism espoused by Russell would open the door to "an armed party within the State taking power"[237]. Since every other nation had put defence before peace, Angell concluded that Britain must do likewise; the corollary of rearmament was a system of military alliances that could stabilize the international situation: if "the instrument of war" was to be avoided, it needed to specify "beforehand under what conditions this instrument [would] be used"[238]. In March 1938, Russell was offered a one-year contract as visiting Professor of Philosophy at the University

---

233 Almost six years had elapsed since Russell's inheritance of the earldom from his brother; in June 1934, Russell told the Danish interviewer Elias Bredsdorff that he believed to be "more effective by keeping [his] political activity outside the House of Lords". See E. Bredsdorff, "En samtale med Bertrand Russell", in *Politiken*, 6 October 1935, p. 1.
234 Lord Arnold issued this plea: "We ought to get out and keep out. Not only ought we to do that in our own interests, but we ought to do it in the interests of Europe". See Lord Arnold, *Foreign Affairs*, Parliamentary Debates (Lords), 24 February 1937, 5th ser., vol. 104, cols. 291–334 (for the quotation, see col. 298).
235 "Russell's speech in House of Lords for British Isolation", Parliamentary Debates (Lords), 24 February 1937, 5th ser., vol. 104, cols. 318–323.
236 Lord Cecil, *Foreign Affairs*, Parliamentary Debates (Lords), 2 March 1937, 5th ser., vol. 104, cols. 391–432 (for the quotation, see col. 418).
237 See B. Russell, N. Angell, "Sir Norman Angell v Mr. Bertrand Russell", in *Oxford Mail*, 2 June 1937, p. 3.
238 Ibid.

of Chicago. In the aftermath of the Anschluss between Germany and Austria, most European countries were preparing for war. On 20 September, Russell sailed for America, leaving Great Britain in the grip of fear over the Czechoslovakian crisis. At the end of the same month, Prime Minister Neville Chamberlain met Hitler in Munich to discuss the secession of the Sudetenland to Nazi Germany. However, the dismemberment of Czechoslovakia in March 1939 signalled the end of appeasement for the Chamberlain Government. In turn, Russell developed serious doubts about his absolute pacifism; two days before Germany's invasion of Poland, he confessed to the publisher Warder Norton that "Europe [could not] go on in this intolerable uncertainty", though he expressed his fear that another world war could lead to "a still more vindictive Versailles"[239]. He later claimed that his unconditional renunciation of all wars was consistent with his non-absolute pacifism because "my objections to the war that was coming were not of principle, but of expediency"[240]. As explained in his autobiography, his excuse for his lack of political insight in the 1930s was that his thinking about war and peace had been "unconsciously insincere"[241]; he had been taking a stand based on a considered and utilitarian calculation. As British historian Martin Ceadel pointed out, the "unconscious insincerity" arose from Russell's conscious denial that "the basis of his pacifism had been humanitarian, or even spiritual, rather than rational"[242]. However, as the Canadian historian Peter Brock and the English historian Nigel Young wrote, in September 1939 "his absolute pacifism was shattered", as it was for those who had "felt that peace-pledging was the surest way to prevent war from breaking out"[243]. Therefore, Russell began to become the interpreter of a relative pacifism, showing a dose of political realism: war represented a great evil, but in some extreme cases the use of force could be justified.

In the 1930s, Russell espoused an "instrumental" and "absolute" pacifism, if we rely on the classifications made by Norberto Bobbio and by Michael Allen Fox examined in the first paragraph of this essay. Instrumental pacifism aimed at the limitation of armaments in order to prevent their unlimited growth, like the disarmament policy and renunciation of compulsory military service – he had already

---

239   Letter from Bertrand Russell to Warder Norton, 30 August 1939, in BRA, Box no. 6.36, Recent acquisition no. 1A, McMaster University Library, Hamilton.
240   See B. Russell, "Long-Time Advocate of Peace Approves Prevent War", in *The New York Times*, 16 February 1941, sec. 4, p. 8.
241   Id., *The Autobiography of Bertrand Russell 1914–1944*, vol. II, p. 191.
242   See M. Ceadel, *Pacifism in Britain, 1914–1945: The Defining of a Faith*, Oxford, Clarendon Press, 1980, p. 218.
243   See P. Brock, N. Young, *Pacifism in the Twentieth Century*, Syracuse, Syracuse University Press, 1999, p. 133.

shown this vision during the years of the Great War – and the Gandhian philosophy of nonviolence. In this period, however, his instrumental pacifism was primarily identified with unconditional support for neutralism: in *Which Way to Peace?* he hoped for UK neutrality in conjunction with unilateral measures of disarmament, for he regarded disarmament as a corollary of neutrality, and in February 1937, he made neutralism the theme of his maiden speech in the House of Lords. Until the outbreak of the Second World War, he advocated an "absolute pacifism" that emphasized an uncompromising condemnation of violence – unlike Fox, who argued that war was utterly inconsistent with morality, in this period Russell's objections seemed not so much of principle as of expediency. He supported this kind of pacifism also in his severe criticism of the contradictory concept of "collective security" defended by the League of Nations – see the 1935 article "Keep Out of War!". In August 1939 he realized, with political realism, that totalitarianisms could only be stopped by force of arms, justifying a "semi-pacifism" and "contingent pacifism", to refer to the concepts coined by Wilhelm Emil Mühlmann, and by James Sterba and Larry May mentioned at the beginning of this essay; the former justified the war under certain conditions – in this case it was a war of "defence" – whereas the latter derived from the just war theory. The evolution of Russell's pacifist thought was concomitant with the end of the Chamberlain Government's appeasement.

CHAPTER THREE

Between Fear and Hope in the Atomic Age

The Hypothesis of a Preventive Nuclear Conflict

In the late 1930s, the idea of a world government was supported especially by the British and American federalists. In Great Britain Charles Kimber, Patrick Ransome, and Derek Rawnsley created the "Federal Union" (1938); the general idea of this movement was that the absolute sovereignty of nation-states – the fundamental cause of international anarchy – was to be replaced by a federal government capable of guaranteeing a lasting peace. This view found concrete expression in the American journalist Clarence Kirshman Streit's pamphlet *Union Now* (1939)[1]; due to the failure of the League of Nations and the Nazi invasion of Czechoslovakia, Streit[2] advocated a federation of the main 15 democracies of North America, North-western Europe and Australasia. After the outbreak of the Second World War, the Federal Union redefined its position – see the ideas of leftist intellectuals such as Henry Noel Brailsford and Leonard Woolf. In *The Federal Idea*, Brailsford saw the European federation as able to "respect the rich variety of a Continent, which ha[d] preserved many stocks, many cultures, many

---

1 See C.K. Streit, *Union Now. A Proposal for a Federal Union of the Democracies of the North Atlantic*, London-New York, Cape and Harper, 1939.
2 Streit was a correspondent in Geneva for *The New York Times* from 1929 to 1939.

tongues [...] and to end the anarchy of our economic life"[3]. In the 1939 article "De Profundis" published in *The Political Quarterly*, Woolf argued that a lasting peace could flourish through a European union that would include federated states governed based on international justice[4]. Brailsford and Woolf made a clear change of perspective; indeed, British federalists rarely argued for a primarily European union because they perceived themselves to be citizens of a self-sufficient empire, remaining tied to the Commonwealth of Nations by their common past, similar institutions, and converging economic interests. Both had probably observed that, twice in a quarter of a century, conflicts between European powers had triggered world wars; hence, the solution had to be found in the Old Continent.

In 1938, Russell began a career as a college lecturer in the United States; at first, he taught at Chicago University while giving several public talks. At that time, he still supported absolute pacifism; in the March 1939 article "The Case for US Neutrality" in *Common Sense Magazine*, he warned that the attempt to defeat fascism through war would be futile for the United States because any belligerent nation could become fascist: "If America bec[a]me a belligerent the first effect [would be] the complete eclipse of liberalism, democracy, and free thought in the United States"[5]. On 15 April 1939, Russell was pleased to read an account of the peace plea that Franklin Delano Roosevelt had issued to Hitler and Mussolini. He sent a letter of appreciation to the US President: "I cannot resist expressing to you my profound gratitude and admiration for your peace plea" and added that as "a humble professor" he never before had expressed "such feelings [...] to any possessor of power"[6]. Three days later, Roosevelt replied that "it was very kind of you to write me that fine letter approving the course which I took"[7]. Before his contract with the University of Chicago ended, Russell contacted the University of California, Los Angeles (UCLA), securing a three-year tenure as a lecturer in philosophy. A week before his move to Los Angeles, the Nazi-Soviet Pact was announced, and on 1 September 1939, Germany invaded Poland; two days later, Britain and France declared war. On 10 May 1940, Winston Churchill took over from Neville Chamberlain as Prime Minister; on 13 May, Churchill made his

---

3   See H.N. Brailsford, *The Federal Idea*, London, Federal Union, 1939, pp. 7–8.
4   See L. Woolf, "De Profundis", in *The Political Quarterly*, October–December 1939, vol. 10, no. 4, pp. 463–476.
5   See B. Russell, "The Case for U.S. Neutrality", in *Common Sense*, March 1939, vol. 8, no. 3, pp. 8–9.
6   Letter from Bertrand Russell to Franklin Delano Roosevelt, 15 April 1939, in BRA, RA3, Recent acquisition no. 88, McMaster University Library, Hamilton.
7   Letter from Franklin Delano Roosevelt to Bertrand Russell, 18 April 1939, in BRA, Class no. 710, Box no. 5.40, Document no. 054924, McMaster University Library, Hamilton.

famous speech to Parliament in which he declared that he had "nothing to offer but blood, toil, tears and sweat"[8]. On the same day, Russell, who was gradually abandoning the idea of absolute pacifism because of the Nazi air war against England, announced his support for the Allied cause to the editor of the *New Statesman* Kingsley Martin: "Ever since the war began, I have felt that I could no longer go on being a pacifist [...]. If I were young enough to fight myself, I should do so"[9]. In a 19 May letter to his old friend Robert Trevelyan, he showed once again his new vision: "I find that this time I am not a pacifist, and consider the future of civilisation bound up with our victory"[10]. A few months after his arrival in Los Angeles, Russell was invited to take up a professorship at the College of the City of New York (CCNY); the appointment would run from 1 February 1941 to 30 June 1942, but it was revoked by law within two months of its announcement[11]. At the beginning of 1941, Russell was invited as a philosophy lecturer to join the Barnes Foundation in Philadelphia, where he stayed until the end of 1942; his Barnes lectures served as the basis for his best-selling book *History of Western Philosophy*. On 7 December 1941, the United States entered the war following Japan's attack on Pearl Harbor.

A fundamental step in the evolution of Russell's pacifism was the article "The Future of Pacifism" published in the quarterly magazine *American Scholar*, in which he introduced a distinction between "absolute pacifism" and "relative pacifism". The former was the doctrine that considered war as always unjustifiable – it had been theorized by Tolstoy, Gandhi and the Quakers – and had been supported by Russell himself during the Great War because at that time "the evils resulting from the

---

8   See W. Churchill, Parliamentary Debates (Commons), 13 May 1940, 5th ser., vol. 360, cols. 1501–1525 (for the quotation, see col. 1502).
9   Bertrand Russell to Kingsley Martin, 13 May 1940, in BRA, Class no. 811, Box no. 6.32, McMaster University Library, Hamilton.
10 Bertrand Russell to Robert Trevelyan, 19 May 1940, in BRA, Class no. 710, Box no. 5.50, Document no. 057040, McMaster University Library, Hamilton.
11 The New York Episcopal Bishop William Thomas Manning conducted a campaign against Russell's appointment. The two had quarrelled during Russell's 1929 lecture tour to promote *Marriage and Morals*. Manning felt outraged that Russell, "a man who [was a] recognised propagandist against both religion and morality", was welcomed by the CCNY. On 18 March 1940 the Board of Higher Education examined the question; the motion to revoke Russell was defeated. A further petition was presented to the State Supreme Court; on 27 March the judge, the Irish Catholic John E. McGeehan, announced his verdict: "Mr Russell ha[d] taught in his books immoral and salacious doctrines" and the Board had acted "arbitrarily". See P. Edwards, "How Betrand Russell was Prevented from Teaching at City College, New York", appendix to B. Russell, *Why I Am Not a Christian and Other Essays*, New York, Simon & Schuster, 1957, pp. 165–199.

war 1914–18 were greater than would have been the evils of making concessions to the Kaiser", as he wrote. The latter was "the doctrine that very few wars [were] worth fighting, and that the evils of war [were] almost always greater than they seem[ed]"[12]. Russell highlighted a further distinction between "individual pacifism" and "political pacifism": the supporters of the former would never fight a war, regardless of the decisions of their country's government, whereas those who espoused the latter, which he considered realistically more important, would be more concerned with keeping their government out of war. On these premises, he argued, "the most useful kind of pacifism" destined to become probably "the one most influential" was "relative political pacifism". This synthetic concept implied that there were few causes that justified war: "I think it [was] worth while to fight to prevent England or America being conquered by the Nazis", even if "it would [be] far better if this end could be secured without war"[13]. To this end, it is worth recalling the reflections of the British historian Martin Ceadel, who highlighted the distinction between "pacifism", namely an "absolute" and "personal" doctrine whereby participation in war could never be justified, and "pacificism", i.e., a relative and "political" doctrine which entailed the advocacy of peaceful policies that would not exclude occasional support for a justified war[14]. From this perspective, Russell defended a "pacificist" policy in "The Future of Pacifism", whereas on the occasion of the Great War he had supported a "pacifist" policy.

In May 1944, Russell set sail for England; the Council of Trinity College, Cambridge, had unanimously agreed to offer him a five-year Fellowship beginning in the autumn. On 6 June, the D-Day offensive began, and within a week Hitler used his secret weapon; every day between 100 and 150 V-1 flying bombs rained down on the South of England, causing a second evacuation of women and children from London. In the 18 November 1944 article "The Thinkers Behind Germany's Sins" published in *Leader Magazine*, Russell identified the philosophers in some way responsible for Nazism: Fichte for having encouraged German nationalism, Hegel for having glorified the Prussian State, and Nietzsche for having developed an "aristocratic doctrine in ethics" that valued the "will to power" over the impulse to sympathy. Russell argued that these doctrines, "combined and vulgarised, had made up most of what [was] distinctive in Nazi political theory"[15].

---

12   See B. Russell, "The Future of Pacifism", in *American Scholar*, 1943–1944, vol. 13, pp. 7–13 (for the quotations, see p. 8).
13   Ibid., pp. 8–9.
14   See M. Ceadel, *Thinking about Peace and War*, Oxford, Oxford University Press, 1987, pp. 4–5.
15   See B. Russell, "The Thinkers Behind Germany's Sins. Can Germany Blame Her Philosophers?", in *Leader Magazine*, 18 November 1944, vol. 2, no. 5, p. 6.

Japan's surrender, announced by Emperor Hirohito on 15 August 1945 after the bombings of Hiroshima and Nagasaki, determined the end of the war; at that time Russell was 73 years of age and continued to campaign for a world government as a means of protecting mankind from the risk of a nuclear war. Moreover, the primacy of international law as a supreme normative system capable of ensuring peace was an idea shared by some prestigious intellectuals. In *The Price of Peace* (1945), William Beveridge emphasized that "international anarchy [was] the soil of war"; therefore, its abolition meant "setting up a supernational authority to decide by justice issues between nations which [were] decided by force"[16]. The failure of the League of Nations had proved that "the establishment of world order require[d], not a League or Confederation of national states, but a Federal Union of Peoples"[17]. In the same year, the Hungarian writer Emery Reves published *The Anatomy of Peace* (1945), in which he claimed that the nation was regarded as the centre of the universe in much the same way as the ancient astronomers had clung to the Ptolemaic theory of the physical universe – i.e., the earth as the centre thereof with all other planets around it. He wrote: "Our Ptolemaic political conceptions in a Copernican industrial world are bankrupt"; therefore, it was necessary to overcome the "dogmatic nation-centric conceptions"[18], and the only way to save the world from utter destruction was a genuine world legal order.

Albert Einstein also emphasized the need to establish a "world government" in order to defeat the nuclear threat; in a November 1945 interview published in the American magazine *The Atlantic Monthly*, he argued that the secret of the atomic bomb should be entrusted not to the United Nations but to "a world government" initially composed of the United States, Great Britain, and the Soviet Union, namely the three powers with the main military strength. As only the first two states had the secret of the new weapon, they had to invite the Soviet Union to prepare "the first draft of a Constitution" in order to dispel Russian distrust; afterwards, this supranational authority would exercise "jurisdiction over all military matters" also in the smaller countries[19]. The apocalyptic vision of civilisation destroying itself through the power of its science and technology, which Russell had foreseen since the 1920s[20], now looked imminent. In a series of speeches and

---

16   See W. Beveridge, *The Price of Peace*, London, Pilot Press, 1945, p. 51.
17   Ibid., p. 64.
18   See E. Reves, *The Anatomy of Peace*, New York-London, Harper & Brothers Publishers, 1945, p. 29.
19   See A. Einstein, "On the Atomic Bomb, as Told to Raymond Swing", before 1 October 1945, in *The Atlantic Monthly*, November 1945, vol. 176, no. 5, pp. 43–45.
20   In *The ABC of Atoms* (1923), Russell made a prescient remark, although he could not yet foresee the development of nuclear fusion: "It is probable that it [the recent work on the structure of

articles, he argued that in order to preserve peace, the United States had to impose its will on the rest of the world and in particular on the Soviet Union; as Ray Monk wrote, behind his comments on the international situation lay "not only a concern to prevent the suicide of humanity, but also a fierce detestation of Stalin's regime"[21]. For example, in his September 1945 article "What Should Be British Policy Towards Russia?", Russell argued that the Soviet Union too would have an atomic bomb in the next few years, and therefore it was of fundamental importance that Soviet power be contained quickly not by a "policy of appeasement such as we pursued towards Germany until after Munich"[22]. A month later, in the article "Humanity's Last Chance" published in the British magazine *Cavalcade*, he argued that American supremacy deriving from "the immense power conferred by the atomic bomb" had to be used by the United States "with no undue shrinking from the responsibilities which this power confer[red]". He also advocated the establishment of a new confederation of nations with membership imposed on the USSR, and warned that in case of its non-adhesion, "the conditions for justifiable war […] would have all been fulfilled"[23].

Russell made his voice heard on this topic in the House of Lords during a two-day debate on "The International Situation" on 27–28 November 1945[24]. The event was attended by prestigious personalities, including former Cabinet Ministers Herbert Samuel and Samuel Hoare, Archbishop Cyril Garbett and Bishop George Bell, Labour leaders Christopher Addison and Lord Strabolgi, opposition spokesmen Lord Llewellin and Lord Cherwell, pacifists Lord Cecil and Lord Pethick-Lawrence. Russell focused on effective international control of nuclear weapons technology; he supported the idea of a world government and stressed the need to prevent the Soviet Union from developing atomic technology. He argued that the "atmosphere of suspicion" between East and West "[could] only be got over by complete and utter frankness"; therefore, an indispensable precondition to the creation of international control of atomic energy was not only technical or diplomatic but also psychological[25]. From this perspective, one of the

the atom] will ultimately be used for making more deadly explosive and projectiles than any yet invented". See Russell, *The ABC of Atoms*, p. 5.
21 See Monk, *Bertrand Russell 1921–1970: The Ghost of Madness*, p. 299.
22 See B. Russell, "What Should Be British Policy Towards Russia?", in *Forward*, 29 September 1945, vol. 39, no. 39, p. 4.
23 Id., "Humanity's Last Chance", in *Cavalcade*, 20 October 1945, vol. 7, no. 398, pp. 8–9.
24 "The International Situation", Parliamentary Debates (Lords), 27–28 November 1945, 5th ser., vol. 138, cols. 17–64 (27th), 68–137 (28th). Russell's House of Lords speech was reprinted in Id., *Has Man a Future?*, pp. 19–25.
25 Ibid., cols. 89–92.

most important proposals was the June 1946 Baruch Plan presented by the US Government to the United Nations Atomic Energy Commission (UNAEC); it was written by the American financier Bernard Baruch but based on the Acheson-Lilienthal Report. This plan proposed to internationalize fission energy through an International Atomic Development Authority controlled by the UNAEC, with an exclusive system of inspection that included monitoring, policing, and sanctions, regardless of any right of veto by the permanent members of the UN Security Council[26].

In the aftermath of the December 1946 Soviet rejection of the Baruch Plan, Russell's articles and lectures appeared to be more aggressive, as on Churchill's famous Iron Curtain speech of 5 March 1946. In his 1947 pamphlet *Towards World Government*, Russell stated that "the only way to prevent great wars […] was the creation of an international authority for the control of atomic energy". He added that if Soviet resistance was to be overcome by "diplomatic pressure", "the international government" would be established "peacefully by gradual degrees", but if diplomatic pressure was to fail, war would be "inevitable"; since the Soviet Union did not as yet have the atomic weapon, a possible war would be "less destructive" for mankind[27]. This statement could be interpreted through a utilitarian vision: the USSR was developing the atomic bomb, and a one-sided nuclear war could be considered less catastrophic than a larger two-sided nuclear war. On 30 April 1947, he made a statement in the House of Lords on the problem of atomic energy. He argued that "to preserve the peace of the world beyond the time when America [had] ceased to have a monopoly of the bomb", it was necessary to establish an "international control over atomic energy"; since he had not "much faith in the United Nations", he advocated a "real international government" composed of states that were prepared to forego the power of veto[28]. As he pointed out, the question that had to be faced was how to force Soviet acceptance of a strict international control and military sanctions: "From all we kn[ew] of Russia [and Mr Gromyko], inspection [was] the one thing they [could] not stand"; therefore, we had to understand "how much pressure of one sort or another it [was] proper to use against them"[29].

26 See M. Rosenbloom, *Peace through Strength: Bernard Baruch and a Blueprint for Security*, New York, Straus and Young, 1953.
27 See B. Russell, *Towards World Government*, London, New Commonwealth, 1948, pp. 11–12.
28 Id., "Atomic Energy Control", Parliamentary Debates (Lords), 30 April 1947, 5th ser., vol. 147, cols. 272–276 (for the quotations, see cols. 273–275). This speech was partially reprinted as "The House of Lords Debates the Control of Atomic Energy", in *Bulletin of the Atomic Scientist*, July 1947, vol. 3, no. 7, pp. 184–185.
29 Ibid., col. 275.

In 1947, the Crusade for World Government was established in England; it was supported by more than 80 members of the British Parliament, whose main exponents were Labour MPs Gordon Lang (chairman) and Henry Charles Usborne (secretary), as well as Wing Commander Ernest Millington. This movement hoped for a constituent procedure; indeed, its fundamental proposal was that "representatives of all countries", more precisely "one for every million of inhabitants", had to form a single Constituent Assembly to draw up "the Charter of the World Government"[30]. In the November 1947 essay "Still Time for Good Sense", submitted to Einstein for comment, Russell wrote that "the human race [was] faced with a new situation: it must alter its political habits or perish"[31]. The main safeguard against possible mass destruction was a world government capable of maintaining control of the nuclear weapons; he identified the Baruch Plan as an "enormously important first step"[32] towards a world government. In his reply on 19 November, Einstein expressed his disagreement; although he referred to Russell's "brilliant article" for "world government propaganda", he argued that "it was very difficult for the Russians to agree to the [Baruch] Plan", despite being "sensible" and "carefully worked out" because it was asymmetric as to demands placed on the Soviets due to the Western presence in their country[33]. In turn, Russell, aware of his underestimation of the danger of Nazi Germany before the Second World War, now rejected a new kind of appeasement, this time towards the USSR. Indeed, in his 24 November 1947 letter to Einstein, he pointed out: "I favoured appeasement before 1930, wrongly, as I know think; I do not want to repeat the same mistake" and added: "I think it is essential that America should assume leadership"[34]. While arguing for peace through world government, Russell's vision was closely related to his anti-Soviet position; the Stalin period had reinforced further his view of communism as a threat to individual liberty.

Both Russell and Einstein advocated the need for a world government. In this regard, Einstein wrote an "Open Letter to the General Assembly of the UN" in October 1947. He argued that to create the preconditions for "control of atomic

---

30 Crusade for World Government, The British Parliamentary Committee, *Crusade for World Government: The Plan in Outline*, London, The Committee, 1947, p. 11.
31 See B. Russell, "Still Time for Good Sense", in *'47: The Magazine of the Year*, November 1947, vol. 1, no. 9, pp. 56–63 (for the quotation, see p. 56).
32 Ibid., p. 59.
33 Letter from Einstein to Russell, *The Lilienthal-Baruch Proposal Was Sensible and Carefully Worked*, 19 November 1947, in Albert Einstein Archives 33–189, Hebrew University of Jerusalem, Jerusalem.
34 Bertrand Russell to Albert Einstein, 24 November 1947, in BRA, Class no. 710, Box no. 5.15, Document no. 049710, McMaster University Library, Hamilton.

energy", it was necessary that the General Assembly increase its authority so that the Security Council, paralyzed by the power of veto of the individual states, was subordinated to it. Secondly, it needed to modify the United Nations' representation method because the appointment procedures by national governments did not permit the appointees to act according to their convictions. Thirdly, the General Assembly could create the foundations for a "real world government" initially composed of "at least two-thirds of the major industrial and economic areas" of the planet. In addition, Einstein recommended that "the doors" remain wide open particularly to Russia for participation on "the basis of complete equality"[35]. A month later, the Soviets made their voices heard in an "Open Letter to Dr. Einstein" signed by four leading scientists: Abram Fedorovich Ioffe, Alexander Naumovich Frumkin, Nikolay Nikolayevich Semyonov, and Sergey Vavilov. They claimed that Einstein's appeal for a world government echoed merely the interests of the capitalist monopolies, which could function only within the framework of the "world markets and sources of raw materials"[36]. As Russell feared, this exchange of open letters showed that the Soviet Union was not available to join any supranational organization capable of managing nuclear power because it wanted to build the atomic bomb on its own; its rejection of the Baruch Plan had proved it.

Russell believed that war was conditional on the Soviets' rejection of an ultimatum to internationalize atomic energy, although he thought that they would agree; due to the Soviet rejection of the Baruch Plan and the 1948 Czech Communist coup, however, he developed doubts about whether the USSR would acquiesce to an overt threat. In a May 1948 letter written to the German American psychoanalyst Walter Marseille, he pointed out: "Communism must be wiped out, and world government must be established [...]. I do not think the Russians will yield without war"[37]. This seemed an expression of a "conditional" preventive war, foreseeing that the Soviets would not accept the proposal for the internationalization of atomic energy. In the November 1948 lecture delivered at Westminster School in London, he advocated a strengthening of the West's defences to show the Soviets that "they [could] not make war successfully"[38]. On this occasion, he outlined three hypotheses: a "war with Russia before she ha[d] the atomic bomb",

---

35 See A. Einstein, "Open Letter to the General Assembly of the United Nations", in *United Nations World*, October 1947, no. 8, pp. 13–14.

36 "Open Letter to Dr. Einstein from Four Soviet Scientist", in *Bulletin of Atomic Scientists*, February 1948, vol. 4, no. 2, p. 34.

37 See B. Russell, "1948 Russell vs. 1954 Russell", in *The Saturday Review*, 16 October 1954, vol. 37, no. 42, pp. 25–26 (for the quotation, see p. 25).

38 Id., "Atomic Energy and the Problems of Europe", in *The Nineteenth Century and After*, January 1949, vol. 145, pp. 39–43 (for the quotation, see p. 41).

with an "inevitably Western victory"; a "war with Russia after she had the atomic bomb", with a Western victory but "after frightful carnage, destruction and suffering"; and a "submission", which was the worst, "so utterly unthinkable that it could be dismissed"[39].

The press reaction to his Westminster speech was not long in coming; *Reynold's News* featured an editorial accusing Russell to advance "the oldest and most blood-drenched fallacy in History: 'the war to end wars' "[40]. He rejected such accusations while admitting that "the democracies [should be] prepared to use force if necessary", and "their readiness" had to be "perfectly clear to Russia"[41]. In his *Autobiography* Russell admitted that during the period of the Baruch Plan he had hypothesized a "conditional preventive war", believing that the Soviets would accept the internationalization proposal of atomic energy and the idea of a world government. He wrote that "the threat of immediate war" by the United States on the Soviet Union with "the purpose of forcing nuclear disarmament" could be considered as a justifiable scenario, since the Soviets "very likely [would] yield to the demands of the West"[42], but added that he had abandoned this hope by mid-1948, as evidenced by his letter to Walter Marseille. At the end of 1948, Russell travelled to both Norway and Berlin, and in December he held the first in a prestigious series of Reith Lectures on "Authority and the Individual" on the BBC. His visit to Berlin was sponsored by the Foreign Office. The city was under blockade by the Soviet Union, and the Allies had kept supply lines open using military aircraft; his task during the airlift was to give morale-boosting lectures to the troops.

The alleged advocacy of a preventive conditional war against the Soviet Union represented one of the most contentious aspect of Russell's public life; this topic was the subject of a controversial discussion involving the US philosophers Ray Perkins and Douglas Lackey in the 1990s. Perkins, Emeritus Professor at Plymouth State University, considered Russell's pronouncements on the possibility of a nuclear war against the Soviets in the 1945–1948 period and highlighted the inability of his critics to recognize the conditional nature of Russell's statements. Perkins distinguished three main scenarios of "preventive war" against the Soviet Union: an "unconditional preventive war" and a "conditional preventive war" before which the Soviets could accept – or reject – the internationalization proposal of atomic energy and the idea of a world government[43]. In those years, Perkins

---

39 Ibid., p. 43.
40 *Reynolds News*, 21 November 1948.
41 See Bertrand Russell's letter to *The Observer*, 28 November 1948, p. 3.
42 See Russell, *The Autobiography of Bertrand Russell*, vol. III, *1944–1967*, p. 7.
43 See R. Perkins, "Bertrand Russell and Preventive War", in *Russell: The Journal of Bertrand Russell Studies*, 1994, vol. 14, no. 2, pp. 135–153 (for the quotations, see pp. 135–136).

noted, Russell had supported the first option of "conditional preventive war" – he never advocated an "unconditional preventive war" – and his hope was that the United States, with a nuclear monopoly, could effectively threaten the Soviets with war in order to make them agree. According to Perkins, it was enough to read Russell's January 1948 article "International Government" published in *The New Commonwealth*; if the whole world insisted upon international control of atomic energy to the point of going to war on this issue, it was highly probable that the Soviet Government would give way on this issue: "If it did not, [...] the war might be so short as not to involve utter ruin"[44]. Two years later, Lackey, Professor at City University of New York (CUNY), criticized Perkins' theses on Russell's preventive war idea, arguing that Perkins' distinction between "unconditional" and "conditional preventive war" was "vacuous"[45]. The enemy's conditional intentions of war could be assessed by focusing on "the actual probability of the conditions, not their perceived probability"; in this regard, Russell had "very little information about how the Soviets would react to such conditional threats". Therefore, Lackey added, nuclear threats could not be "morally permissible" only because they had a low probability of occurring, and in any case, those who made these claims had "no rational grounds for assuming that the probabilities were so low"[46]. In the same year, Perkins replied to Lackey: "I did not claim that Russell was without blame, only that he was less blameworthy than commonly charged"; in fact, in 1948 he stopped advocating his preventive war proposal when he came to believe that "the Soviets would be unlikely to accede to the ultimatum"[47].

On 29 August 1949, the Soviets detonated their first atomic bomb, ending the nuclear monopoly enjoyed by the United States for the previous four years; this event had wide repercussions for the prospects of world peace and public opinion. The alleged scenario of a preventive war was no longer conceivable; at that moment more than before, mankind had to face and prevent the risk of total annihilation deriving from the danger of an atomic war between the West and the East. The concept of "relative political pacifism" developed a few years earlier by Russell represented in this new geopolitical context a valuable compass for orientation.

---

44   See B. Russell, "International Government", in *The New Commonwealth*, January 1948, vol. 9, pp. 77–80.
45   See D. Lackey, "Reply to Perkins on 'Conditional Preventive War'", in *Russell: The Journal of Bertrand Russell Studies*, 1996, vol. 16, no. 1, pp. 85–88 (for the quotation, see p. 86).
46   Ibid., pp. 86–88.
47   See R. Perkins, "Response to Lackey on 'Conditional Preventive War'", in *Russell: The Journal of Bertrand Russell Studies*, 1996, vol. 16, no. 2, pp. 169–170.

The Futility of War and the Need for a World Government

Russell's initial antinuclear activism was characterized by a troubled relationship between pro-Soviet and independent peace organizations. The communist-led movement existed under the umbrella of the World Peace Council (WPC), founded as a successor of the Partisans of Peace at the Second World Peace Congress held in Warsaw in November 1950 and presided by the French Nobel laureate in physics Frédéric Joliot-Curie. One of its most significant initiatives was the Stockholm Peace Appeal of March 1950, a petition that called for unconditional prohibition of nuclear weapons. The general thrust of WPC propaganda was to present the Soviet Government as a pillar of peace; therefore, its affiliates were viewed with suspicion by many potential sympathizers in the West. In turn, pro-Soviet groups considered Western pacifists as supporters of a world government and servants of American imperialism. We should note Russell's involvement in the birth of the Congress for Cultural Freedom (CCF) dating back to June 1950. The CCF was a Cold War organization that carried the ideological battle against communism into CIA-sponsored academic conferences and seminars, writers' congresses, and literary and political journals; he represented it as honorary president. Russell believed that the benefits of cooperation outweighed the risks of being labelled as an apologist for communism; he occupied the middle ground between those nonaligned organizations and activists who, like Linus Carl Pauling, endorsed "all peace movements, even those conducted by communists"[48] and those who steadfastly opposed such alliances. Therefore, he supported a fair balance between accommodating and excluding pro-Soviet elements in the wider peace movement: as British writer Ronald William Clark wrote, it was "a tricky operation" that the "aristocratic" Russell would have attempted "with equanimity" and could have carried out "with some chance of success"[49].

In June 1950, Russell arrived in Australia for a nine-week tour promoted by the Australian Institute of International Affairs (AIIA), particularly by Edward Clarence Dyason, one of the main advocates in the 1933 establishment of the AIIA; Russell agreed to lecture in Canberra, Brisbane, Adelaide, Perth, Sydney and Melbourne. Since the Second World War, the main thrust of Australian foreign policy had been towards striking a military alliance with the United States; during his Australian tour, the Korean War broke out and this signalled an extension of

---

48 See L.S. Wittner, *The Struggle against the Bomb. Resisting the Bomb: A History of the World Nuclear Disarmament Movement, 1954–1970*, vol. 2, Stanford, Stanford University Press, 1997, p. 92.

49 See Clark, *The Life of Bertrand Russell*, pp. 545–546.

American containment policy. Russell's discussion of world government (Sydney) and his fears for the nuclear age (Melbourne) suited the mission to "foster in Australia a greater understanding of its situation in the world", as the Canadian philosopher Nicholas Griffin recalled[50]. After returning to London at the end of August, Russell began a speaking tour of the United States two months later; after his arrival in New York on 22 October, he delivered a lecture at Mount Holyoke College in South Hadley, Massachusetts, and sounded out his contacts at Yale, Harvard and Princeton, as well as at Columbia. During his American lecture tour, he was informed that he had been awarded the Nobel Prize in Literature – in June 1949 he had been awarded the Order of Merit by King George VI.

On 11 December 1950 in Stockholm, he received the prestigious prize "In recognition of his varied and significant writings in which he champions humanitarian ideals and freedom of thought". On this occasion, he argued that a peaceful society could be promoted through "harmless outlets for the impulses" because two closely related passions conditioned human behaviour, namely "fear and hate"; they were all the more dangerous when considering the possession of nuclear weapons by the United Stated and the Soviet Union. He stated that the world was obsessed with the conflict between communist and capitalist ideologies, but it was only an apparent cause of the tension between the two superpowers; indeed, war was intrinsic to human nature rather than being a historical social construct. In this way, he once again supported a "scientific pacifism" – if we consider Norberto Bobbio's concept – whereby the real reason for war was to be found in the primitive impulses of human nature; Russell had already formulated a similar theory in *Why Men Fight*[51]. He further explored the theme of human impulsiveness, particularly with reference to American society of the early 1950s, in an article published in *The New York Times*; more precisely, he analysed the political hysteria to which the United States had succumbed, lamenting – with implicit reference to McCarthyism – how "the atmosphere of suspicion [was] poisoning public life" in this country[52].

The discovery of the hydrogen bomb, tested almost simultaneously for the first time by the United States and the Soviet Union between 1952 and 1953, instilled even more fears in the international community and raised the nuclear peril to a new level. Britain's defence planners feared that the European scenario would be

---

50   See N. Griffin, "Russell in Australia", in *Russell: The Journal of Bertrand Russell Studies*, 1974, no. 16, pp. 3–12 (for the quotation, see p. 3).
51   See B. Russell, "What Desires Are Politically Important?" (1950), in H. Frenz (ed.), *Nobel Lectures, Literature 1901–1967*, Amsterdam, Elsevier Publishing Company, 1969, pp. 259–270.
52   Id., "To Face Danger without Hysteria", in *The New York Times*, 21 January 1951, sec. 6, pp. 7, 42, 44–45.

left exposed by the diversion of American military resources to Asia due to the conflict in Korea; they remained concerned that the United States' growing vulnerability to nuclear attack might make them reluctant to guarantee the defence of Western Europe. In June 1954, the Defence Policy Committee chaired by Prime Minister Churchill declared: "We must maintain and strengthen our position as a world power so that Her Majesty's Government can exercise a powerful influence in the counsels of the world"[53]; thus, the British Government decided to proceed with the development of the hydrogen bomb. Despite this scenario, some strategic analysts inside the British and American defence believed that war could be limited by holding the exponentially greater threat of thermonuclear weapons in reserve according to the logic of deterrence. Russell was sceptical of the very notion of deterrence; in a BBC interview with William Donaldson Clark[54] on 24 February 1955, he pointed out that nuclear weapons "[were] valuable deterrents if they enable you to inflict damage upon the enemy greater than he [could] inflict upon you […]"[55]. Yet, elsewhere he seemed prepared to grant the plausibility of this strategic doctrine; in September 1954 he wrote: "I do not […] advocate either appeasement or a slackening in rearmament, since either might encourage the Communist Powers in aggressive designs and would therefore make war more likely"[56]. Therefore, his thinking about nuclear weapons was not always linear, although Alan Ryan noted that Russell's "argumentative record" on nuclear weapons, disarmament and international security in the mid-1950s was "all of a piece"[57].

Russell's critique of Soviet tyranny was evident especially under Stalin; after the latter's death in 1953 and the 1954 Bikini test, he "was brought around to being more favourable to Communism" and came "gradually" to attribute, more and more, "the danger of nuclear war to the West, to the United States of America, and less to Russia"[58]. After all, the new Republican Administration led by President Dwight David Eisenhower supported the nuclear doctrine of "massive retaliation", which gained traction after a speech given by Secretary of State John Foster Dulles to the Council on Foreign Relations in January 1954. This shift was implemented also on grounds of economy: reliance on hydrogen bombs could be less costly than the maintenance of military manpower at existing or higher

53 See L. Arnold, K. Pyne, *Britain and the H-Bomb*, Basingstoke, Palgrave, 2001, p. 53.
54 William Donaldson Clark was a diplomatic correspondent for *The Observer* and Anthony Eden's press secretary.
55 *The Collected Papers of Bertrand Russell. Man's Peril 1954–55*, vol. 28, London, Routledge, 2003, p. 262.
56 Ibid., p. 73.
57 See A. Ryan, *Bertrand Russell: A Political Life*, New York, Hill and Wang, 1988, p. 177.
58 See Russell, *The Autobiography of Bertrand Russell 1944–1967*, vol. III, p. 20.

levels[59]. For this reason, Russell was positively impressed by Soviet Premier Georgy Maximilianovich Malenkov's March 1954 public statement pointing out that another world war, "with the present means of warfare, mean[t] the destruction of world civilization"[60].

In the article "The Danger to Mankind" published in January 1954 in the *Bulletin of the Atomic Scientists*, Russell highlighted three central ideas about the Cold War. Firstly, he underlined the vital role of neutral nations because they were able to "diminish the tension" between Western and Communist governments; moreover, the "genuinely" neutral countries had a "legitimate interest" in seeking to prevent a possible Third World War, a "calamity" that would destroy not only the belligerents[61]. Secondly, he emphasized the uselessness of any agreement to prohibit nuclear weapons; in fact, they could be manufactured again, since mutual suspicion between the great powers persuaded them to consider "the enemy worthy of being destroyed in a holy crusade". Lastly, he hoped for an international authority with the "monopoly" of weapons of mass destruction[62].

In the mid-1950s, Russell explored the theme of the "futility" of war according to a utilitarian logic. In the 14 August 1954 article "A Study in Futility: H-Bomb Politics" published in *Saturday Night*, he highlighted the uselessness of war due to the possible use of the H-bomb; the new issue with which "the conscience of mankind" was confronted was not "the morality of war" because "it had always been morally a horror", he argued. War fought with modern means could no longer achieve the aims of any of the belligerents; it was likely that "neither Democracy nor Communism [...] would emerge", while "chaos, anarchy and madness" would prevail in "the surviving remnant of mankind"[63]. In a November 1954 article published in *Britain To-day*, Russell once again stressed the "futility" of war due to the destructiveness of the H-bomb and highlighted the role of the neutral countries. More precisely, he affirmed that "Clausewitz's dictum that war [was] the continuation of policy by other means [...] was no longer true", but neither communist nor anti-communist countries alone could support all this, for they would give "an impression of weakness". Instead, the neutral countries could dialogue with governments on both sides of the Iron Curtain without being "actuated by

---

59 See L. Freedman, *The Evolution of Nuclear Strategy*, New York, St. Martin's Press, 1989, pp. 78–86.
60 See H. Dinerstein, *War and the Soviet Union: Nuclear Weapons and the Revolution in Soviet Military and Political Thinking*, New York-London, Praeger, 1962, p. 71.
61 See B. Russell, "The Danger to Mankind", in *Bulletin of the Atomic Scientists*, January 1954, vol. 10, no. 1, pp. 8–9 (for the quotations, see p. 8).
62 Ibid., p. 9.
63 See B. Russell, "A Study in Futility: H-Bomb Politics", in *Saturday Night*, 14 August 1954, vol. 69, no. 45, pp. 7–8.

bias". The first step should be the appointment of a commission composed of military, naval, and air experts; a nuclear physicist; a bacteriologist; an economist; and an expert in international politics. It would draw up a report to highlight "the futility of world war"[64]. In his 14 April 1955 address to the Standing Committees of the Inter-Parliamentary Union in the Italian Chamber of Deputies held in Rome, he similarly pointed out: "War [could] no longer be regarded as an instrument of policy" because it had become "a danger to the further existence of mankind". In this regard, a small committee composed of a nuclear physicist, a bacteriologist, a chemist, a geneticist, an economist and an expert in international affairs was to draw up a report about the effects caused by a nuclear war. Furthermore, it was necessary to involve the neutral powers that were not conditioned by political bias and were capable of fostering dialogue between the governments of the great powers, especially the United States, Russia and China[65]. In his 23 June 1955 address at the World Assembly for Peace in Helsinki – which was read *in absentia* by William Wainwright, a representative of the pro-Soviet British Committee – Russell once again criticized Carl von Clausewitz's assertion: in the face of danger of "annihilation of human race", the governments on either side of the Iron Curtain could simultaneously admit that "war [could] no longer serve a continuation of policy". Since mankind formed "one family", the governmental divisions could be overcome through "the creation of a World Authority", already attempted "first by the League of Nations and then by UNO"[66].

The very idea of a world government had represented "one of the strongest lines of continuity in his political thought"[67] since the First World War. Russell also pursued this idea under the auspices of some organizations such as the Inter-Parliamentary Union, the British Parliamentary Group for World Government (PGWG) – namely the British wing of the World Association of Parliamentarians for World Government (WAPWG) – and the World Movement for World Federal Government. The PGWG had over 200 members from the House of Commons and the House of Lords; two of its executive committee members in 1955 were Liberal Party leader Clement Davies and former Conservative minister Walter Elliot. Russell established working relations primarily with PGWG founder and Honorary Secretary Henry Charles Usborne and WAPWG Secretary-General Gilbert McAllister. In "The Hydrogen Bomb and World Government", which

64 Id., "What Neutrals Can Do to Save the World", in *Britain To-day*, November 1954, no. 223, pp. 6–10.
65 Id., "The Road to Peace", in *Inter-Parliamentary Bulletin*, 1955, vol. 25, no. 2, pp. 49–53.
66 Id., "Creating Climate of Peace", in *The Manchester Guardian*, 27 June 1955, p. 7.
67 See A.G. Bone (Introduction to), *The Collected Papers of Bertrand Russell. Man's Peril 1954–55*, vol. 28, pp. xiii–xliv (for the quotation, see p. xxxv).

was broadcast on 13 July 1954 on the BBC's European Service and published in *The Listener*, Russell pointed out that the "essence" of a world government – "the only long-run alternative to the extinction of the human race" – involved a "coercive power" unlike the UNO, which had been deprived of it due to the power of veto that could be exercised within the Security Council. The world government should be a "world federation" composed of "large federations" such as the Western Hemisphere, the British Commonwealth, and the communist world. It should hold the "monopoly of armed force" – with the exception of such minor weapons as might be necessary for police action – the power to ratify the international treaties between "national States or federation of States", and in the event of a dispute between national states or between federations, it had "to pronounce a decision of arbitration"; furthermore, "all mining of fissionable material" was to be managed by this "international authority"[68]. On the same wavelength we can consider his 28 August 1954 article "A Prescription for the World" in *The Saturday Review*, in which he expressed his hope for a world government with "the monopoly of armed force" – leaving to national states "only such forces necessary for internal police purposes" – and the "control over treaties". The "Central Government" should take the form of a "Federal Authority" with powers defined by a "written constitution". The "world federation" was not to be composed of national states but of "subordinate federations of States" capable of deciding "matters concerning States" that belonged to it. Indeed, it could investigate "every dispute between States belonging to different subordinate federations" and also between states of the same subordinate federation, if the latter was unable to impose a solution[69].

He explored the idea of a world government especially in the article "The Road to Peace" (1955), published in the collection of essays *The Bomb: Challenge and Answer* commissioned by WAPWG Secretary-General Gilbert McAllister. Since mankind was faced with an alternative that had never before arisen in human history, namely "peace by agreement or the peace of universal death", an International Commission – appointed by an "international conference of scientists" composed of a nuclear physicist, a chemist, a physiologist, a bacteriologist, an expert in guided missiles, a geneticist, and an economist – would highlight the effects of a thermonuclear war. The conference would propose the establishment of a World Authority conceived as a World Federation composed of eight

---

68 See B. Russell, "The Hydrogen Bomb and World Government", in *The Listener*, 22 July 1954, vol. 52, pp. 133–134.
69 Id., "A Prescription for the World", in *The Saturday Review*, 28 August 1954, vol. 37, no. 35, pp. 9–11 and 38–40.

"subordinate federations" closely similar to one suggested by Ely Culbertson[70]: the United States, the USSR and its European satellites, the British Commonwealth, China, Latin America, Latin Europe (France, Italy, Spain, Portugal, and Belgium), the Mohammedan World, and Germany, together with Scandinavia, Austria, Switzerland, and Holland. Africa could not as yet be included due to the presence of the colonial empires of Great Britain, France, Belgium and Portugal. The World Authority would hold "legal powers" defined by a Federal Constitution, first of all "the power required for the preservation of peace" involving the "monopoly" of nuclear weapons and the possibility to "revise or abrogate treaties"; it would give "each national State and each subordinate Federation complete freedom in everything not affecting the peace of the world"[71]. In these last writings and speeches, he seemed to tolerate a potential degree of coercion deriving from the establishment of a world government as an acceptable price for ending international anarchy. In this regard, Mark Lippincott of Toronto University highlighted "Russell's appropriation of elements from Thomas Hobbes' theory of domestic peace", in particular "the image of a rational leviathan wielding an awe-inspiring monopoly of armed forces"[72].

The essence of Russell's thought on mid-1950s international politics can be found in the 23 December 1954 speech "Man's Peril from the Hydrogen Bomb" broadcast by the BBC and published in *The Listener*[73]. The main points raised were the devastation of a hydrogen-bomb war, the uselessness of nonbinding agreements to prohibit nuclear weapons, and the vital role of neutral states to ease mutual suspicion among the great powers. Drawing inspiration from this discourse, on 11 February 1955 he wrote a letter to Einstein in which he affirmed some ideas

---

70   In 1943 Culbertson had proposed a World Federation composed of 11 "Regional Federations"; each of them was an economic unit often bound by a common heritage of history, culture, law, psychology and language. The countries were the following: America (the United States and the Latin American republics), British Commonwealth (the United Kingdom and the British Dominions), Latin Europe (France, Italy, Spain, Portugal, Belgium), Northern Europe (Germany, Austria, the Netherlands, Scandinavia, Finland), Middle Europe (Poland, Lithuania, Czechoslovakia, Hungary and the Balkans), the Middle East (Turkey, Persia, Afghanistan, Syria, Arabia, a sovereign Jewish state of Palestine, and Egypt), the Soviet Union, China, Japan, India, and Malaysia. See E. Culbertson, *Summary of the World Federation Plan*, New York, Garden City, 1943.
71   See B. Russell, "The Road to Peace", in G. McAllister (ed.), *The Bomb: Challenge and Answer*, London, Batsford, 1955, pp. 47–68.
72   See M. Lippincott, "Russell's Leviathan", in *Russell: The Journal of Bertrand Russell Studies*, 1990, vol. 10, no. 1, pp. 6–29 (for the quotation, see p. 8).
73   See B. Russell, "Man's Peril from the Hydrogen Bomb", in *The Listener*, 30 December 1954, vol. 52, pp. 1, 135–136.

already expressed in his previous writings and speeches. He proposed that "six men of the very highest scientific repute, headed by yourself", free from pro-communist or anti-communist bias, could make "a very solemn statement about the imperative necessity of avoiding war"[74]. More precisely, this commission was to be composed of a nuclear physicist, a bacteriologist, a geneticist, an authority on air warfare, a man with international experience matured in the United Nations, and a chairman chosen for his cultural prowess. He proposed that their reports were to be presented to all governments of the world so that "the impossibility of modern war might come to be generally acknowledged"[75]. Einstein reacted enthusiastically to this proposal; a few days later, in response he advocated a "public declaration" signed by "a small number of people" to "make an impression on the general public as well as on political leaders"[76]. Even if it could be helpful to propose signatories in the United States and in the Soviet Union, he advised Russell on the need to involve neutral countries because it was fundamental to emphasize "the neutral character of the whole project"[77].

Russell sent him the text of the Manifesto; Einstein did not live long enough to witness the developments of this important initiative because he died on 18 April 1955, a week after he had signed it. Nine other scientists signed the declaration: the Americans Percy Williams Bridgman, Herman Joseph Muller and Linus Carl Pauling; the British Cecil Frank Powell and Joseph Rotblat; the French Jean Frédéric Joliot-Curie; the Polish Leopold Infeld; the Japanese Hideki Yukawa; and the German Max Born. Russell delivered the statement at a press conference in London on 9 July 1955. The Russell-Einstein Manifesto described the potential scenario deriving from the use of the H-bomb: faced with "the tragic situation which confronted humanity", scientists were to assemble in conference to assess the perils arising from the development of the new weapon of mass destruction and to discuss a resolution, not "as members of this or that nation, continent or creed, but as human beings, [...] whose existence [was] in doubt"[78]. A single H-bomb was up to 2,500 times more powerful than the nuclear bombs that had destroyed Hiroshima and Nagasaki; by annihilating cities such as London, New York and Moscow, it could "put an end to the human race". Despite this, the Manifesto stated that there was not a real understanding of the gravity of

---

74 Id., *In Common with Every Other Thinking Person*, 11 February 1955, Albert Einstein Archives 33–199, Hebrew University of Jerusalem, Jerusalem.
75 Ibid.
76 Letter from Albert Einstein to Bertrand Russell, 16 February 1955, Albert Einstein Archives 33–201, Hebrew University of Jerusalem, Jerusalem.
77 Ibid.
78 Russell's 9 July 1955 statement was published in *The New York Times* on 10 July 1955.

the situation because the concept of "mankind [was felt] vague and abstract"; in fact, public opinion scarcely realized that the danger also concerned their children and grandchildren. Emphasizing the goal of bridging the ideological gap that was separating communists and anti-communists, it called on the governments of the world to publicly acknowledge that "their purposes [could not] be furthered by a world war" and, at the same time, to find "peaceful means for the settlement of all matters of dispute between them"[79]. The Manifesto received widespread publicity in the world; Russell sent copies of the declaration to US President Dwight David Eisenhower, Soviet Premier Nikolai Alexandrovich Bulganin, British Prime Minister Anthony Eden, French President René Coty, Chinese Chairman Mao Zedong, and Canadian Prime Minister Louis Saint-Laurent.

Some scientists voiced anti-communist sentiments to explain their unwillingness to sign. The Swedish physicist Manne Siegbahn stated: "The eastern side ha[d] misused 'peace resolution' and 'peace-conference' for propagandistic purposes", and for this reason it had very little to do with "the work for a lasting peace"[80]. The American Nobel laureate in chemistry Harold Urey expressed his perplexity to Russell: "I dislike Communists from the democratic countries"[81]. An initiative similar to the Russell-Einstein Manifesto was the Göttingen Manifesto of 12 April 1957; it was a declaration signed, on the initiative of Otto Hahn, by 18 leading nuclear scientists of West Germany against the proposal of Chancellor Konrad Adenauer and Defence Minister Franz-Josef Strauss to equip the Federal Republic of Germany with tactical nuclear weapons[82]. Russell applauded this initiative but pointed out: "Einstein and I had hoped to show that political differences do not prevent a large and important measure of agreement among men of science"[83]. At any rate, the Russell-Einstein Manifesto enhanced the role of scientists in their mission as upholders of conscience. Russell highlighted the link between internationalism and science in the opening address to the conference of scientists held by the WAPWG at Country Hall in London on 3–5 August 1955. Unlike

---

79 Ibid.
80 Manne Siegbahn to Bertrand Russell, 30 June 1955, in BRA, Class no. 600, Box no. 1.36, McMaster University Library, Hamilton.
81 Harold Urey to Bertrand Russell, 7 July 1955, in BRA, Class no. 600, Box no. 1.36, McMaster University Library, Hamilton.
82 The 18 nuclear scientists were the following: Fritz Bopp, Max Born, Rudolf Fleischmann, Walther Gerlach, Otto Hahn, Otto Haxel, Werner Karl Heisenberg, Hans Kopfermann, Max von Laue, Heinz Maier-Leibnitz, Josef Mattauch, Friedrich Adolf Paneth, Wolfgang Ernst Pauli, Wolfgang Riezler, Fritz Strassmann, Wilhelm Walcher, Carl Friedrich von Weizsäcker, and Karl Wirtz.
83 See B. Russell, "Scientists' Warning", in *The Sunday Times*, 17 July 1955.

in the past, he argued, "scientists [were] organized nationally", and their main aim was not the "advancement of knowledge" but the "perfecting of means of slaughter in the hands of a nation or group of nations". Since a nuclear war would not bring victory to either side, the governments of the great powers, with the help of men of science, could admit that "war [could] no longer serve as a continuation of policy", and the defeat of communism or capitalism was not of such importance as to justify "the extermination of the human race"[84]. As Ray Monk wrote, by giving the scientific community a pivotal role to maintain peace, Russell showed "his deepseated view that science itself was neutral"[85].

In the first half of the 1950s, Russell advocated a "utilitarian pacifism" and a "juridical" pacifism. He implicitly supported a "utilitarian pacifism" through the concept of the "futility" of war because it could no longer be considered as the continuation of politics by other means – in Carl von Clausewitz's thought – because the destructiveness of the H-bomb would determine not winners and losers but only the annihilation of humanity. He reproposed the idea of the uselessness of war already analysed by Norman Angell a few decades earlier; however, their ideological perspectives had become different. In his essay "The Great Illusion", (1911) Angell had proposed the model of uneconomic war: in a world increasingly influenced by the "economic interdependence of civilized nations", conflicts that strengthened the political supremacy had become futile and anachronistic. For these reasons, states were not to fall into the "great illusion" of the traditional policy of imperialism, nationalism and colonialism. However, Russell no longer justified his "utilitarian pacifism" through the uneconomic nature of the war, like during the Great War; he now considered the futility of war as a moral issue because it was linked to the survival of humanity – see the August 1954 article "A Study in Futility: H-Bomb Politics". His "juridical pacifism" – to refer to Norberto Bobbio's theory – can be traced back to his idea of the "world government": since the main cause of the wars afflicting mankind was represented by the existence of absolute sovereign states, it would be possible to overcome international anarchy through the establishment of a world authority; this aim had become a need rather than an ideal due to the danger posed by the H-bomb. Russell referred primarily to a World Federation composed of "subordinate federations" with the monopoly of nuclear weapons and the power to revise or abrogate treaties, leaving each subordinate federation and national state freedom in everything that did not involve world peace, and with the right to resolve disputes and impose its resolutions – he mainly shared the idea of World

---

84 *The Collected Papers of Bertrand Russell. Man's Peril 1954–55*, vol. 28, p. 347 and pp. 349–350.
85 See Monk, *Bertrand Russell 1921–1970: The Ghost of Madness*, p. 375.

Federation supported by Ely Culbertson. Both communist and anti-communist powers should understand that their aims could not be realized because of mutual destruction; for this reason, Russell emphasized the role of the neutral countries as an appropriate diplomatic solution to overcome mutual suspicion on both sides of the Iron Curtain. In it ensuring a lasting peace, the idea of a world government called to mind Thomas Hobbes's contractualism in the Kantian sense – see *Perpetual Peace*, 1795 – giving it a cosmopolitan value.

The Disarmament Policy and Beyond

The 18 July 1955 Geneva Summit seemed to herald signs of a thaw in the Cold War; it was a meeting of the Big Four, whose main purpose was to bring together world leaders to begin discussions on peace and global security. US President Dwight David Eisenhower, UK Prime Minister Anthony Eden, Soviet Premier Nikolai Alexandrovich Bulganin, and French Prime Minister Edgar Faure were accompanied by their Foreign Ministers John Foster Dulles, Harold Macmillan, Vyacheslav Molotov and Antoine Pinay. In the two years following the signing of the Russell-Einstein Manifesto and the Geneva Conference, Russell's political energy was expended in planning an international scientific congress on the real risks of a nuclear war. His effort involved primarily two fellow signatories of the Manifesto, Polish physicist Joseph Rotblat and British physicist Cecil Frank Powell, and Australian physicist Eric Burhop. On 10 September, Russell wrote to Rotblat that "further steps" should be "taken by scientists", while his "further work" should be restricted to "the political field"[86]. On 12 November, Russell made Burhop aware of the need to invite "a Russian, a Chinese and an Indian"[87] because no scientists from these countries had signed the Russell-Einstein Manifesto. Burhop replied that Soviet Academy of Sciences President Alexander Nikolaevich Sesmeyanov, with three other academicians, would "probably accept an invitation to join the Initiating Committee"[88].

---

86 Letter from Bertrand Russell to Jospeh Rotblat, 10 September 1955, in BRA, Class no. 750, Box no. 11.14, Document no. 2, McMaster University Library, Hamilton.
87 Letter from Bertrand Russell to Eric Burhop, 12 November 1955, in BRA, Class no. 750, Box no. 11.14, Document no. 6, McMaster University Library, Hamilton.
88 Letter from Eric Burhop to Bertrand Russell, 23 November 1955, in BRA, Class no. 600, Box no. 1.36, McMaster University Library, Hamilton.

The "oscillatory antagonism"[89] characterizing superpower relations in the mid-1950s persuaded Russell to support the strengthening of the United Nations. In his 1 January 1956 article published in the Japanese newspaper *Sangyo Keizai Shimbun*, he wrote that the "reformed United Nations" should abolish "the veto" and appoint "a small commission" made up of representatives of the "two sides" and of the "disinterested nations" so that its decisions would be "impartial"[90]. Banning or destroying H-bombs through an international agreement was not enough, for no practicable method of inspection could ensure that bombs were not being manufactured secretly, and even if the bans were observed in peacetime, no power would consider them binding in wartime: if the ban on H-bombs was "inadequate", their reduction was no more than a "temporary palliative"[91]. On 9 May 1956, *The Current Digest of the Soviet Press* published an article by Russell alongside its reply from the Soviet physicist Dmitri Vladimirovich Skobeltzyn. On this occasion, Russell argued that neither side dared "embark upon global war" because they possessed means of "annihilating each other", and it was this "uneasy balance" that was preventing the employment of nuclear weapons. An agreement between the two superpowers to prohibit the use of H-bombs or prescribe their destruction, "if unaccompanied by a general détente, did not seem to me desirable"[92]; in fact, "very elaborate inspections" would be necessary. Secondly, if war could not cause a "total catastrophe", it would become "more likely". Thirdly, each side could feel "released from previous agreements" and manufacture "as many H-bombs as possible"[93]. Skobeltzyn criticized Russell's "paradoxical thesis" that "an agreement to ban [nuclear] weapons" would make their use "more probable"[94]. In a September 1956 article published in the *Moscow New Times*, Russell asserted that "mutual suspicions" between the two superpowers had prevented a nuclear-weapons agreement that could "serve any useful purpose". Moreover, he advocated an "international tribunal" composed of Eastern and Western representatives in equal numbers and representatives of "uncommitted nations" to guarantee an international "balance", whose authority could solve international disputes and ensure a "world peace"[95].

---

89 See F. Halliday, *The Making of the Second Cold War*, London, Verso, 1983, p. 3.
90 See B. Russell, "Nuclear Weapons and World Peace", in *Sangyo Keizai Shimbun*, 1 January 1956.
91 Ibid.
92 See B. Russell, "A Dispute in *Pravda* on Disarmament", in *The Current Digest of the Soviet Press*, 9 May 1956, vol. 8, no. 13, pp. 8–10.
93 Ibid.
94 See D.V. Skobeltzyn, "Problem of Disarmament Must Be Solved", in *Current Digest of the Soviet Press*, 9 May 1956, vol. 8, no. 13, pp. 9–10 (for the quotation, see p. 9).
95 See B. Russell, "Nuclear Weapons Must Be Not Used", in *New Times*, September 1956, vol. 14, no. 39, pp. 8–9.

The Soviet physicist Pyotr Kapitza, who had just been rehabilitated by the Soviet Union, published a "reasoned comment" on this article in the same issue of the newspaper. He did not share Russell's reservations about banning the H-bomb, affirming instead that measures to prohibit its manufacture and use should be "welcomed and wholeheartedly supported"[96].

Meanwhile, Russell had retired to North Wales[97]. The Suez Crisis and the Hungarian Revolution further convinced him of the urgent need for more effective mechanisms of international governance while causing the postponement of the scientists' meeting for which he had been working for more than a year. Nasser's announcement of the nationalization of the Suez Canal on 26 July 1956 was regarded by Eden's government as a direct challenge to British political and economic interests in the region to be forcibly revoked. Russell denounced Franco-British politics but also criticised Nasser's rejection of an international users' consortium to operate the canal: the Middle East was "entirely justified in resisting imperialism", but no country could inflict "wanton damage" upon the world in "the supposed pursuit of purely national interests"[98]. Most of the Labour parliamentary opposition hesitated to rule out the use of force. In the Commons debate on Suez, which began on 2 August, Hugh Gaitskell echoed Eden's comparison of Nasser with the fascist dictators of the 1930s: if in the past he "ha[d] not hesitated to express [his] disagreement with the Government", at that moment it was possible to justify "in no way Colonel Nasser's action in seizing the Canal"[99]. Russell's public reaction to the Suez Crisis appeared on 11 August 1956 in *The Manchester Guardian*. He drew attention to a small group of left-wing Labour MPs' call for a peaceful solution to the conflict and, with implicit reference to the institutional weakness of the United Nations Security Council, he stated that a "constructive internationalism" demanded the creation of "an authority" capable of taking "enforceable decisions by a majority" when "unanimity [was] unattainable"[100]. In the

---

96 See P. Kapitza, "The Paramount Task", in *New Times*, September 1956, vol. 14, no. 39, pp. 10–11 (for the quotation, see p. 11).
97 As he aged, Russell became increasingly reluctant to travel – except between London and Plas Penrhyn. From 1956, his house in North Wales became Russell's principal residence with his wife Edith.
98 See B. Russell, "Every Nation Is a Bully at Heart", in *Maclean's Magazine*, 2 March 1957, vol. 70, no. 5, pp. 2, 48.
99 See H. Gaitskell, *Suez Canal*, Parliamentary Debates (Commons), 2 August 1956, vol. 557, cols. 1609–1617 (for the quotation, see col. 1609).
100 See B. Russell, Letter to the Editor, in *The Manchester Guardian*, 11 August 1956, p. 4; this document is also in BRA, 9 August 1956, Class no. 220, Box no. 3.58, Document no. 022082, McMaster University Library, Hamilton.

article "Every Nation Is a Bully at Heart" published in *Maclean's Magazine* on 2 March 1957, we find Russell's thoughts on nationalism and imperialism regarding the Suez Crisis. This event had led to a conflict between "the passions of British imperialists and Egyptian nationalists" in an "acute form". The Middle East was "entirely justified" in "resisting Western or Communist imperialism", but no country could inflict "wanton damage" upon the world in the pursuit of "purely national interests". Therefore, it was necessary to "dissociate internationalism from imperialism": Egypt should have "ownership" of the Canal, but an "International Authority" should take care of its management[101]. Russell did not fail to make his voice heard on the occasion of the Hungarian Revolution. Some three weeks after the Red Army had entered Budapest on 4 November 1956, he warned that the political repression in Hungary proved to the West the limits of de-Stalinization and showed Russian communism as "a brutal, ruthless, hypocritical, and treacherous, conquering imperialism". He showed his solidarity with Hungarian intellectuals, protesting against the communist authorities' ongoing persecution: "The forcible subjection of Hungary" had instilled in the majority of British intellectuals "feelings of very deep horror and revulsion"[102]. It was a "disaster to mankind" that, while the Soviet Government was displaying its "ruthless imperialism", Britain and France had chosen to embark on an "illegal war of aggression" against Egypt; humanity could be saved from this disaster only by "substituting law for force in international affairs"[103].

Due to the arms race, the two superpowers were progressing towards a state of "mutual atomic plenty"[104]. In this "present critical condition", Russell stated, scientists had an "exceptional duty", namely, to ensure that statesmen and peoples were informed about the "universal destruction" of a nuclear war[105]. In these years, the leading organization of politically active scientists in the United States was the Federation of American Scientists (FAS), for which the *Bulletin of the Atomic Scientists* served as an official mouthpiece; its British equivalent was the Atomic Scientists' Association (ASA). Mounting concern followed the accumulation of

---

101 Id., "Every Nation Is a Bully at Heart", in *Maclean's Magazine*, 2 March 1957, vol. 70, no. 5, pp. 2, 48.
102 Letter from Bertrand Russell to Central Office of Information, 29 November 1956, in BRA, Class no. 410, Box no. 1.21, McMaster University Library, Hamilton.
103 Ibid.
104 See A. Wenger, *Living with Peril: Eisenhower, Kennedy and Nuclear Weapons*, Lanham, Rowan & Littlefield, 1997, p. 102.
105 See B. Russell, "Science and Human Life" (1955), in A.G. Bone (ed.), *The Collected Papers of Bertrand Russell. Détente or Destruction, 1955–57*, vol. 29, London-New York, Routledge, 2005, pp. 10–18 (for the quotations, see p. 15).

scientific data after the US hydrogen-bomb test at Bikini Atoll in March 1954; by 1956 the Indian, Japanese and Indonesian Parliaments passed resolutions urging the suspension of all tests[106]. Britain's first series of hydrogen-bomb tests was announced on 7 June 1956; Prime Minister Eden reassured the Commons: "All safety precautions will be taken in the light of our knowledge and of experience gained from the tests of other countries"[107]. In the following year, the new Prime Minister Harold Macmillan instructed the Minister of Defence, Duncan Sandys, to conduct a thorough review of Britain's armed forces; in the March 1957 White Paper, Sandys attached great weight to Britain's "independence" as a nuclear power. The British hydrogen-bomb tests were carried out on 15 and 31 May, and on 19 June 1957 at the uninhabited Malden Island in the central Pacific – Operation Grapple was the culmination of a military strategy widely supported by the UK Parliament that had begun in June 1954 with Churchill's decision to develop the hydrogen bomb. The protests against the planned series of hydrogen-bomb tests in the central Pacific coincided with the growth of the National Council for the Abolition of Nuclear Weapons Tests (NCANWT). Three days before the first Grapple test, the NCANWT led a public demonstration through central London and a rally in Trafalgar Square; the development of a British hydrogen bomb raised the spectre of an uncontrolled proliferation of nuclear weapons. In his 21 March 1957 letter to the editor of *The Manchester Guardian*, Russell declared his willingness to join in the protests against the British Government's decision to carry out a nuclear test at Christmas Island, since the hazards were "unknown" and the arguments in favour appeared to be only those of a "rather foolish national vanity". In contrast, Richard Rapier Stokes, a Labour backbencher who had been Minister of Works, replied that it was necessary to show UK war potential "without hesitation", should Russia contemplate "to engulf Europe without fighting on the mainland"[108].

The risk of proliferation of nuclear weapons deriving from UK possession of the H-bomb, together with the Suez Crisis and the Hungarian Revolution, revealed the United Nations' institutional weakness. A United Nation reform, conceived as a necessary step for the establishment of a world government, was

---

106 In 1957, the United States conducted 32 nuclear tests compared to the 18 carried out in the previous year; in the same period, the number of Soviet tests increased from 9 to 15.

107 See A. Eden, *Thermo-Nuclear Weapons (Tests)*, Parliamentary Debates (Commons), 7 June 1956, vol. 553, cols. 1283–1286 (for the quotation, see col. 1283).

108 See B. Russell, "Letter to the Editor ("Britain's Bomb")", in *The Manchester Guardian*, 21 March 1957, p. 6; this document is also in BRA, 19 March 1957, Class no. 750, Box no. 11.14, Document no. 1, McMaster University Library, Hamilton. See R.R. Stokes, "Britain's Bomb", Letter to *The Manchester Guardian*, 27 March 1957, p. 6.

once again advocated by Russell in June 1957, when the Hugo Grotius Foundation chose him as the recipient of its award dedicated to the ideals of international law and human rights. On that occasion, he stated that the "first step" was to increase "the authority" of the United Nations, more precisely of its Assembly as opposed to the Security Council, which could not become the "germ of a world government" due to its power of veto. He asserted that "unrestricted nationalism" was "incompatible" with world peace; "the rights of nations" must not be regarded as "absolute", since the result would be "international anarchy"; however, the pursuit of "national interests" could coexist under a "world government", as the pursuit of "sectional interests" in a "democracy", within "the limits of law"[109].

Russell's planning of an international scientific congress culminated in the first "Pugwash Conference on Science and World Affairs" on 7–10 July 1957, when 22 scientists[110] were invited to the summer retreat of Canadian-born American industrialist and financier Cyrus Stephen Eaton in Pugwash, Nova Scotia. Russell was asked to record a formal statement because he did not intend to travel to Canada on health grounds. He underlined the relevance of this conference, as "leading scientists coming from many countries" were "seriously consider[ing] the dangers of an atomic war"; since the participants represented "only themselves", they could put forward "their point of view with frankness", creating the conditions to overcome "the present futile competition" from which "nothing but catastrophe [could] result"[111]. The participants met in three committees: the first analysed the radiation hazards and the catastrophic effects, both somatic and genetic, deriving from a nuclear war; the second called for the suspension of nuclear weapon tests; the third highlighted the moral responsibilities of Western and Eastern scientists. The editor of the *Bulletin of the Atomic Scientists* Eugene Rabinowitch drafted an 11-point working paper as a basis for discussion of "beliefs shared by scientists of all countries", which would allow them "to work for radical change in the convictions

---

109 This paper was published with the title "The Next Steps in International Relations", in Bone (ed.), *The Collected Papers of Bertrand Russell. Détente or Destruction, 1955–57*, vol. 29, pp. 319–322.
110 There were seven Americans: jurist David Farquhar Cavers, chemist Paul Mead Doty, geneticist Hermann Joseph Muller, biophysicist Eugene Rabinowitch, physicists Walter Selove, Leó Szilárd, and Victor Weisskopf; three Soviets: biophysicist Alexander Kuzin, physicist Dmitri Vladimirovich Skobeltzyn, and chemist Alexander Vasilievich Topchiev; three Japanese: physicists Iwao Ogawa, Shinichiro Tomonaga, and Hideki Yukawa; two British: physicists Cecil Frank Powell and Joseph Rotblat; two Canadians: psychiatrist George Brock Chisholm and physicist John Stuart Foster. The other participants were Chinese physicist Peiyuan Zhou, Polish physicist Marian Danysz, French biologist Antoine Lacassagne, Australian physicist Mark Oliphant, and Austrian physicist Hans Thirring.
111 See B. Russell, "Message to First Pugwash Conference", in *The New York Times*, 10 July 1967, p. 6.

of their peoples and the policies of their governments"[112]. The Soviet Academy of Sciences emphasized the importance of Pugwash to "the fight of world public opinion against atomic dangers"[113]. The Pugwash delegates elected a Continuing Committee to organize further conferences in the following years; this included Skobeltzyn, Rabinowitch and two of the original organizers, Rotblat and Powell. Russell was elected chairman of the committee and subsequently president of the Pugwash Movement, even if he remained an inspirational figurehead rather than an active participant. As the Pugwash movement became "part of the respectable progress of the scientific relations with international affairs", he stated, his interests turned to "new plans" aimed at persuading peoples and governments to "banish war"[114].

In the new political climate inaugurated by the first Pugwash Conference, in November 1957 Russell wrote an open letter to US President Dwight D. Eisenhower and to the Secretary of the Communist Party of the Soviet Union Nikita S. Khrushchev, which was published in the *New Statesman*. Believing that they had a joint interest to overcome "the pall of fear" that was dimming "the hopes of mankind", he called for a meeting of the two leaders to favour "a frank discussion of the conditions of coexistence" and limit "future occasions of strife"[115]. Khrushchev shared Russell's arguments: the danger of an atomic war could be removed "finally and completely" only when the manufacture and use of nuclear weapons were to be "completely prohibited"[116]. Replying on Eisenhower's behalf, US Secretary of State John Foster Dulles underlined the violent aspects of communism – for instance, its commitment to class warfare and revolution – in contrast to "the creed of the United States", which was based "on moral law"; it was necessary to abandon "at least that part of the Soviet Communist creed" to achieve a "peaceful result"[117]. In his 5 April 1958 letter, Russell described Khrushchev and Dulles as "rival fanatics", each "blinded to obvious facts by mental blinkers";

---

112   See E. Rabinowitch, "Pugwash – History and Outlook", in *Bulletin of the Atomic Scientist*, September 1957, vol. 13, no. 7, pp. 243–248 (for the quotation, see p. 247).
113   See "Resolution of the Presidium of the Academy of Sciences of the USSR", in *Bulletin of the Atomic Scientist*, November 1957, vol. 13, no. 9, p. 316.
114   See Russell, *The Autobiography of Bertrand Russell 1944–1967*, vol. III, pp. 86–87.
115   Id., "Open Letter to Eisenhower and Khrushchev", in *New Statesman*, 23 November 1957, vol. 54, p. 638.
116   See N.S. Khrushchev, "Nikita Khrushchev replies to Bertrand Russell", in *New Statesman*, 21 December 1957, vol. 54, pp. 845–846.
117   See J.F. Dulles, "Mr Dulles replies to Russell and Khrushchev", in *New Statesman*, 8 February 1958, vol. 55, pp. 158–159.

however, he was most impressed by the Soviet leader's letter: "Khrushchev [came] nearer than Mr. Dulles to advocating the sort of policy which [was] called for"[118].

No less relevant was Russell's commitment as the president of the Campaign for Nuclear Disarmament (CND)[119], with public talks and journalistic articles. CND had welcomed several affiliates of the World Peace Council; after the crisis of world communism triggered by Khrushchev's revelations about Stalin to the 20th Party Congress in February 1956, the World Peace Council had undermined its own position by refusing to condemn the Soviet action in Hungary, becoming "a marginal force" among pacifist organizations, as US historian Lawrence S. Wittner wrote[120]. Russell advocated a balance between accommodation and exclusion of pro-Soviet elements within the broader peace movement. In this regard, Ronald William Clark pointed out: "It was a tricky operation which only the aristocratic [...] Russell had the background and resolution to carry out with some chance of success"[121]. As Russell wrote in his *Autobiography*, CND sought to influence primarily Labour Party politics as most of its upholders came from its ranks, even though "the matter [...] transcend[ed] Party politics and even national boundaries"[122]. Due to the British possession of the H-bomb, he no longer assessed the nuclear peril exclusively in terms of the two superpowers. He began to espouse a unilateralist policy for Britain, and in his article published in *The Times* on 18 March 1958, he argued that "British renunciation" of the bomb would allow the United States and the Soviet Union to prevent the uncontrolled spread of nuclear weapons[123]. Consistently with this political vision, on 29 March 1958 he

---

118 See B. Russell, "Bertrand Russell replies", in *New Statesman*, 5 April 1958, vol. 55, pp. 426–427.
119 The Campaign for Nuclear Disarmament (CND) was an organization established in November 1957 to advocate UK unilateral nuclear disarmament; its committee included Canon John Collins as chairman, Bertrand Russell as president, and Peggy Duff as organising secretary. Between 1958 and 1965, the CND organized the Aldermaston Marches, which were held over the Easter weekend from the Atomic Weapons Establishment near Aldermaston to Trafalgar Square. See F. Parkin, *Middle Class Radicalism: The Social Bases of the British Campaign for Nuclear Disarmament*, Manchester, Manchester University Press, 1968; R. Taylor, C. Pritchard, *The Protest Makers: The British Nuclear Disarmament of 1958–1965, Twenty Years On*, Oxford, Pergamon Press, 1980; J. Minnion, P. Bolsover (eds.), *The CND Story*, London, Allison & Busby, 1983; P. Byrne, *The Campaign for Nuclear Disarmament*, London-New York-Sidney, Croom Helm, 1988; J. Mattausch, *A Commitment to Campaign: A Sociological Study of CND*, Manchester, Manchester University Press, 1989; K. Hudson, *CND. Now More Than Ever: The Story of a Peace Movement*, London, Vision Paperbacks, 2005.
120 See Wittner, *The Struggle against the Bomb. Resisting the Bomb*, p. 95.
121 See Clark, *Life of Bertrand Russell*, pp. 545–546.
122 See Russell, *The Autobiography of Bertrand Russell 1944–1967*, vol. III, p. 102.
123 Id., "Nuclear Dilemma", in *The Times*, 18 March 1958, p. 11.

wrote to Frédéric Joliot-Curie that, in the long run, "the only solution" that would make "the world safe" was the establishment of "a World Government with a monopoly of the major weapons of war"[124]. On 11 February 1959, Russell promoted a debate on Britain's nuclear deterrence in the House of Lords together with Lord Simon, but their motion for unilateralism gained little support[125].

Some of the main ideas that can be referred to Russell's pacifism of the second half of the 1950s can be found in his book *Common Sense and Nuclear Warfare* (1959); the perspective it offered was "resolutely global" because it concerned the "choices" of "mankind as a whole", as Ray Monk emblematically wrote[126]. Russell analysed the problem of an "agreed disarmament", declaring his support for the ban of the H-bombs and the immediate cessation of nuclear tests, but warned that multilateral disarmament could be "a palliative rather than a solution" as new decision-making mechanisms had not been introduced worldwide. However, there were at least three reasons for desiring a reduction of armaments: firstly, negotiations between East and West would bear "fruit" in measures that "all sane men must welcome"; secondly, there would be a reduction of the risk of an "unintended war" deriving, for example, from a "mechanical defect" in the radars or a "sudden nervous breakdown" of some important officer as a result of the stress caused by appalling responsibility; thirdly, there were economic reasons, for so long as the arms race remained "a matter of life and death" to both superpowers, military expenditures would increase, reducing both sides to a "subsistence level"[127]. Russell once again supported the idea of a world federation, even though he highlighted a preliminary "difficulty" of any federal organization; since some member states could be "more powerful" or "more populous" than others, they could refuse to have "equal weight". In this regard, the framers of the US Constitution had adopted a "compromise solution", he argued: in the Senate, all states had been equally represented, but in the House of Representatives their weight had been proportional to their population. In contrast, inside the UN General Assembly all states counted "equally", while the five member states of the Security Council had a "veto power". A "World-wide Federation" – a sort of reconstituted UNO – could be divided into "subordinate Federations" framed in accordance with two principles: they were to be "approximately equal in population" and with "internal interests outweighing those concerning its external relations". Due to the veto power of its Security Council, the

---

124 Letter from Bertrand Russell to Frédéric Joliot-Curie, 29 March 1958, in BRA, Class no. 750, Box no. 11.15, Document no. 9, McMaster University Library, Hamilton.
125 "Nuclear Disarmament", Parliamentary Debates (Lords), 11 February 1959, vol. 214 (for the speeches of Lord Simon and Russell, see cols. 71–78 and cols. 97–102).
126 See Monk, *Bertrand Russell 1921–1970: The Ghost of Madness*, p. 389.
127 See Russell, *Common Sense and Nuclear Warfare*, pp. 46–48.

United Nations lacked an "essential characteristic of any Government". Indeed, an "International Authority" could not be penalized by the unanimity vote because otherwise it would be "unable to settle any dispute"; a "well-defined Constitution" should decide the federal powers involving the "prevention of war", without interference with "religion or economic structure". The International Authority should be free to create the "armed forces" and "impose taxation", with a "legal right" to "limit the armed forces of national States"[128]. He added that its "ultimate aim" was to preserve the world from the disasters of nuclear war, although it could be hampered by "disruptive forces": the opposition between capitalism and communism was "the most notable obstacle to world unity", as well as nationalism, which now appeared to be an "intrinsic part of human nature"[129].

In the second half of the 1950s, Russell supported a "positive pacifism" – the term used by Johan Galtung and David Boersma – that involved the construction and consolidation of harmonious relations between states to prevent war instead of mere absence of violence ("negative pacifism"). Furthermore, he supported "instrumental pacifism" and "juridical pacifism", with reference to Norberto Bobbio's concepts: the former aimed at drastically limiting the instruments of war – in this regard, he supported this kind of pacifism through a disarmament policy, like during the Great War, rather than through a support for neutralism, like in the 1930s; the latter aimed at establishing a world government capable of resolving conflicts between sovereign countries[130]. The disarmament policy seemed to Russell theoretically useful to reduce the risks of a nuclear war, but at the same time, he considered it realistically difficult to implement. It was not enough to reach an international agreement to ban or destroy H-bombs without first reducing the mutual suspicion between the two superpowers; any strategic disarmament could prove to be no more than a temporary solution. Therefore, he believed that British renunciation of the H-bomb, through a UK unilateralist policy, would make it easier for the two superpowers to prevent the risk of proliferation of nuclear weapons. On these premises, Russell's support for juridical pacifism was equally passionate: he reproposed the idea of a world government in the form of a world federation to overcome the absolute sovereignty of nation-states, the main cause of the international anarchy, and secure a lasting peace; the Suez Crisis and the Hungarian Revolution further convinced him of this need. He hoped for an institutional reform of the United Nations, for the Security Council could not become a world government *in nuce* due to the veto power of its member states. In this way,

---

128 Ibid., pp. 66–69.
129 Ibid., pp. 71, 77–79.
130 On the concepts of Galtung, Boersma and Bobbio, see the first paragraph of chapter one.

he implicitly espoused the theory of *The Federalist* (1788) developed by Alexander Hamilton, James Madison and John Jay, who had made a clear distinction between interstate collaborations and forms of true unification, emphasizing the superiority of the federal model over the confederal one. Russell's federalism was influenced by the cosmopolitan vision of Immanuel Kant; however, Kant's analysis was purely structural and his federalism an abstract model, whereas Russell's reflections constituted not just an idea of reason but a distinct political proposal. Russell's proposal could also be traced back to the Federal Union, although he did not join it, more precisely to that part of the British movement that had advocated a world government; indeed, the guiding idea of the Federal Union was that the absolute sovereignty of nation-states had to be replaced by a federal government to guarantee a durable peace.

From the Committee of 100 to the International War Crimes Tribunal

In the early 1960s, Russell pointed out that he did not consider himself an absolute pacifist: "I have never been opposed to all war", so much so that he thought that "the Second World War was justified, but the First was not". In this way, he did not accept "complete pacifism as a creed" because "each war must be judged on its merits"[131], but in the current situation, it was not possible to support any war because of the modern weapons of mass extermination[132]. In his July 1960 article "The Case for Neutralism" published in *The New York Times*, Russell urged Great Britain to withdraw from NATO, thereby moving from unilateralism to neutralism: "Both as a patriot and as a friend of humanity", he hoped for the United Kingdom to be "officially neutral" between the United States and the Soviet Union. From the patriotic point of view, "no sensible man" wished to see his country "obliterated". With reference to humanity, anything tending to mitigate the hostility between

---

131 Letter from Bertrand Russell to Michael A. Freeman, 30 April 1960, in BRA, Class no. 750, Box no. 11.16, Document no. 00000011, McMaster University Library, Hamilton.

132 In a letter dated November 1962, Russell stressed once again that he was not an absolute pacifist. He wrote: "I abhor violence", but "my attitude to it [was] not based on dogma"; indeed, there were "occasions when the use of force m[ight] be necessary", as, for example, a "world government" would require "some kind of world force in order to give its authority any meaning". Letter from Bertrand Russell to Kim Johnson, 26 November 1962, in BRA, Class no. 720, Box no. 6.10, McMaster University Library, Hamilton.

Russia and America "turn[ed] men aside from collective suicide"[133]. Russell also developed a new strategy within the CND; some of its activists, including he himself, had supported the Direct Action Committee against Nuclear War, the pacifist organisation set up in 1957 with the aim of preventing the risk of nuclear war through nonviolent action. On 21 July Ralph Schoenman[134], a member of the CND dissatisfied by its methods, wrote to Russell proposing a campaign of mass civil disobedience inspired by a committee composed of prominent people prepared to break the law and go to prison to avoid the annihilation of the human race[135]. Russell saw in Schoenman's proposal a method of propaganda more effective than the legitimate protests of CND; on 16 August he replied that civil disobedience would not appear to ordinary people so "subversive or anarchical" as to "cause serious inconvenience to average unpolitical people"[136]. In his *Autobiography*, Russell affirmed that if "only constitutional methods" were used, it would be very difficult "to allow the public opinion to know the pacifist cause"[137]. He had already highlighted the risks and the potential benefits of civil disobedience in *Which Way to Peace?* (1936): "I know well that this is a dangerous doctrine" that could lead to "anarchy", but "all great advances ha[d] involved illegality", as in the case of "the early Christians, Galileo and the French revolutionaries", who had "broke[n] the law"[138].

On 11 September 1960, Russell announced that The Committee of 100 for Civil Disobedience against Nuclear Warfare was being formed; CND chairman Canon John Collins distanced himself from this initiative because he believed that the campaign against nuclear war was to be based on "legal and democratic methods"[139]. The practice of civil disobedience could not find fertile ground within the Labour Party, which, in its conference held in Scarborough on 3–7 October 1960, approved the policy of unilateral nuclear disarmament supported especially by the trade union leader Frank Cousins. On 21 October, the Committee of 100

---

133 See B. Russell, "The Case for Neutralism", in *The New York Times*, 24 July 1960, sec. 6, pp. 10, 35–36.
134 Schoenman studied philosophy at Princeton and enrolled as a postgraduate student at the London School of Economics; his tutor was Ralph Miliband, one of the founding members of the British New Left movement, whose fundamental aim was to establish a genuinely Socialist Labour Party independent from the Communist Party.
135 Ralph Schoenman to Bertrand Russell, 21 July 1960, in BRA, Class no. 710, Box no. 5.43, Document no. 055602, McMaster University Library, Hamilton.
136 Bertrand Russell to Ralph Schoenman, 16 August 1960, in BRA, Class no. 710, Box no. 5.44, Document no. 055665, McMaster University Library, Hamilton.
137 See Russell, *The Autobiography of Bertrand Russell 1944–1967*, vol. III, p. 139.
138 Id., *Which Way to Peace?*, p. 207.
139 See C. Driver, *The Disarmers: A Study in Protest*, London, Hodder and Stoughton, 1964, p. 113.

was launched at a meeting in London; Russell, who had resigned from the CND, was elected president and Michael Randle secretary. Its members included film director Lindsay Anderson; playwrights Robert Bolt, Arnold Wesker and John Osborne; poet and art historian Herbert Edward Read; sculptor Reg Butler; writer Doris Lessing; poet John Berger; novelist John Braine; painter Augustus John. The general aims of the new movement can be found in the pamphlet *Act or Perish: A Call to Non-violent Action* drawn up by Russell and Michael Scott: "Our immediate purpose" was to persuade Britain "to abandon reliance upon the illusory protection of nuclear weapons" and become aware of "the immense possibilities of nature" thanks to "the purposes and arts of peace"[140].

Russell further explored the concept of civil disobedience as a nonviolent method of struggle that characterized the Committee of 100 in a 17 February 1961 article published in *New Statesman*. On the one hand, he highlighted a "[civil] disobedience to a law" that commanded "an action" considered by some people "profoundly [...] wicked" – the most relevant example was conscientious objection. On the other hand, there was another kind of civil disobedience that was now "necessary", namely a "means of propaganda" the employment of which would involve "a change in the law or in public policy"[141]. In the first case, civil disobedience was considered as a matter of principle, whereas in the second, an issue of tactics and strategy; Russell was more in favour of the second meaning, for he conceived civil disobedience as an aid to the pacifist cause. Conversely, Schoenman conceived the practice of civil disobedience as an issue of principle; in fact, in *Peace News* he affirmed that the purpose of illegal protests against nuclear weapons was to reaffirm "the right of individuals to resist the technological society that alienated them"[142]. On the same wavelength, Randle asserted that "unilateral nuclear disarmament" implied "a profound political and social upheaval" that, however, could not be achieved "within the framework of existing parties" but through "mass civil disobedience"[143]. The committee's first demonstration was a four-hour sit-down outside the Air Ministry, planned for 18 February 1961, the day on which the US Proteus, a submarine tender, arrived in Holy Loch, Scotland. At the First Annual Conference of the Midlands Region Youth Campaign for Nuclear Disarmament held in Birmingham on 5 April 1961, Russell justified civil disobedience in this way: "Kennedy and Macmillan and others both in the East

---

140 See B. Russell, M. Scott, "Act or Perish: A Call to Non-Violent Action", in Russell, *The Autobiography of Bertrand Russell 1944–1967*, vol. III, pp. 137–139.
141 Id., "Civil Disobedience", in *New Statesman*, 17 February 1961, vol. 61, pp. 245–246.
142 See R. Schoenman, "Civil Disobedience to Halt Polaris", in *Peace News*, 17 February 1961.
143 See M. Randle, "Is It Revolution We're After?", in *Peace News*, 10 March 1961.

and in the West" could be deemed "much more wicked than Hitler" because they were pursuing policies that "[would] probably lead to killing not only all the Jews but all the rest of us too"; therefore, it was not possible "to obey a government which [was] organising the massacre of the whole of mankind"[144]. On Hiroshima Day, held in London on 6 August 1961, 37 members of the Committee, including Russell, Schoenman, Randle and Scott, were charged under the Justices of the Peace Act of 1361; Russell was sentenced to two months in prison – the sentence was reduced to seven days due to his health conditions. Two months later, the Labour Party conference held at Blackpool on 2–6 October 1961 reversed its decision to support UK unilateralism; the new Labour Party strategy, advocated by Hugh Gaitskell, undermined CND members' faith in constitutional methods, while the Committee of 100 became a mass movement perceived as a threat by the Conservative Government led by Harold Macmillan. In short, if Russell had distanced himself from absolute pacifism, it was not so regarding nonviolent civil disobedience. As he pointed out in a letter dated 28 October 1961 sent to the India High Commission for the celebration of Gandhi's Anniversary, since "the other methods" had already made "people aware of the disaster that threaten[ed] them, methods of non-violent civil disobedience ha[d] seemed to me necessary in order to accomplish our aims quickly enough to be of any use"; for this reason, "I very greatly hope that our employment of such methods m[ight] be as successful as was Gandhi's"[145].

In his opening address at the 22nd Congress of the Communist Party on 17 October 1961, Khrushchev announced the upcoming test of a 50-megaton bomb; Russell sent a letter of protest signed by himself and Scott to the Soviet Embassy in London[146]. He had a keen layman's understanding of the physics of nuclear weapons; his essay *Has Man a Future?* (1961) contained "perhaps the clearest couple of propaganda on the nature of nuclear fusion and on the difference between atomic and hydrogen bombs that anyone ever wrote", as Alan Ryan noted[147]. On 30 October, the Tsar Bomb, a 56-megaton hydrogen bomb – over 3,000 times more powerful than the Hiroshima bomb – was tested at the Novaya Zemlya

---

144 See Russell, "Civil Disobedience", in Id., *The Autobiography of Bertrand Russell 1944–1967*, vol. III, pp. 139–145 (for the quotation, see p. 144).
145 Letter from Bertrand Russell to A.M. Keswani (India High Commission), 28 October 1961, in BRA, Class no. 640, Box no. 1.51, McMaster University Library, Hamilton.
146 See B. Russell, M. Scott, *Statement on Soviet Bomb*, 22 October 1961, in BRA, Class no. 640, Box no. 1.55, McMaster University Library, Hamilton.
147 See Ryan, *Bertrand Russell: A Political Life*, p. 177.

archipelago[148]. Some delegates of the Committee of 100 attended the "World Congress for General Disarmament and Peace" in Moscow on 9–14 July 1962, and in a pamphlet headed *Against All Bombs*, they denounced the Soviet regime. In it, we read that for both the East and the West, the H-bomb had served to defend the interests of "privileged minorities" at the expense of the working class. Appealing to common class interests, it concluded: "Together we must act – or we shall perish together. Workers of the world, unite!"[149]. Underestimating the role of Russell's personal charisma, the members of the London committee conceived themselves as a popular movement of anarchist rebellion. Based on this misconception, the committee planned a massive sit-down at the Air Ministry in central London on 9 September 1962, causing a "growing dissipation of the Committee's policies"[150]. In January 1963, Russell resigned as president of the Committee of 100.

Meanwhile, Russell announced his support for the 1958 Cuban Revolution. In February 1962, he wrote an article for the Havana newspaper *Revolución* in which he argued that "the Cuban revolution deserve[d] hope and encouragement, not blind hostility" because Cuba was "a sovereign and independent nation" with the "inalienable right to solve her own problems"[151]. Kennedy made no secret of his desire to see the overthrow of the Castro regime and of his willingness to support its exiles, such as those involved in the Bay of Pigs affair. In summer 1962, the Cubans signalled their alarm to the Soviet Union and the United Nations; the Soviet Union, at Castro's request, provided its armed support. On 22 October, Kennedy announced the naval blockade of the island while calling on Khrushchev to remove the missiles; the latter replied that the Soviet Union would instruct its vessels bound for Cuba not to obey the orders of US naval forces and, in case of interference, to take "all actions that [were] necessary"[152]. Russell recalled those dramatic days when the world was on the brink of nuclear war: "I decided that I must telegraph Kennedy and Khrushchev beseeching them to let the human

---

148 The Tsar Bomb was the culmination of a series of high-yield thermonuclear tests designed by the Soviet Union and the United States – the most powerful US nuclear test had been "Castle Bravo", a 15-megaton bomb detonated on 1 March 1954 at the Bikini Atoll. On 5 August 1963, the Treaty Banning Nuclear Weapon Tests in the Atmosphere, Outer Space and Under Water was signed in Moscow by the Soviet Union, the United States and Great Britain.
149 See Committee of 100, *Against All Bombs*, 7 July 1962, in BRA, Class no. 630, Box no. 1.46, McMaster University Library, Hamilton.
150 See Russell, *The Autobiography of Bertrand Russell 1944–1967*, vol. III, p. 125.
151 Id., "Atacar a Cuba Llevaria a una Guerra Nuclear", in *Revolución*, 15 February 1962, pp. 1, 6; the English translation ("Attacking Cuba Will Lead to a Nuclear War") was published in Feinberg, Kasrils, *Bertrand Russell's America: His Transatlantic Travels and Writings*, vol. 2, pp. 146–147.
152 See R.F. Kennedy, *Thirteen Days: A Memoir of the Cuban Missile Crisis*, New York, W.W. Norton, 1969, p. 58.

race continue to exist"[153]. On 23 October he cabled Kennedy: "Your action [was] desperate" as well as a "threat to human survival" and invited him to "end this madness"[154]. Russell's telegram to Khrushchev had a more conciliatory tone: "I appeal to you not to be provoked by the unjustifiable action of the United States in Cuba. [...]. Precipitous action could mean annihilation for mankind"[155]. On 24 October, Khrushchev delivered a public statement in the form of a reply to Russell's telegram, in which he wrote that "the question of war and peace" was "so vital" as to "consider a top-level meeting in order to discuss all the problems which have arisen, to [...] remove the danger of unleashing a thermonuclear war"[156]. Russell cabled Khrushchev, praising him for his "caution" and suggesting, as a possible compromise, the simultaneous renunciation of Cuban and Turkish military bases by the Soviet Union and the United States[157]. In contrast, Russell received a dismissive reply from Kennedy, who argued that Russell had made "no mention" of the installation of Soviet missiles in Cuba: "Your attention might well be directed to the burglars rather than to those who caught the burglars"[158]. On 27 October, Russell replied that he would appeal to Castro "to accept UN inspection in exchange for your solemn pledge that Cuba will not be invaded"[159]; on the same day, he asked the Cuban leader to agree on UN protection: "I ask humbly to accept unwarranted American demands [...]. They would remove the pretext of invasion"[160].

On 28 October, the US Government was surprised when the Soviet Union declared that it would remove its bases from Cuba in exchange for US removal of the missiles in Turkey and their nonaggression pledge on the island[161]. This was the "compromise" suggested by Russell two days earlier; he probably offered Khrushchev a fundamental way out of the crisis by acting as an intermediary.

153 See B. Russell, *Unarmed Victory*, London, Allen & Unwin, 1963, p. 8.
154 From Bertrand Russell to John Fitzgerald Kennedy (telegram), 23 October 1962, in BRA, Class no. 650, Box no. 1.57, McMaster University Library, Hamilton.
155 From Bertrand Russell to Nikita Khrushchev (telegram), 23 October 1962, in BRA, Class no. 650, Box no. 1.57, McMaster University Library, Hamilton.
156 Letter from Nikita Khrushchev to Bertrand Russell, 24 October 1962, in BRA, Class no. 650, Box no. 1.60, McMaster University Library, Hamilton.
157 From Bertrand Russell to Nikita Khrushchev (telegram), 26 October 1962, in BRA, Class no. 650, Box no. 1.60, McMaster University Library, Hamilton.
158 From John Fitzgerald Kennedy to Bertrand Russell (telegram), 27 October 1962, in BRA, Class no. 650, Box no. 1.57, McMaster University Library, Hamilton.
159 From Bertrand Russell to John Fitzgerald Kennedy (telegram), 27 October 1962, in BRA, Class no. 650, Box no. 1.57, McMaster University Library, Hamilton.
160 From Bertrand Russell to Fidel Castro (telegram), 27 October 1962, in BRA, Class no. 650, Box no. 1.57, McMaster University Library, Hamilton.
161 See Kennedy, *Thirteen Days: A Memoirs of the Cuban Missile Crisis*, p. 94.

In this regard, UN Secretary-General U Thant affirmed: "Khrushchev's positive reply [...] was due to Earl Russell's repeated pleadings to him"[162]. In more recent times, Barry Feinberg and Ronald Kasrils, two members of the African National Congress, pointed out that "Russell's unique status" enabled him to play "an important role in the crisis"; his voice had been heard due to "his tireless efforts ever since 1945 to arouse humanity to the dangers of nuclear warfare"[163]. In contrast, Ronald William Clark argued that there was "no evidence to suggest that Russell's intervention affected the course of events"[164]. In any case, the Cuban Missile Crisis marked a turning point in Russell's political outlook; he distanced himself from neutralism, sympathizing with revolutionary movements in their struggles against "US imperialism" – a locution widely used in *Unarmed Victory*. Russell also appeared as an arbitrator during the October–November 1962 Sino-Indian war caused by a disputed Himalayan border; on 8 November 1962, he wrote to Prime Ministers Jawaharlal Nehru and Chou En-lai, urging them "to accept cease-fire"[165] to avoid the risk of a global war. Celebrating China's withdrawal from the disputed territory at the end of November 1962 as a unilateral gesture for peace, Russell also criticised India for its bellicose nationalism: it "ha[d] ceased, though not in form, to be neutral as between East and West, and ha[d], thereby, increased the chance of world war"[166].

In early 1963, a series of reports from Vietnam demonstrated the scale of US military involvement and the nature of the Ngo Dinh Diem regime. On 22 March, Russell sent a letter to *The Washington Post* in which he argued that the US Government was conducting "a war of annihilation" in Vietnam, whose "sole purpose" was to retain "a brutal and feudal regime in the South"[167]. *The Washington Post* declined to publish the letter, unlike the journal of the British-Vietnam Committee *Vietnam Bulletin* and the North Vietnamese magazine *Cun Quoc Weekly*. Even before the Cuban Crisis, he had advocated the creation of an organization capable of attracting financial support from all parts of the world to undertake "the co-ordination of efforts on behalf of peace internationally" through journals, newspapers, and films in order to raise public awareness, as he wrote to Albert

---

162 See U Thant, *View from the U.N.: The Memoirs of U Thant*, Garden City-N.Y., Doubleday, 1978, pp. 171–172.
163 See Feinberg, Kasrils, *Bertrand Russell's America: 1945–1970*, vol. 2, p. 158.
164 See Clark, *Bertrand Russell and His World*, p. 110.
165 From Bertrand Russell to Jawaharlal Nehru and Chou En-lai (telegrams), 8 November 1962, in BRA, Class no. 650, Box no. 1.57, McMaster University Library, Hamilton.
166 See Russell, *Unarmed Victory*, p. 105.
167 Bertrand Russell to the editor of *The Washington Post*, 23 March 1963, in BRA, Class no. 383, Box no. 10.14, Document no. 175424, McMaster University Library, Hamilton.

Schweitzer on 11 October 1962[168]. In September 1963, the Bertrand Russell Peace Foundation was established in London, with Ken Coates as its director and Ralph Schoenman as its general secretary; *The Spokesman* became its journal. In light of the Cuban Crisis, the Sino-Indian conflict, the Arab-Israeli dispute, and the problem of Berlin as a symbol of the world division in two blocs, the foundation appeared as an international voice supporting nuclear disarmament. Russell wrote that the foundation had the task of teaching "the conception of Man as one family [...] both to individuals and Governments" so that "mankind [might] prosper as never before", and to be "representative of all the interests concerned in the prevention of war"[169]. Educational work should also be carried out by intellectuals as moral consciences for mankind and potential builders of peace among states. In his 1964 article "The Duty of a Philosopher in This Age", Russell implicitly supported the practice of civil disobedience: the main "duty" of a philosopher was "to persuade other people to agree with him" on the real risks of a nuclear war, "joining him in whatever protest show[ed] the most chance of success". With reference to scientific and juridical pacifism, he added that "the chief conflict [was] between Communists and their opponents", but man was "a quarrelsome animal"; therefore, if the present source of conflict were resolved, he might find some other "equally futile basis for war" – "wickedness [was] not a geographical phenomenon". The only "long-term cure" for this situation was "the creation of a World Government" that would be able to "substitute law" instead of "lawless force" in deciding disputes between nations; in this scenario, the philosopher should favour "a mood of mutual tolerance" among men by "painting a glorious and a peaceful world"[170].

The Vietnam War determined Russell's break with the Labour Party because he also regarded the Labour Government led by Harold Wilson as subservient to the United States; in his 1 November 1965 letter to Lord Shepherd, then Chief Whip of the House of Lords, he announced: "I have decided to resign from the Labour Party on the ground that I cannot support its agreement with American policy in Vietnam"[171]. It was the issue of US foreign policy that animated the

---

168 From Bertrand Russell to Albert Schweitzer, 11 October 1962, in BRA, Document no. 20, McMaster University Library, Hamilton.
169 See B. Russell, "The Cold War and the Bertrand Russell Peace Foundation", in *Russell: The Journal of Bertrand Russell Studies*, 1995, vol. 15, no. 1, pp. 7–20 (for the quotations, see pp. 12–13).
170 See B. Russell, "The Duty of a Philosopher in This Age" (1964), in E. Freeman (ed.), *The Abdication of Philosophy: Philosophy and the Public Good. Essays in Honor of Paul Arthur Schilpp*, La Salle, Open Court, 1976, pp. 15–22.
171 Letter from Bertrand Russell to Lord Shepherd and the Labour Party, 1 November 1965, in BRA, Class no. 750, Box no. 11.17, Document no. 2, McMaster University Library, Hamilton.

"Tricontinental Conference" held in Havana on 3–16 January 1966[172], at which Ernesto Guevara asserted that there was no alternative but to battle against US imperialism; the "dispossessed masses" of the Third World must prepare themselves for "a long, cruel war". If one wanted to "look into a bright future", he added, "two, three or many Vietnams" should "flourish throughout the world"[173]. Russell sent a message marked by revolutionary rhetoric, although over time he had opposed Marxism and campaigned for peace. He wrote that Cuba had demonstrated its "utter determination" against "brutal foreign domination and rapacious economic exploitation" and concluded that Fidel Castro and Ernesto Guevara were men "whose example will be followed by struggling people everywhere"[174]. Both Russell and Schoenman admitted that some of the writings published in this period under Russell's signature were written mainly by Schoenman, who stated that their revolutionary appeals were motivated by a desire to combat the "spread of the power of American imperialism"[175]. In April 1966, Russell argued that due to "the overwhelming exploitive power exercised by American capitalism", men had "the responsibility to support the oppressed"[176]. In turn, Schoenman pointed out that Russell had "many aristocratic attributes which infused his entire sensibility", and therefore "he did not believe in the creative energy [...] in the great masses"; only "great evils" such as a nuclear war or the genocide against the Vietnamese moved him to support "the moral imperative of action against barbarity"[177].

At a press conference held in London on 16 November 1966, Russell announced the establishment of an independent tribunal, also known as the Russell-Sartre Tribunal or the International War Crimes Tribunal, which aimed to avoid

---

172 The Tricontinental Conference aimed to gather delegates from all the revolutionary guerrilla movements throughout Latin America, Asia and Africa in order to promote solidarity between them and the Cuban Government; it was attended by some 500 delegates from 82 countries. See A.G. Mahler, *From the Tricontinental to the Globe South: Race, Radicalism, and Transnational*, Durham-London, Duke University Press, 2018.

173 See E. Che Guevara, *Vinceremos! The Speeches and Writings of Che Guevera*, edited by John Gerassi, New York, Macmillan, 1968, p. 581.

174 "Bertrand Russell's message to the First Tri-Continental Conference of the Revolutionary Peoples of the World", 10 January 1966, in BRA, Class no. 320, Box no. 9.43, Document no. 177586, McMaster University Library, Hamilton.

175 See R. Schoenman, "Bertrand Russell and the Peace Movement", in G. Nakhnikian (ed.), *Bertrand Russell's Philosophy*, London, Duckworth, 1974, pp. 227–252 (for the quotation, see p. 250).

176 From Bertrand Russell to V.V. Ramana Murthi, 21 April 1966, in BRA, Class no. 410, Box no. 10.38, Document no. 144071, McMaster University Library, Hamilton.

177 See Schoenman, "Bertrand Russell and the Peace Movement", in Nakhnikian (ed.), *Bertrand Russell's Philosophy*, pp. 227–252 (for the quotations, see p. 233).

committing "the crime of silence" over Vietnam[178]. It was composed of prestigious intellectuals from 18 countries[179] and was to investigate and assess US military intervention in Vietnam. The Bertrand Russell Peace Foundation was transformed into a limited company that lent the tribunal the necessary funds; before the tribunal began to work, its members moved its executive base to Paris. Russell described its main characteristics in his September 1966 article "My Conscience of Mankind" published in *Vietnam Solidarity Bulletin*: "our situation" was "analogous to the circumstances which [had] made necessary the Nuremberg trials" after the Third Reich atrocities. The tribunal, which was not "the spokesman of any government", would be "an international commission of enquiry" that the "witnesses [...] under accusation [were] free to attend, not compelled", which ruled out "adversary procedure"; its members were "experts in international law", particularly with knowledge of "war crimes". Russell concluded: "People of all the countries: help the War Crimes Tribunal to make it [...] the conscience of Mankind"[180]. In May 1967, he told the Cuban press that "the historical perspective of our Tribunal" was to provide "a voice for the conscience of humanity" capable of judging "the continuous crimes and aggression of counter-revolutionary power"[181]. In order to lend support to the National Liberation Front (NLF), the Bertrand Russell Peace Foundation set up the Vietnam Solidarity Campaign led by Tariq Ali.

The tribunal was held in two sessions, the first in Stockholm on 2–10 May 1967 and the second in Roskilde, Denmark, on 20 November – 1 December; North Vietnamese witnesses testified to US brutality, while some US soldiers confessed to having committed war crimes. On 1 December 1967, the tribunal announced that the United States was found guilty; in his final address to the Stockholm

---

178 The main members were Bertrand Russell (Tribunal Honorary President), Ralph Schoenman (Secretary-General), French philosopher Jean-Paul Sartre (Tribunal Executive President), and Yugoslav human-rights activist Vladimir Dedijer (Tribunal chairman and President of Sessions).

179 The other members were the following: German jurist Wolfgang Abendroth, Pakistani writer Tariq Ali, Member of Turkish Parliament Mehmet Ali Aybar, British philosopher Alfred Jules Ayer, African-American novelist James Baldwin, Italian Parliament Member Lelio Basso, French philosopher Simone de Beauvoir, former Mexican President Lázaro Cárdenas, American pacifist David Dellinger, UNESCO ambassador Miguel Ángel Estrella, Israeli politician Haika Grossman, Cuban revolutionary Melba Hernandez, Swedish novelist Sara Lidman, Japanese lawyer Kinju Morikawa, US writer Carl Preston Oglesby, and Japanese physicist Shoichi Sakata.

180 See B. Russell, "The Conscience of Mankind", in *Vietnam Solidarity Bulletin*, September 1966, vol. 1, no. 5, pp. 1, 6 (for the quotations, see p. 1).

181 See B. Russell, "Message to Cuba, Answer to Marta Rojas", May 1967, in BRA, Class no. 320, Box no. 9.43, Document no. 177621, McMaster University Library, Hamilton.

session, Russell stated: "The International War Crimes Tribunal must do for the peoples of Vietnam, Asia, Africa and Latin America what no tribunal did while Nazi crimes were committed and plotted"[182]. In this regard, the international-law expert Richard Anderson Falk wrote that "an unofficial and symbolic application" of the Nuremberg principles characterized "the proceedings of the Bertrand Russell War Crimes Tribunal held in 1966–1967" in the two Scandinavian countries[183]. Russell made his voice heard following the escalation of the Arab-Israeli conflict; after the Six-Day War, he condemned the Israeli air raids on Egypt and harshly criticized the treatment of Palestine refugees. In his February 1970 message to the "International Conference of Parliamentarians in Cairo" – his last political statement – he argued that Israel's aggression must be condemned not only because "no State ha[d] the right to annex foreign territory", but also because "every expansion [was] also an experiment to discover how much more aggression the world [would] tolerate". Even if the Soviet Union was equipping the Arab armies, it was not possible "to sympathise with Israel because of the suffering of the Jews in Europe at the hands of the Nazis"; indeed, "invok[ing] the horrors of the past to justify those of the present [was] gross hypocrisy"[184].

In summary, in the last ten years of his life, Russell's pacifism took on further nuances. Due to his early-1960s commitment in the Committee of 100, he supported "instrumental pacifism" and "non-political pacifism": Norberto Bobbio used the former concept as a way of replacing violent means with nonviolent ones; in contrast, according to Mulford Quickert Sibley, the latter meant that political institutions were unable to avoid war, and therefore the peace movements should be engaged at the forefront. These two principles can be traced back to the strategy and action that Russell adopted within the Committee of 100: an "instrumental pacifism" can be identified in his support for civil disobedience, rather than in his struggle for disarmament policy or neutralism in previous decades, since this practice appeared more effective than parliamentary debate and constitutional methods – means traditionally adopted by political institutions – to oppose the danger of nuclear warfare; more precisely, he conceived civil disobedience as an issue of tactics and strategy more than as a matter of principle. If we consider the Cuban Missile Crisis, Russell supported a "realistic pacifism". As already observed

182   Id., "Towards a New Morality", in *London Bulletin of the Bertrand Russell Peace Foundation*, 1 August 1967, p. 2.
183   See R.A. Falk, "A Nuremberg Perspective on the Trial of Karl Armstrong", in Id., *A Global Approach to National Policy*, Cambridge, Harvard University Press, 1975, pp. 133–145 (for the quotation, see p. 133).
184   See B. Russell, "Message from Bertrand Russell to the International Conference of Parliamentarians in Cairo", February 1970, in *Spokesman*, April 1970, no. 2, p. 5.

at the beginning of this book, this concept was coined by the peace activist David Cortright to claim the essential and vital need to avoid war in the nuclear age; Russell's staunch commitment and fundamental role as an intermediary between the two superpowers during the Cuban Crisis was proof of that. If we refer to the International War Crimes Tribunal, he supported a pacifism that was ethical enough to take on the features of a secular religion; it showed an affinity with the integral and absolute pacifism advocated a few decades earlier by Lev Tolstoy and Romain Rolland. Therefore, we are conceptually far from the utilitarian pacifism that Russell espoused in the early 1950s; in fact, this tribunal was a kind of sounding board for the conscience of humanity, which did not judge whether war was useful or futile while considering it immoral.

A Pragmatic and Active Pacifism in Various Shades

Chronologically, Russell's pacifism ideally corresponded to five periods of his life: the first coincided with the Great War and the Russian Revolution; the second with the 1920s and 1930s, and the crisis of the League of Nations; the third with the initial British appeasement towards Nazi Germany and the Second World War; the fourth with the decade between the Baruch Plan and the drafting of the Russell-Einstein Manifesto; and the fifth with the Hungarian Revolution and the Suez Crisis, the Cuban Missile Crisis, the Committee of 100, and the International War Crimes Tribunal. Throughout these phases, he advocated five main forms of pacifism, each of which intersected with some of those periods.

Firstly, Russell espoused an "absolute pacifism" (see Michael Allen Fox) that expressed an uncompromising condemnation of war; it developed throughout those periods, except for the third. His pacifist commitment began with the outbreak of the First World War, when he condemned the secret plots of British diplomacy headed by Foreign Secretary Edward Grey, which led Great Britain into war. Russell believed that the Asquith Government's authoritarian measures, notably the Defence of the Realm Act approved on 8 August 1914, could inflict a mortal blow to the Victorian values of tolerance and internationalism while ending an era of progressive evolution of democratic institutions and personal liberties. It was only in his January 1915 article "The Ethics of War" that he did not advocate his idealistic "absolute pacifism", by justifying wars of colonization, of principle and of self-defence – against an inferior civilization – but not of prestige. With the affirmation of the Third Reich and other totalitarian regimes, Russell advocated a "relative pacifism" or "semi-pacifism" (see Wilhelm Emil Mühlmann) for a few years, showing political realism; only a militarily united Europe could convince the

Nazi regime that its rearmament programme was doomed to failure. In his 1944 article "The Future of Pacifism", he highlighted the distinction between "absolute pacifism" and "relative pacifism": the former was the doctrine that considered war as always unjustifiable, which had been theorized by Tolstoy, Gandhi and the Quakers; the latter was the theory that very few wars were worth fighting since the evils were almost always greater than they seemed to be. At the same time, he pointed out the difference between "individual pacifism" and "political pacifism": the former meant that one would never fight a war, regardless of the decisions of one's own country's government; the latter meant that one's concern would be keeping one's own government out of war. On these premises, Russell developed the concept of "relative political pacifism", his main pacifist idea during the Second World War. The escalation of the Cold War caused growing mutual suspicion between the two superpowers; Russell feared that the Soviet Union would have an atomic bomb in the years immediately following, and therefore its power was to be quickly contained. In his *Autobiography*, he admitted that, during the period of the Baruch Plan in 1946, he had hypothesized a "conditional preventive war", believing that the Soviets would accept the internationalization proposal regarding atomic energy. When in August 1949 the Soviet Union detonated its first atomic bomb, ending US nuclear monopoly, an alleged preventive war was no longer conceivable because mankind had to face the risk of annihilation. So, in the early 1950s he embraced once again an "absolute pacifism", which can be ascribed more precisely to a "realistic pacifism" (see David Cortright) to claim the imperative need to avoid war in the nuclear age. The discovery of the hydrogen bomb, tested almost simultaneously for the first time by the United States and the Soviet Union between 1952 and 1953, instilled even more fears in the international community. It is in this new scenario that the July 1955 Russell-Einstein Manifesto can be placed. Signed by 11 prestigious intellectuals, it aimed to raise public awareness of the perils posed by the new weapon of mass destruction and to discuss a resolution, not as members of this or that nation, continent or creed, but as human beings. Although the first "Pugwash Conference on Science and World Affairs" in 1957 had inaugurated a new political climate, the danger of nuclear warfare reached its peak in the wake of the Cuban Missile Crisis, which was resolved on 28 October 1962 when the Soviet Union declared that it would remove its bases from Cuba in exchange for US removal of the missiles in Turkey and their nonaggression pledge on the island. This was the compromise suggested by Russell to Khrushchev and Kennedy, through which he offered a fundamental way out of the crisis as he acted as an intermediary. The Cuban Missile Crisis marked a turning point in Russell's political outlook; he distanced himself from neutralism, sympathizing with revolutionary movements in their struggles against US imperialism. The foreign policy of the United States determined the establishment of the International War Crimes Tribunal, or Russell-Sartre Tribunal, in 1966 to investigate and assess US military intervention in Vietnam. On that occasion, he argued that it was a situation analogous to the circumstances that had made the Nuremberg trials necessary after Third Reich atrocities.

Secondly, Russell advocated a "scientific pacifism" (Norberto Bobbio) whereby the real reasons for war were to be found in the primitive impulses of human nature; he embraced this kind of pacifism especially in the first period and occasionally in the second and fourth. In two 1915 writings, "Triebe und Triebschicksale" (*Instincts and Their Vicissitudes*) and "Zeitgemäßes über Krieg und Tod" (*Thoughts for the Times on War and Death*), Sigmund Freud identified aggression as an inherent impulse of man. It was only in the essay "Jenseits des Lustprinzips" (*Beyond the Pleasure Principle*, 1920) that he showed this new orientation: human nature could be conceived through the antagonistic action of two opposing instincts, namely Eros and death. Russell supported Freud's theses; indeed, already in *Principles of Social Reconstructions* (1916) he had underlined the distinction between "creative" and "possessive" impulses, together with the conviction that "liberation of creativeness" should be the principle of reform both in politics and in economics. In *Political Ideas* (1917), he analysed the psychological causes of war, noting two different types of impulses: the "possessive" ones, which satisfied the acquisition of private goods not always available because they were limited, and the "creative" or "constructive" ones, which helped in acquiring knowledge and therefore could always be satisfied. Institutions rested upon "property and power"; political institutions should increase "the opportunities for the creative impulses" by shaping education to reduce "the outlets for the possessive instincts". On the same wavelength, in *Why Men Fight* (1917) he asserted that "impulses", which were at the basis of our life much more than "desires", could be divided into those that could be attributed to "life" and "death": the former favoured art and science, the latter were embodied in war. In "Is Nationalism Moribund?" (1917), he explored the darker side of human nature, once again addressing the issue of human impulses, particularly with reference to the destructive ones. He argued that the British, the French and the Germans had considered themselves as the "champions" of, respectively, parliamentary institutions, the intellectual enlightenment brought about by the 1789 Revolution, and *Kultur* as a synonym for knowledge. However, the belief that the nation was a sort of a "special guardian of some important idea" was nothing more than an idea fostered by "pride and self-interest"; he believed that under "the illusory beliefs of nationalism" there was "a substructure of the herd instinct" that was part of the fundamental structure of human nature. Russell's criticism of Bolshevism can be ascribed in part to "scientific pacifism". Although in 1918 he considered the Russian Revolution as a great opportunity because Europe was on the verge of realizing the brotherhood of men (see *Roads to Freedom: Socialism, Anarchism, and Syndicalism*), he quickly developed a deep criticism of Bolshevism due to its maximalist vision. So much so that in 1920 he regarded it more as a kind of religion than a political movement, for the people who had accepted it had become "impervious to scientific evidence", committing an "intellectual suicide" (see *The Practice and Theory of Bolshevism*). Despite his growing condemnation of Soviet communism, Russell believed that the Great War had signalled the end of traditional European liberalism and made clear the need to replace capitalism – the idea that it was associated with peace had been overcome by the war – with international socialism. Thus, he abandoned his inherited liberalism to move to the Labour Party. Russell once again embraced a "scientific pacifism" in the 1927 article "The Danger of Creed Wars". In it, he affirmed that the ideological dispute between the United States and the Soviet Union, namely between capitalism and communism, was excessively based on economic reflections to the detriment of biological ones. He argued that the strife between these two economic systems could cease only if public opinion acknowledged that both were inadequate "to recognise biological needs". A few decades later, when he received the Nobel Prize in December 1950, Russell argued that a peaceful society could be promoted through "harmless outlets for the impulses". Two closely related passions such as "fear and hate" were conditioning human behaviour and were all the more dangerous when considering the possession of nuclear weapons by the United States and the Soviet Union. The world was obsessed with the conflict between communist and capitalist ideologies, but it was only an apparent cause of the tension between the United States and the Soviet Union; indeed, war was more intrinsic to human nature than a historical social construct.

Thirdly, Russell supported an "instrumental pacifism" that can be traced back to the first, second and fifth periods; this kind of pacifism was aimed at limiting the means of war such as the struggle against compulsory military service and the disarmament policy. With the outbreak of the First World War, Russell became involved in campaigning against conscription; he joined the British pacifist movement No-Conscription Fellowship, and the British authorities regarded him as a political agitator. In 1916, he criticized the Military Service Act approved by the second Asquith Government, which introduced conscription for all single men between 18 and 41 years of age who were liable to be called up for service in the army unless they were married or widowed with children; in the same year, he defined compulsory military service as "perhaps the extreme example of the power of State" (see *Principles of Social Reconstructions*). In the second half of the 1920s, the struggle for disarmament and against compulsory military service became a growing leitmotif in Russell's life. Indeed, in 1926 he signed the Manifesto against Conscription and the Military System, in which we read that in "the name of humanity", all people were encouraged to emancipate themselves from the military system and apply "methods of non-violent resistance on the lines of Mahatma Gandhi and Martin Luther King". In October 1930, Russell signed the Manifesto against Conscription and the Military Training of Youth supported by the Joint Peace Council, a coalition of international peace organizations that included the Quakers, the War Resisters' International and the Women's International League for Peace and Freedom. In the 1930s, his "instrumental pacifism" was identified primarily with support for neutralism more than with the disarmament policy and renunciation of compulsory military service. In *Which Way to Peace?* (1936), he hoped for UK neutrality in conjunction with unilateral measures of disarmament, for he regarded disarmament as a corollary of neutrality; in February 1937, he made neutralism the theme of his maiden speech in the House of Lords. He also criticized the principle of "collective security", which meant that if any country belonging to the League of Nations was involved in war, all the others were also; in this way, however, collective security could no longer be considered as a method for preserving peace but a means of making any conflict the premise of a full-scale war. In the early 1960s, Russell developed a new strategy within the Campaign for Nuclear Disarmament, supporting a campaign of mass civil disobedience inspired by the Committee of 100. He conceived the practice of civil disobedience as a means of protest and propaganda that was more effective than the constitutional methods of CND because it would allow public opinion to really understand the pacifist cause, even if he considered civil disobedience as an issue of tactics and strategy more than a matter of principle. In his 1964 article "The Duty of a Philosopher in This Age", Russell supported the practice of civil disobedience; he pointed out that the main duty of philosophers was to persuade public opinion of the real risks of a nuclear war, asking people to join him "in whatever protest" with the best chance of success. Thus, Russell's "instrumental pacifism" can now be identified with his support for civil disobedience – instead of his struggle for disarmament policy or neutralism as in previous decades – because he deemed this practice more effective than parliamentary debate traditionally adopted by political institutions to fight the danger of nuclear warfare.

Fourthly, Russell embraced a "utilitarian pacifism" that sporadically emerged in the first, second and fourth periods. In this regard, Norman Angell was a relevant point of reference for him. Before the Great War, Angell had proposed the model of uneconomic war: in a world increasingly influenced by the "economic interdependence of civilized nations", wars of conquest between industrial countries had become futile; they were not justifiable because of their destructiveness, which almost always outweighed any potential benefits regardless of whether they were moral or immoral. In other words, Angell feared the risks of a conflict, even more likely if states fell into the "great illusion" of the traditional policy of imperialism, nationalism and colonialism. In 1918, Russell supported the thesis that war was uneconomical because "the destructiveness of war" increased while "its profits" diminished (see *Roads to Freedom: Socialism, Anarchism, and Syndicalism*); therefore, during the Great War Russell's utilitarian pacifism was justified from an economic point of view. Moreover, this vision was rooted in English liberal thought, which, based on a utilitarian logic, reached the optimistic conclusion that trade would make wars costly and futile. Russell implicitly also shared Richard Cobden's conviction that peace and British interests were most effectively protected through the international diffusion of free trade. In his June 1922 article "The Prevention of War", however, Russell argued that Angell's thought was based on a limited view because it did not give due consideration to the effects of human impulses. Embracing a scientific pacifism, he stated that "greed" as a motive for war could be eliminated by "the arguments which Norman Angell ha[d] made familiar", but instincts such as "hatred and envy" required to be treated by using "different methods". In the early 1950s, Russell underlined the concept of the "futility" of war (see "A Study in Futility: H-Bomb Politics" and "What Neutrals Can Do to Save the World", 1954), which could no longer be considered as the continuation of politics by other means – as he argued by quoting the famous dictum of Carl von Clausewitz – because the destructiveness of the H-bomb would cause the annihilation of humanity. In this way, Russell reproposed the idea of the uselessness of war, but now he conceived "utilitarian pacifism" as a moral issue, unlike in the years of the Great War, because it was linked to the survival of humanity while appearing as a sort of "realistic pacifism" (see Cortright) through which to claim the essential and vital need to avoid war in the nuclear age.

Finally, Russell advocated a "juridical pacifism" (see Bobbio), one of the most relevant lines of his political thought characterizing all five periods; this concept can also be ascribed to "positive pacifism" (see Johan Galtung, David Boersma) because it involved the construction and consolidation of harmonious relations among states to prevent war. In the August 1915 article "War and Non-Resistance", Russell advocated the establishment of a "central government of the world" capable of securing "obedience by force", for the great majority of men would recognize that it was better than international anarchy. In May 1916, he supported *in nuce* the idea of a "world federation": the presence of many sovereign states, each with its own army, would make war inevitable (see "War as an Institution"). In the following year, he highlighted the need for an "international government" to overcome the anarchy between states endowed with "legislative" and "judicial" functions and one "only army and navy" (see *Political Ideals*). On several occasions, Russell made his voice heard on the League of Nations. At first, he considered it as a potential keeper of peace capable of imposing the resolution of international disputes, but from the early 1920s he predicted its institutional weakness because it represented a sort of alliance between states that was unable to guarantee a lasting peace; only through renunciation of the absolute sovereignty of the European countries would it be possible to overcome international anarchy and avoid new wars. In 1923, he wrote that the League of Nations would reproduce in its debates only a "diplomatic tug of war between the nations" (see *The Prospects of Industrial Civilization*). In the 1950s, he similarly criticized the United Nations' institutional weakness; in a more precise and determined way, he supported the idea of world government – "the only long-run alternative to the extinction of the human race" in the face of the danger of a nuclear war – with "coercive powers", unlike the UNO, which was paralyzed by the veto power of its Security Council. In 1955, he reproposed the idea of world government in the form of a World Federation composed of eight "subordinate federations" closely similar to one suggested by Ely Culbertson in his *Summary of the World Federation Plan* (1943): the United States, the USSR and its European satellites, the British Commonwealth, China, Latin America, Latin Europe (France, Italy, Spain, Portugal, and Belgium), the Mohammedan World, and Germany, together with Scandinavia, Austria, Switzerland, and Holland; Africa could not as yet be included due to the presence of the colonial empires of Great Britain, France, Belgium, and Portugal. The World Federation should hold "legal powers" defined by a Federal Constitution, namely the monopoly of nuclear weapons to preserve peace and the possibility to revise or abrogate treaties; it should leave each nation state and subordinate federation "complete freedom in everything not affecting the peace of the world" (see *The Road to Peace*). The risk of the proliferation of nuclear weapons that derived from the United Kingdom's possession of the H-bomb, together with the Suez Crisis and the Hungarian Revolution, led Russell to advocate a juridical pacifism. From this perspective, he conceived the reform of the United Nations as a necessary step for the establishment of a world government by increasing the authority of the UN General Assembly compared to the Security Council, which could not become the "germ of a world government" because of its veto power. In the late 1950s, Russell underlined the preliminary difficulties inherent in establishing a world federation, stating that the framers of the US Constitution had adopted a "compromise solution": in the Senate all states had been equally represented, but in the House of Representatives their weight had been proportional to their population. In contrast, within the UN General Assembly all states counted equally, whereas the Security Council, which had to vote unanimously, lacked an essential characteristic of any international authority, namely the power to settle disputes between states; only a "well-defined Constitution" should decide the federal powers (see *Common Sense and Nuclear Warfare*). In this way, Russell espoused the theory of *The Federalist* (1788) developed by Alexander Hamilton, James Madison and John Jay, who had underlined the superiority of the federal model over the confederal one. As in the case of the crisis of the League of Nations, Russell confirmed the ideas of those who, over the century, had interpreted international relations on the premise that states could be considered as citizens belonging to the same community. Hence the need to transfer the traditional model of natural law from the individual level to the interstate one, as individual countries were still in a sort of belligerent and potentially unsafe state of nature. Thus, he applied Hobbesian contractualism in the Kantian sense; he gave it a cosmopolitan value through the concept of world government with at least the legitimate monopoly of the international force. Russell's idea of a federal world government could be regarded as a model to legalise international relations, an institution whose decisions and rules had to be binding upon the individual member states, unlike the United Nations. He argued that to move from international anarchy to a peaceful and stable political system, it was necessary for the individual nation-states to subscribe to both a *pactum societatis*, which involved a preliminary agreement of nonaggression between them for the resolution of disputes, and a *pactum subjectionis*, which implied the subjection of the individual countries under a common power that would be able to enforce the pact signed and coercively regulate their relationships. However, the UNO – like the League of Nations – had been the result of a *pactum societatis*, not of a *pactum subjectionis*; indeed, through the Security Council, its members states had maintained their sovereignty by not transferring the monopoly of force to a higher authority. In other words, the individual countries had not entrusted "a third" one with the power to coercively regulate their relationships and disputes and, consequently, to ensure peace between them.

During his long and tenacious pacifist battle that lasted over half a century, Russell did not conceive peace as a mere absence of war; from this point of view, he implicitly shared Baruch Spinoza's thought. In his *A Political Treatise* (1677), Spinoza had written: "Peace is not just the absence of war, but a virtue which comes from strength of mind"; through the formula *Pax enim non belli privatio*, he had announced a fundamental paradigm shift of political theory. Through various kinds of pacifism, Russell sought to encapsulate in a pragmatic way the dilemmas and problems that derived from the changed political conditions of his time: the beginning of the Great War, the creation and failure of the League of Nations, the affirmation of totalitarian regimes, the outbreak of the Second World War, the origin of the atomic age and the escalation of the Cold War, the establishment of the UN with its institutional weakness, and the need for a world government in the form of a world federation. His multifaceted and original form of pacifism still retains all its validity and topicality more than 50 years after his death.

Bibliography

Archival Sources

Albert Einstein Archives, Hebrew University of Jerusalem, Jerusalem.
Bertrand Russell Archives, McMaster University Library, Hamilton.
Cabinet Papers, Public Record Office, London.
Catherine Marshall Papers, Cumbria County Record Office, Carlisle.
David Lloyd George Papers, House of Lords Record Office, London.
Lord Lothian Papers, National Records of Scotland, Edinburgh.
Parliamentary Debates (Commons), UK Parliament, London.
Parliamentary Debates (Lords), UK Parliament, London.

Publications on Bertrand Russell

Ahmed M., *Bertrand Russell's Neutral Monism*, New Delhi, Mittal Publications, 1989.
Aiken L.W., *Bertrand Russell's Philosophy of Morals*, New York, Humanities Press, 1963.
Alcaro M., *Bertrand Russell*, San Domenico di Fiesole, Cultura della Pace, 1990.
Alter T., Nagasawa Y. (eds.), *Consciousness in the Physical World: Perspectives on Russellian Monism*, New York, Oxford University Press, 2015.

Anellis I.H., "Bertrand Russell's Theory of Numbers, 1896–1898", in *Epistemologia*, 1987, vol. 10, no. 2, pp. 303–322.

Id., "Russell and Engels: Two Approaches to a Hegelian Philosophy of Mathematics", in *Philosophia Mathematica*, January 1987, vol. 2, no. 2, pp. 151–179.

Arthur R.T.W., "Russell's Conundrum: On the Relation of Leibniz's Monads to the Continuum in An Intimate Relation", in *Boston Studies in the Philosophy of Science*, 1989, vol. 116, pp. 171–201.

Ayer A.J., *Russell and Moore: The Analytical Heritage*, London, Macmillan, 1971.

Id., *Russell*, London, Fontana-Collins, 1972.

Id., "Bertrand Russell as a Philosopher", in *Proceedings of the British Academy*, 1972, vol. 58, pp. 127–151.

Baldwin T., "Russell on Memory", in *Principia: An International Journal of Epistemology*, 2001, vol. 5, no. 1–2, pp. 187–208.

Banks E.C., *The Realistic Empiricism of March, James and Russell: Neutral Monism Reconceived*, London-New York, Cambridge University Press, 1996.

Barnes A.C., *The Case of Bertrand Russell Versus Democracy and Education*, Merion, Barnes, 1944.

Belgion M., *Notre foi contemporaine: Bernard Shaw, André Gide, Sigmund Freud, Bertrand Russell*, translated from the English by L. Delavis, Paris, Gallimard, 1934.

Bell D.R., *Bertrand Russell*, Valley Forge, Judson Press, 1972.

Benmakhlouf A., *Bertrand Russell: l'atomisme logique*, Paris, Puf, 1996.

Blackwell K., *The Spinozistic Ethics of Bertrand Russell*, London, Allen & Unwin, 1985.

Blackwell K., Ruja H., *A Bibliography of Bertrand Russell*, 3 vols., London, Routledge, 1994.

Blackwell K., Spadoni C., *A Detailed Catalogue of the Second Archives of Bertrand Russell*, Bristol, Thoemmes Press, 1992.

Blitz D., "Russell, Einstein and the Philosophy of Non-Absolute-Pacifism", in *Russell: The Journal of Bertrand Russell Studies*, 2000, vol. 20, no. 2, pp. 101–128.

Bonino G., "On Russell's Robust Sense of Reality", in J. Cumpa, G. Jesson, G. Bonino (eds.), *Defending Realism: Ontological and Epistemological Investigations*, Boston-Berlin-Munich, De Gruyter, 2014, pp. 363–378.

Bornet G., *Naive Semantik und Realismus: Eine sprachphilosophische Untersuchung der Frühphilosophie von Bertrand Russell (1903–04)*, Bern-Stuttgart, Haupt, 1991.

Bradford D.E., "Moore, Russell, and the Foundation of Analytic Metaphysics", in *Philosophy Research Archives*, 1981, vol. 7, pp. 553–581.

Bradie M.P., "Russell's Scientific Realism", in *Russell: The Journal of Bertrand Russell Studies*, 1988, vol. 8, no. 1, pp. 195–208.

Brink A., *Bertrand Russell: The Psychobiography of a Moralist*, Atlantic Highlands, Humanities Press International, 1989.

Burke T., "Dewey and Russell on the Possibility of Immediate Knowledge", in *Studies in Philosophy and Education*, 1998, vol. 17, no. 2–3, pp. 149–153.

Byrd M., "Russell, Logicism, and the Choice of Logical Constants", in *Notre Dame Journal of Formal Logic*, 1989, vol. 30, no. 3, pp. 343–361.
Candlish S., *The Russell/Bradley Dispute and Its Significance for Twentieth-Century Philosophy*, New York, Palgrave Macmillan, 2007.
Cappio J., "Russell's Philosophical Development", in *Synthese*, February 1981, vol. 46, no. 2, pp. 185–205.
Carey R., *Russell and Wittgenstein on the Nature of Judgment*, London, Continuum, 2007.
Carey R., Ongley J., *Russell*, London, Bloomsbury, 2013.
Carr B., *Bertrand Russell: An Introduction*, London, Allen & Unwin, 1975.
Chomsky N., *Problems of Knowledge and Freedom: The Russell Lectures*, New York, Vintage Books, 1971.
Id., *Spheres of Influence in the Age of Imperialism: Papers Submitted to the Bertrand Russell Centenary Symposium, Linz, Austria, September 11th to 15th, 1972*, Nottingham, Spokesman, 1972.
Clack R.J., *Bertrand Russell's Philosophy of Language*, The Hague, Nijhoff, 1969.
Clark C.H.D., *Christianity and Bertrand Russell: A Critique of the Essay: "Why I Am Not a Christian"*, London, Lutterworth Press, 1958.
Clark R.W., *The Life of Bertrand Russell*, London, Jonathan Cape-Weidenfeld & Nicolson, 1975.
Id., *Bertrand Russell and His World*, London, Thames & Hudson, 1981.
Coates K. (ed.), *Essays on Socialists Humanism in Honour of the Centenary of Bertrand Russell, 1872–1970*, Nottingham, Spokesman, 1972.
Cocchiarella N., "Whither Russell's Paradox of Predication?", in M.K. Munitz (ed.), *Logic and Ontology*, New York, New York Press, 1973, pp. 133–158.
Id., "Frege, Russell and Logicism: A Logical Reconstruction", in L. Haaparanta, J. Hintikka (eds.), *Frege Synthesized*, Dordrecht, Reidel Publishing Company, 1986, pp. 197–252.
Coniglione F., "Bertrand Russell e la nascita dell'idea di filosofia scientifica", in G. Bentivegna, S. Burgio, G. Magnano San Lio (eds.), *Filosofia, scienza, cultura. Studi in onore di Corrado Dollo*, Soveria Mannelli, Rubbettino, 2002, pp. 181–218.
Corsano A., *Introduzione a Bertrand Russell*, Manduria, Lacaita, 1972.
Cosimo G., *La pedagogia di Bertrand Russell*, Lecce, Milella, 1974.
Costelloe K., "Complexity and Synthesis: A Comparison of the Data and Philosophical Methods of Mr. Russell and M. Bergson", in *Proceedings of the Aristotelian Society*, June 1915, vol. 15, no. 1, pp. 271–303.
Crankshow E., "How Russell Saw Russia", in *The Observer*, 3 April 1949, p. 4.
Crawshay-Williams R., *Russell Remembered*, London-New York, Oxford University Press, 1970.
Croddy S., "Russell on the Meaning of Descriptions", in *Notre Dame Journal of Formal Logic*, 1976, vol. 17, no. 3, pp. 424–428.
Cunningham S., "Herbert Spencer, Bertrand Russell, and the Shape of Early Analytic Philosophy", in *Russell: The Journal of Bertrand Russell Studies*, 1994, vol. 14, no. 1, pp. 7–29.
Dahms H.-J., "Das Verhältnis von Beobachtungs und theoretischer Sprache in der Erkenntnistheorie Bertrand Russell", in *Erkenntnis*, 1982, vol. 17, no. 3, pp. 405–411.

Dau P., "Russell's First Theory of Denoting and Qualification", in *Notre Dame Journal of Formal Logic*, 1986, vol. 27, no. 1, pp. 133–166.

Dejnožka J., *Bertrand Russell on Modality and Logical Relevance*, Aldershot-Brookfield, Ashgate, 1999.

Demopoulos W., Clark P., "The Logicism of Frege, Dedekind, and Russell", in S. Shapiro (ed.), *The Oxford Handbook of Philosophy of Mathematics and Logic*, New York, Oxford University Press, 2005, pp. 129–165.

Demopoulos W., Friedman M., "Bertrand Russell's The Analysis of Matter: Its Historical Context and Contemporary Interest", in *Philosophy of Science*, 1985, vol. 52, no. 4, pp. 621–639.

Demos R., "Mr. Russell and Dogmatism", in *Journal of Philosophy*, October 1945, vol. 42, no. 22, pp. 589–594.

Denton P.H., *The A B C of Armageddon: Bertrand Russell on Science, Religion, and the Next War, 1919–1938*, New York, State University of New York Press, 2001.

Devaux P., *Bertrand Russell ou la paix dans la vérité. Présentation, choix de textes, bio-bibliographique*, Paris, Seghers, 1967.

Dewar L., *Marriage without Morals: A Reply to Mr. Bertrand Russell*, London, Society for Promoting Christian Knowledge, 1931.

Dewey J., Kallen H.M. (eds.), *The Bertrand Russell Case*, New York, Da Capo Press, 1972.

Di Francesco M., *Introduzione a Russell*, Roma-Bari, Laterza, 1990.

Id., "Russell, l'idealismo e l'origine della filosofia analitica", in *Rivista di Storia della Filosofia*, 1992, vol. 47, no. 4, pp. 761–774.

Donati S., *I fondamenti della matematica nel logicismo di Bertrand Russell*, Firenze, Firenze Atheneum, 2003.

Id., *Il logicismo di Bertrand Russell e il suo contesto filosofico*, 2 vols., North Charleston, CreateSpace, 2016.

Dorward A., *Bertrand Russell: A Short Guide to His Philosophy*, London, Longmans-Green & Company, 1951.

Duncan M., "Two Russellian Arguments for Acquaintance", in *Australasian Journal of Philosophy*, 2017, vol. 95, no. 3, pp. 461–474.

Durant W., *Contemporary European Philosophers: Bergson, Croce and Bertrand Russell*, Girard, Haldeman-Julius, 1925.

Eames E.R., *Bertrand Russell's Theory of Knowledge*, London, Allen & Unwin, 1969.

Id., "Russell on 'What There Is'", in *Revue Internationale de Philosophie*, 1972, vol. 26, no. 102, pp. 483–498.

Id., *Bertrand Russell's Dialogue with His Contemporaries*, Carbondale-Edwardsville, Southern Illinois University Press, 1989.

Eames E.R., Dematteis P.B., "Bertrand Russell", in P.B. Dematteis, P.S. Fosl, L.B. McHenry (eds.), *British Philosophers, 1800–2000*, Columbia, Bruccoli Clark Layman, 2002, pp. 262–303.

Eastman M., "Nietzsche, Plato, and Bertrand Russell", in *The Liberator*, 27 September 1920, vol. 3, no. 9, pp. 6–10.

Eisler L. (ed.), *Russell: Pensieri*, Roma, Newton, 1997.

Elkind L.D.C., Landini G. (eds.), *The Philosophy of Logical Atomism. A Centenary Reappraisal*, Basingstoke-New York, Palgrave Macmillan, 2018.

Esteves O., "Bertrand Russell, The Utilitarian Pacifist", in *French Journal of British Studies*, 2015, vol. XX, no. 1, pp. 1–13.

Falk A.E., "The Judger in Russell's Theories of Judgment", in *Russell: The Journal of Bertrand Russell Studies*, 1998, vol. 17, no. 2, pp. 101–122.

Feibleman J.K., "Knowing About Semipalatinsk", in *Dialectica*, December 1955, vol. 9, no. 3–4, pp. 279–286.

Feinberg B. (ed.), *A Detailed Catalogue of the Archives of Bertrand Russell*, London, Continuum, 1967.

Feinberg B., Kasrils R., *Bertrand Russell's America: His Transatlantic Travels and Writings*, 2 vols., London, Allen & Unwin, 1973–1984.

Flathman R.E., "Russell's Empiricism and Its Relation to His and Our Ethics and Politics", in *Philosophy of the Social Sciences*, June 1996, vol. 26, no. 2, pp. 162–180.

Fritz C.A., *Bertrand Russell's Construction of the External World*, London, Routledge, 1952.

Fuhrmann A., "Russell's Way Out of the Paradox of Propositions", in *History and Philosophy of Logic*, 2002, vol. 23, no. 3, pp. 197–213.

Ganapathy T.N., *Bertrand Russell's Philosophy of Sense-Data*, Madras, Vivekananda College, 1984.

Gandon S., "Toward a Topic Logicism? Russell's Theory of Geometry in the Principles of Mathematics", in *Philosophia Mathematica*, February 2009, vol. 17, no. 1, pp. 35–72.

Garciadiego A.R., *Bertrand Russell and the Origins of the Set-theoretic "Paradoxes"*, Basel-Boston-Berlin, Birkhäuser Verlag, 1992.

Giaquinto M., "Russell on Knowledge of Universals by Acquaintance", in *Philosophy*, October 2012, vol. 87, no. 4, pp. 497–508.

Giaretta P., "Analysis and Logical Form in Russell: The 1913 Paradigm", in *Dialectica*, 1997, vol. 51, no. 4, pp. 273–293.

Gödel K., "Russell's Mathematical Logic", in S. Feferman, J. Dawson, S. Kleene (eds.), *Journal of Symbolic Logic*, Evanston, Northwestern University Press, 1944, pp. 119–141.

Goethe N.B., "How Did Bertrand Make Leibniz into a 'Fellow Spirit'?", in P. Phemister, S. Brown (eds.), *Leibniz and the English-Speaking World*, Dordrecht, Springer, 2007, pp. 195–205.

Gotlind E., *Bertrand Russell's Theories of Causation: Inaugural Dissertation*, Uppsala, Almqvist & Wiksells Boktryckeri AB, 1952.

Gottschalk H., *Bertrand Russell: A Life*, translated from the German by Edward Fitzgerald, London, Allen & Unwin, 1967.

Graham P.J., "Russell's Logical Construction of the World", in D. Machuca, B. Reed (eds.), *Skepticism: From Antiquity to the Present*, London, Bloomsbury, 2018, pp. 454–466.

Grant G., "Pursuit of An Illusion: A Commentary on Bertrand Russell", in *Collected Works of George Grant*, edited by Arthur Davis and Henry Roper, 4 vols., Toronto, University of Toronto Press, 2002, vol. II, pp. 34–48.

Grattan-Guinness I., *Dear Russell, Dear Jourdain: A Commentary on Russell's Logic, Based on His Correspondence with Philip Jourdain*, New York, Columbia University Press, 1977.

Id., "Georg Cantor's on Bertrand Russell", in *History and Philosophy of Logic*, 1980, vol. 1, no. 1–2, pp. 61–93.

Id., "Bertrand Russell's Logical Manuscripts: An Apprehensive Brief", in *History and Philosophy of Logic*, 1985, vol. 6, no. 1, pp. 53–74.

Grayling A.C., *Russell*, Oxford, Oxford University Press, 1996.

Green J.L., "Dewey, Russell, and the Integration of 'the Social'", in *Educational Theory*, October 1979, vol. 29, no. 4, pp. 285–296.

Green K., *Bertrand Russell, Language and Linguistic Theory*, London-New York, Continuum, 2007.

Greenspan L., *The Incompatible Prophecies: An Essay on Science and Liberty in the Political Writings of Bertrand Russell*, Oakville, Mosaic Press, 1978.

Id., "Bertrand Russell and the End of Nationalism", in *Philosophy of the Social Sciences*, September 1996, vol. 26, no. 3, pp. 348–368.

Grelling K., "Realism and Logic: An Investigation of Russell's Metaphysics", in *The Monist*, October 1929, vol. 39, no. 4, pp. 501–520.

Griffin N., "Russell's Later Political Thought", in *Russell: The Journal of Bertrand Russell Studies*, 1972, no. 5, pp. 3–6.

Id., "Russell's Multiple Relation Theory of Judgment", in *Philosophical Studies*, March 1985, vol. 47, no. 2, pp. 213–247.

Id., *Russell's Idealist Apprenticeship*, Oxford, Clarendon Press, 1991.

Id. (ed.), *The Cambridge Companion to Bertrand Russell*, Cambridge, Cambridge University Press, 2003.

Griffin N., Jacquette D. (eds.), *Russell Vs. Meinong: The Legacy of "On Denoting"*, London-New York, Routledge, 2008.

Griffin N., Lewis A.C., "Bertrand Russell's Mathematical Education", in *Notes and Records of the Royal Society of London*, January 1990, vol. 44, no. 1, pp. 51–71.

Griffin N., Zak G., "Russell on Specific and Universal Relations: The Principles of Mathematics", in *History and Philosophy of Logic*, 1982, vol. 3, no. 1, pp. 55–67.

Griffiths D.A., "Russell on Existence and Descriptions", in *The Philosophical Quarterly*, April 1976, vol. 26, no. 103, pp. 157–162.

Hager P.J., *Continuity and Change in the Development of Russell's Philosophy*, Dordrecht, Nijhoff, 1994.

Halbasch K., "A Critical Examination of Russell's View of Facts", in *Noûs*, November 1971, vol. 5, no. 4, pp. 395–409.

Hardy G.H., *Bertrand Russell and Trinity*, London, Cambridge University Press, 1942.

Hare W., "Bertrand Russell on Critical Thinking", in *Journal of Thought*, 2001, vol. 36, no. 1, pp. 7–16.
Harrison B., "Bertrand Russell: The False Consciousness of a Feminist", in *Russell: The Journal of Bertrand Russell Studies*, 1984, vol. 4, no. 1, pp. 157–206.
Harrison R., "Bertrand Russell: From Liberalism to Socialism?", in *Russell: The Journal of Bertrand Russell Studies*, 1986, vol. 6, no. 1, pp. 5–38.
Harwood L.D., "Russell's Reticence with Religion", in *Russell: The Journal of Bertrand Russell Studies*, 1997, vol. 17, no. 1, pp. 27–41.
Hatfield G., "Russell's Progress: Spatial Dimensions", in D. Emundts (ed.), *Self, World, and Art: Metaphysical Topics in Kant and Hegel*, Berlin-Boston, De Gruyter, 2013, pp. 321–344.
Id., "Psychology, Epistemology, and the Problem of the External World: Russell and Before", in E.H. Reck (ed.), *The Historical Turn in Analytic Philosophy*, Basingstoke, Palgrave-Macmillan, 2013, pp. 171–200.
Hattiangadi J.N., "The Realism of Popper and Russell", in *Philosophy of the Social Sciences*, December 1985, vol. 15, no. 4, pp. 461–486.
Hayhurst S., "Russell's Anti-Communist Rhetoric Before and after Stalin's Death", in *Russell: The Journal of Bertrand Russell Studies*, 1991, vol. 11, no. 1, pp. 67–82.
Hazen A.P., Davoren J.M., "Russell's 1925 Logic", in *Australasian Journal of Philosophy*, December 2000, vol. 78, no. 4, pp. 534–556.
Hellman G., "How to Gödel a Frege-Russell: Godel's Incompleteness Theorems and Logicism", in *Noûs*, November 1981, vol. 15, no. 4, pp. 451–468.
Hendley B.P., *Dewey, Russell, Whitehead: Philosophers as Educators*, Carbondale-Edwardsville, Southern Illinois University Press, 1986.
Hide Ø. (ed.), *Bertrand Russell om krig fred og pasifisme*, Oslo, Humanist Forlag, 2006.
Hill C.O., *Word and Object in Husserl, Frege and Russell: The Roots of Twentieth-Century Philosophy*, Athens, Ohio University Press, 1991.
Hillman T.A., "The Early Russell on the Metaphysics of Substance in Leibniz and Bradley", in *Synthese*, 2008, vol. 163, no. 2, pp. 245–261.
Hinderliter H., "More on Russell's Hypothesis", in *Philosophy of Science*, December 1990, vol. 57, no. 4, pp. 703–711.
Hintikka J., Kulas J., "Russell Vindicated: Towards a General Theory of Definite Description", in *Journal of Semantics*, 1982, vol. 1, no. 3–4, pp. 387–397.
Hochberg H., "Strawson, Russell, and the King of France", in *Philosophy of Science*, September 1970, vol. 37, no. 3, pp. 363–384.
Id., "Russell, Ramsey, and Wittgenstein on Ramification and Quantification", in *Erkenntnis*, September 1987, vol. 27, no. 2, pp. 257–281.
Id., "Propositions, Truth and Belief: The Wittgenstein-Russell Dispute", in *Theoria*, April 2000, vol. 66, no. 1, pp. 3–40.
Id., "Russell and Ramsey on Distinguishing between Universals and Particulars", in *Grazer Philosophische Studien*, 2004, vol. 67, no. 1, pp. 195–207.

Hookway C., "Russell et la possibilité du scepticisme", in *Hermès*, 1990, no. 7, pp. 103–118.
Hope V., "The Picture Theory of Meaning in the Tractatus as a Development of Moore's and Russell's Theories of Judgment", in *Philosophy*, April 1969, vol. 44, no. 168, pp. 140–148.
Horowitz I.L., "Bertrand Russell on War and Peace", in *Science & Society*, 1957, vol. 21, no. 1, pp. 30–51.
Hylton P., "Russell's Substitutional Theory", in *Synthese*, September 1980, vol. 45, no. 1, pp. 1–31.
Id., *Russell, Idealism, and the Emergence of Analytic Philosophy*, Oxford, Clarendon Press, 1990.
Id., *Propositions, Functions, and Analysis: Selected Essays on Russell's Philosophy*, Oxford, Clarendon Press, 2005.
Imaguire G., *Russells Frühphilosophie: Propositionen, Realismus und die Sprachontologische Wende*, Hildesheim-Zürich-New York, Olms, 2001.
Id., "O Platonismo de Russell na metafísica e na matemática", in *Kriterion: Journal of Philosophy*, 2005, vol. 46, no. 111, pp. 9–28.
Id., "A crítica de Russell à concepção leibniziana das relações", in *Manuscrito*, 2006, vol. 29, no. 1, pp. 153–183.
Ironside P., *The Social and Political Thought of Bertrand Russell: The Development of an Aristocratic Liberalism*, Cambridge, Cambridge University Press, 1996.
Irvine A.D. (ed.), *Bertrand Russell: Critical Assessments*, 4 vols., London, Routledge, 1999.
Irvine A.D., Wedeking G.A. (eds.), *Russell and Analytic Philosophy*, Toronto, University of Toronto Press, 1993.
Irvine W.B., "Russell's Construction of Space from Perspectives", in *Synthese*, September 1984, vol. 60, no. 3, pp. 333–347.
Jacquette D., "Wittgenstein's Critique of Propositional Attitudes and Russell's Theory of Judgment", in *Brentano Studien*, 1992, vol. 4, pp. 193–220.
Jadacki J.J., "Leon Chwistek-Russell's Scientific Correspondence", in *Dialectics and Humanism*, 1986, vol. 13, no. 1, pp. 239–263.
Jager R. (ed.), *Essays in Logic from Aristotle to Russell*, Englewood Cliffs, Prentice Hall, 1963.
Id., *The Development of Bertrand Russell's Philosophy*, London-New York, Allen & Unwin-Humanity Press, 1972.
Jha A., *Social Philosophy of Bertrand Russell*, Delhi, Ajanta Books International, 1978.
Johnston C., "Russell, Wittgenstein, and Synthesis in Thought", in J.L. Zalabardo (ed.), *Wittgenstein's Early Philosophy*, Oxford, Oxford University Press, 2012, pp. 15–36.
Jorgensen L.M., "Russell's Leibnizian Concept of Vagueness", in *History of Philosophy Quarterly*, July 2011, vol. 28, no. 3, pp. 289–301.
Judson L., "Russell on Memory", in *Proceedings of the Aristotelian Society*, 1987, vol. 88, pp. 65–82.
Julka K.L., *The Political Ideas of Bertrand Russell*, Patna, Associated Book Agency, 1977.
Jung D., "Russell, Presupposition, and the Vicious-Circle Principle", in *Notre Dame Journal of Formal Logic*, 1999, vol. 40, no. 1, pp. 55–80.
Kaplan D., "What is Russell's Theory of Descriptions?", in W. Yourgrau, A.D. Breck (eds.), *Physics, Logic, and History*, New York, Plenum Press, 1970, pp. 277–295.

Kemp G., "Propositions and Reasoning in Russell and Frege", in *Pacific Philosophical Quarterly*, September 1998, vol. 79, no. 3, pp. 218–235.
Kennedy T.C., "Nourishing Life: Russell and the Twentieth-Century British Peace Movement, 1900-18", in *Russell: The Journal of Bertrand Russell Studies*, 1984, vol. 4, no. 1, pp. 223–236.
Kinrade A.D., *Discipline and Freedom in Education: A Comparison of Theories of John Dewey and Bertrand Russell*, Toronto, University of Toronto Press, 1963.
Kitchener R.F., "Bertrand Russell's Flirtation with Behaviorism", in *Behavior and Philosophy*, 2004, vol. 32, no. 2, pp. 273–291.
Klein A., "Russell on Acquaintance with Spatial Properties: The Significance of James", in S. Lapointe, C. Pincock (eds.), *Innovations in the History of Analytical Philosophy*, London, Palgrave Macmillan, 2017, pp. 229–264.
Klembe E.D. (ed.), *Essays on Bertrand Russell*, Urbana, University of Illinois Press, 1970.
Klement K.C., "Putting Form before Function: Logical Grammar in Frege, Russell and Wittgenstein", in *Philosophers' Imprint*, August 2004, vol. 4, no. 2, pp. 1–47.
Id., "The Paradoxes and Russell's Theory of Incomplete Symbols", in *Philosophical Studies*, June 2014, vol. 169, no. 2, pp. 183–207.
Kneale W.C., "Russell's Paradox and Some Others", in *The British Journal for the Philosophy of Science*, November 1971, vol. 22, no. 4, pp. 321–338.
Knight F.H., "Bertrand Russell on Power", in *Ethics*, April 1939, vol. 49, no. 3, pp. 253–285.
Knight M.K. (ed.), *Humanist Anthology: From Confucius to Bertrand Russell*, London, Barrie & Rockliff, 1961.
Koehler C.J., "Studies in Bertrand Russell's Theory of Knowledge", in *Revue Internationale de Philosophie*, 1972, vol. 26, no. 102, pp. 499–512.
Korhonen A., "Russell's Early Metaphysics of Propositions", in *Prolegomena*, December 2009, vol. 8, no. 2, pp. 159–192.
Kovacs D., "Memory and Imagery in Russell's *The Analysis of Mind*", in *Prolegomena*, December 2009, vol. 8, no. 2, pp. 193–206.
Kripke S.A., "Russell's Notion of Scope", in *Mind*, October 2005, vol. 114, no. 456, pp. 1005–1037.
Kuntz P.G., *Bertrand Russell*, Boston, Twayne, 1986.
Lackey D., "Russell's 1913 Map of the Mind", in *Midwest Studies in Philosophy*, September 1981, vol. 6, no. 1, pp. 125–142.
Id., "Russell's Contribution to the Study of Nuclear Weapons Policy", in *Russell: The Journal of Bertrand Russell Studies*, 1984, vol. 4, no. 2, pp. 243–252.
Id., "Reply to Perkins on 'Conditional Preventive War'", in *Russell: The Journal of Bertrand Russell Studies*, 1996, vol. 16, no. 1, pp. 85–88.
Landini G., *Russell's Hidden Substitutional Theory*, New York-Oxford, Oxford University Press, 1998.
Id., *Wittgenstein's Apprenticeship with Russell*, Cambridge, Cambridge University Press, 2007.
Id., "Russell's Schema, Not Priest's Inclosure", in *History and Philosophy of Logic*, April 2009, vol. 30, no. 2, pp. 105–139.

Id., *Russell*, London-New York, Routledge, 2011.

Lebens S., *Bertrand Russell and the Nature of Propositions: A History and Defence of the Multiple Relation Theory of Judgment*, New York-London, Routledge, 2017.

Leggett H.W., *Bertrand Russell: A Pictorial Biography*, New York, Philosophical Library, 1950.

Levine J., "From Absolute Idealism to 'The Principles of Mathematics'", in *International Journal of Philosophical Studies*, 1998, vol. 6, no. 1, pp. 87–127.

Id., "On Russell's Vulnerability to Russell's Paradox", in *History and Philosophy of Logic*, 2001, vol. 22, no. 4, pp. 207–231.

Lewis J., *Bertrand Russell: Philosopher and Humanist*, London, Lawrence and Wishart, 1968.

Link G. (ed.), *One Hundred Years of Russell's Paradox: Mathematics, Logic, Philosophy*, Berlin-New York, De Gruyter, 2004.

Linsky B., "The Resolution of Russell's Paradox in 'Principia Mathematica'", in *Noûs*, October 2002, vol. 36, no. 16, pp. 395–417.

Id., *The Evolution of Principia Mathematica: Bertrand Russell's Manuscripts for the Second Edition*, Cambridge, Cambridge University Press, 2011.

Lipkind D., "Russell on the Notion of Cause", in *Canadian Journal of Philosophy*, December 1979, vol. 9, no. 4, pp. 701–720.

Lippincott M., "Russell's Leviathan", in *Russell: The Journal of Bertrand Russell Studies*, 1990, vol. 10, no. 1, pp. 6–29.

Lück U., "Continu'ous Time Goes by Russell", in *Notre Dame Journal of Formal Logic*, 2006, vol. 47, no. 3, pp. 397–434.

MacBride F., "The Russell-Wittgenstein Dispute: A New Perspective", in M. Textor (ed.), *Judgment and Truth in Early Analytic Philosophy and Phenomenology*, London, Palgrave Macmillan, 2013, pp. 206–241.

Madigan T., Stone P. (eds.), *Bertrand Russell: Public Intellectual*, Rochester, Tiger Bark Press, 2016.

Makin G., *The Metaphysicians of Meaning: Russell and Frege on Sense and Denotation*, London-New York, Routledge, 2000.

Mancosu P., Zach R., Badesa C., "The Development of Mathematical Logic from Russell to Tarski 1900–1935", in L. Haaparanta (ed.), *The Development of Modern Logic*, New York-Oxford, Oxford University Press, 2004, pp. 318–470.

Maracchia S., "Plato and Russell on the Definition of Mathematics", in *Scientia*, 1971, vol. 106, no. 6, pp. 216–223.

Marjolin R., "Liberté et organisation par Bertrand Russell", in *Revue de Métaphysique et de Morale*, January 1936, vol. 43, no. 1, pp. 131–148.

Martin G., "Bertrand Russell und die Platonischen Ideen", in *Studi Internazionali di Filosofia*, 1973, vol. 5, pp. 169–180.

Martin W., *Bertrand Russell: A Bibliography of His Writings. Eine Bibliographie seiner Schriften: 1895–1976*, München-New York, Linnet Books, 1981.

Martins A., "Conhecimento e Experiência no Empirismo de Russell", in *Revista Portuguesa de Filosofia*, 1972, vol. 28, no. 4, pp. 397–420.

Mckenney J.L., "Dewey and Russell: Fraternal Twins in Philosophy", in *Educational Theory*, January 1959, vol. 9, no. 1, pp. 24–30.
Mckeon M., "Bertrand Russell and Logical Truth", in *Philosophia*, 1999, vol. 27, no. 3–4, pp. 541–553.
McLendon H.J., "Has Russell Answered Hume?", in *The Journal of Philosophy*, February 1952, vol. 49, no. 5, pp. 145–159.
McMichael A., "A Set Theory with Frege-Russell Cardinal Numbers", in *Philosophical Studies*, September 1982, vol. 42, no. 2, pp. 141–149.
Miah S., *Russell's Theory of Perception 1905–1919*, Dhaka, Dhaka University Press, 1998.
Milkov N., "The History or Russell's Concepts 'Sense-Data' and 'Knowledge by Acquaintance'", in *Archiv für Begriffsgeschichte*, 2001, vol. 43, pp. 221–231.
Id., "The Joint Philosophical Program of Russell and Wittgenstein and Its Demise", in *Nordic Wittgenstein Review*, August 2013, vol. 2, no. 1, pp. 81–105.
Id., "The 1900 Turn in Bertrand Russell's Logic, the Emergence of His Paradox, and the Way Out", in *Siegener Beiträge zur Geschichte und Philosophie der Mathematik*, 2016, vol. 7, pp. 29–50.
Monk R., *Bertrand Russell: 1872–1920. The Spirit of Solitude*, London, Jonathan Cape, 1996.
Id., *Russell. Mathematics: Dreams and Nightmares*, London, Phœnix, 1997.
Id., "Was Russell an Analytical Philosopher?", in H.J. Glock (ed.), *The Rise of Analytic Philosophy*, Oxford, Blackwell, 1997, pp. 35–50.
Id., *Bertrand Russell 1921–1970: The Ghost of Madness*, London, Jonathan Cape, 2000.
Monk R., Palmer A. (eds.), *Bertrand Russell and the Origins of Analytical Philosophy*, Bristol, Thoemmes Press, 1996.
Monro D.H., "Russell's Moral Theories", in *Philosophy*, January 1960, vol. 35, no. 132, pp. 30–50.
Moorehead C., *Bertrand Russell: A Life*, London, Sinclair-Stevenson, 1992.
Mormann T., "Russell's Many Points", in A. Hieke, H. Leitgeb (eds.), *Reduction, Abstraction, Analysis*, Frankfurt-Paris-Lancaster-New Brunswick, Ontos Verlag, 2009, pp. 239–258.
Morris C.W., "Has Russell Passed the Tortoise?", in *The Journal of Philosophy*, August 1929, vol. 26, no. 17, pp. 449–459.
Morris W.E., "Moore and Russell on Philosophy and Science", in *Metaphilosophy*, April 1979, vol. 10, no. 2, pp. 111–138.
Muehlmann R., "Russell and Wittgenstein on Identity", in *The Philosophical Quarterly*, July 1969, vol. 19, no. 76, pp. 221–230.
Mumford S. (ed.), *Russell on Metaphysics: Selections from the Writings of Bertrand Russell*, London-New York, Routledge, 2003.
Myers O.F., *The Significance of the Mathematical Element in the Philosophy of Bertrand Russell*, Chicago, Chicago University Press, 1926.
Nacci M., *Strade per la felicità: il pensiero politico di Bertrand Russell*, Roma, Nuova Cultura, 2012.
Id., "Il volo di Icaro. Scienza, tecnica, potere nel pensiero di Bertrand Russell", in *Rivista di Politica*, 2012, no. 2, pp. 127–148.

Nagel E., "Mr. Russell on Meaning and Truth", in *The Journal of Philosophy*, May 1941, vol. 38, no. 10, pp. 253–270.
Nakhnikian G. (ed.), *Bertrand Russell's Philosophy*, London, Duckworth, 1974.
Narskii I.S., Pomogaeva E.F., "Bertrand Russell – Philosopher and Humanist", in *Russian Studies in Philosophy*, 1973, vol. 12, no. 1, pp. 33–53.
Nasim O.W., *Bertrand Russell and the Edwardian Philosophers: Constructing the World*, Basingstoke, Palgrave Macmillan, 2008.
Id., "The Spaces of Knowledge: Bertrand Russell, Logical Construction, and the Classification of the Sciences", in *British Journal for the History of Philosophy*, 2012, vol. 20, no. 6, pp. 1163–1182.
Nelson M.T., "Bertrand Russell's Defence of the Cosmological Argument", in *American Philosophical Quarterly*, January 1998, vol. 35, no. 1, pp. 87–100.
Nicod J., "Les tendances philosophiques de M. Bertrand Russell", in *Revue de Métaphysique et de Morale*, Janvier-Mars 1992, vol. 29, no. 1, pp. 77–84.
Oaklander L.N., Miracchi S., "Russell, Negative Facts, and Ontology", in *Philosophy of Science*, 1980, vol. 47, no. 3, pp. 434–455.
Oberdan T., "Russell's Principles of Mathematics and the Revolution in Marburg Neo-Kantianism", in *Perspectives on Science*, 2014, vol. 22, no. 4, pp. 523–544.
Ogbozo C.N., *Knowing and Believing as Degrees of Probability in Bertrand Russell: Prolegomena to a Complementary Epistemology*, Roma, Tip. Poliglotta della Pontificia Università Gregoriana, 1995.
Ogden S., "The Sage in the Inkpot: Bertrand Russell's and China's Social Reconstruction in the 1920's", in *Modern Asian Studies*, 1982, vol. 16, no. 4, pp. 529–600.
Orayen R., "Tres dificultades en la Teoria de las Descripciones de Bertrand Russell", in *Critica: Revista Hispanoamericana de Filosofía*, Abril 1975, vol. 7, no. 19, pp. 69–104.
Orilia F., "Type-Free Property Theory, Exemplification and Russell's Paradox", in *Notre Dame Journal of Formal Logic*, 1991, vol. 32, no. 3, pp. 432–447.
Overskeid G., "Psychological Hedonism and the Nature of Motivation: Bertrand Russell's Anhedonic Desires", in *Philosophical Psychology*, 2002, vol. 15, no. 1, pp. 77–93.
Padia C., "Is Russell a Political Philosopher?", in *Russell: The Journal of Bertrand Russell Studies*, 1986, vol. 6, no. 2, pp. 134–143.
Palazón Mayoral M.R., *Bertrand Russell Empirista (las ideas)*, México, Universidad Nacional Autónoma de México, 1975.
Park J., *Bertrand Russell on Education*, Columbus, Ohio State University Press, 1963.
Patterson W.A., *Bertrand Russell's Philosophy of Logical Atomism*, New York, Peter Lang, 1993.
Patton L., "Russell's Method of Analysis and the Axioms of Mathematics", in S. Lapointe, C. Pincock (eds.), *Innovations in the History of Analytical Philosophy*, London, Palgrave Macmillan, 2017, pp. 105–126.
Pears D.F., "Logical Atomism: Russell and Wittgenstein", in Various Authors, *The Revolution in Philosophy*, New York, St. Martin's Press, 1956, pp. 44–55.

Id., *Bertrand Russell and the British Tradition in Philosophy*, London, Collins, 1967.
Id. (ed.), *Bertrand Russell: A Collection of Critical Essays*, Garden City, Anchor Books, 1972.
Id., "The Function of Acquaintance in Russell's Philosophy", in *Synthese*, February 1981, vol. 46, no. 2, pp. 149–166.
Pelham J., "Russell, Frege, and the Nature of Implication", in *Topoi*, September 1999, vol. 18, no. 2, pp. 175–184.
Perkins R., "Bertrand Russell and Preventive War", in *Russell: The Journal of Bertrand Russell Studies*, 1994, vol. 14, no. 2, pp. 135–153.
Id., "Response to Lackey on 'Conditional Preventive War'", in *Russell: The Journal of Bertrand Russell Studies*, 1996, vol. 16, no. 2, pp. 169–170.
Perry L.R. (ed.), *Bertrand Russell, A.S. Neil, Homer Lane, W.H. Kilpatrick: Four Progressive Educators*, London, Collier-Macmillan, 1967.
Peters F., "Russell on Class Theory", in *Synthese*, 1963, vol. 15, no. 1, pp. 327–335.
Pickel B., "Russell on Incomplete Symbols", in *Philosophy Compass*, October 2013, vol. 8, no. 10, pp. 909–923.
Pigden C.R., "Bertrand Russell: Meta-Ethical Pioneer", in *Philosophy of the Social Sciences*, June 1996, vol. 26, no. 2, pp. 181–204.
Id., "Bertrand Russell: Moral Philosopher or Unphilosophical Moralist?", in Griffin (ed.), *The Cambridge Companion to Bertrand Russell*, pp. 475–506.
Id., "Desiring to Desire: Russell Lewis and G.E. Moore", in S.Nuccetelli, G. Seay (eds.), *Themes from G.E. Moore: New Essays in Epistemology and Ethics*, Oxford, Oxford University Press, 2007, pp. 244–260.
Pitt J., "Russell on Religion", in *International Journal for Philosophy of Religion*, March 1975, vol. 6, no. 1, pp. 40–53.
Ponticelli L., "Il dualismo di soggetto e il suo rifiuto in Bertrand Russell", in *Rivista di Filosofia Neo-Scolastica*, 1981, no. 2, pp. 418–434.
Potter M.K., *Bertrand Russell's Ethics*, London-New York, Continuum, 2006.
Pratt S.L., "Inquiry and Analysis: Dewey and Russell on Philosophy", in *Studies in Philosophy and Education*, June 1998, vol. 17, no. 2–3, pp. 101–122.
Price H., Corry R. (eds.), *Causation, Physics, and the Constitution of Reality: Russell's Republic Revisited*, Oxford, Oxford University Press, 2007.
Prichard H.A., "Mr. Bertrand Russell on our Knowledge of the External World", in *Mind*, April 1915, vol. 24, no. 94, pp. 145–185.
Id., "Mr. Bertrand Russell's Outline of Philosophy", in *Mind*, July 1928, vol. 37, no. 147, pp. 265–282.
Proops I., "Russell and the Universalist Conception of Logic", in *Noûs*, March 2007, vol. 41, no. 1, pp. 1–32.
Id., "Russellian Acquaintance Revisited", in *Journal of the History of Philosophy*, October 2014, vol. 52, no. 4, pp. 779–811.
Pujia R., *Bertrand Russell e l'eredità idealista inglese*, Messina, La Libra, 1977.

Pulkkinen J., "Russell and the Neo-Kantians", in *Studies in History and Philosophy of Science*, March 2001, vol. 32, no. 1, pp. 99–117.
Quine W.V.O., "Russell's Ontological Development", in *The Journal of Philosophy*, November 1966, vol. 63, no. 21, pp. 657–667.
Quinton A., "Russell's Philosophical Development", in *Philosophy*, January 1960, vol. 35, no. 132, pp. 1–13.
Radner M., "Philosophical Foundations of Russell's Logicism", in *Dialogue*, 1975, vol. 14, no. 2, pp. 241–253.
Ready W.B., *Necessary Russell*, Toronto, Copp Clark, 1969.
Reinhardt L., "Bertrand Russell's Triumph and Failure", in *Think*, 2016, vol. 15, no. 42, pp. 79–95.
Ribeiro H.J., "The Present Relevance of Bertrand Russell's Criticism of Logical Positivism", in *Revista Portuguesa de Filosofia*, 1999, vol. 55, no. 4, pp. 427–458.
Riverso E., *Il pensiero di Bertrand Russell: esposizione storico-critica*, Napoli, Istituto editoriale del Mezzogiorno, 1958.
Rizzacasa A., *Il pacifismo nella dottrina politico-pedagogica di Bertrand Russell*, Bologna, Leonardi, 1969.
Roberts G.W. (ed.), *Bertrand Russell Memorial Volume*, London-New York, Allen & Unwin-Humanities Press, 1979.
Robinson D., Groves J., *Introducing Bertrand Russell*, Cambridge, Icon Books, 2002.
Robles J.A., "B. Russell: Relaciones y universals", in *Critica: Revista Hispanoamericana de Filosofía*, September 1971, vol. 5, no. 15, pp. 65–81.
Rodriguez-Consuegra F.A., *The Mathematical Philosophy of Bertrand Russell: Origins and Development*, Basel-Boston-Berlin, Birkhäuser Verlag, 1991.
Id., "El impacto de Wittgenstein sobre Russell", in *Theoria*, 1992, vol. 7, no. 16–18, pp. 875–911.
Id., "Bertrand Russell 1920–1948: una filosofia de la cienca del atomismo al holismo", in *Diálogos: Revista de Filosofía de la Universidad de Puerto Rico*, 1992, vol. 27, no. 59, pp. 135–186.
Rolf B., "Russell's Theses on Vagueness", in *History and Philosophy of Logic*, 1982, vol. 3, no. 1, pp. 69–83.
Rosenbaum S.P., "Bertrand Russell in Bloomsbury", in *Russell: The Journal of Bertrand Russell Studies*, 1984, vol. 4, no. 1, pp. 11–29.
Rosenberg J.F., "Russell on Negative Facts", in *Noûs*, March 1972, vol. 6, no. 1, pp. 27–40.
Ross D., Spurrett D., "Notions of Cause: Russell's Thesis Revisited", in *The British Journal for the Philosophy of Science*, March 2007, vol. 58, no. 1, pp. 45–76.
Rota Ghibaudi S., *Bertrand Russell*, Milano, FrancoAngeli, 1985.
Rouilhan (de) P., *Russell et le cercle des paradoxes*, Paris, Puf, 1996.
Ruja H., "Principles of Polemic in Russell", in *Inquiry: An Interdisciplinary Journal of Philosophy*, 1968, vol. 11, no. 1–4, pp. 282–294.
Russell H., "Russell's Power", in *Philosophy of the Social Sciences*, September 1996, vol. 26, no. 3, pp. 322–347.

Ryan A., *Bertrand Russell: A Political Life*, New York, Hill and Wang, 1988.
Id., "La politique de Russell", in *Hermès*, 1990, no. 7, pp. 189–201.
Id., "Russell: The Last Great Radical?", in *Philosophy of the Social Sciences*, June 1996, vol. 26, no. 2, pp. 247–266.
Saarinen E., "How to Frege a Russell-Kaplan", in *Noûs*, May 1982, vol. 16, no. 2, pp. 253–276.
Sainsbury R.M., *Russell*, London-Boston, Routledge and Kegan, 1979.
Id., "Russell on Constructions and Fictions", in *Theoria*, April 1980, vol. 46, no. 1, pp. 19–36.
Id., "Russell on Acquaintance", in *Royal Institute of Philosophy Supplements*, March 1986, vol. 20, pp. 219–244.
Santamaría Velasco F.O., "Russell y el problema de la referencia", in *Escritos*, 2008, vol. 16, no. 37, pp. 390–417.
Santayana G., "Russell's Philosophical Essays", in *The Journal of Philosophy, Psychology and Scientific Methods*, August 1911, vol. 8, no. 3, pp. 57–63.
Savage C.W., Anderson C.A. (eds.), *Rereading Russell: Essays on Bertrand Russell's Metaphysics and Epistemology*, Minneapolis, University of Minnesota Press, 1989.
Schaar (van der) M., "GF Stout and Russell's Earliest Account of Judgment", in Textor (ed.), *Judgment and Truth in Early Analytic Philosophy and Phenomenology*, pp. 137–156.
Schiller F.C.S., "Mr. Russell's Psychology", in *The Journal of Philosophy*, May 1922, vol. 19, no. 11, pp. 281–292.
Schilpp P.A. (ed.), *The Philosophy of Bertrand Russell*, Illinois, Open Court, 1944.
Id., "Some Reflections of Bertrand Russell 1872–1970", in *Journal of Thought*, April 1971, vol. 6, no. 2, pp. 68–79.
Schmid A.-F., "La correspondence inédite entre Bertrand Russell et Louis Couturat", in *Dialectica*, June 1983, vol. 37, no. 2, pp. 75–109.
Id. (ed.), *Bertrand Russell: correspondence sur la philosophie, la logique et la politique avec Louis Couturat (1897–1913)*, 2 vols., Paris, Kimé, 2001.
Schoenman R. (ed.), *Bertrand Russell: Philosopher of the Century. Essays in His Honour*, London, Allen and Unwin, 1967.
Id., "Bertrand Russell and the Peace Movement", in Nakhnikian (ed.), *Bertrand Russell's Philosophy*, pp. 227–252.
Schultz B., "Bertrand Russell in Ethics and Politics", in *Ethics*, April 1992, vol. 102, no. 3, pp. 594–634.
Schwarcz V., "Between Russell and Confucius: China's Russell Expert, Zhang Shenfu", in *Russell: The Journal of Bertrand Russell Studies*, 1991, vol. 11, no. 2, pp. 117–146.
Schwerin A. (ed.), *Bertrand Russell on Nuclear War, Peace and Language: Critical and Historical Essays*, Westport-London, Praeger, 2002.
Id., *Russell Revisited: Critical Reflections on the Thought of Bertrand Russell*, Newcastle, Cambridge Scholars Press, 2008.
Seckel A., "Russell and the Cuban Missile Crisis", in *Russell: The Journal of Bertrand Russell Studies*, 1984, vol. 4, no. 2, pp. 253–261.

Senofonte C., *Scienza, religione e morale in Bertrand Russell*, Napoli, Vivarium, 2002.
Shaw J.L., "Number: From the Nyāya to Frege-Russell", in *Studia Logica*, 1982, vol. 41, no. 2–3, pp. 283–291.
Shearn M., "Russell's Analysis of Existence", in *Analysis*, 1950–1951, vol. 11, pp. 124–131.
Shosky J., "Russell and the Contemplation of Philosophy", in *Free Inquiry*, 1995, vol. 15, no. 4, pp. 41–42.
Shukla J., "Failure of Russell's Theory of External Relations", in *Indian Philosophical Quarterly*, July 1979, vol. 6, no. 4, pp. 697–704.
Shute C., *Bertrand Russell: "Education as the Power of Independent Thought"*, Nottingham, Educational Heretics Press, 2002.
Sierra Mejía H., "La noción de sujeto en Bertrand Russell", in *Ideas y Valores*, 1986, vol. 35, no. 71–72, pp. 107–121.
Singh A., *The Political Philosophy of Bertrand Russell*, New Delhi, Mittal Publications, 1987.
Slater J.G., "Russell's Conception of Philosophy", in *Russell: The Journal of Bertrand Russell Studies*, 1988, vol. 8, no. 1–2, pp. 163–178.
Id., *Bertrand Russell*, Preface by Ray Monk, Bristol, Thoemmes Press, 1994.
Id., "Is Bertrand Russell a Logical Fiction?", in T. Mathien, D.G. Wright (eds.), *Autobiography as Philosophy: The Philosophical Uses of Self-Presentation*, London, Routledge, 2006, pp. 253–265.
Smart H.R., "Cassirer versus Russell", in *Philosophy of Science*, July 1943, vol. 10, no. 3, pp. 167–175.
Smith H.M., "Bertrand Russell on Perception", in *Proceedings of the Aristotelian Society*, June 1932, vol. 32, no. 1, pp. 207–226.
Smith J.F., "The Russell-Meinong Debate", in *Philosophy and Phenomenological Research*, March 1985, vol. 45, no. 3, pp. 305–350.
Soames S., "What Is the Frege/Russell Analysis of Quantification?", in Id., *Analytic Philosophy in America: And Other Historical and Contemporary Essays*, Princeton, Princeton University Press, 2014, pp. 191–199.
Spiegelberg H., "The Correspondence between Bertrand Russell and Albert Schweitzer", in *International Studies in Philosophy*, 1980, vol. 12, no. 1, pp. 1–45.
Stapledon O., "Mr. Bertrand Russell's Ethical Beliefs", in *International Journal of Ethics*, July 1927, vol. 37, no. 4, pp. 390–402.
Stevens G., *The Russellian Origins of Analytical Philosophy: Bertrand Russell and the Unity of the Proposition*, London, Routledge, 2005.
Id., "Russell's Repsychologising of the Proposition", in *Synthese*, July 2006, vol. 151, no. 1, pp. 99–124.
Id., "Russell's Ontological Development Reconsidered", in *British Journal for the History of Philosophy*, 2010, vol. 18, no. 1, pp. 113–137.
Stol A., *De beulen staan terecht: Bertrand Russell Tribunaal II over Latijns-Amerika*, Den Haag, Manteau, 1975.

Stone I.F., "Bertrand Russell as a Moral Force in Word Politics", in *Russell: The Journal of Bertrand Russell Studies*, 1981, vol. 1, no. 1, pp. 1–25.
Stone P. (ed.), *Bertrand Russell's Life and Legacy*, Wilmington, Vernon Press, 2017.
Strachey O., "Mr. Russell and Some Recent Criticisms of His Views", in *Mind*, January 1915, vol. 24, no. 93, pp. 16–28.
Stroll A., "Russell's 'Proof'", in *Canadian Journal of Philosophy*, June 1975, vol. 4, no. 4, pp. 653–662.
Strong C.A., "Mr. Russell's Theory of the External World", in *Mind*, July 1922, vol. 31, no. 123, pp. 307–320.
Sullivan P., Johnston C., "Judgments, Facts and Propositions: Theories of Truth in Russell, Wittgenstein and Ramsey", in M. Glanzberg (ed.), *The Oxford Handbook of Truth*, New York-Oxford, Oxford University Press, 2018, pp. 150–192.
Sumares M., "Revisiting Bertrand Russell's Refusal of the Christian Faith: A Reappraisal", in *Revista Portuguesa de Filosofia*, 2006, vol. 62, no. 2–4, pp. 851–864.
Tait K., *My Father Bertrand Russell*, New York, Harcourt Brace Jovanovich, 1975.
Id., "Russell and Feminism", in *Russell: The Journal of Bertrand Russell Studies*, 1978, no. 29–32, pp. 5–16.
Tallon H.J., "Russell's Doctrine of the Logical Proposition", in *The New Scholasticism*, 1939, vol. 13, no. 1, pp. 31–48.
Taylor G.G., "The Analytic and Synthetic in Russell's Philosophy of Mathematics", in *Philosophical Studies*, January 1981, vol. 39, no. 1, pp. 51–59.
Tempini N., *La relazione di implicazione e la teoria della deduzione nella logica di Bertrand Russell*, Venezia, Istituto Veneto di Scienze, Lettere ed Arti, 1973.
Thomas J.E., Blackwell K. (eds.), *Russell in Review: The Bertrand Russell Centenary Celebrations at McMaster University, October 12–14, 1972*, Toronto, Samuel Stevens-Hakkert & Company, 1976.
Trejo W., "Russell: descripcion y existencia", in *Crítica: Revista Hispanoamericana de Filosofía*, 1968, vol. 2, no. 4, pp. 89–124.
Tugnoli C., "Bertrand Russell e l'analisi dell'esperienza temporale", in *Rivista di Filosofia*, April 1998, vol. 89, no. 1, pp. 53–86.
Tully R.E., "Russell's Alter Ego", in *Dialogue: Canadian Philosophical Review*, 1988, vol. 27, no. 4, pp. 701–709.
Turcon S., "Like a Shattered Vase: Russell's 1918 Prison Letters", in *Russell: The Journal of Bertrand Russell Studies*, 2010, vol. 30, no. 2, pp. 101–125.
Unna S., "Bertrand Russell – Then and Now", in *Journal of Philosophy, Psychology and Scientific Methods*, July 1919, vol. 16, no. 15, pp. 393–403.
Urbaniak R., "Lesniewski and Russell's Paradox: Some Problems", in *History and Philosophy of Logic*, 2008, vol. 29, no. 2, pp. 115–146.
Urmson J.O., "Russell on Acquaintance with the Past", in *The Philosophical Review*, October 1969, vol. 78, no. 4, pp. 510–515.

Ushenko A., "Comments on Russell's: *An Inquiry Into Meaning and Truth*", in *Philosophy and Phenomenological Research*, September 1941, vol. 2, no. 1, pp. 98–101.

Id., "The Logics of Hegel and Russell", in *Philosophy and Phenomenological Research*, September 1949, vol. 10, no. 1, pp. 107–114.

Van Patten J., "Some Reflections on Bertrand Russell's Philosophy", in *Educational Theory*, January 1965, vol. 15, no. 1, pp. 58–65.

Vax L., *L'empirisme logique de Bertrand Russell à Nelson Goodman*, Paris, Puf, 1970.

Vellacott J., *Bertrand Russell and the Pacifists in the First World War*, New York, St. Martin's Press, 1980 (reprinted as *Conscientious Objection: Bertrand Russell and the Pacifists in the First World War*, Nottingham, Spokesman Books, 2015).

Vernant D., *La philosophie mathématique de Bertrand Russell*, Paris, Librairie philosophique J. Vrin, 1993.

Id., "Le statut de la vérité dans le calcul implicationnel de Russell en 1903", in *Revue Internationale de Philosophie*, June 1997, vol. 51, no. 200, pp. 221–229.

Vuillemin J., *Leçons sur la première philosophie de Russell*, Paris, Colin, 1968.

Id., "Logical Flaws on Philosophical Problems: On Russell's *Principia Mathematica*", in *Revue Internationale de Philosophie*, 1972, vol. 26, no. 102, pp. 534–556.

Id., "Le «platonisme» dans la première philosophie de Russell et le «principe d'abstraction»", in *Dialogue: Canadian Philosophical Review*, 1975, vol. 14, no. 2, pp. 222–240.

Id., "Difficultés logiques et problèmes philosophiques dans les Principia Mathematica de Russell", in *Hermès*, 1990, no. 7, pp. 39–60.

Wahl R., "Bertrand Russell's Theory of Judgment", in *Synthese*, September 1986, vol. 68, no. 3, pp. 383–407.

Wang H., "Russell and Philosophy", in *The Journal of Philosophy*, November 1966, vol. 63, no. 21, pp. 670–673.

Waterlow S., "Some Philosophical Implications of Mr. Bertrand Russell's Logical Theory of Mathematics", in *Proceedings of the Aristotelian Society*, 1909–1910, vol. 10, pp. 132–188.

Watling J., *Bertrand Russell*, Edinburgh, Oliver & Boyd, 1970.

Weiss B., "On Russell's Arguments for Restricting Modes of Specification and Domains of Qualification", in *History and Philosophy of Logic*, 1994, vol. 15, no. 2, pp. 173–188.

Id., "On the Demise of Russell's Multiple Relations Theory of Judgment", in *Theoria*, December 1995, vol. 61, no. 3, pp. 261–282.

Westphal K.R., "Hegel, Russell, and the Foundations of Philosophy", in A. Nuzzo (ed.), *Hegel and the Analytic Tradition*, London-New York, Continuum, 2010, pp. 174–194.

Wettstein H., "Frege-Russell Semantics?", in *Dialectica*, 1990, vol. 44, no. 1–2, pp. 113–135.

Whitehead A.N., "To the Master and Fellows of Trinity College, Cambridge", in *Russell: The Journal of Bertrand Russell Studies*, 1986, vol. 6, no. 1, pp. 62–70.

Wickham H., *The Unrealists: James, Bergson, Santayana, Einstein, Bertrand Russell, John Dewey, Alexander and Whitehead*, New York, Lincoln MacVeagh-The Dial Press, 1930.

Wielenberg E.J., *God and the Reach of Reason: C.S. Lewis, David Hume, and Bertrand Russell*, Cambridge, Cambridge University Press, 2007.

Willis K., "The Critical Reception of German Social Democracy", in *Russell: The Journal of Bertrand Russell Studies*, 1976, no. 21–22, pp. 35–45.

Id., "Russell in the Lords", in *Russell: The Journal of Bertrand Russell Studies*, 2002, vol. 22, no. 2, pp. 101–141.

Wilson M., "Frege and Russell: Does Science Talk Sense?", in *European Journal of Analytic Philosophy*, October 2007, vol. 3, no. 2, pp. 179–190.

Wilson W.K., "Incomplete Symbols and Russell's Proof", in *Canadian Journal of Philosophy*, 1980, vol. 10, no. 2, pp. 233–250.

Winchester I., "The Antinomy of Dynamical Causation in Leibniz and the Principles and Russell's Early Picture of Physics", in *Russell: The Journal of Bertrand Russell Studies*, 1988, vol. 8, no. 1, pp. 35–45.

Wishon D., Linsky B. (eds.), *Acquaintance, Knowledge, and Logic: New Essays on Bertrand Russell's "The Problems of Philosophy"*, Stanford, Centre for the Study of Language & Information, 2015.

Wolf L.O., "Mr. Russell's Theory of Facts", in *New Scholasticism*, 1931, vol. 5, no. 4, pp. 342–354.

Wood A., *Bertrand Russell: The Passionate Sceptic*, London, Allen & Unwin, 1957.

Woodger J.H., "Mr. Russell's Theory of Perception", in *The Monist*, October 1930, vol. 40, no. 4, pp. 621–636.

Woodhouse H., "Science as Method: The Conceptual Link Between Russell's Philosophy and His Educational Thought", in *Russell: The Journal of Bertrand Russell Studies*, 1985, vol. 5, no. 2, pp. 150–161.

Yibao X., "Bertrand Russell and the Introduction of Mathematical Logic in China", in *History and Philosophy of Logic*, 2003, vol. 24, no. 3, pp. 181–196.

Yourgrau P., "Russell and Kaplan on Denoting", in *Philosophy and Phenomenological Research*, December 1985, vol. 46, no. 2, pp. 315–321.

Zając M., "Dwa rodzaje wypełnienia i dwa typy wiedzy: Husserl i Russell", in *Studia Filozoficzne*, 1988, no. 10, pp. 23–32.

Zalabardo J.L., "Davidson, Russell and Wittgenstein on the Problem of Predication", in C. Verheggen (ed.), *Wittgenstein and Davidson on Thought, Language and Action*, Cambridge, Cambridge University Press, 2017, pp. 226–249.

Zavadivker N., "La Teoría Emotivista de los Valores de Bertrand Russell", in *Revista de Filosofía y Teoría Política*, 2008, no. 39, pp. 53–72.

Zhou L., Linsky B., "Russell's Two Lectures in China on Mathematical Logic", in *Russell: The Journal of Bertrand Russell Studies*, 2018, vol. 38, no. 1, pp. 52–68.

Zijiang D., "A Comparison of Dewey's and Russell's Influences on China", in *Dao: A Journal of Comparative Philosophy*, June 2007, vol. 6, no. 2, pp. 149–165.

Zouhar M., "The Relationship between Epistemology and Logic in Russell's Philosophy", in *Filozofia*, January 1999, vol. 54, no. 10, pp. 731–741.

Zürcher J.M., "Lenguaje y realidad en filosofía del atomismo lógico de Bertrand Russell", in *Revista de Filosofía de la Universidad de Costa Rica*, 1977, no. 40, pp. 11–22.

Publications by Bertrand Russell

"The A Priori in Geometry", in *Proceedings of the Aristotelian Society*, 1895–1896, vol. 3, no. 2, pp. 97–112.
German Social Democracy: Six Lectures, London-New York-Bombay, Longman-Green and Company, 1896.
"The Logic of Geometry", in *Mind*, January 1896, vol. 5, no. 17, pp. 1–23.
An Essay on the Foundations of Geometry, Cambridge, Cambridge University Press, 1897.
"On the Relations of Number and Quantity", in *Mind*, July 1897, vol. 6, no. 23, pp. 326–341.
"Les axiomes propres à Euclide, sont-ils empiriques?", in *Revue de Métaphysique et de Morale*, November 1898, vol. 6, no. 6, pp. 759–776.
"Sur les axiomes de la géométrie", in *Revue de Métaphysique et de Morale*, November 1899, vol. 7, no. 6, pp. 684–707.
A Critical Exposition of the Philosophy of Leibniz: With an Appendix of Leading Passages, Cambridge, Cambridge University Press, 1900.
"Sur la logique des relations avec des applications à la théorie des séries", in *Revue de mathématiques*, 1901, vol. 7, no. 2–3, pp. 115–136, 137–148.
"On the Notion of Order", in *Mind*, January 1901, vol. 10, no. 37, pp. 30–51.
"Is Position in Time and Space Absolute or Relative?", in *Mind*, July 1901, vol. 10, no. 39, pp. 293–317.
"Recent Work on the Principles of Mathematics", in *The International Monthly*, July 1901, vol. 4, pp. 83–101.
"Théorie générale des séries bien-ordonnées", in *Revue de mathématiques*, 1902, vol. 8, no. 1–2, pp. 12–24, 25–43.
"The Teaching of Euclid", in *The Mathematical Gazette*, May 1902, vol. 2, no. 33, pp. 165–167.
"On Finite and Infinite Cardinal Numbers", in *American Journal of Mathematics*, October 1902, vol. 24, pp. 378–383.
The Principles of Mathematics, Cambridge, Cambridge University Press, 1903.
"Comments on Definitions of 'Cause', 'Contenu' and 'Convergence'", in *Bulletin de la Société française de Philosophie*, 1903, vol. 3, pp. 163, 192–193, 197.
"Recent Work on the Philosophy of Leibniz", in *Mind*, April 1903, vol. 12, no. 46, pp. 177–201.
"The Free Man's Worship", in *The Independent Review*, December 1903, vol. 1, pp. 415–424.
"The Tariff Controversy", in *The Edinburgh Review*, January 1904, vol. 199, no. 407, pp. 169–196.
"Mr. Charles Booth's Proposals for Fiscal Reform", in *The Contemporary Review*, February 1904, vol. 85, pp. 198–206.
"The Meaning of Good", in *The Independent Review*, March 1904, vol. 2, pp. 328–333.

"Meinong's Theory of Complexes and Assumptions", in *Mind*, April–July–October 1904, vol. 13, no. 50–51–52, pp. 204–219, 336–354, 509–524.
"The Axiom of Infinity", in *Hibbert Journal*, July 1904, vol. 2, pp. 809–812.
"On History", in *The Independent Review*, July 1904, vol. 3, pp. 207–215.
"Non-Euclidean Geometry", in *The Athenaeum*, 29 October 1904, no. 4018, pp. 592–593.
"Comment on Abstracts of Two Papers", in *Sociological Papers*, 1905, vol. 1, p. 244.
"Comments on Definitions of 'Epistemologie' and 'Evidence'", in *Bulletin de la Société française de Philosophie*, 1905, vol. 5, pp. 221, 235.
"The Existential Import of Propositions", in *Mind*, July 1905, vol. 14, no. 55, pp. 398–401.
"On Denoting", in *Mind*, October 1905, vol. 14, no. 56, pp. 479–493.
"Sur la relation des mathématiques à la logistique", in *Revue de Métaphysique et de Morale*, November 1905, vol. 13, no. 2, pp. 906–916.
"Comments on Definitions of 'Figure' and 'Force'", in *Bulletin de la Société française de Philosophie*, 1906, vol. 6, pp. 307, 320.
"Marriage and Eugenics", in *Sociological Papers*, 1906, vol. 2, p. 47.
"On Some Difficulties in the Theory of Transfinite Numbers and Order Types", in *Proceedings of the London Mathematical Society*, 7 March 1906, vol. 4, series 2, pp. 29–53.
"Religion and Metaphysics", in *The Independent Review*, April 1906, vol. 9, pp. 109–116.
"The Theory of Implication", in *American Journal of Mathematics*, April 1906, vol. 28, no. 2, pp. 159–202.
"Les paradoxes de la logique", in *Revue de Métaphysique et de Morale*, September 1906, vol. 14, no. 5, pp. 627–650.
"The Nature of Truth", in *Mind*, October 1906, vol. 15, no. 60, pp. 528–533.
To the Electors of the Wimbledon Division of Surrey, London, George Falkner and Sons, 1907.
"One Some Difficulties in the Theory of Transfinite Numbers and Order Types", in *Proceedings of the London Mathematical Society*, 1907, vols. 2–4, no. 1, pp. 29–53.
"On the Nature of Truth", in *Proceedings of the Aristotelian Society*, 1907, vol. 7, no. 1, pp. 28–49.
"The Development of Morals", in *The Independent Review*, February 1907, vol. 12, pp. 204–210.
"Garibaldi's Defence of the Roman Republic", in *The Edinburgh Review*, April 1907, vol. 205, no. 420, pp. 489–507.
"The Study of Mathematics", in *The New Quarterly*, November 1907, vol. 1, pp. 29–44.
"After the Second Reading", in *Women's Franchise*, 12 March 1908, vol. 1, p. 429.
"Mr. Haldane on Infinity", in *Mind*, April 1908, vol. 17, no. 66, pp. 238–242.
"'If' and 'Imply', a Reply to Mr. MacColl", in *Mind*, April 1908, vol. 17, no. 66, pp. 300–301.
"Mr. Asquith's Pronouncement", in *Women's Franchise*, 28 May 1908, vol. 1, p. 565.
"Mathematical Logic as Based on the Theory of Types", in *American Journal of Mathematics*, July 1908, vol. 30, no. 3, pp. 222–262.
"Liberalism and Women's Suffrage", in *The Contemporary Review*, July 1908, vol. 94, pp. 11–16.
"Determinism and Morals", in *The Hibbert Journal*, October 1908, vol. 7, pp. 113–121.
"Pragmatism", in *The Edinburgh Review*, April 1909, vol. 209, pp. 363–388.

"Should Suffragists Welcome the People's Suffrage Federation?", in *The Common Cause*, 9 December 1909, vol. 1, pp. 463–464.

Philosophical Essays, London-New York-Bombay-Calcutta, Longmans-Green and Company, 1910.

Anti-Suffragist Anxieties, London, People's Suffrage Federation, 1910.

"Ethics", in *The New Quarterly*, February and May 1910, vol. 3, pp. 21–34, 131–143.

"La théorie des types logiques", in *Revue de Métaphysique et de Morale*, May 1910, vol. 18, no. 3, pp. 263–301.

"Some Explanations in Reply to Mr. Bradley", in *Mind*, July 1910, vol. 19, no. 75, pp. 373–378.

"The Philosophy of William James", in *The Nation*, 3 September 1910, vol. 7, pp. 793–794.

"Spinoza", in *The Nation*, 12 November 1910, vol. 8, pp. 278, 280.

"Knowledge by Acquaintance and Knowledge by Description", in *Proceedings of the Aristotelian Society*, 1910–1911, vol. 11, no. 1, pp. 108–128.

"Sur les axiomes de l'infini et du transfini", in *Société Mathématique de France*, 1911, no. 2, pp. 22–35.

"Le réalisme analytique", in *Bulletin de la Société française de Philosophie*, March 1911, vol. 11, pp. 53–82.

"The Basis of Realism", in *Journal of Philosophy, Psychology and Scientific Methods*, 16 March 1911, vol. 8, no. 6, pp. 158–161.

"L'importance philosophique de la logistique", in *Revue de Métaphysique et de Morale*, May 1911, vol. 19, no. 3, pp. 281–291.

"On the Relations of Universals and Particulars", in *Proceedings of the Aristotelian Society*, 1911–1912, vol. 12, no. 1, pp. 1–24.

The Problems of Philosophy, New York-London, Holt and Company-Williams and Norgate, 1912.

"Truth and Falsehood", in M.P. Lynch (ed.), *The Nature of Truth: Classic and Contemporary Perspectives*, Cambridge, MIT Press, 1912, pp. 17–24.

"A Medical Logician", in *The Nation*, 23 March 1912, vol. 10, pp. 1029–1030.

"The Philosophy of Bergson", in *The Monist*, July 1912, vol. 22, no. 3, pp. 321–347.

"Réponse à M. Koyré", in *Revue de Métaphysique et de Morale*, September 1912, vol. 20, pp. 725–726.

"The Essence of Religion", in *The Hibbert Journal*, October 1912, vol. 11, pp. 46–62.

"On the Notion of Cause", in *Proceedings of the Aristotelian Society*, 1912–1913, vol. 13, no. 1, pp. 1–26.

"The Nature of Sense-Data – Reply to Dr. Dawes Hicks", in *Mind*, January 1913, vol. 22, no. 85, pp. 76–81.

"The Twilight of the Absolute", in *The Nation*, 22 February 1913, vol. 12, p. 864.

"Metaphysics and Intuition", in *The Cambridge Review*, 17 April 1913, vol. 34, pp. 376–377.

"Mr. Wildon Carr's Defence of Bergson", in *The Cambridge Magazine*, 26 April 1913, vol. 2, pp. 490, 492.

"Course Descriptions", in *Official Register of Harvard University*, 20 May 1913, vol. 10, no. 1, pp. 16–17, 21.
"Science as an Element in Culture", in *New Statesman*, 24, 31 May 1913, vol. 1, pp. 202–204, 234–236.
"The Philosophical Importance of Mathematical Logic", in *The Monist*, October 1913, vol. 23, no. 4, pp. 481–493.
"The Ordination Service", in *The Cambridge Magazine*, 6 December 1913, vol. 3, pp. 229, 231.
Our Knowledge of the External World as a Field for Scientific Method in Philosophy, London, Allen & Unwin, 1914.
War the Offspring of Fear, London, Union of Democratic Control, 1914.
"Competitive Logic", in *The Nation*, 31 January 1914, vol. 14, pp. 771–772.
"On the Nature of Acquaintance", in *The Monist*, January 1914, vol. 24, no. 1, pp. 1–16; *ib.*, April 1914, vol. 24, no. 2, pp. 161–187; *ib.*, July 1914, vol. 24, no. 3, pp. 435–453.
"Mr. Balfour's Natural Theology", in *The Cambridge Review*, 4 March 1914, vol. 35, pp. 338–339.
"The Relation of Sense-Data to Physics", in *Scientia*, July 1914, vol. 16, pp. 1–27.
"Mysticism and Logic", in *The Hibbert Journal*, July 1914, vol. 12, pp. 780–803.
"Friends of Progress Betrayed, 4 August, 1914", in B. Russell, *The Collected Papers of Bertrand Russell. Prophecy and Dissent, 1914–16*, vol. 13, edited by Richard A. Rempel, London, Routledge, 1988, pp. 3–5.
"The Rights of War", in *The Nation*, 15 August, 1914.
"Will This War End War?", in *The Labour Leader*, 10 September 1914, vol. 11, no. 37, p. 2.
"War: The Cause and the Cure", in *The Labour Leader*, 24 September 1914, vol. 11, no. 39, p. 2.
"Definitions and Methodological Principles in Theory of Knowledge", in *The Monist*, October 1914, vol. 24, no. 4, pp. 582–593.
"Our Foreign Office: The Need of Democratic Control", in *The Labour Leader*, 8 October 1914, vol. 11, no. 41, p. 5.
"Armaments and National Security", in *The Labour Leader*, 15 October 1914, vol. 11, no. 42, p. 5.
"Why Nations Love War", in *War and Peace*, November 1914, vol. 2, no. 14, pp. 20–21.
"Christianity and the War", in *The Labour Leader*, 24 December 1914, vol. 11, no. 52, p. 7.
The Philosophy of Pacifism, London, League of Peace and Freedom, 1915.
The Policy of the Entente, 1904–1914: A Reply to Professor Gilbert Murray, Manchester, The National Labour Press, 1915.
"An Appeal to the Intellectuals of Europe", in *International Review*, 1915, vol. 1, no. 4–5, pp. 145–151, 223–230 (published also in *Justice in War-Time*, pp. 1–19).
"Sensation and Imagination", in *The Monist*, January 1915, vol. 25, no. 1, pp. 28–44.
"The Ethics of War", in *The International Journal of Ethics*, January 1915, vol. 25, no. 2, pp. 127–142.
"Can England and Germany Be Reconciled after the War?", in *The Cambridge Review*, 10 February 1915, vol. 36, pp. 185–186.
"Is a Permanent Peace Possible?", in *The Atlantic Monthly*, March 1915, vol. 115, pp. 367–376.
"A True History of Europe's Last War", in *The Labour Leader*, 11 March 1915, vol. 12, no. 10, p. 5.

"On the Experience of Time", in *The Monist*, April 1915, vol. 25, no. 2, pp. 212–233.
"To Avoid Future Wars", in *The Herald*, 8 May 1915, no. 790, p. 4.
"A Notable Gathering", in *The Cambridge Magazine*, 22 May 1915, vol. 4, p. 419.
"Lord Northcliffe's Triumph", in *The Labour Leader*, 27 May 1915, vol. 12, no. 21, p. 1.
"The Ultimate Constituents of Matter", in *The Monist*, July 1915, vol. 25, no. 3, pp. 399–417.
"The Future of Anglo-German Rivalry", in *The Atlantic Monthly*, July 1915, vol. 116, pp. 127–133.
"Letter from Bertrand Russell", in *The Journal of Philosophy, Psychology and Scientific Methods*, July 1915, vol. 12, no. 14, pp. 391–392.
"War and Non-Resistance", in *The Atlantic Monthly*, August 1915, vol. 116, pp. 266–274.
"On Justice in War-Time, An Appeal to the Intellectuals of Europe", in *The International Review*, 10 August and 1 September 1915, vol. 1, pp. 145–151, 223–230.
"The War and Non-Resistance: A Rejoinder to Professor Perry", in *The International Journal of Ethics*, October 1915, vol. 26, no. 1, pp. 23–30.
"Edith Cavell", in *The Labour Leader*, 28 October 1915, vol. 12, no. 43, p. 3.
"The Nature of the State in View of Its External Relations", in *Proceedings of the Aristotelian Society*, 1915–1916, vol. 16, pp. 301–310.
Justice in War-Time, Chicago-London, The Open Court Publishing Company, 1916.
Principles of Social Reconstructions, London, Allen & Unwin, 1916.
"Conscription", in *The Labour Leader*, 6 January 1916, vol. 13, no. 1, p. 7.
"The Danger to Civilisation", in *The Open Court*, March 1916, vol. 30, pp. 170–180.
"A Clash of Consciences", in *The Nation*, 15 April 1916, vol. 19, p. 76.
"Practical War Economy", in *The Labour Leader*, 20 April 1916, vol. 13, no. 16, p. 6.
"Religion and the Churches", in *The Unpopular Review*, April–June 1916, vol. 5, pp. 392–409.
"War as an Institution", in *The Atlantic Monthly*, May 1916, vol. 117, pp. 603–613.
"Education as a Political Institution", in *The Atlantic Monthly*, June 1916, vol. 117, pp. 750–757.
"Trial of Mr. Bertrand Russell: Brilliant Defence of Anti-Militarists", in *The Labour Leader*, 8 June 1916, vol. 13, no. 23, p. 5.
"Marriage and the Population Question", in *The International Journal of Ethics*, July 1916, vol. 26, no. 4, pp. 443–461.
"What Bertrand Russell Was Not Allowed to Say", in *The Tribunal*, 6 July 1916, no. 16, p. 2.
"British Politics", in *The Ploughshare*, August 1916, vol. 1, pp. 210–213.
"Hon. Bertrand Russell Says When Fate of Constantinople Is Settled", in *Forward*, 5 August 1916, vol. 10, no. 39, p. 3.
"Clifford Allen and Mr. Lloyd George", in *The Tribunal*, 17 August 1916, no. 22, p. 1.
"Mr. Bertrand Russell and the War Office", in *The Manchester Guardian*, 27 September 1916, p. 6.
"An Open Letter to President Wilson", in *Survey*, October 1916–March 1917, vol. 37, pp. 372–373.
"Syllabus of Lectures by Bertrand Russell", in *War and Peace*, October 1916, vol. 4, no. 37, p. 7.
"What We Stand For", in *The Tribunal*, 12 October 1916, no. 30, p. 1.
"The N.C.P. and the Political Outlook", in *The Tribunal*, 7 December 1916, no. 38, p. 2.

"The Momentum of War", in *The Tribunal*, 14 December 1916, no. 39, pp. 1, 3.
Political Ideals, New York, The Century Company, 1917.
Why Men Fight. A Method of Abolishing the International Duel, New York, The Century Company, 1917.
Mysticism and Logic and Other Essays, London, Allen & Unwin, 1917.
"I Appeal unto Caesar", in Id., *The Collected Papers of Bertrand Russell. Prophecy and Dissent, 1914–1916*, 1917, vol. 13, pp. 206–211.
"The Logic of Armaments", in *The Ploughshare*, January 1917, vol. 1, pp. 366–369.
"Two Ideals of Pacifism", in *War and Peace*, January 1917, vol. 4, no. 40, pp. 58–60.
"For Conscience Sake", in *The Independent*, 15 January 1917, vol. 89, pp. 101–103.
"The Future of The Tribunal", in *The Tribunal*, 25 January 1917, no. 44, p. 2.
"Why the War Continues", in *The U.D.C.*, February 1917, vol. 2, pp. 41–42.
"President Wilson's Statement", in *The Tribunal*, 1 February 1917, no. 45, p. 1.
"The Prospects of the N.C.F. in the New Year", in *The Tribunal*, 1 February 1917, no. 45, p. 2.
"The Government and Absolute Exemption", in *The Tribunal*, 8 February 1917, no. 46, p. 2.
"National Service", in *The Tribunal*, 15 February 1917, no. 47, p. 2.
"Liberty and National Service", in *The Tribunal*, 22 February 1917, no. 48, p. 2.
"The Position of the Absolutists", in *The Tribunal*, 1 March 1917, no. 49, p. 2.
"War and Individual Liberty", in *The Tribunal*, 8 March 1917, no. 50, p. 2.
"Saul among the Prophets", in *The Tribunal*, 15 March 1917, no. 51, p. 2.
"Conscientious Objectors", in *The Manchester Guardian*, 19 March 1917, p. 8.
"Russia Leads the Way", in *The Tribunal*, 22 March 1917, no. 52, p. 2.
"The Evils of Persecution", in *The Tribunal*, 29 March 1917, no. 53, p. 2.
"The Conscientious Objector: A Reply to Mr. E.A. Wodehouse", in *The Herald of the Star*, April 1917, vol. 6, pp. 181–183.
"The New Hope", in *The Tribunal*, 5 April 1917, no. 54, p. 2.
"America's Entry into the War", in *The Tribunal*, 19 April 1917, no. 55, p. 1.
"The Importance of Mental Growth", in *The Tribunal*, 19 April 1917, no. 55, p. 2.
"Should the N.C.F. Abstain from All Political Action?", in *The Tribunal*, 26 April 1917, no. 56, p. 2.
"National Independence and Internationalism", in *The Atlantic Monthly*, May 1917, vol. 119, pp. 622–628.
"Message to Russia", in *The Tribunal*, 3 May 1917, no. 57, p. 2.
"Resistance and Service", in *The Tribunal*, 3 May 1917, no. 57, p. 2.
"How to Destroy Prussian Militarism", in *The Tribunal*, 10 May 1917, no. 58, p. 2.
"The Value of Endurance", in *The Tribunal*, 17 May 1917, no. 59, p. 2.
"Russia and Peace", in *The Tribunal*, 24 May 1917, no. 60, p. 2.
"No-Conscription Fellowship", in *News Sheet*, June 1917, no. 9, pp. 7–8.
"Lord Derby and Leeds", in *The Tribunal*, 7 June 1917, no. 61, p. 2.
"The Chances of Peace", in *The Tribunal*, 14 June 1917, no. 62, p. 2.

"The Price of Vengeance", in *The Tribunal*, 21 June 1917, no. 63, p. 2.
"The Military Authorities and the Absolutists", in *The Tribunal*, 28 June 1917, no. 64, p. 2.
"Individual Liberty and Public Control", in *The Atlantic Monthly*, July 1917, vol. 120, pp. 112–120.
"Pacifism and Economic Revolution", in *The Tribunal*, 5 July 1917, no. 65, p. 2.
"The Renewed Ill-Treatment of C.O.'s", in *The Tribunal*, 12 July 1917, no. 66, p. 2.
"A Pacifist Revolution?", in *The Tribunal*, 19 July 1917, no. 67, p. 2.
"Pacifism and Revolution", in *The Tribunal*, 19 July 1917, no. 67, pp. 2–3.
"The Fall of Bethmann-Hollweg", in *The Herald*, 21 July 1917, no. 905, p. 9.
"The International Situation", in *The Tribunal*, 26 July 1917, no. 68, p. 2.
"Chancellor and Premier", in *The Herald*, 28 July 1917, no. 906, p. 9.
"The Russian Revolution and International Relations", in *The U.D.C.*, August 1917, vol. 2, pp. 118–120.
"Crucify Him! Crucify Him!", in *The Tribunal*, 2 August 1917, no. 69, p. 2.
"The International Situation: The Pope's Peace Note", in *The Tribunal*, 23 August 1917, no. 71, pp. 1, 4.
"Imperialist Anxieties", in *The Tribunal*, 30 August 1917, no. 72, p. 2.
"Self-Discipline and Self-Government", in *The Herald of the Star*, September 1917, vol. 6, pp. 484–488.
"Six Months for Spreading Truth", in *The Tribunal*, 6 September 1917, no. 73, p. 2.
"Secret Diplomacy", in *The Tribunal*, 13 September 1917, no. 74, p. 2.
"The Charge of Anarchy", in *The Tribunal*, 20 September 1917, no. 75, p. 2.
"The Kaiser's Reply to the Pope", in *The Tribunal*, 27 September 1917, no. 76, p. 2.
"Is Nationalism Moribund?", in *The Seven Arts*, October 1917, vol. 2, no. 12, pp. 673–687.
"Asia and the War", in *The Tribunal*, 4 October 1917, no. 77, p. 2.
"The Times on Revolution", in *The Pioneer*, 6 October 1917, no. 342, p. 1.
"Count Czernin's Speech", in *The Tribunal*, 11 October 1917, no. 78, p. 2.
"A Valuable Suggestion by the Bishop of Exeter", in *The Tribunal*, 18 October 1917, no. 79, p. 2.
"The People and Peace", in *The Tribunal*, 25 October 1917, no. 80, p. 2.
"Saul among the Prophets", in *The Tribunal*, 1 November 1917, no. 81, p. 2.
"Will Conscription Continue After the War?", in *The Tribunal*, 8 November 1917, no. 82, p. 2.
"The International Outlook", in *The Pioneer*, 10 November 1917, no. 347, p. 3.
"A New Tribunal for Gaol Delivery", in *The Tribunal*, 15 November 1917, no. 83, p. 2.
"Who Is the British Bolo?", in *The Tribunal*, 22 November 1917, no. 84, p. 2.
"Boloism in Power", in *The Tribunal*, 29 November 1917, no. 85, p. 2.
"The Sanctity of Conscience", in *The Herald*, 1 December 1917, no. 924, p. 19.
"Lord Lansdowne's Letter", in *The Tribunal*, 6 December 1917, no. 86, p. 2.
"The Government's 'Concessions'", in *The Tribunal*, 13 December 1917, no. 87, p. 2.
"Freedom or Victory?", in *The Pioneer*, 15 December 1917, no. 352, p. 2.
"International Opinion During 1917", in *The Tribunal*, 27 December 1917, no. 89, pp. 1, 3.
Roads to Freedom: Socialism, Anarchism, and Syndicalism, London, Allen & Unwin, 1918.

"The German Peace Offer", in *The Tribunal*, 3 January 1918, no. 90, p. 1.
"The Bolsheviks and Mr. Lloyd George", in *The Tribunal*, 10 January 1918, no. 91, p. 2.
"Human Character and Social Institutions", in *The Ploughshare*, May 1918, vol. 3, pp. 100–104.
"The Philosophy of Logical Atomism (Lectures 1–2)", in *The Monist*, October 1918, vol. 28, no. 4, pp. 495–527.
Introduction to the Mathematical Philosophy, London-New York, Allen & Unwin-Macmillan, 1919.
"Professor Dewey's 'Essays in Experimental Logic'", in *The Journal of Philosophy, Psychology and Scientific Methods*, 1919, vol. 16, no. 1, pp. 5–26.
"On Propositions: What They Are and How They Mean", in *Proceedings of the Aristotelian Society, Supplementary Volumes*, 1919, vol. 2, pp. 1–43.
"The Philosophy of Logical Atomism (Lectures 3–4)", in *The Monist*, January 1919, vol. 29, no. 1, pp. 32–63.
"On 'Bad Passions'", in *The Cambridge Magazine*, 1 February 1919, vol. 8, pp. 491–492.
"Why Are the C.O.'s Not Released?", in *The Labour Leader*, 6 February 1919, vol. 16, no. 6, p. 7.
"The Philosophy of Logical Atomism (Lectures 5–6)", in *The Monist*, April 1919, vol. 29, no. 2, pp. 190–222.
"Dreams and Facts", in *The Athenaeum*, 18 and 25 April 1919, no. 4642–4643, pp. 198–199, 232–233.
"What the Conscientious Objector Has Achieved", in *The Tribunal*, 24 April 1919, no. 154, p. 2.
"Democracy and Direct Action", in *The English Review*, May 1919, vol. 28, pp. 396–403.
"New Powers and Old Frontiers", in *The Nation*, 7 June 1919, vol. 25, p. 2935.
"The Philosophy of Logical Atomism (Lectures 7–8)", in *The Monist*, July 1919, vol. 29, no. 3, pp. 345–380.
"Why I Am a Guildsman", in *The Guildsman: a Journal of Social and Industrial Freedom*, September 1919, no. 33, p. 3.
"The Analysis of Mind", in *Morley College Magazine*, November 1919, vol. 29, pp. 30–35.
"Einstein's Theory of Gravitation", in *The Athenaeum*, 14 November 1919, no. 4672, p. 1189.
"The Philosopher King", in *The Athenaeum*, 21 November 1919, no. 4673, p. 1221.
"The Anatomy of Desire", in *The Athenaeum*, 12, 19 and 26 December 1919, no. 4676–4677–4678, pp. 1340–1341, 1372–1373, 1402–1403.
The Practice and Theory of Bolshevism, London, Allen & Unwin, 1920.
"The Relativity Theory of Gravitation", in *The English Review*, January 1920, vol. 30, pp. 11–18.
"What the C.O. Stands For", in *The Tribunal*, 8 January 1920, no. 182, p. 9.
"La Civilisation et la lutte des classes", in *Clarté*, 21 February 1920, no. 11, p. 1.
"Food and the Man", in *McCall's Magazine*, April 1920, vol. 47, no. 8, p. 24.
"Socialism and Liberal Ideals", in *The English Review*, May–June 1920, vol. 30, pp. 449–455, 499–508.
"Impressions of Bolshevik Russia", in *The Nation*, 10, 17, 24, 31 July and 7 August 1920, vol. 27, pp. 460–462, 493–494, 520–521, 547–548, 576–577.

"British Labour Delegation to Russia and the Illness of Mr. Clifford Allen", in *The Lancet*, 17 July 1920, vol. 199, pp. 159–160.
"Why Russia Endures Bolshevism", in *Illustrated Sunday Herald*, 8 August 1920, p. 5.
"Daily Life in Moscow", in *Common Sense*, 4 September 1920, vol. 9, p. 122.
"Bolshevik Theory", in *The New Republic*, 15 September, 3 and 17 November 1920, vol. 24, pp. 67–69, 239–241, 296–298.
"The Meaning of 'Meaning'", in *Mind*, October 1920, vol. 29, no. 116, pp. 398–404.
"Industry in Undeveloped Countries", in *The Chinese Social and Political Science Review*, December 1920, vol. 5, pp. 239–254.
"First Impressions of China", in *The Peking Leader*, 16 December 1920.
The Analysis of Mind, London-New York, Allen & Unwin-Macmillan, 1921.
"The Happiness of China", in *The Nation*, 8 January 1921, vol. 28, pp. 505–506.
"The Prospects of Bolshevik Russia", in *Kaizo*, February 1921, vol. 3, no. 2, pp. 1–14.
"Causes of the Present Chaos", in *Kaizo*, March 1921, vol. 3, no. 3, p. 116.
"Why I Support the Labour Party", in *Labour Leader*, 17 March 1921, p. 1.
"What Makes a Social System Good or Bad?", in *Kaizo*, April 1921, vol. 3, no. 4, pp. 1–16.
"Some Traits in the Chinese Character", in *The Atlantic Monthly*, July–December 1921, vol. 128, no. 6, pp. 771–777.
"China's Road to Freedom", in *The Peking Leader*, 7 July 1921, p. 3.
"Inherent Tendencies of Industrialism", in *Kaizo*, August 1921, vol. 3, no. 9, pp. 1–15.
"Industrialism and Private Property", in *Kaizo*, September 1921, vol. 3, no. 10, pp. 109–119.
"Interactions of Industrialism and Nationalism", in *Kaizo*, October 1921, vol. 3, no. 11, pp. 123–137.
"Communist Ideals", in *The Daily Herald*, 19 October 1921, p. 4.
"China and the Powers", in *Foreign Affairs*, November 1921, vol. 3, pp. 69–70.
"The Future of China", in *The Labour News*, 10 November 1921, p. 1.
"A Plea for China", in *The Sun*, 24 November 1921, p. 8.
"China and Chinese Influence", in *The Manchester Guardian*, 29 November 1921, p. 6.
"The Problems of China", in *The Manchester Guardian*, 30 November 1921, p. 6.
"Chinese Independence", in *The Manchester Guardian*, 2 December 1921, p. 16.
"Sketches of Modern China", in *The Nation and the Athenaeum*, 3, 10 and 17 December 1921, pp. 375–376, 429–430, 461–463.
"'Vorwort', Logisch-philosophische Abhandlung von Ludwig Wittgenstein", in *Annalen der Naturphilosophie*, 14 December 1921, vol. 14, pp. 186–198.
"How Washington Could Help China", in *Daily Herald*, 16 December 1921, p. 4.
The Problem of China, London, Allen & Unwin, 1922.
Free Thought and Official Propaganda: Delivered at South Place Institute on March 24, 1922, London, Watts, 1922.
"The Chinese Intelligentsia", in *Time and Tide*, 13 January 1922, vol. 3, pp. 29–31.
"Present Anglo-American Policy in China", in *Daily Herald*, 26 January 1922, p. 4.

"Reconstruction in China", in *The Chinese Students' Monthly*, February 1922, vol. 17, pp. 283–285.
"The Washington Conference and the Future", in *Kaizo*, March 1922, vol. 4, no. 3, pp. 135–147.
"As a European Radical Sees It", in *The Freeman*, 8 March 1922, vol. 4, pp. 608–610.
"Hopes and Fears as Regards America", in *The New Republic*, 15 and 22 March 1922, vol. 30, pp. 70–72, 99–101.
"Chinese Civilization and the West", in *The Dial*, April 1922, vol. 72, no. 4, pp. 356–364.
"Socialism in Undeveloped Countries", in *The Atlantic Monthly*, May 1922, vol. 129, pp. 664–671.
"The Prevention of War", in *No More War*, June 1922, vol. 1, no. 5, p. 5.
"How Can Internationalism Be Brought About?", in *The Century Magazine*, June 1922, vol. 104, pp. 195–202.
"Socialism in Advanced Countries", in *Kaizo*, July 1922, vol. 4, no. 7, pp. 104–114.
"The World and the War-Dragon: Next War Would Wipe Out Civilization. Have the People Learned Their Lesson?", in *Labour Leader*, 27 July 1922, vol. 19, no. 30, p. 5.
"Chinese Problems", in *The Labour Magazine*, September 1922, vol. 1, pp. 229–231.
"The Theory of Relativity", in *Kaizo*, October 1922, vol. 4, no. 10, pp. 61–73.
"Physics and Perception", in *Mind*, October 1922, vol. 31, no. 124, pp. 478–485.
"Toward an Understanding of China", in *Century Magazine*, October 1922, vol. 104, pp. 912–916.
"Bring Us Peace: An Appeal to American Students", in *The New Student*, 7 October 1922, vol. 2, no. 1, pp. 1–2.
"Motive in Industry: A Reply to Professor Einstein", in *The New Leader*, 13 October 1922, vol. 1, no. 2, pp. 11–12.
"The Outlook for China", in *The Century Magazine*, November 1922, vol. 105, pp. 141–146.
"Instinct and the Unconscious", in *The New Leader*, 3 November 1922, vol. 1, no. 5, p. 12.
"Dr. Schiller's Analysis of The Analysis of Mind", in *Journal of Philosophy*, 23 November 1922, vol. 19, no. 24, pp. 645–651.
"Herd Instinct and Acquisitiveness", in *The New Leader*, 15 December 1922, vol. 1, no. 11, p. 10.
The Prospects of Industrial Civilization, in collaboration with Dora Russell, London, Allen & Unwin, 1923.
The ABC of Atoms, New York, Dutton & Company, 1923.
"Can Men Be Rational?", in *The Rationalist Annual*, 1923, pp. 23–28.
"Bertrand Russell Hits Back", in *The New Generation*, January 1923, vol. 2, p. 12.
"Lord Balfour on Methodological Doubt", in *The Nation and the Athenaeum*, 6 January 1923, vol. 32, pp. 542–544.
"Freedom in Education: A Protest Against Mechanism", in *The Dial*, February 1923, vol. 74, no. 2, pp. 153–164.
"The Structure of the Atom", in *The New Leader*, 9, 16, 23 February – 2, 9 March 1923, vol. 2, no. 6–10, pp. 10–11, 11–12, 10–11, 10–11, 14–15.
"Birth Control and the Law", in *The Arena*, March 1923, vol. 1, no. 1, pp. 8–9.
"Una Revista de la Situación Europea", in *La Nación*, 4 March 1923, sec. 2, p. 13.
"The Boxer Indemnity and Chinese Education", in *The Manchester Guardian*, 4 April 1923, p. 12.

"The Sources of Power", in *The Freeman*, 2, 9, 16 May 1923, vol. 7, pp. 176–179, 200–202, 224–226.
"Vagueness", in *The Australasian Journal of Psychology and Philosophy*, June 1923, vol. 1, no. 2, pp. 84–92.
"Preparándonos para la Guerra Próxima", in *La Nación*, 8 July 1923, sec. 3, p. 2.
"Slavery or Self-Extermination: A Forecast of Europe's Future", in *The Nation*, 11 July 1923, vol. 117, pp. 32–34.
"Leisure and Mechanism", in *The Dial*, August 1923, vol. 75, no. 2, pp. 105–122.
"Posibilidades del Fascismo", in *La Nación*, 1 August 1923, sec. 1, p. 4.
"Labour and the Universities: A Practical Policy", in *The New Leader*, 14 September 1923, vol. 4, no. 11, p. 4.
"Life as an Art", in *The Outlook*, 15 September 1923, vol. 52, pp. 213–214.
"The Atom: Its Structure and Its Problems", in *The Observer*, 16 September 1923, p. 9.
"An Essay on Behaviourism", in *Vanity Fair*, October 1923, vol. 21, no. 2, pp. 47, 96, 98.
"Workhouse for Disabled!", in *Daily Herald*, 1 October 1923, p. 6.
"La Carrera de Europa Hacia el Desastre", in *La Nación*, 7 October 1923, sec. 3, p. 3.
"En Torno a la Nota Britanica del 13 de Agosto", in *La Nación*, 14 October 1923, sec. 3, p. 2.
"The Revival of Puritanism", in *The Freeman*, 17 October 1923, vol. 8, pp. 128–130.
"El Fracaso de la Legalidad Internacional", in *La Nación*, 28 October 1923, sec. 3, p. 2.
"Socialism and Birth Control", in *The New Generation*, November 1923, vol. 2, p. 127.
"Science and Civilisation", in *Daily Herald*, 16, 19, 20, 21 November 1923, p. 4.
"Mr. Baldwin ante las Elecciones Generales", in *La Nación*, 25 November 1923, sec. 3, p. 2.
"Las Dificultades Económicas de Gran Bretaña", in *La Nación*, 30 December 1923, sec. 3, p. 2.
Icarus or The Future of Science, London-New York, Kegan Paul-Trench-Trubner & Co., 1924.
"Logical Atomism", in J.H. Muirhead, *Contemporary British Philosophers*, London, Allen & Unwin, 1924, pp. 356–383.
"Dogmatic and Scientific Ethics", in *The Outlook*, 5 January 1924, vol. 53, pp. 9–10.
"The Need for Political Scepticism", in *The Freeman*, 23, 30 January 1924, vol. 8, pp. 464–467, 489–490.
"An Impression of Lenin", in *The New Leader*, 25 January 1924, vol. 6, no. 4, p. 3.
"The Case Against Islam", in *The Nation and the Athenaeum*, 16 February 1924, vol. 34, p. 704.
"Psychology and Politics", in *The Outlook*, 23 February 1924, vol. 53, pp. 124–126.
"Lo que puede y lo que no puede hacer un gobierno laborista", in *La Nación*, 24 February 1924, sec. 3, p. 2.
"How to Read History", in *The Bermondsey Book*, March 1924, vol. 1, no. 2, pp. 10–13.
"Machines and the Emotions", in *The Outlook*, 22 March 1924, vol. 53, pp. 200–202.
"Problemas internos del gobierno laborista", in *La Nación*, 23 March 1924, sec. 3, pp. 1–2.
"If We Are to Prevent the Next War", in *The Century Magazine*, May 1924, vol. 108, pp. 3–12.
"Bertrand Russell expone las consecuencias del informe de Dawes", in *La Nación*, 18 May 1924, sec. 3, p. 2.

"Por primera vez, desde 1914, hay indicios de una verdadera paz en Europa", in *La Nación*, 6 July 1924, sec. 3, p. 2.
"Impressions of America", in *The New Leader*, 22 August 1924, vol. 8, no. 8, pp. 4–5.
"Los problemas internacionales que debe ir resolviendo Macdonald", in *La Nación*, 31 August 1924, sec. 3, p. 1.
"British Imperialism in China", in *The New Leader*, 19 September 1924, vol. 8, no. 12, p. 3.
"Philosophy in the Twentieth Century", in *The Dial*, October 1924, vol. 77, no. 4, pp. 271–290.
"Materialism, Past and Present", in *Psyche*, October 1924, vol. 5, pp. 111–120.
"Future Cultural Relations of East and West", in *The New Orient*, October–December 1924, vol. 2, no. 2, pp. 1–6.
"The American Intelligentsia", in *The Nation and the Athenaeum*, 11 October 1924, vol. 36, pp. 50–51.
"Why I Believe in Labour: A Great Work Begun", in *The New Leader*, 17 October 1924, vol. 9, no. 3, p. 10.
"La Restauración de la Paz en Europa", in *La Nación*, 23 October 1924, sec. 1, p. 6.
"The International Debate of the Day!", in *Life and Letters*, November 1924, vol. 3, no. 3, pp. 1, 4–8.
"Sobre la Democracia y el Gobierno", in *La Nación*, 9 November 1924, sec. 3, p. 5.
"Under Which Flag?", in *The New Leader*, 21 November 1924, vol. 9, no. 8, p. 6.
"Los Resultados del Primer Gobierno Laborista", in *La Nación*, 23 November 1924, sec. 3, p. 2.
"Préface à La Géométrie dans le monde sensible de Jean Nicod", in *Revue Philosophique*, November–December 1924, vol. 98, pp. 450–454.
"Freedom or Authority in Education", in *The Century Magazine*, December 1924, vol. 109, pp. 172–180.
"Appreciation of E.D. Morel", in *Foreign Affairs*, December 1924, vol. 6, p. 125.
"The Far Eastern Problem", in *Foreign Affairs*, December 1924, vol. 6, pp. 131–132.
"Why He Distrusts 'Gentlemen'", in *Daily Herald*, 3 December 1924, p. 9.
"Anguiskie Poutiki i Pisateli ob Otkaze Konservativnogo Pravitelstva Ratifitsirovat Anglo-Sovetskii Dogover", in *Izvestiia*, 10 December 1924, p. 1.
"A Dawes Plan for China?", in *The New Leader*, 26 December 1924, vol. 9, no. 13, p. 6.
"British Labor's Lesson", in *The New Republic*, 31 December 1924, vol. 41, pp. 138–139.
The ABC of Relativity, New York, Harper & Brothers, 1925.
What I Believe, New York, Dutton & Company, 1925.
"El Nuevo Gobierno Británico", in *La Nación*, 13 January 1925, sec. 1, p. 4.
"La Política Británica Bajo el Nuevo Gobierno", in *La Nación*, 16 February 1925, sec. 1, p. 4.
"Socialism and Education", in *The Socialist Review*, March 1925, vol. 25, pp. 124–134.
"The Novels We Read", in *John O'London's Weekly*, 28 March 1925, vol. 12, p. 951.
"El Imperio Britanico y la Liga de las Naciones", in *La Nación*, 10 May 1925, sec. 3, p. 2.
"The Chinese Amritsar", in *The New Leader*, 19 June 1925, vol. 11, no. 12, p. 9.
"Is the Universe Finite?", in *Psyche*, July 1925, vol. 6, pp. 46–51.

"Deliver China from Her Bondage: Peace or Shame for Britain", in *The New Leader*, 10 July 1925, vol. 12, no. 2, pp. 3–4.
"Fair Play for the Chinese: We Can Only Hurt Ourselves as well as Them by Refusing It", in *Daily Herald*, 18 July 1925, p. 7.
"British Policy in China", in *The Nation and the Athenaeum*, 18 July 1925, vol. 37, pp. 480–482.
"China Asserts Herself", in *The New Leader*, 28 August 1925, vol. 12, no. 9, p. 9.
On Education, Especially in Early Childhood, London, Allen & Unwin, 1926.
"Perception", in *Journal of Philosophical Studies*, January 1926, vol. 1, no. 1, pp. 78–86.
"Psychology and Politics", in *The Dial*, March 1926, vol. 80, no. 3, pp. 179–188.
"Freedom in Society", in *Harper's Magazine*, March 1926, vol. 152, pp. 438–444.
"What is Happening in China?", in *The Socialist Review*, March 1926, no. 2, pp. 11–18.
"What Shall We Educate For?", in *Harper's Magazine*, April 1926, vol. 152, pp. 586–597.
"A Vigorous Attempt to Free Education from the Taint of Class", in *Daily Herald*, 28 April 1926, p. 9.
"Capitalism – Or What?", in *The Bankers Magazine*, May 1926, vol. 112, pp. 679–680, 725, 727.
"On the Use of a General Strike", in *The New Leader*, 28 May 1926, vol. 13, no. 33, pp. 3–4.
"Bertrand Russell Tells How General Strike Affected the British People", in *Jewish Daily Forward*, 30 May 1926, p. 1.
"Bertrand Russell Tells Why England Is Friendly to Jews", in *Jewish Daily Forward*, 27 June 1926, p. 1.
"Is Carlyle's Fame Enduring?", in *Daily Herald*, 7 July 1926, p. 9.
"Bertrand Russell Explains True Meaning of Education", in *Jewish Daily Forward*, 1 August 1926, p. 1.
"When Science Rules Us", in *The Sunday Chronicle*, 5 September 1926, p. 8.
"Bertrand Russell Thinks America Will Rule the World in the Future", in *Jewish Daily Forward*, 12 September 1926, p. 1.
"The White Peril in China", in *The New Leader*, 17 September 1926, vol. 13, no. 49, pp. 9–10.
"The Harm That Good Men Do", in *Harper's Magazine*, October 1926, vol. 153, pp. 529–534.
"What I Think of America", in *Jewish Daily Forward*, 31 October 1926, p. 1.
"Behaviorism: Its Effect on Ordinary Mortals Should It Become a Craze", in *The Century Magazine*, December 1926, vol. 113, pp. 148–153.
"Are We Living in a Decadent Age?", in *Jewish Daily Forward*, 5 December 1926, p. 1.
"The Institution of Marriage Is Here to Stay", in *Jewish Daily Forward*, 19 December 1926, p. 1.
The Analysis of Matter, London-New York, Kegan Paul-Trench-Trubner & Co., 1927.
An Outline of Philosophy, London, Allen & Unwin, 1927.
Why I Am Not a Christian, London, Rationalist Press, 1927.
Selected Papers of Bertrand Russell, New York, The Modern Library, 1927.
Philosophy, New York, Norton & Co., 1927.
"Substance", in *Journal of Philosophical Studies*, January 1927, vol. 2, no. 5, pp. 20–27.
"Rewards and Punishments in Education", in *The Teachers World*, 14 January 1927, pp. 797, 815.

"Bertrand Russell on the Decalogue", in *Jewish Daily Forward*, 23 January 1927, pp. 1, 3.
"The Case for Withdrawing Our Forces", in *New Leader*, 4 February 1927, vol. 14, no. 15, p. 10.
"Where Is China Going?", in *Jewish Daily Forward*, 13 February 1927, p. 1.
"Democracy of the Future", in *The Oriental Magazine*, March 1927, vol. 1, pp. 3–5.
"British Folly in China", in *The Nation*, 2 March 1927, vol. 124, pp. 227–228.
"Why Psychoanalysis Is Popular", in *Jewish Daily Forward*, 13 March 1927, pp. 1–2.
"From the Stone Age to 1927", in *The Sunday Chronicle*, 20 March 1927, p. 3.
"Events, Matter, and Mind", in *The Referee*, 27 March 1927, p. 9.
"Had Newton Never Lived", in *The Radio Times*, 8 April 1927, vol. 15, pp. 49–50.
"Is Literature a Dead Art?", in *Jewish Daily Forward*, 10 April 1927, p. 1.
"Bertrand Russell's Confession of Faith", in *Jewish Daily Forward*, 24 April 1927, pp. 3, 11.
"The Danger of Creed Wars", in *The Socialist Review*, May 1927, no. 16, pp. 7–19.
"The Babies Nobody Wants: But Is Sterilization the Way to Avoid Them?", in *The Sunday Chronicle*, 8 May 1927, p. 3.
"The New Life That Is America's", in *The New York Times*, 22 May 1927, sec. 4, pp. 1–2.
"Are Men and Women Equal?", in *Jewish Daily Forward*, 12 June 1927, p. 1.
"The Future", in *Jewish Daily Forward*, 26 June – 3, 10, 17 July 1927, pp. 1, 1, 1–2, 2.
"The Training of Young Children", in *Harper's Magazine*, August 1927, vol. 155, pp. 313–319.
"Russell Opposed to Bolshevism", in *Jewish Daily Forward*, 7 August 1927, pp. 1, 3.
"Things That Have Moulded Me", in *The Dial*, September 1927, vol. 83, no. 3, pp. 181–186.
"British Aristocracy Will Last as Long as the Monarchy", in *Jewish Daily Forward*, 18 September 1927, p. 1.
"A Bold Experiment in Child Education", in *The New York Times*, 2 October 1927, sec. 4, pp. 8–9, 22.
"Are Old Men Fit to Rule the World?", in *Jewish Daily Forward*, 9 October 1927, pp. 1, 4.
"A Real Philosopher", in *The City College Alumnus*, November 1927, vol. 23, p. 378.
"Russell Tells Why Eugenics Is Not Popular", in *Jewish Daily Forward*, 13 November 1927, pp. 1, 4.
"Education Without Sex Taboos", in *The New Republic*, 16 November 1927, vol. 52, pp. 346–348.
"Does the World Progress?", in *Jewish Daily Forward*, 4 December 1927, pp. 1, 3.
Sceptical Essays, London, Allen & Unwin, 1928.
"Bertrand Russell Catches the Tortoise", in *The Forum*, February 1928, vol. 79, pp. 262–263.
"The Road to Universal Peace", in *Jewish Daily Forward*, 26 February 1928, pp. 1–2.
"Is America Giving a Chance to Individuality?", in *Nation's Business*, March 1928, vol. 16, no. 3, pp. 23–24, 121–123.
"My Own View of Marriage", in *The Outlook*, 7 March 1928, vol. 148, pp. 376–377.
"Is Life Worth Living?", in *Jewish Daily Forward*, 25 March 1928, p. 1.
"How Will Science Change Morals?", in *The Menorah Journal*, April 1928, vol. 14, pp. 321–329.
"Nationalism – Is It a Blessing or a Curse?", in *Jewish Daily Forward*, 6 May 1928, p. 1.
"Optimistic America", in *New York Herald Tribune*, 6 May 1928, sec. 13, pp. 1–2.

"Physics and Metaphysics", in *The Saturday Review of Literature*, 26 May 1928, vol. 4, pp. 910–911.
"Bertrand Russell on Future of Science", in *Jewish Daily Forward*, 17 June 1928, p. 1.
"World's Greatest Need Is Permanent Peace", in *Jewish Daily Forward*, 24 June 1928, pp. 1–2.
"The Hon. Bertrand Russell", in *The Literary Guide and Rationalist Review*, July 1928, no. 385, pp. 122–123.
"School and the Very Young Child", in *The Outlook*, 11 July 1928, vol. 149, pp. 418–420, 433.
"Tolstoy – A Modern Hebrew Prophet", in *Jewish Daily Forward*, 9 September 1928, p. 1.
"The Value of Skepticism", in *Plain Talk*, October 1928, vol. 3, pp. 423–430.
"Romance – And So to the Divorce Court!", in *The Evening News*, 20 October 1928, p. 8.
"On Catholic and Protestant Sceptics", in *Life and Letters*, November 1928, vol. 1, no. 6, pp. 468–476.
"What Faith Means", in *Cassell's Magazine*, December 1928, no. 201, pp. 34–41.
"For Better or Worse – The Choice before Mankind", in *Daily Herald*, 7 December 1928, p. 4.
"Science and Education", in *St. Louis Post-Dispatch*, 9 December 1928, suppl. pp. 4–5.
"The Americanization of Europe Is Inevitable", in *Jewish Daily Forward*, 9 December 1928, pp. 1–2.
"Bertrand Russell on Aims of Modern Education", in *Jewish Daily Forward*, 23 December 1928, pp. 1–2.
Has Religion Made Useful Contributions to Civilizations?, Girard, Haldeman-Julius, 1929.
Marriage and Morals, London, Allen & Unwin, 1929.
"The Grave Mistake of Inculcating Fear", in *The Daily Telegraph*, 4 January 1929, p. 8.
"Has Man A Soul?", in *Jewish Daily Forward*, 10 February 1929, p. 1.
"Why Mr. Wood Is Not a Freethinker", in *The Literary Guide and Rationalist Review*, March 1929, no. 393, pp. 47–48.
"Your Child and the Fear of Death", in *The Forum*, March 1929, vol. 81, no. 3, pp. 174–178.
"When Bertrand Russell Goes to the Movies", in *Jewish Daily Forward*, 24 March 1929, pp. 1–2.
"Russell on Westernization of Turkey", in *Jewish Daily Forward*, 7 April 1929, p. 1.
"Confessions", in *The Little Review*, May 1929, vol. 12, no. 2, pp. 72–73.
"Is Religion Desirable?", in *Everyman*, 9 May 1929, vol. 1, no. 15, p. 5.
"Does Mankind Need a New God?", in *Jewish Daily Forward*, 19 May 1929, pp. 1–2.
"Has Religion Made Useful Contributions to Civilization?", in *The Debunker*, June 1929, vol. 10, no. 1, pp. 3–16.
"Russell Sees Menace in Lateran Treaties", in *Jewish Daily Forward*, 2 June 1929, pp. 1–2.
"Socialist Government in England", in *Jewish Daily Forward*, 9 June 1929, pp. 1–2.
"What Is Western Civilization?", in *Scientia*, July 1929, vol. 46, no. 7, pp. 35–41.
"The Twilight of Science", in *The Century Magazine*, July 1929, vol. 118, no. 3, pp. 311–315.
"How I Came by My Creed", in *The Realist*, September 1929, vol. 1, no. 6, pp. 14–29.
"The Sedentary Age", in *Illustrated, Nation's Business*, September 1929, vol. 17, no. 10, pp. 35–37, 142.

"MacDonald Government Makes Rapid Strides – Russell", in *Jewish Daily Forward*, 8 September 1929, pp. 1–2.
"What You Should Know About – Marriage and Sex", in *T.P.'s Weekly*, 26 October 1929, vol. 13, no. 313, p. 4.
"Anatole France", in *Tambour*, Novembre 1929, no. 5, pp. 30–31.
"Religion and Morals", in *Jewish Daily Forward*, 3 November 1929, pp. 1–2.
"Idealism for Children", in *The Saturday Review of Literature*, 14 December 1929, vol. 6, p. 575.
The Conquest of Happiness, London, Allen & Unwin, 1930.
"British Philosopher Explains Why So Many Modern Marriages Are Thoroughgoing Failures", in *Jewish Daily Forward*, 19 January 1930, pp. 1–2.
"Bertrand Russell the Famous Philosopher and Writer Advocates Mutual Consent as the Soundest Reason for Dissolving Marriage", in *Daily Express*, 20 January 1930, p. 8.
"Homogeneous America", in *The Outlook and Independent*, 19 February 1930, vol. 154, pp. 285–287, 318.
"Bertrand Russell Tells How He Was Educated as a Child", in *Jewish Daily Forward*, 9 March 1930, pp. 1–2.
"Politics and Theology", in *The Political Quarterly*, April 1930, vol. 1, no. 2, pp. 179–185.
"My Ten Commandments", in *Everyman*, 3 April 1930, vol. 3, no. 62, pp. 291, 296.
"Your Child in the School Room", in *The Household Magazine*, May 1930, vol. 30, no. 5, pp. 3, 46.
"Are Parents Bad for Children?", in *The Parents' Magazine*, May 1930, vol. 5, no. 5, pp. 18–19, 69.
"Why Is Modern Youth Cynical?", in *Harper's Magazine*, May 1930, vol. 160, pp. 720–724.
"What I Am Teaching My Children about War", in *Daily Express*, 1 May 1930, p. 10.
"Will the British Empire Last?", in *Jewish Daily Forward*, 11 May 1930, p. 1.
"Bertrand Russell Despairs of Europe's Future", in *Jewish Daily Forward*, 13 July 1930, pp. 1–2.
"Heads or Tails", in *The Atlantic Monthly*, August 1930, vol. 146, pp. 163–170.
"Russell on True Function of Modern Education", in *Jewish Daily Forward*, 24 August 1930, p. 1.
"Do Men Want Children?", in *The Parents' Magazine*, October 1930, vol. 5, no. 10, pp. 14–15.
"Thirty Years from Now", in *The Virginia Quarterly Review*, October 1930, vol. 6, no. 4, pp. 575–585.
"Symposium on War Responsibility", in *The World Tomorrow*, October 1930, vol. 13, pp. 399–400.
"Religion and Happiness", in *The Spectator*, 15 November 1930, vol. 145, pp. 714–715.
The Scientific Outlook, London, Allen & Unwin, 1931.
"Barriers to Culture", in *The Clarion*, 3 January 1931, pp. 7–8.
"Don't Tell the Children, Children and the Truth", in *Child Study*, February 1931, vol. 8, pp. 161–162.
"What I Believe", in *The Nation*, 29 April 1931, vol. 132, pp. 469–471.
"Free Speech in Childhood", in *The New Statesman and Nation*, 30 May 1931, vol. 1, pp. 486–488.
"On a Survey of Clergymen's Attitudes Towards War", in *The World Tomorrow*, June 1931, vol. 14, pp. 196–197.
"Modern Tendencies in Education", in *The Spectator*, 13 June 1931, vol. 146, pp. 926–927.

"Nice People", in *Harper's Magazine*, July 1931, vol. 163, pp. 226–230.
"Sex and Happiness", in *New York American*, 5 August 1931, p. 15.
"In Praise of Artificiality", in *New York American*, 9 September 1931, p. 15.
"Who May Use Lipstick?", in *New York American*, 14 September 1931, p. 13.
"Hope and Fear", in *New York American*, 7 October 1931, p. 17.
"Are Criminals Worse Than Other People?", in *New York American*, 29 October 1931, p. 15.
"The Advantages of Cowardice", in *New York American*, 2 November 1931, p. 13.
"The Decay of Meditation", in *New York American*, 4 November 1931, p. 17.
"Whose Admiration Do You Desire?", in *Nash's Pall Mall Magazine*, December 1931, vol. 88, p. 8.
"Who Gets Our Savings?", in *New York American*, 1 December 1931, p. 13.
"On Politicians", in *New York American*, 16 December 1931, p. 17.
"Keeping Pace?", in *New York American*, 23 December 1931, p. 15.
Education and the Social Order, London, Allen & Unwin, 1932.
"Christmas at Sea", in *New York American*, 13 January 1932, p. 17.
"How Science Has Changed Society", in *The Listener*, 13 January 1932, vol. 7, pp. 39–42.
"On National Greatness", in *New York American*, 20 January 1932, p. 15.
"Is the World Going Mad?", in *New York American*, 27 January 1932, p. 13.
"Are We Too Passive?", in *New York American*, 3 February 1932, p. 13.
"Why We Enjoy Mishaps", in *New York American*, 10 February 1932, p. 15.
"Does Education Do Harm?", in *New York American*, 17 February 1932, p. 15.
"Do Scientists Err?", in *New York American*, 24 February 1932, p. 13.
"Why We Read", in *New York American*, 2 March 1932, p. 13.
"Illegal? On Attempted Suicide", in *New York American*, 9 March 1932, p. 17.
"Will Capitalism Crash?", in *The New Leader*, 18 March 1932, vol. 21, no. 10, p. 4.
"As Others See Us", in *New York American*, 23 March 1932, p. 15.
"Taking Long Views", in *New York American*, 30 March 1932, p. 13.
"How to End War", in *New World: Journal of the No More War Movement*, April 1932, vol. 2, no. 12, pp. 1–2.
"Sex Education in Schools", in *The New Generation*, April 1932, vol. 11, no. 4, p. 38.
"On Mental Differences", in *New York American*, 6 April 1932, p. 13.
"On the Fierceness of Vegetarians", in *New York American*, 13 April 1932, p. 13.
"Furniture and the Ego", in *New York American*, 20 April 1932, p. 13.
"Why Are We Discontent?", in *New York American*, 27 April 1932, p. 13.
"How People Economize", in *New York American*, 4 May 1932, p. 13.
"On Locomotion", in *New York American*, 11 May 1932, p. 13.
"Of Cooperation", in *New York American*, 18 May 1932, p. 15.
"Our Woman Haters", in *New York American*, 25 May 1932, p. 13.
"Should Children Be Happy?", in *Nash's Pall Mall Magazine*, June 1932, vol. 89, no. 469, p. 57.
"Influence of Fathers", in *New York American*, 1 June 1932, p. 13.
"On Societies", in *New York American*, 8 June 1932, p. 13.

"On Being Edifying", in *Time and Tide*, 11 June 1932, vol. 13, p. 642.
"Do Dogs Think?", in *New York American*, 15 June 1932, p. 23.
"On Sales Resistance", in *New York American*, 22 June 1932, p. 15.
"Dangers of Feminism", in *New York American*, 6 July 1932, p. 13.
"On Expected Emotions", in *New York American*, 13 July 1932, p. 15.
"Modern Uncertainty", in *New York American*, 20 July 1932, p. 13.
"On Imitating Heroes", in *New York American*, 27 July 1932, p. 13.
"The Sophistication of the Young", in *Nash's Pall Mall Magazine*, August 1932, vol. 89, no. 471, p. 65.
"Vicarious Asceticism", in *New York American*, 3 August 1932, p. 13.
"On Labeling People", in *New York American*, 10 August 1932, p. 13.
"On Smiling", in *New York American*, 17 August 1932, p. 15.
"Who Wants War? Do Governments?", in *New York American*, 24 August 1932, p. 13.
"Corporal Punishment. Crime and Punishment", in *New York American*, 7 September 1932, p. 13.
"What Animals Would Think", in *New York American*, 14 September 1932, p. 15.
"On Insularity", in *New York American*, 21 September 1932, p. 13.
"On Astrologers", in *New York American*, 28 September 1932, p. 13.
"In Praise of Idleness", in *Harper's Magazine*, October 1932, vol. 165, no. 10, pp. 552–559.
"Protecting Children from Reality", in *New York American*, 5 October 1932, p. 15.
"The Decay of Standards. Rules of Thought", in *New York American*, 19 October 1932, p. 15.
"Pride in Illness", in *New York American*, 26 October 1932, p. 15.
"Comments on the Basis of the Sexology Group of the Promethean Society", in *On Education, Twentieth Century*, November 1932, vol. 4, no. 21, p. 22.
"On Charity. Where Charity Fails", in *New York American*, 2 November 1932, p. 15.
"On Reverence", in *New York American*, 9 November 1932, p. 19.
"On Proverbs", in *New York American*, 16 November 1932, p. 15.
"On Clothes", in *New York American*, 23 November 1932, p. 17.
"Should Socialists Smoke Good Cigars?", in *New York American*, 30 November 1932, p. 17.
"A Sense of Humor", in *New York American*, 7 December 1932, p. 15.
"Love and Money", in *New York American*, 14 December 1932, p. 15.
"Interest in Crime", in *New York American*, 21 December 1932, p. 15.
"How to Become a Genius", in *New York American*, 28 December 1932, p. 13.
"The Future of the Family", in *Nash's Pall Mall Magazine*, January 1933, vol. 90, no. 476, pp. 27, 80.
"On Old Friends", in *New York American*, 4 January 1933, p. 13.
"Success and Failure", in *New York American*, 11 January 1933, p. 15.
"On Feeling Ashamed", in *New York American*, 18 January 1933, p. 15.
"On Economic Security", in *New York American*, 25 January 1933, p. 15.
"The Modern Midas", in *Harper's Magazine*, February 1933, vol. 166, pp. 327–334.
"On Tact", in *New York American*, 1 February 1933, p. 17.
"Changing Fashions in Reserve", in *New York American*, 8 February 1933, p. 13.

"On Honor", in *New York American*, 15 February 1933, p. 13.
"The Consolations of History", in *New York American*, 22 February 1933, p. 17.
"The Governmental Mentality", in *Sunday Referee*, 26 February 1933, p. 6.
"How People Take Failure", in *New York American*, 1 March 1933, p. 13.
"The Influence of Technique on Politics", in *The Twentieth Century*, 1 March 1933, vol. 1, no, 7, pp. 3–6.
"On Conceit", in *New York American*, 8 March 1933, p. 10.
"This Way to Chaos", in *Sunday Referee*, 12 March 1933, p. 6.
"On Bores", in *New York American*, 15 March 1933, p. 10.
"Sport and Politics", in *New York American*, 22 March 1933, p. 10.
"Freedom of the Press. Power of the Plutocrats", in *Sunday Referee*, 26 March 1933, p. 6.
"On Reticence", in *New York American*, 29 March 1933, p. 10.
"Should the Public Schools Be Abolished? Debate", in *The Listener*, 29 March 1933, vol. 9, pp. 477–480.
"The Good Old Days", in *New York American*, 5 April 1933, p. 12.
"History's Lesson for the Nazis", in *Sunday Referee*, 9 April 1933, p. 6.
"Civilization", in *New York American*, 12 April 1933, p. 12.
"Art of Persuading", in *Los Angeles Examiner*, 19 April 1933, sec. 1, p. 8.
"If You Were Charged With Murder! Reflections on the Moscow Trial", in *Sunday Referee*, 23 April 1933, p. 6.
"Democracy. Its prospects", in *New York American*, 26 April 1933, p. 10.
"Strong Man Cult", in *New York American*, 3 May 1933, p. 13.
"Wisdom from the West. Will Roosevelt Lead World?", in *Sunday Referee*, 7 May 1933, p. 6.
"Stupidity Rules", in *New York American*, 10 May 1933, p. 13.
"On Utilitarianism", in *New York American*, 17 May 1933, p. 17.
"How to Avoid War. Harmful Political Creeds", in *Sunday Referee*, 21 May 1933, p. 6.
"On Race Hatred", in *New York American*, 24 May 1933, p. 15.
"The Spirit of Adventure", in *New York American*, 31 May 1933, p. 11.
"The Only Alternative to Internationalism Is Death!", in *Sunday Referee*, 4 June 1933, p. 6.
"What Makes People Likeable", in *New York American*, 7 June 1933, p. 13.
"On Self-Righteousness", in *New York American*, 14 June 1933, p. 19.
"Rise and Fall of Big Business. Limitations of Self-Help", in *Sunday Referee*, 18 June 1933, p. 6.
"On Spending Money", in *New York American*, 21 June 1933, p. 15.
"Origin of Victorianism", in *New York American*, 28 June 1933, p. 15.
"Cause of the World's Troubles. Economic Fallacies", in *Sunday Referee*, 2 July 1933, p. 6.
"On Propriety", in *New York American*, 5 July 1933, p. 11.
"I Escape from Progress", in *New York American*, 12 July 1933, p. 13.
"America Turns Its Back on Europe. It's the Right Policy", in *Sunday Referee*, 16 July 1933, p. 6.
"Experts and Oligarchs", in *New York American*, 19 July 1933, p. 13.
"Cloistered Virtue", in *New York American*, 26 July 1933, p. 13.

"Socialism Over the White House. A Revolution", in *Sunday Referee*, 30 July 1933, p. 6.
"Ashamed of Virtue", in *New York American*, 2 August 1933, p. 13.
"Men Versus Insects", in *New York American*, 9 August 1933, p. 13.
"If I Were Dictator of Housing", in *Sunday Referee*, 13 August 1933, p. 6.
"Paralysis of Statesmanship", in *New York American*, 16 August 1933, p. 13.
"On Orthodoxies", in *New York American*, 23 August 1933, p. 15.
"Democracy Is In Eclipse. Men Prefer Persecuting Others", in *Sunday Referee*, 27 August 1933, p. 6.
"Means to Ends", in *New York American*, 30 August 1933, p. 13.
"Individualistic Ethics", in *New York American*, 6 September 1933, p. 15.
"Marriage and the Serfdom of Women", in *Sunday Referee*, 10 September 1933, p. 6.
"Cult of the Individual", in *New York American*, 13 September 1933, p. 15.
"On Being Argumentative", in *New York American*, 20 September 1933, p. 15.
"There Need Be No War", in *Sunday Referee*, 24 September 1933, p. 6.
"On Mediaevalism", in *New York American*, 27 September 1933, p. 19.
"Nash's Commentary. Let's cooperate", in *Nash's Pall Mall Magazine*, October 1933, vol. 92, no. 485, p. 5.
"In Praise of Dullness", in *New York American*, 4 October 1933, p. 15.
"Why Are Alien Groups Hated?", in *Everyman*, 6 October 1933, no. 2, p. 22.
"Social Importance of Culture", in *Sunday Referee*, 8 October 1933, p. 6.
"The End of Pioneering", in *New York American*, 11 October 1933, p. 17.
"Combating Cruelty", in *New York American*, 18 October 1933, p. 15.
"Ideals of Fascism", in *Sunday Referee*, 22 October 1933, p. 14.
"How to Keep Mentally Young", in *New York American*, 25 October 1933, p. 17.
"Dangers of Discipline", in *New York American*, 30 October 1933, p. 15.
"The Age of Stagnation", in *Sunday Referee*, 5 November 1933, p. 14.
"The Next Billion Years", in *New York American*, 10 November 1933, p. 23.
"War Mentality and Armament Firms", in *Sunday Referee*, 19 November 1933, p. 6.
"Do Children Need Fathers?", in *Daily Herald*, 21 November 1933, p. 10.
"The Churches and War", in *New York American*, 24 November 1933, p. 19.
"Can the World Be Saved? The Role of Force", in *Sunday Referee*, 3 December 1933, p. 8.
"A Benefit of Prohibition", in *New York American*, 6 December 1933, p. 19.
"'Kings in a Republic'. Loving our Neighbors", in *New York American*, 14 December 1933, p. 19.
"The World Is in a Mad Mood", in *Sunday Referee*, 17 December 1933, p. 8.
"Impulse vs. Self-Control", in *New York American*, 21 December 1933, p. 19.
"The Essence of Law", in *New York American*, 28 December 1933, p. 15.
"The Balance of Power", in *Sunday Referee*, 31 December 1933, p. 6.
Freedom and Organization 1814–1914, London, Allen & Unwin, 1934.
"Is Euthanasia Justifiable?", in *New York American*, 1 January 1934, p. 21.
"Equality", in *New York American*, 8 January 1934, p. 15.

"The Father of the Family", in *New York American*, 15 January 1934, p. 15.
"The Sphere of Liberty in the Modern World", in *Berwick Mercury*, 20 January 1934, p. 3.
"The Origin of Mourning and Other Customs", in *New York American*, 22 January 1934, p. 13.
"Why I Am Neither a Communist Nor a Fascist", in *New Britain*, 31 January 1934, vol. 2, pp. 310–311.
"They Are Beating the Cross into a Swastika in Germany. Religious Persecution", in *Sunday Referee*, 4 February 1934, p. 6.
"Transferring Anger", in *New York American*, 5 February 1934, p. 15.
"Dangers of Adult Education", in *New York American*, 12 February 1934, p. 19.
"The Next 200 Years. Is progress assured?", in *New York American*, 19 February 1934, p. 17.
"This Modern World. Curious Beliefs", in *New York American*, 26 February 1934, p. 17.
"The Technique for Politicians", in *Esquire*, March 1934, vol. 1, pp. 26, 133.
"Pioneer Ethics", in *New York American*, 19 March 1934, p. 15.
"Queer People. Sanity and Otherwise", in *New York American*, 26 March 1934, p. 15.
"'That's Different', Justifying One's Actions", in *New York American*, 2 April 1934, p. 13.
"Back to Nature", in *New York American*, 30 April 1934, p. 13.
"Education and Civilisation", in *The New Statesman and Nation*, 5 May 1934, vol. 7, pp. 666–668.
"A Bill Which Says Britons Shall Be Slaves!", in *Sunday Referee*, 6 May 1934, p. 6
"Parental Love", in *New York American*, 7 May 1934, p. 15.
"Japan and China", in *No More War*, June 1934, vol. 1, no. 6, pp. 4–5.
"The Sphere of Liberty", in *Esquire*, July 1934, vol. 2, p. 29.
"British in India like Nazis, Bertrand Russell Charges", in *New York Post*, 6 July 1934.
"Possessiveness", in *New York American*, 13 July 1934, p. 19.
"Superstitions", in *New York American*, 20 July 1934, p. 19.
"Science's Goal", in *New York American*, 27 July 1934, p. 19.
"Social Sciences", in *New York American*, 3 August 1934, p. 19.
"Racial Bunk", in *New York American*, 10 August 1934, p. 19.
"Spare Time", in *New York American*, 17 August 1934, p. 19.
"What to Believe", in *New York American*, 24 August 1934, p. 19.
"'Human Instincts' – Pleasure v. Needs", in *New York American*, 31 August 1934, p. 19.
"Virtue's Fashions", in *New York American*, 7 September 1934, p. 19.
"Comets", in *New York American*, 14 September 1934, p. 23.
"Duels. A Proposal for Politicians", in *New York American*, 20 September 1934, p. 17.
"Useless Wisdom", in *New York American*, 27 September 1934, p. 21.
"Was Europe a Success?", in *The Nation*, 3 October 1934, vol. 139, pp. 373–374.
"'Great Men' – Men Who Shaped History", in *New York American*, 4 October 1934, p. 19.
"Europe and Africa", in *Heckmondwike Herald*, 6 October 1934, p. 3.
"Contemplation", in *New York American*, 26 October 1934, p. 23.
"Uniformity", in *New York American*, 2 November 1934, p. 21.
"Obscure Fame", in *New York American*, 9 November 1934, p. 23.

"Protean Truth. Genius and Madness", in *New York American*, 16 November 1934, p. 23.
"Stilted Manners", in *New York American*, 23 November 1934, p. 25.
"Bertrand Russell on India and the West", in *Sunday Referee*, 25 November 1934, p. 7.
"Materialism. Love of Money", in *Los Angeles Examiner*, 30 November 1934, sec. 1, p. 19.
"When Men Die For Religion", in *Sunday Referee*, 2 December 1934, p. 12.
"Strangers. On married Couples", in *New York American*, 7 December 1934, p. 25.
"Polite Lies", in *New York American*, 14 December 1934, p. 27.
"Shall We See A New Aristocracy?", in *Sunday Referee*, 16 December 1934, p. 12.
"How To Be Insulting", in *New York American*, 21 December 1934, p. 25.
"Peace Will Come to Europe if Germany Tires of Hitler", in *Sunday Referee*, 30 December 1934, p. 10.
In Praise of Idleness and Other Essays, London, Allen & Unwin, 1935.
Religion and Science, London, Thornton Butterworth, 1935.
"The Revolt Against Reason", in *The Political Quarterly*, January 1935, vol. 6, no. 1, pp. 1–19.
"The Limits of Empiricism", in *Proceedings of the Aristotelian Society*, 1935–1936, vol. 36, pp. 131–150.
"The Revolt Against Reason", in *The Political Quarterly*, January 1935, vol. 6, no. 1, pp. 1–19.
"The Plunder of Abyssinia", in *Sunday Referee*, 13 January 1935, p. 2.
"'New Faith' – On vigorous v. Feeble Epochs", in *New York American*, 16 January 1935, p. 19.
"Light on Japan's Aims", in *Sunday Referee*, 27 January 1935, p. 11.
"England's Duty to India", in *Asia*, February 1935, vol. 35, pp. 69–70.
"The Men Who Want War", in *Sunday Referee*, 10 February 1935, p. 10.
"The Tragedy of Peace", in *Sunday Referee*, 24 February 1935, p. 10.
"Bertrand Russell on the World Chaos", in *Sunday Referee*, 10 March 1935, p. 12.
"Saving Europe From Disaster", in *Sunday Referee*, 31 March 1935, p. 11.
"'Let Us Stand by the League' – On Isolationism", in *Sunday Referee*, 14 April 1935, p. 12.
"'Knowledge'. On Decrease of Knowledge", in *New York American*, 19 April 1935, p. 21.
"Take the Profits Out of War", in *Sunday Referee*, 28 April 1935, p. 11.
"'Fear of Freedom'. A Problem of Education", in *The Berwick Mercury*, 11 May 1935, p. 4.
"Why Be Afraid of Socialism?", in *Sunday Referee*, 12 May 1935, p. 12.
"A Weekly Diary", in *The New Statesman and Nation*, 25 May, 1–8–15–22 June, vol. 9, pp. 742–743, 798–799, 854–855, 886–887, 918–919.
"Hitler's Thirteen Points", in *Sunday Referee*, 26 May 1935, p. 12.
"Dangers in the Far East", in *Sunday Referee*, 9 June 1935, p. 10.
"Menace of Secret Pacts", in *Sunday Referee*, 23 June 1935, p. 12.
"Are We Any Happier?", in *Nash's Pall Mall Magazine*, July 1935, vol. 95, no. 506, pp. 12–13, 120, 122.
"If You Were Foreign Minister What Would You Do about Abyssinia?", in *Sunday Referee*, 7 July 1935, p. 12.
"Your Duty in the Next War", in *Sunday Referee*, 21 July 1935, p. 12.

"Britain Must Be Neutral", in *Sunday Referee*, 4 August 1935, p. 10.
"How to Keep the Peace", in *Sunday Referee*, 18 August 1935, p. 12.
"Bertrand Russell Applauds U.S. Neutrality Decision", in *New York Post*, 27 August 1935, p. 4.
"Keep Out of War!", in *Sunday Referee*, 1 September 1935, p. 10.
"'The New Alliance' Between Italy and Germany", in *Sunday Referee*, 15 September 1935, p. 4.
"'The Dangers of Bluff' Between Britain and Italy", in *Sunday Referee*, 29 September 1935, p. 10.
"How to Keep Peace", in *Sunday Referee*, 13 October 1935, p. 4.
"'In Lands Where Slums and Wars Are Unknown' – Scandinavia", in *Sunday Referee*, 23 October 1935, p. 18.
"Science Is Tottering", in *Sunday Referee*, 10 November 1935, p. 12.
"When a Marriage Crashes", in *Sunday Express*, 17 November 1935, p. 15.
"Our Grandfathers Would Not Have Put Up With It", in *Sunday Referee*, 24 November 1935, p. 12.
"Who Should Bring Up Our Children", in *The Listener*, 27 November 1935, vol. 14, pp. 951–953.
"'These Rights Husbands Had Once', Wife-Beating", in *Sunday Referee*, 15 December 1935, p. 12.
"Resistance to Authority", in *Sunday Referee*, 29 December 1935, p. 12.
Which Way to Peace?, London, Michael Joseph, 1936.
"The Prospects of a Permanent Peace", in *The Lecture Recorder*, January 1936, vol. 5, pp. 163–167.
"Peace in the World", in *Sunday Sun*, 12 January 1936, p. 10.
"Hysterics While You Wait", in *Sunday Referee*, 19 January 1936, p. 12.
"Why Radicals Are Unpopular", in *Common Sense*, March 1936, vol. 5, no. 3, pp. 13–15.
"Determinism and Physics", in *Proceedings of the University of Durham Philosophical Society*, March 1936, vol. 9, pp. 228–245.
"Our Brave Impatient World!", in *Sunday Referee*, 29 March 1936, p. 12.
"Empirismens gränser", in *Theoria*, April 1936, vol. 2, no. 1–2, pp. 107–127.
"Is Life No Longer Sacred?", in *Sunday Referee*, 19 April 1936, p. 12.
"Our Sexual Ethics", in *The American Mercury*, May 1936, vol. 38, pp. 36–41.
"On Order in Time", in *Proceedings of the Cambridge Philosophical Society*, May 1936, vol. 32, pp. 216–228.
"Dangerous Passions", in *Sunday Referee*, 24 May 1936, p. 12.
"Dictatorships That Pass in the Night", in *Sunday Referee*, 9 August 1936, p. 14.
"The Last Survivor of a Dead Epoch", in *The Listener*, 12 August 1936, vol. 16, p. 289.
"Spanish Conspiracy", in *New York American*, 15 August 1936, vol. 12, p. 218.
"A Turning Point in Foreign Policy", in *Berwick Mercury*, 22 August 1936, p. 4.
"Your Freedom Is in Danger", in *Sunday Sun*, 25 October 1936, p. 10.
"Paralysis of England", in *Coronet*, December 1936, vol. 1, no. 2, pp. 3–8.
"No Continental Entanglements", in *The Yorkshire Post*, 5 December 1936, p. 8.
"On Being Modern-Minded", in *The Nation*, 9 January 1937, vol. 144, pp. 47–48.
"Philosophy's Ulterior Motives", in *Atlantic Monthly*, February 1937, vol. 159, no. 2, pp. 149–155.

"Collective 'Security'", in *Peace News*, 13 February 1937, no. 35, p. 6.
"Law and Conscience", in *Birmingham Mail*, 16 February 1937, p. 8.
"Russell Speech in House of Lords for British Isolation", Parliamentary Debates (Lords), 24 February 1937, vol. 104, cols. 318–323.
"Power, Ancient and Modern", in *The Political Quarterly*, April 1937, vol. 8, no. 2, pp. 155–164.
"The Future of Democracy", in *The New Republic*, 5 May 1937, vol. 90, pp. 381–382.
"Plato in Modern Dress", in *The New Statesman and Nation*, 22 May 1937, vol. 13, p. 850.
"Humanizing Warfare", in *Peace News*, 29 May 1937, no. 50, p. 6.
"The Superior Virtue of the Oppressed", in *The Nation*, 26 June 1937, vol. 144, pp. 731–732.
Power: A New Social Analysis, London, Allen & Unwin, 1938.
"My Religious Reminiscences", in *The Rationalist Annual*, 1938, pp. 3–8.
"The Relevance of Psychology to Logic", in *Aristotelian Society, Supplementary Volume: Action, Perception and Measurement*, 1938, vol. 17, pp. 42–53.
"The Crisis in Foreign Policy", in *Peace News*, 5 March 1938, no. 90, p. 8.
"What Is Happiness?", in *News Chronicle*, 18 March 1938, p. 6.
"Has the League a Future?", in *Sunday Sun*, 15 May 1938, p. 12.
"On Verification: The Presidential Address", in *Proceeding of the Aristotelian Society*, June 1938, vol. 38, no. 1, pp. 1–20.
"'The Persecution of the Jews' – What Can Be Done", in *The Berwick Mercury*, 9 July 1938, p. 3.
"Power Over Opinion", in *The Saturday Review of Literature*, 13 August 1938, vol. 18, no. 16, pp. 13–14.
"What We Should Teach Our Children", in *Lilliput*, September 1938, vol. 3, pp. 241–243.
"The Taming of Power", in *The Atlantic Monthly*, October 1938, vol. 162, no. 4, pp. 439–449.
"Dewey's New Logic", in P.A. Schilpp (ed.), *The Philosophy of John Dewey*, Evanston, Northwestern University Press, 1939, pp. 137–156.
"The Role of the Intellectual in the Modern World", in *The American Journal of Sociology*, January 1939, vol. 44, no. 4, pp. 491–498.
"Is Security Increasing?", in *The University of Chicago Round Table*, 15 January 1939, no. 44, pp. 2–9, 11.
"Democracy and Economics", in *Survey Graphic*, February 1939, vol. 28, pp. 130–132.
"Munich Rather Than War", in *The Nation*, 14 February 1939, vol. 148, pp. 173–175.
"Individual Freedom in England and America", in *Berwick Mercury*, 25 February 1939, p. 3.
"The Case for U.S. Neutrality", in *Common Sense*, March 1939, vol. 8, no. 3, pp. 8–9.
"Can Power Be Humanized?", in *Forum and Century*, October 1939, vol. 102, pp. 184–185.
An Inquiry Into Meaning and Truth: The William James Lectures for 1940 Delivered at Harvard University, London, Allen & Unwin, 1940.
"The Philosophy of Santayana", in P.A. Schilpp (ed.), *The Philosophy of George Santayana*, Evanston, Northwestern University Press, 1940, pp. 453–474.
"Freedom and the Colleges", in *The American Mercury*, May 1940, vol. 50, pp. 24–33.
"Do I Preach Adultery?", in *Liberty*, 18 May 1940, vol. 17, no. 20, p. 579.

"The Functions of a Teacher", in *Harper's Magazine*, June 1940, vol. 181, no. 1081, pp. 11–16.
"Education in Democracy", in *The California Monthly*, September 1940, vol. 45, no. 1, pp. 8–9.
Let the People Think, London, Watts & Co., 1941.
"Education in America", in *Common Sense*, June 1941, vol. 10, no. 6, pp. 163–166.
"Blueprint for an Enduring Peace", in *The American Mercury*, June 1941, vol. 52, pp. 666–676.
"Russell Condemns Policy of Isolation", in *The New York Times*, 21 September 1941, sec. 1, p. 13.
"Bertrand Russell Urges Creation of World Federation Controlling All Armaments", in *The New Leader*, 27 September 1941, vol. 24, no. 39, p. 4.
"A Philosophy for You in These Times", in *Reader's Digest*, October 1941, vol. 39, no. 234, pp. 5–7.
"Messages for India Independence Day", in *India To-Day*, January 1942, vol. 2, p. 2.
"To End the Deadlock in India", in *Asia*, January 1942, vol. 42, pp. 338–340.
"Proposals for an International University", in *The Fortnightly*, July 1942, vol. 152, pp. 8–16.
"Freedom in a Time of Stress", in *The Rotarian*, September 1942, vol. 61, no. 3, pp. 23–24.
"Non-Materialistic Naturalism", in *The Kenyon Review*, Autumn 1942, vol. 4, no. 3, pp. 361–365.
"The International Significance of the Indian Problem", in *Free World*, January 1943, vol. 5, pp. 63–69.
"Some Problems of the Post-War World", in *Free World*, April 1943, vol. 5, pp. 297–301.
"If You Fall in Love With a Married Man", in *Glamour*, April 1943, vol. 9, no. 4, pp. 68, 94, 99–100.
"An Outline of Intellectual Rubbish", in *The American Freeman*, June 1943, no. 2049, pp. 1–3.
"Zionism and the Peace Settlement", in *The New Palestine*, 11 June 1943, vol. 33, no. 15, pp. 5–7.
"My Grandmother and Mr. Gladstone", in *Vogue*, 15 July 1943, vol. 102, no. 2, pp. 35, 81.
"Eccentrics Preferred", in *Vogue*, 1 September 1943, vol. 102, no. 5, pp. 103, 162.
"'The Russian Realities'- Russia and the U.S. after the War", in *Common Sense*, October 1943, vol. 12, no. 10, pp. 351–354.
"Our World after the War: A Plan for International Action", in *The New Leader*, 27 November 1943, vol. 26, no. 48, pp. 5, 7.
"Citizenship in a Great State", in *Fortune, Chicago*, December 1943, vol. 28, no. 6, pp. 167–185.
"Britain's Shrunken Economy Makes Her Dependent on U.S.", in *The New Leader*, 4 December 1943, vol. 26, no. 49, p. 5.
"Experience Among Freaks", in *Vogue*, 15 December 1943, vol. 102, no. 12, pp. 53, 70–71.
"The Future of Pacifism", in *American Scholar*, 1943–1944, vol. 13, pp. 7–13.
"My Mental Development" (1944), in Schilpp (ed.), *The Philosophy of Bertrand Russell*, pp. 1–20.
"Reply to Criticisms" (1944), in Schilpp (ed.), *The Philosophy of Bertrand Russell*, pp. 679–746.
"Cooperate With Soviet Russia", in *The New Leader*, 5 February 1944, vol. 27, no. 6, pp. 8–9.
"Western Hegemony in Post-War Asia", in *The New Leader*, 26 February 1944, vol. 27, no. 9, p. 7.
"Victors and Vanquished", in *The New Leader*, 18 March 1944, vol. 27, no. 12, p. 9.
"Education in International Understanding", in *Tomorrow*, June 1944, vol. 3, no. 10, pp. 19–21.
"Can Americans and Britons Be Friends?", in *The Saturday Evening Post*, 3 June 1944, vol. 216, no. 49, pp. 14–15, 57–59.

"How War Has Changed the British People", in *Reynolds News*, 23 July 1944, p. 6.
"The Value of Free Thought", in *The American Freeman*, August 1944, no. 2063, pp. 1–4.
"Four-Power Alliance: Step to Peace", in *The New Leader*, 12 August 1944, vol. 27, no. 33, p. 9.
"The Disarmament of Education", in *The New Leader*, 2 September 1944, vol. 27, no. 36, p. 9.
"Britain – U.S.A.", in *Leader Magazine*, 28 October 1944, vol. 2, no. 2, pp. 12–13.
"The Thinkers Behind Germany's Sins. Can Germany Blame Her Philosophers?", in *Leader Magazine*, 18 November 1944, vol. 2, no. 5, p. 6.
"Twilight of British Empire", in *Forward*, December 1944, vol. 2, p. 4.
A History of Western Philosophy and Its Connection with Political and Social Circumstances from the Earliest Times to the Present Day, London, Allen & Unwin, 1945.
"British and American Nationalism", in *Horizon*, January 1945, vol. 11, pp. 17–30.
"Where Do We Go Now?", in *The Listener*, 11 January 1945, vol. 33, pp. 31–32.
"Can We Re-Educate Germany?", in *Maclean's Magazine*, 15 March 1945, vol. 58, no. 6, pp. 16, 20–21.
"Democracy in Liberated Europe", in *Forward*, 17 March 1945, vol. 39, no. 11, p. 3.
"The Future in China and Japan", in *Forward*, 21 April 1945, vol. 39, no. 16, pp. 4–5.
"Bertrand Russell on the Problems of Peace", in *Picture Post*, 21 April 1945, vol. 27, no. 3, pp. 16–18.
"Should Scientists Be Public Servants?", in *The Listener*, 10 May 1945, vol. 33, pp. 516–520.
"Whose Guilt? The Problem of Cruelty", in *Picture Post*, 16 June 1945, vol. 27, no. 11, pp. 10–13.
"The Bomb and Civilisation", in *Forward*, 18 August 1945, vol. 39, no. 33, pp. 1, 3.
"What Should Be British Policy Towards Russia?", in *Forward*, 29 September 1945, vol. 39, no. 39, p. 4.
"How to Avoid the Atomic War", in *Common Sense*, October 1945, vol. 14, no. 9, pp. 3–5.
"Peace or Atomisation?", in *Cavalcade*, 6 October 1945, vol. 7, no. 396, pp. 8–9.
"Humanity's Last Chance", in *Cavalcade*, 20 October 1945, vol. 7, no. 398, pp. 8–9.
"Logical Positivism", in *Polemic*, November 1945, no. 1, pp. 6–13.
"Britain and the Atomic Bomb", in *The Manchester Guardian*, 7 November 1945, p. 4.
"The German Disaster", in *Forward*, 17 November 1945, vol. 39, no. 46, p. 3.
"The Atomic Bomb", Parliamentary Debates (Lords), 28 November 1945, vol. 138, cols. 87–92.
"'Filosofiens Värde' – Philosophy's value", in *Samtid och Framtid*, December 1945, vol. 2, pp. 606–608.
"On Central Europe", Parliamentary Debates (Lords), 5 December 1945, vol. 138, cols. 376–380.
Physics & Experience, Cambridge, Cambridge University Press, 1946.
"Mind and Matter in Modern Science", in *The Rationalist Annual*, 1946, pp. 13–23.
"The Problem of Universals", in *Polemic*, January 1946, no. 2, pp. 21–35.
"What Should Now Be Our Policy Towards Germany?", in *World Review*, January 1946, pp. 19–23.
"The One Way Out", in *Sunday Pictorial*, 3 February 1946, p. 4.
"What Is Democracy?", in *The Manchester Guardian*, 4 May 1946, p. 4.

"Should a Scientist Be Free to Tell? A Debate", in *Picture Post*, 15 June 1946, vol. 31, no. 11, p. 18.
"The Atomic Bomb and the Prevention of War", in *Polemic*, July–August 1946, no. 4, pp. 15–22.
"Wells: The Man As I Knew Him", in *Daily Graphic and Daily Sketch*, 14 August 1946, p. 2.
"Soviet Genetics", in *The Guardian*, 18 October 1946, vol. 101, pp. 496–497.
"Philosophy for Laymen", in *Universities Quarterly*, November 1946, no. 1, pp. 38–49.
"Good and Bad", in *Polemic*, November–December 1946, no. 6, pp. 2–8.
Philosophy and Politics. Fourth National Book League Lecture: delivered at Friends House, London, October 23, 1946, Cambridge, Cambridge University Press, 1947.
"A Scientist's Plea for Democracy", in *The Listener*, 16 January 1947, vol. 37, pp. 107–108.
"Dangers of State Power", in *The Listener*, 13 February 1947, vol. 37, pp. 281–282.
"The Outlook for Mankind", in *The Listener*, 13 March 1947, vol. 37, pp. 370–372.
"A Plea for Clear Thinking", in *The Listener*, 3 April 1947, vol. 37, p. 500.
"Atomic Energy Control", Parliamentary Debates (Lords), 30 April 1947, vol. 147, cols. 272–276.
"The Faith of a Rationalist", in *The Listener*, 29 May 1947, vol. 37, pp. 826, 836.
"German Recovery: A European Interest, BBC transcript", in *The Listener*, 2 October 1947, vol. 38, p. 565.
"Still Time for Good Sense", in *'47: The Magazine of the Year*, November 1947, vol. 1, no. 9, pp. 56–63.
Human Knowledge: Its Scope and Limits, London, Allen & Unwin, 1948.
Towards World Government, London, New Commonwealth, 1948.
"A Turning-Point in My Life", in *The Saturday Book*, 1948, vol. 8, pp. 142–146.
"International Government", in *The New Commonwealth*, January 1948, vol. 9, pp. 77–80.
"'The International Bearings of Atomic Warfare' – Address to Royal Empire Society", in *United Empire*, January–February 1948, vol. 39, pp. 18–21.
"A Period of Dread and Doubt", in *The Listener*, 5 February 1948, vol. 39, pp. 211–212.
"The Future of Mankind", in *The New Leader*, 6 March 1948, vol. 31, no. 10, pp. 8–9.
"Rewards of Philosophy", in *The Listener*, 18 March 1948, vol. 39, p. 459.
"Whitehead and Principia Mathematica", in *Mind*, April 1948, vol. 57, no. 226, pp. 137–138.
"The Outlook for Mankind", in *Horizon*, April 1948, vol. 17, no. 100, pp. 238–246.
"Toleration", in *The Listener*, 29 April 1948, vol. 39, pp. 695–697.
"Science as a Product of Western Europe", in *The Listener*, 27 May 1948, vol. 39, pp. 865–866.
"Det Internationella Läget", in *Dagens Nyheter*, 30 May 1948, p. 5.
"Förebyggandet Av Krig", in *Dagens Nyheter*, 1 June 1948, p. 4.
"Det Marxistiska Giftet", in *Samtid och Framtid*, June–August 1948, vol. 5, pp. 299–301.
"The Existence of God", in *Humanitas*, Autumn 1948, vol. 2, no. 3–4, pp. 2–17.
"The Way of the World", in *World Review*, September 1948, pp. 11–15.
"Can Foreign Policy Be Democratic?", in *American Perspective*, September 1948, vol. 2, pp. 149–154.
"Why Fanaticism Brings Defeat", in *The Listener*, 23 September 1948, vol. 40, pp. 452–453.
"Resisting Russia", in *The Observer*, 28 November 1948, p. 3.

"Social Cohesion and Human Nature", in *The Listener*, 30 December 1948, vol. 40, pp. 991–992, 1010.

Authority and the Individual: The Reith Lectures for 1948–49, London, Allen & Unwin, 1949.

"Atomic Energy and the Problems of Europe", in *The Nineteenth Century and After*, January 1949, vol. 145, pp. 39–43.

"Social Cohesion and Government", in *The Listener*, 6 January 1949, vol. 41, pp. 7–9.

"The Role of Individuality", in *The Listener*, 13 January 1949, vol. 41, pp. 57–59.

"Conflict of Technique and Human Nature", in *The Listener*, 20 January 1949, vol. 41, pp. 97–98, 103.

"Control and Initiative", in *The Listener*, 27 January 1949, vol. 41, pp. 137–139.

"Individual and Social Ethics", in *The Listener*, 3 February 1949, vol. 41, pp. 179–181.

"Einstein and the Theory of Relativity", in *The Listener*, 17 March 1949, vol. 41, pp. 452–453.

"'First Sign of Decay' – Science in Russia", in *News Review*, 17 March 1949, vol. 27, no. 11, pp. 10–11.

"The Future of Europe", in *European Affairs*, April 1949, vol. 1, no. 1, pp. 3–4.

"Unity of Western Culture", in *World Review*, April 1949, no. 2, pp. 5–8.

"Germany's Generals: Justice or Vengeance?", in *News Review*, 26 May 1949, vol. 27, no. 21, pp. 3–4.

"Bertrand Russell Writes for the Daily Graphic on the Life of His Mind", in *Daily Graphic and Daily Sketch*, 1 June 1949, p. 4.

"Agnosticism v. Atheism", in *The Literary Guide and Rationalist Review*, July 1949, vol. 64, pp. 115–116.

"Freedom: At the Price of Freedoms", in *Leader Magazine*, 23 July 1949, vol. 6, no. 38, pp. 24–26.

"Ten Years since the War Began", in *The New Leader*, 3 September 1949, vol. 32, no. 36, pp. 6–7.

"The American Mentality", in *News Review*, 15 September 1949, vol. 28, no. 11, pp. 7–8.

"I Would Tell Stalin", in *Leader Magazine*, 17 September 1949, vol. 6, no. 46, pp. 26–28.

"Towards a New Loyalty", in *United Nations World*, October 1949, vol. 2, pp. 10–12.

"William of Occam: Empiricist and Democrat", in *The Listener*, 1 December 1949, vol. 42, pp. 949–951.

"Political and Cultural Influence of U.S.A.", in *The Listener*, 8 December 1949, vol. 42, pp. 991–993.

"Can a Scientific Society Be Stable?", in *British Medical Journal*, 10 December 1949, no. 4640, pp. 1307–1311.

Unpopular Essays, London, Allen & Unwin, 1950.

"What Desires Are Politically Important?" (1950), in H. Frenz (ed.), *Nobel Lectures, Literature 1901–1967*, Amsterdam, Elsevier Publishing Company, 1969, pp. 259–270.

"Le principe d'individuation", in *Revue de Métaphysique et de Morale*, January–March 1950, vol. 55, no. 1, pp. 1–15.

"'The Next Fifty Years'. Tolerance is Needed", in *European Affairs*, January 1950, vol. 1, no. 1, pp. 5–7.

"Logical Positivism", in *Revue Internationale de Philosophie*, January 1950, vol. 4, no. 12, pp. 3–19.
"Man of the Half-Century? I Choose Einstein", in *Leader Magazine*, 7 January 1950, vol. 7, no. 10, pp. 7–8.
"The Next Fifty Years", in *Illustrated*, 7 January 1950, pp. 7–9.
"La démocratie politique, peut-elle s'adapter aux problèmes de 1950?", in *Politique étrangère*, February–March 1950, vol. 15, no. 1, pp. 5–13.
"Is a World State Still Possible?", in *The Listener*, 23 February 1950, vol. 43, pp. 326–327.
"Is a Third World War Inevitable?", in *United Nations World*, March 1950, no. 3, pp. 11–13.
"The Science to Save Us from Science", in *The New York Times*, 19 March 1950, sec. 6, pp. 9, 31–33.
"En Filosof Spørger: Hvad Er Man Pligt?", in *Fremtiden*, June 1950, vol. 5, no. 6, pp. 22–27.
"George Orwell", in *World Review*, June 1950, no. 16, pp. 5–7.
"Crime and the Community", in *The Listener*, 1 June 1950, vol. 43, pp. 939, 953.
"Can We Afford to Keep Open Minds?", in *The New York Times*, 11 June 1950, sec. 6, pp. 9, 37–39.
"Bertrand Russell's Blueprint for Australia's Future", in *The Daily Telegraph*, 26 June 1950, p. 6.
"Only Birth Control Will Check Over-Population", in *The Daily Telegraph*, 27 June 1950, p. 6.
"Belief in Man's Omnipotence Is Delusion Which Creates Dictators", in *The Daily Telegraph*, 3 July 1950, p. 6.
"How the Races Could Live Side by Side", in *The Daily Telegraph*, 4 July 1950, p. 8.
"Communist Fanaticism Is the Chief Threat to Peace Today", in *The Daily Telegraph*, 6 July 1950, p. 6.
"A World Split in Two", in *The Daily Telegraph*, 10 July 1950, p. 6.
"We and U.S. Can Lead and Help Asian People", in *The Daily Telegraph*, 13 July 1950, p. 8.
"Intelligent Democracy Can Create a Good World", in *The Daily Telegraph*, 17 July 1950, p. 8.
"Science Can Help Australia Support More People", in *The Daily Telegraph*, 21 July 1950, p. 8.
"Bertrand Russell Tells Us What Communism Is", in *The Argus*, 31 July 1950, p. 2.
"Private Monopoly Is Bane of Capitalism", in *The Argus*, 1 August 1950, p. 2.
"The Atom, World Hatreds, and You", in *The Argus*, 2 August 1950, p. 1.
"Greater Democracy Is Socialism's Purpose", in *The Argus*, 2 August 1950, p. 2.
"Land With a Future for Ambitious Youth", in *The Daily Telegraph*, 23 August 1950, p. 8.
"I Leave Your Shores With More Hope for Man", in *The Daily Telegraph*, 24 August 1950, p. 8.
"If We Are to Survive This Dark Time", in *The New York Times*, 3 September 1950, sec. 6, pp. 5, 17–18.
"Happy Australia", in *The Observer*, 22 October 1950, p. 4.
"The Kind of Fear We Sorely Need", in *The New York Times*, 29 October 1950, sec. 6, pp. 9, 52–55.
"Light and Shade of Fifty Years", in *London Calling*, 9 November 1950, no. 581, p. 12.
"Thoughts on Liberty Then and Now. Broadcast Lecture on Mill", in *London Calling*, 7 December 1950, no. 585, p. 10.
"To Replace Our Fears With Hope", in *The New York Times*, 31 December 1950, sec. 6, pp. 5, 23, 25.
New Hopes for a Changing World, London, Allen & Unwin, 1951.

"What We Should Do Now", in *European Digest*, January 1951, vol. 1, no. 2, p. 37.
"My Plan for Peace", in *Daily Herald*, 15 January 1951, p. 4.
"To Face Danger without Hysteria", in *The New York Times*, 21 January 1951, sec. 6, pp. 7, 42, 44–45.
"Why America Is Losing Her Allies", in *The Wichita Beacon*, 5 February 1951, p. 1.
"The Future of Man", in *The Atlantic Monthly*, March 1951, vol. 187, no. 2, pp. 48–51.
"What Can I Do?", in *Mademoiselle*, March 1951, vol. 32, no. 5, pp. 107, 160–162.
"Hvad Betyder det Enkelte Individ?", in *Fremtiden*, March 1951, vol. 6, no. 3, pp. 7– 9.
"Soviet 'Humor' Offers a Moral for Us", in *The New York Times*, 1 April 1951, sec. 6, pp. 9, 26.
"World Sighs with Relief at Firing of Macarthur", in *The Daily Compass*, 18 April 1951, p. 2.
"Lord Russell and the Atom Bomb", in *New Statesman*, 21 April 1951, pp. 448, 450.
"What's Wrong with Americans?", in *Look*, 24 April 1951, vol. 15, no. 9, pp. 34–35.
"Bertrand Russell on 'How I Write'", in *London Calling*, 10 May 1951, no. 607, p. 12.
"Present Perplexities", in *The Listener*, 17 May 1951, vol. 45, pp. 787–788.
"Are These Moral Codes Out of Date?", in *Evening Standard*, 22 May 1951, p. 9.
"Obsolete Ideas", in *The Listener*, 24 May 1951, vol. 45, pp. 822–823.
"The Modern Mastery of Nature", in *The Listener*, 31 May 1951, vol. 45, pp. 881, 883.
"The Limits of Human Power", in *The Listener*, 7 June 1951, vol. 45, pp. 911–912.
"Conflict and Unification", in *The Listener*, 14 June 1951, vol. 45, pp. 954–955.
"The Achievement of Harmony", in *The Listener*, 21 June 1951, vol. 45, pp. 984–985.
"Ludwig Wittgenstein", in *Mind*, July 1951, vol. 60, no. 239, pp. 297–298.
"China and History", in *The Saturday Review of Literature*, 4 August 1951, vol. 34, no. 31, p. 39.
"Competition and Co-Operation in Politics and Economics", in *Progress*, Autumn 1951, vol. 42, no. 232, pp. 13–16.
"Prof. Gilbert Murray Honoured", in *The Manchester Guardian*, 12 September 1951, p. 10.
"Are Human Beings Necessary?", in *Everybody's Weekly*, 15 September 1951, p. 13.
"Denies Categorization as a 'Humanist'", in *The Humanist*, October 1951, vol. 11, p. 199.
"British Philosopher Calls for Development of New Beliefs to Fit Techniques", in *New York Herald Tribune*, 28 October 1951, sec. 9, pp. 16, 18.
"Democracy and the Teachers", in *The Manchester Guardian*, 30 October 1951, pp. 6, 8.
"L'éducation sexuelle est souhaitable", in *Science et vie*, November 1951, vol. 80, p. 303.
"My Faith in the Future", in *John O'London's Weekly*, 9 November 1951, vol. 60, p. 706.
"The Corsican Ordeal of Miss X", in *Go*, December 1951–January 1952, no. 5, pp. 69–74, 76–77.
"The Best Answer to Fanaticism: Liberalism", in *The New York Times*, 16 December 1951, sec. 6, pp. 9, 40–42.
"The Narrow Line", in *New York Herald Tribune*, 16 December 1951, sec. 7, pp. 7, 22, 35.
The Impact of Science on Society, London, Allen & Unwin, 1952.
Bertrand Russell's Dictionary of Mind, Matter and Morals, edited and with an introduction by Lester E. Denonn, New York, Philosophical Library, 1952.
"The Road to Happiness", in *The Listener*, 31 January 1952, vol. 47, pp. 177–178.

"Is America in the Grip of Hysteria?", in *The New Leader*, 3 March 1952, vol. 35, no. 9, p. 23.
"Advice to Those Who Want To Attain 80", in *The New York Times*, 18 May 1952, sec. 6, p. 13.
"The Next Eighty Years", in *The Observer*, 18 May 1952, p. 4.
"Reflections on My Eightieth Birthday", in *The Listener*, 22 May 1952, vol. 47, pp. 823–824.
"The American Way (a Briton Says) Is Dour", in *The New York Times*, 15 June 1952, sec. 6, pp. 12, 30.
"Academic Freedom in America and Britain", in *The University of Chicago Round Table*, 22 June 1952, no. 743, pp. 1–11.
"Alfred North Whitehead", in *The Listener*, 10 July 1952, vol. 48, pp. 51–52.
"Maynard Keynes and Lytton Strachey", in *The Listener*, 17 July 1952, vol. 48, pp. 97–98.
"D.H. Lawrence", in *The Listener*, 24 July 1952, vol. 48, pp. 135–136.
"Completely Married", in *The Listener*, 31 July 1952, vol. 48, pp. 177–178.
"Three Essentials for a Stable World", in *The New York Times*, 3 August 1952, sec. 6, pp. 11, 53.
"The Next Eighty Years", in *The Saturday Review of Literature*, 9 August 1952, vol. 35, no. 32, pp. 8–9, 48–49.
"'The Faultless Max' at 80", in *The New York Times*, 24 August 1952, sec. 6, pp. 18–19, 41.
"Britain Can Lead Europe to Equality with America", in *European and Atlantic Digest*, Autumn 1952, vol. 2, no. 4, pp. 3–6.
"The Medieval Mind of Gandhi", in *Institute of Social Studies*, Autumn-Winter 1952, vol. 1, no. 7–8, pp. 73, 80, 88–89.
"As School Opens: The Educators Examined", in *The New York Times*, 7 September 1952, sec. 6, pp. 9, 44–45.
"Reason and Passion", in *The Listener*, 25 September 1952, vol. 48, pp. 495–496.
"Mahatma Gandhi", in *The Atlantic Monthly*, December 1952, vol. 190, no. 6, pp. 35–39.
"How to Be Happy in 1953", in *Sunday Graphic*, 28 December 1952, p. 2.
Satan in the Suburbs and Other Stories, London, The Bodley Head, 1953.
"What Shall We Teach Our Children?", in *News Chronicle*, 5 January 1953, p. 4.
"Young People in a Changing Civilisation", in *Picture Post*, 10 January 1953, vol. 58, no. 2, pp. 5–7.
"The Infra-Redioscope", in *Daily Mail*, 12–16 January 1953, pp. 6, 6, 6, 4, 6.
"De Vrijheid is Drieërlei", in *Elseviers Weekblad*, 31 January 1953, vol. 9, no. 5, p. 5.
"The Cult of 'Common Usage'", in *The British Journal for the Philosophy of Science*, February 1953, vol. 3, no. 12, pp. 303–307.
"Education's Place in a New Age", in *Saturday Night*, 7 March 1953, vol. 68, no. 22, pp. 1, 7–8.
"The Idea of Progress", in *The Manchester Guardian*, 14 March 1953, p. 4.
"'G' Is For Gobbledegook", in *New York Herald Tribune*, 12 April 1953, sec. 7, pp. 23, 64.
"Looking Backward: To the 1950's", in *The New York Times*, 26 April 1953, sec. 6, pp. 12, 58–59.
"Benefit of Clergy", in *Harper's Bazaar*, June 1953, vol. 87, no. 6, pp. 86–87, 124, 130.
"Are the World's Troubles Due to Decay of Faith?", in *El Nacional*, 3 August 1953, p. 75.
"Cambridge in the Eighteen-Nineties", in *The Listener*, 20 August 1953, vol. 50, pp. 307–308.
"Cambridge Friendships", in *The Listener*, 27 August 1953, vol. 50, pp. 337–338.

"Bernard Shaw, the Admirable Iconoclast", in *The Listener*, 3 September 1953, vol. 50, pp. 380–381.
"H.G. Wells: Liberator of Thought", in *The Listener*, 10 September 1953, vol. 50, pp. 417–418.
"Joseph Conrad", in *The Listener*, 17 September 1953, vol. 50, pp. 462–463.
"George Santayana", in *The Listener*, 24 September 1953, vol. 50, pp. 503, 511.
"What Would Help Mankind Most?", in *The New York Times*, 27 September 1953, sec. 6, pp. 10, 47–49.
"Bertrand Russell and 'Preventive War'", in *The Nation*, October 1953, vol. 177, p. 320.
"What Is an Agnostic?", in *Look*, 3 November 1953, vol. 17, no. 22, pp. 96, 98–101.
"A World I'd Like", in *The Nation*, 7 November 1953, vol. 177, pp. 367–369.
"Mr. Bowdler's Family Bliss", in *Courier*, December 1953, vol. 21, no. 5, pp. 69–72.
"A Philosophy for Our Time", in *London Calling*, 17 December 1953, no. 737, pp. 8, 18.
Human Society in Ethics and Politics, London, Allen & Unwin, 1954.
Nightmares of Eminent Persons and Other Stories, London, The Bodley Head, 1954.
History as an Art, Aldington, Hand and Flower Press, 1954.
"The Danger to Mankind", in *Bulletin of the Atomic Scientists*, January 1954, vol. 10, no. 1, pp. 8–9.
"Atomic Energy and the Future of the World", in *The Asahi Shimbun*, 1 January 1954.
"The Corroding Effects of Suspicion", in *The New York Times*, 14 February 1954, sec. 6, pp. 7, 55–56.
"What next? The Summing Up", in *London Calling*, 4 March 1954, no. 748, p. 10.
"The Psycho-Analyst's Nightmare", in *Courier*, April 1954, vol. 22, no. 4, pp. 81–87.
"Segreti del domani", in *Corriere della Sera*, 22 June 1954, p. 3.
"Secrets of Happiness", in *Everybody's Weekly*, 26 June 1954, pp. 20–21.
"Virtue and the Censor", in *Encounter*, July 1954, vol. 3, no. 10, pp. 8–11.
"You and Your Work", in *Everybody's Weekly*, 3 July 1954, pp. 18–19.
"You and Your Leisure", in *Everybody's Weekly*, 10 July 1954, pp. 28–29.
"You and the State", in *Everybody's Weekly*, 17 July 1954, pp. 19, 45.
"The Hydrogen Bomb and World Government", in *The Listener*, 22 July 1954, vol. 52, pp. 133–134.
"The Most Hopeful Road to Peace", in *Picture Post*, 24 July 1954, vol. 64, no. 4, pp. 13–14.
"Reflections on the Re-Awakening East", in *Pakistan Quarterly*, August 1954, vol. 4, no. 3, pp. 4–7.
"A Study in Futility: H-Bomb Politics", in *Saturday Night*, 14 August 1954, vol. 69, no. 45, pp. 7–8.
"A Prescription for the World", in *The Saturday Review*, 28 August 1954, vol. 37, no. 35, pp. 9–11 and 38–40.
"Birth Control and World Problems", in *Crux*, Autumn 1954, vol. 9, no. 1, pp. 4, 6.
"Knowledge and Wisdom", in *The Listener*, 9 September 1954, vol. 52, p. 390.
"1948 Russell vs. 1954 Russell", in *The Saturday Review*, 16 October 1954, vol. 37, no. 42, pp. 25–26.

"What Neutrals Can Do to Save the World", in *Britain To-day*, November 1954, no. 223, pp. 6–10.
"Will Marriage Survive?", in *Everybody's Weekly*, 25 December 1954, pp. 10–11.
"Man's Peril from the Hydrogen Bomb", in *The Listener*, 30 December 1954, vol. 52, pp. 1, 135–136.
"Religionen och Sanningskravet", in *Dagens Nyheter*, 31 December 1954, p. 4.
"The Road to Peace", in *Inter-Parliamentary Bulletin*, 1955, vol. 25, no. 2, pp. 49–53.
"John Stuart Mill", in *Proceedings of the British Academy*, 1955, vol. 41, pp. 43–59.
"A Statement for the New Year", in *Bulletin of the Atomic Scientists*, January 1955, vol. 11, no. 1, p. 4.
"What Will Happen to Liberty?", in *Everybody's Weekly*, 1 January 1955, pp. 9–10.
"Kan Kristendomen Bota Världens Bekymmer?", in *Dagens Nyheter*, 2 January 1955, p. 4.
"What Power Will Britain Have?", in *Everybody's Weekly*, 8 January 1955, pp. 20, 33.
"Will Your Children Have This Kind of Education?", in *Everybody's Weekly*, 15 January 1955, pp. 18–19.
"Influence of John Stuart Mill", in *The Times*, 20 January 1955, p. 11.
"Philosophers and Idiots", in *The Listener*, 10 February 1955, vol. 53, pp. 247, 249.
"Promoting Virtuous Conduct", in *The Observer*, 20 February 1955, p. 6.
"No Victory in H-Bomb War", in *The Statesman*, 25 February 1955, pp. 1, 7.
"Why I Took to Philosophy", in *London Calling*, 3 March 1955, no. 800, p. 9.
"A Pacifist in Wartime", in *London Calling*, 17 March 1955, no. 802, p. 10.
"Can the Liberal Survive?", in *The Saturday Review*, 19 March 1955, vol. 38, no. 12, pp. 22, 35.
"War and the Pursuit of Peace", in *London Calling*, 24 March 1955, no. 803, p. 8.
"A Philosophy of My Own", in *London Calling*, 31 March 1955, no. 804, p. 10.
"So I Go On Writing Books", in *London Calling*, 7 April 1955, no. 805, p. 10.
"Albert Einstein", in *The Observer*, 24 April 1955, p. 8.
"The Greatness of Albert Einstein", in *The Listener*, 28 April 1955, vol. 53, pp. 745–746.
"The Choice Is Ours", in *The Nation*, 18 June 1955, vol. 180, pp. 515–517.
"Creating Climate of Peace", in *The Manchester Guardian*, 27 June 1955, p. 7.
"'Texts of Scientists' – Appeal for Abolition of War", in *The New York Times*, 10 July 1955, p. 25.
"Is the Nightmare Ending?", in *News Chronicle*, 19 July 1955, p. 4.
"China, Geen Oord voor Tyrannen", in *Vrij Nederland*, 26 November 1955, vol. 16, no. 14, p. 3.
Portraits from Memory and Other Essays, New York, Simon and Schuster, 1956.
Logic and Knowledge: Essays 1901–1950, edited by Robert C. Marsh, New York, Macmillan Company, 1956.
"Nuclear Weapons and World Peace", in *Sangyo Keizai Shimbun*, 1 January 1956.
"How to Avoid a Nuclear War", in *Everybody's Weekly*, 21 January 1956, pp. 9–11.
"The Marxist Fraud", in *News Chronicle*, 26 March 1956, p. 4.
"A Great English Historian", in *London Calling*, 3 May 1956, no. 861, p. 8.

"A Dispute in *Pravda* on Disarmament", in *The Current Digest of the Soviet Press*, 9 May 1956, vol. 8, no. 13, pp. 8–10.
"Philosophical Analysis", in *The Hibbert Journal*, July 1956, vol. 54, pp. 320–329.
"In the Company of Cranks", in *The Saturday Review*, 11 August 1956, vol. 39, no. 32, pp. 7–8.
"Nuclear Weapons Must Not Be Used", in *New Times*, September 1956, vol. 14, no. 39, pp. 8–9.
"Human Intelligence and Genius", in *L'Âge nouveau*, October 1956, no. 98, p. 68.
"State of Civil Liberties in USA", in *Daily Worker*, 30 October 1956, pp. 6–7.
Why I am not a Christian and Other Essays on Religion and Related Subjects, with an appendix on the Bertrand Russell case by Paul Edwards, New York, Simon and Schuster, 1957
Understanding History and Other Essays, New York, Philosophical Library, 1957.
"Do Men Survive Death?", in *The Sunday Times*, 13 January 1957, p. 10.
"The State of US Civil Liberties", in *The New Leader*, 18 February 1957, vol. 40, no. 7, pp. 16–18.
"Every Nation Is a Bully at Heart", in *Maclean's Magazine*, 2 March 1957, vol. 70, no. 5, pp. 2, 48.
"The Tests Should Be Stopped", in *The New Scientist*, 28 March 1957, vol. 1, no. 19, pp. 24–25.
"Logic and Ontology", in *The Journal of Philosophy*, April 1957, vol. 54, no. 9, pp. 225–230.
"An Education in History", in *London Calling*, 4 April 1957, no. 909, p. 6.
"Hope and Fear", in *Everybody's Weekly*, 18 May 1957, pp. 9, 27.
"Mr. Strawson and Referring", in *Mind*, July 1957, vol. 66, no. 263, pp. 385–389.
"Three Reasons Why They Dislike Us", in *The New York Times*, 8 September 1957, sec. 6, pp. 20, 115.
"Can Scientific Man Survive?", in *The Sunday Times*, 10 November 1957, p. 14.
"Open Letter to Eisenhower and Khrushchev", in *New Statesman*, 23 November 1957, vol. 54, p. 638.
"Just One Bomb and One Hothead", in *Oxford Mail*, 17 December 1957, p. 4.
The Will to Doubt, New York, Philosophical Library, 1958.
Bertrand Russell's Best: Silhouettes in Satire, selected and introduced by Robert E. Egner, London, Allen & Unwin, 1958.
"Voltaire's Influence on Me", in *Studies on Voltaire and the Eighteenth Century*, 1958, vol. 6, pp. 157–162.
"What is Mind?", in *The Journal of Philosophy*, January 1958, vol. 55, no. 1, pp. 5–12.
"The Two Visions", in *The Montreal Star*, 3 January 1958, p. 11.
"The Divorce of Science and Culture", in *The Unesco Courier*, February 1958, vol. 11, no. 2, p. 4.
"The World and the Observer", in *The Listener*, 6 February 1958, vol. 59, pp. 223–226.
"Message on Nuclear Disarmament", in *Backwards*, March 1958, p. 1.
"Science and Coexistence", in *International Affairs*, March 1958, vol. 29, no. 3, p. 42.
"Why I Have Changed My Mind", in *News Chronicle*, 21 March 1958, p. 4.
"Choice in Nuclear Arms Race: Either Disarmament or Disaster", in *The Globe and Mail*, 3 April 1958, p. 7.
"World Government", Parliamentary Debates (Lords), 14 May 1958, vol. 209, cols. 332–336.

"World Communism and Nuclear War", in *The New Leader*, 26 May 1958, vol. 41, no. 21, pp. 9–10.
"Mankind versus the H-Bomb", in *International Journal*, Summer 1958, vol. 13, pp. 175–178.
"Aufruf an die Europäischen Intellektuellen", in *Die Kultur*, 15 June 1958, vol. 6, p. 2.
"Mathematical Infinity", in *Mind*, July 1958, vol. 67, no. 267, p. 385.
"Views on Nuclear Disarmament", in *United Nations News*, July–September 1958, vol. 13, no. 3, pp. 5–6.
"Freedom to Survive", in *The New Leader*, 7 July 1958, vol. 41, no. 27, pp. 23–25.
"Progress", in *The Observer*, 20 July 1958, p. 21.
"Progress and the Bomb", in *The Observer*, 27 July 1958, p. 2.
"The Dangers of Nuclear Warfare", in *Fifteen Nations*, October 1958, no. 7, pp. 63–65.
"My Philosophical Development", in *Maclean's Magazine*, October 1958, vol. 57, no. 1, pp. 2–8.
Common Sense and Nuclear Warfare, New York, Simon & Schuster, 1959.
My Philosophical Development, London, Allen & Unwin, 1959.
Wisdom of the West, edited by Paul Foulkes, London, Macdonald, 1959.
"My Plan to End Nuclear War Race", in *Reynolds News and Sunday Citizen*, 11, 18, 25 January 1959, pp. 8, 8, 10.
"Nuclear Disarmament", Parliamentary Debates (Lords), 11 February 1959, vol. 214, cols. 97–102.
"The Influence and Thought of G.E. Moore", in *The Listener*, 30 April 1959, vol. 61, pp. 755–756.
"The Expanding Mental Universe", in *Saturday Evening Post*, 18 July 1959, vol. 322, no. 3, pp. 24–25, 91–93.
"Snobbery", in *Encounter*, August 1959, vol. 13, no. 71, p. 71.
"Planetary Effulgence", in *New Statesman*, 5 September 1959, vol. 58, p. 272.
"Khrushchev Has Inaugurated a New Period of Peaceful Cooperation", in *New Times*, October 1959, vol. 17, no. 41, p. 6.
"Russell Tells of Need for World Authority", in *New York Journal-American*, 2 October 1959, p. 4.
"V Silakh Lyudei Sozdat Khorozhie Mir", in *Ogonek*, 1 November 1959, no. 1690, p. 8.
"Dare We Disarm?", in *John Bull*, 19 December 1959, vol. 106, no. 2783, pp. 9–10, 24.
Bertrand Russell Speaks His Mind, Cleveland-New York, The World Publishing Company, 1960.
"The Great Intrusion: Democracy in Higher Education", in *Brown Alumni Monthly*, January 1960, vol. 60, no. 4, pp. 8–10.
"The Possible Future of Mankind", in *Harper's Bazaar*, January 1960, vol. 93, pp. 122–123.
"The Social Responsibilities of Scientists", in *Science*, 12 February 1960, vol. 131, no. 3398, pp. 391–392.
"4 Minute Madness", in *Sunday Dispatch*, 28 February 1960, p. 10.
"The Issue of Nuclear Testing", in *New York Post*, 6 March 1960, p. 10.
"Report With an X-Certificate", in *Sunday Dispatch*, 13 March 1960, p. 10.
"Nado Proyavyt Dobruyu Volyu", in *Ogonek*, 8 May 1960, no. 1716, p. 6.
"Peace? And Freedom?", in *The New Leader*, 9 May 1960, vol. 43, no. 19, pp. 13–14.

"Praises Nehru in issue devoted to Nehru", in *Wisdom*, June 1960, vol. 34, p. 2.
"The Case for Neutralism", in *The New York Times*, 24 July 1960, sec. 6, pp. 10, 35–36.
"Saving World from Brink of Nuclear War", in *The Hindu*, 24 July 1960, pp. 1, 111.
"Edenstvennyi Put", in *Izvestiia*, 20 September 1960, p. 3.
"Prospects of Mankind", in *The Listener*, 6 October 1960, vol. 64, pp. 543–548.
"Bertrand Russell Tells Why British Labor Voted to Renounce the Bomb", in *I.F. Stone's Weekly*, 31 October 1960, vol. 8, no. 39, pp. 1–3.
"The Russell-Scott Call for Non-Violent Resistance", in *Peace News*, 4 November 1960, no. 1271, p. 6.
Fact and Fiction, London, Allen & Unwin, 1961.
Has Man a Future?, New York, Simon & Schuster, 1961.
The Basic Writings of Bertrand Russell: 1903–1959, edited by Robert E. Egner and Lester E. Denonn, London, Allen & Unwin, 1961.
"Approaches to Disarmament", in *Post War World Council Newsletter*, January 1961, pp. 2–4.
"The Importance of Disarmament", in *International Affairs*, January 1961, vol. 7, no. 1, pp. 83–85.
"Civil Disobedience", in *New Statesman*, 17 February 1961, vol. 61, pp. 245–246.
"Bertrand Russell on Unilateralism", in *The New Republic*, 6 March 1961, vol. 144, no. 10, pp. 13–14.
"Thermonuclear War: Battle of the Experts", in *The New Republic*, 3 April 1961, vol. 144, no. 14, pp. 17–18.
"Differences on Disarmament", in *The Guardian*, 11 April 1961, p. 8.
"Human Life Is in Danger", in *Protest*, May 1961, vol. 3, no. 1, p. 1516.
"Sollte Großbritannien Einseitig Abrüsten?", in *Blätter für deutsche und internationale Politik*, May 1961, vol. 6, pp. 439–445.
"Message to New Zealanders", in *New Zealand Rationalist*, May–June 1961, p. 5.
"Protest to President", in *The Guardian*, 6 June 1961, p. 7.
"Address to CND Conference", in *Pour la paix*, July 1961, no. 8, pp. 6–13.
"Here's How to Put on the Brakes", in *Today*, 14 October 1961, vol. 4, no. 86, pp. 2–4.
"Thoughts on the 50–Megaton Bomb", in *New Statesman*, 3 November 1961, vol. 62, p. 638.
"Can Man Survive?", in *The Sunday Times*, 5, 12 November 1961, pp. 25–27, 27.
"'Is Canada Still Puritanical?' Russell Asks", in *Toronto Daily Star*, 4 December 1961, p. 7.
"What Are Humanity's Chances of Survival?", in *Toronto Daily Star*, 9 December 1961, pp. 12–13, 15, 23.
"Prison Sentences", in *Peace News*, 22 December 1961, no. 1330, p. 5.
Essays in Skepticism, New York, Wisdom Library-Philosophical Library, 1962.
"The Misfortune of Being Out-of-Date", in *Harper's Bazaar*, January 1962, no. 3002, pp. 126, 148, 150.
"The Case for British Nuclear Disarmament", in *Bulletin of the Atomic Scientists*, March 1962, vol. 18, no. 3, pp. 6–10.
"Nuclear Disarmament: What I Think", in *Labour Monthly*, March 1962, vol. 44, pp. 123–125.

"Global Butchery", in *Liberation*, April 1962, vol. 7, no. 2, p. 5.
"For and Against Being 90", in *The Observer*, 13 May 1962, p. 10.
"This Great Englishman Bertrand Russell", in *Daily Herald*, 17 May 1962, p. 8.
"Bertrand Russell at 90 Still Fighting On", in *The Irish Times*, 18 May 1962, p. 8.
"Bertrand Russell Contesta a *Tierra y Libertad*", in *Tierra y Libertad*, June 1962, no. 229, pp. 10–11.
"Has Man a Future?", in *Gandhi Marg*, July 1962, vol. 6, pp. 256–258.
"Nuclear Disarmament: What I Think", in *The Socialist*, July–September 1962, no. 4, pp. 66–68.
"What Are the Few to Do?", in *Peace News*, 28 September 1962, no. 1370, p. 12.
"Bertrand Russell's Message to America", in *National Guardian*, 15 October 1962, vol. 15, no. 1, p. 3.
"Russell Pleads for End to American Madness", in *The Globe and Mail*, 24 October 1962, p. 8.
"Earl Russell's Reply", in *The Daily Telegraph*, 25 October 1962.
"Statement from Russell", in *Peace News*, 26 October 1962, no. 1374, p. 12.
"Mr. Khrushchev Averted War", in *The Daily Telegraph*, 26 October 1962.
"Can Nuclear War Be Prevented?", in *New Statesman*, 26 October 1962, vol. 64, pp. 560, 562.
"Behold the Burglars, Kennedy Tells Russell", in *The Evening Star*, 27 October 1962, p. 3.
"Scrap NATO – Russell", in *Daily Herald*, 29 October 1962.
"Telegrama Bertrana Rassela", in *Pravda*, 30 October 1962, p. 1.
"Sanity in the Nuclear Age", in *Man and Society*, November 1962, vol. 2, no. 2, pp. 9–10.
"China 'Always Attacked', Chou En-Lai Tells Russell", in *The Sun*, 23 November 1962, p. 11.
"Mass Murder, Systematic Genocide", in *The Statesman Week-End Review*, 8 December 1962, vol. 8, no. 2, p. 5.
"China: Russell Speaks", in *Peace News*, 14 December 1962, no. 1381, p. 9.
"Bertrand Russell's Memorable Message on Getting the ECLC Tom Paine Award", in *I.F. Stone's Weekly*, 17 December 1962, vol. 10, no. 46, p. 4.
"Whole People Enslaved", in *The Times*, 29 December 1962.
Unarmed Victory, London, Allen & Unwin, 1963.
"Messages to Kennedy and Khrushchev", in *Encounter*, January 1963, vol. 20, no. 112, pp. 88, 91.
"Concerning Cuba/Messages Concernant Cuba", in *Pour la paix*, January–June 1963, vol. 4, no. 14–15, pp. 9–19.
"Russell's Appeal to India", in *The Statesman Week-End Review*, 5 January 1963, vol. 8, no. 6, p. 3.
"Resigns from Committee of 100", in *Peace News*, 11 January 1963, no. 1385, p. 12.
"Britain Must Lead", in *Union Voice*, March 1963, p. 3.
"Letters between Russell and Khrushchev", in *The Jewish Chronicle*, 8 March 1963, p. 1.
"Stop the Race Towards Death", in *Toronto Daily Star*, 23 March 1963, pp. 18–19.
"Is Communism a Menace?", in *The New York Times*, 7 April 1963, sec. 6, pp. 35, 168–173.
"Vietnam Policy Protested", in *The New York Times*, 8 April 1963, p. 46.
"Russell Repeats Atrocity Charges", in *The New York Times*, 9 April 1963, p. 12.

"Bertrand Russell on the Sinful Americans", in *Harper's Magazine*, June 1963, vol. 226, no. 1357, pp. 20–30.
"Unarmed Victory", in *The Spectator*, 28 June 1963, vol. 210, pp. 834–835.
"Russell Protests", in *New Generation*, July–August 1963, no. 12, p. 2.
"Earl Russell Condemns Arms for Iraqis", in *Daily Worker*, 2 July 1963, p. 3.
"Chemical Warfare in Vietnam", in *The New Republic*, 6 July 1963, vol. 149, no. 1, pp. 30–31.
"U.S. Negroes' Plight", in *Globe and Mail*, 28 August 1963.
"Nightmare of Terror", in *Daily Worker*, 2 September 1963, p. 1.
"Peace Foundations Launched", in *The Times*, 30 September 1963, p. 8.
"The Menace to Human Survival", in *Frontier*, November 1963, vol. 15, no. 1, pp. 9–10.
"Sequel to the Test-Ban Treaty?", in *The Minority of One*, November 1963, vol. 5, no. 11, pp. 27–28.
"Russell's Statement", in *Peace News*, 29 November 1963, no. 1431, p. 4.
"Will Man Survive?", in *The Minority of One*, December 1963, vol. 5, no. 12, pp. 4–5.
"The Duty of a Philosopher in This Age" (1964), in E. Freeman (ed.), *The Abdication of Philosophy: Philosophy and the Public Good. Essays in Honor of Paul Arthur Schilpp*, La Salle, Open Court, 1976, pp. 15–22.
"Post-Kennedy World Outlook", in *The Minority of One*, January 1964, vol. 6, no. 1, pp. 4–5.
"Time: The Weekly Fiction Magazine", in *Fact*, January–February 1964, vol. 1, no. 1, p. 5.
"On the Avoidance of World War III", in *The Dong-a Ilbo*, 1 January 1964, p. 5.
"Lord Russell Sends Back Peace Medal", in *The Times*, 8 January 1964, p. 14.
"Rethinking for Peace", in *The Guardian*, 29 January 1964, p. 5.
"Scientists and World Peace", in *The Minority of One*, February 1964, vol. 6, no. 2, p. 5.
"Tribute to Linus Pauling", in *The Minority of One*, February 1964, vol. 6, no. 2, pp. 14–15.
"The Assassination", in *The Minority of One*, February 1964, vol. 6, no. 2, p. 22.
"Stop M.E. Nuclear Race!", in *New Outlook*, February 1964, vol. 7, no. 2, pp. 2–3.
"War in Vietnam", in *The Observer*, 9 February 1964, p. 30.
"The Bomb Has Blunted Our Moral Sense", in *Toronto Daily Star*, 22 February 1964, pp. 11–13.
"War and Atrocity in Vietnam", in *Views*, Spring 1964, no. 4, pp. 73–79.
"War and Peace in the Nuclear Age", in *The Minority of One*, March 1964, vol. 6, no. 3, pp. 18–19.
"On the Cold War", in *The Minority of One*, April 1964, vol. 6, no. 4, pp. 16–17.
"The American Empire", in *The Minority of One*, May 1964, vol. 6, no. 5, p. 10.
"Kennedy Data", in *The Sunday Times*, 31 May 1964, p. 18.
"Jawaharlal Nehru 1889–1964", in *The Minority of One*, July 1964, vol. 6, no. 7, pp. 12–13.
"Detente or New Entanglements?", in *The Minority of One*, August 1964, vol. 6, no. 8, p. 8.
"On Vietnam Peace", in *The Guardian*, 6 August 1964.
"Russell Condemns U.S. Vietnam Action", in *The New York Times*, 8 August 1964, p. 3.
"South Vietnam Shot First", in *New York Herald Tribune*, 23 August 1964.
"Anomalies of the Cold War", in *Bent*, Autumn 1964, no. 1, pp. 11–12.
"Redbook Dialogue", in *Redbook*, September 1964, vol. 123, no. 5, pp. 66–67, 145–149.

"Sixteen Questions on the Assassination", in *The Minority of One*, September 1964, vol. 6, no. 9, pp. 6–8.
"A Question of Proof", in *Evening Standard*, 28 September 1964.
"Africa Can Stop This Nuclear Madness!", in *Africa and the World*, October 1964, vol. 1, no. 1, pp. 8–11.
"Colonialism, Oppression and South Arabia", in *The Minority of One*, October 1964, vol. 6, no. 10, pp. 6–7.
"Who Spawned Goldwater", in *American Dialog*, October–November 1964, vol. 1, no. 2, pp. 5–6.
"Tarafsizlik Türkiyeyi tek Basyina Birakmaz", in *Cumhuriyet*, 18 October 1964, pp. 1, 7.
"Open Letter to Pres. Johnson", in *St. Louis Post-Dispatch*, 25 October 1964, p. 2.
"Freedom in Iran", in *The Minority of One*, November 1964, vol. 6, no. 2, pp. 12–13.
"The Cold War and World Poverty", in *Africa and the World*, November 1964, vol. 1, no. 2, pp. 7–11.
"How Much Democracy Have We in Britain?", in *The Journal*, November 1964, no. 216, p. 1.
"Lord Russell Attacks Soviet Anti-Semitism", in *The Jewish Advocate*, 5 November 1964, pp. 1, 17.
"Russell Chides U.S. on Vietnam Aims", in *The New York Times*, 28 November 1964, p. 9.
"Bertrand Russell Asks Africans to Renounce Tshombe", in *The Guardian*, 30 November 1964, p. 9.
"Free World Barbarism", in *The Minority of One*, December 1964, vol. 6, no. 12, pp. 8–12.
"Another Cold War if China Treated as Pariah", in *Sanity*, December 1964, vol. 2, no. 5, p. 4.
"Semantics and the Cold War", in *Playboy*, December 1964, vol. 11, no. 12, pp. 175, 206, 251.
"War Criminals", in *The Daily Telegraph*, 1 December 1964, p. 14.
"A Hearing for Oswald", in *The Sunday Times*, 20 December 1964, p. 8.
"Russell's Advice to World: Stop Hating", in *The Sacramento Bee*, 20 December 1964, p. 1.
On the Philosophy of Science, edited by Charles A. Fritz, Indianapolis-New York-Kansas City, The Bobbs-Merrill Company, 1965.
Legitimacy Versus Industrialism 1814–1848, London, Allen & Unwin, 1965.
"The Ethos of Violence", in *The Minority of One*, January 1965, vol. 7, no. 1, pp. 6–7.
"India and the Chinese Bomb", in *Gandhi Marg*, January 1965, vol. 9, no. 33, pp. 4–5.
"Prospects for Peace, 1965", in *British-Soviet Friendship*, January 1965, pp. 5–6.
"The Cold War: A New Phase?", in *The Minority of One*, February 1965, vol. 7, no. 2, pp. 7–8.
"US Has Shocked Mankind", in *Daily Worker*, 27 March 1965, p. 2.
"Need for the Bertrand Russell Peace Foundation", in *PazAhora*, April 1965, no. 1, p. 6.
"The Labor Party's Foreign Policy", in *The Minority of One*, April 1965, vol. 7, no. 4, pp. 15–18.
"Prospects of Escalation in Southeast Asia", in *The Minority of One*, May 1965, vol. 7, no. 5, p. 9.
"Lord Russell Says US Seeks China War", in *Victoria Daily Times*, 29 June 1965, p. 29.
"Bertrand Russell: The Threat to World Peace is American Imperialism", in *Peking Review*, 23 July 1965, vol. 8, no. 30, p. 21.
"Bertrand Russell on Vietnam", in *Frontier*, September 1965, vol. 16, no. 11, pp. 12–13.

"The Future of the United Nations", in *The Illustrated Weekly of India*, 28 November 1965, vol. 86, no. 48, p. 28.
"Let Us Join Together to Resist US Imperialism", in *Peking Review*, 10 December 1965, vol. 8, no. 50, pp. 9–11.
"Bertrand Russell's Reply to Premier Chou En-Lai", in *Peking Review*, 10 December 1965, vol. 8, no. 50, p. 9.
"Lord Russell on Kashmir", in *The Statesman Week-End Review*, 25 December 1965, vol. 2, no. 4, p. 3.
"A Century of General Civil War", in *The Minority of One*, April 1966, vol. 8, no. 4, p. 19.
"The 'Yellow Peril'", in *The Minority of One*, May 1966, vol. 8, no. 5, p. 9.
"The Only Honorable Policy in Vietnam", in *The Minority of One*, June 1966, vol. 8, no. 6, pp. 12–13.
"The Economics of Hunger", in *Inheritance*, July 1966, no. 3, pp. 25–28.
"Speech on Vietnam Solidarity Campaign", in *Vietnam Solidarity Bulletin*, July 1966, vol. 1, no. 4, pp. 2–5.
"An Appeal to the American Conscience", in *World Outlook*, 1 July 1966, vol. 4, pp. 26–32.
"Pakistan's Independent Policy", in *Morning News*, 14 August 1966, suppl. 1, p. 11.
"The Conscience of Mankind", in *Vietnam Solidarity Bulletin*, September 1966, vol. 1, no. 5, pp. 1, 6.
"An Exclusive Interview with Lord Bertrand Russell", in *The Forum*, 12 September 1966, vol. 1, no. 1, p. 2.
"American Murder Über Alles", in *Marcha*, 30 September 1966, no. 1323, pp. 3–6.
"Bertrand Russell's Appeal to Negro Soldiers in Vietnam", in *World Outlook*, 14 October 1966, vol. 4, pp. 27–28.
"Le Tribunal", in *Le Monde*, 15 October 1966, p. 2.
"Four Questions and Lord Russell's Replies", in *Toronto Daily Star*, 21 October 1966, p. 7.
"Mensaje a los Pueblos de Tercer Mundo", in *Marcha*, 18 November 1966, no. 1330, p. 23.
"Russell's Statement on War Crimes Tribunal", in *National Guardian*, 3 December 1966.
"Cable to Hanoi", in *International War Crimes Tribunal Bulletin*, 15 December 1966, no. 1, pp. 3, 5.
The Autobiography of Bertrand Russell, 3 vols., London, Allen & Unwin, 1967–1969.
War Crimes in Vietnam, London, Allen & Unwin, 1967.
Russell's Peace Appeals, edited by Tsutomu Makino and Kazuteru Hitaka, Tokyo, Eichosha's New Current Books, 1967.
Bertrand Russell: una antologia dagli scritti, edited by Enrico Musacchio, Torino, Loescher, 1967.
"The Western Press and U.S. Crimes", in *World Outlook*, 24 February 1967, vol. 5, pp. 201–204.
"Negotiations or Withdrawal: Which Way to Peace in Vietnam?", in *Morning News*, 22 March 1967, p. 30.
"Russell Condemns U.S. Brutality", in *The Daily Telegraph*, 3 May 1967, p. 25.
"Johnson Likadan som Hitler!", in *Expressen*, 6 May 1967, p. 14.

"Final Address by Bertrand Russell to Tribunal", in *Foundation Bulletin*, 1 June 1967, no. 12–13, pp. 1–3.
"Tribunalen", in *Aftonbladet*, 24 November 1967, p. 4.
"Genocide Finding by Russell Tribunal", in *The Times*, 2 December 1967, p. 5.
"U.S. Aggression in Vietnam a 'Pure Crime of Conquest'", in *World Outlook*, 8 December 1967, vol. 5, pp. 1009–1010.
"John Stuart Mill", in J.B. Schneewind (ed.), *Mill: A Collection of Critical Essays*, London, Palgrave Macmillan, 1968, pp. 1–21.
"Nato Forever?", in *New Statesman*, 15 March 1968, vol. 75, p. 329.
"Bertrand Russell on the War", in *Voice*, 1 May 1968, p. 3.
"Inside the Shah's Prisons", in *London Bulletin*, Autumn 1968, no. 6, pp. 51–54.
"Labour's Goldwater", in *Tribune*, 28 November 1969, p. 1.
Dear Bertrand Russell: A Selection of his Correspondence with the General Public 1950–1968, edited by Barry Feinberg and Ronald Kasrils, Boston, Houghton Mifflin Company, 1969.
Bertrand Russell, 1872–1970, Nottingham, Bertrand Russell Peace Foundation, 1970.
Il pensiero filosofico di Bertrand Russell: antologia di scritti, edited by Giuseppe Magnano, Bologna, Calderini, 1970.
"Message to February 1970 Parliamentarian Conference", in *The New York Times*, 23 February 1970, p. 21.
"On American Violence", in *Ramparts*, March 1970, vol. 8, no. 9, pp. 55–57.
"Bertrand Russell's Political Testament", in *Black Dwarf*, 5 September 1970, vol. 14, no. 37, pp. 7–10.
The Collected Stories of Bertrand Russell, compiled and edited by Barry Feinberg, London, Allen & Unwin, 1972.
The Life of Bertrand Russell in Pictures and in His Own Words, edited by Christopher Fraley, David Hodgson, Nottingham, Bertrand Russell Peace Foundation, 1972.
Essays in Analysis, edited by Douglas Lackey, London, Allen & Unwin, 1973.
Mortals and Others: Bertrand Russell's American Essays 1931–1935, edited by Harry Ruja, London, Allen & Unwin, 1975.
A Free Man's Worship, and Other Essays, London, Unwin Books, 1976.
The Collected Papers of Bertrand Russell, 20 vols., London-New York, Routledge-Allen & Unwin, 1983–2020.
Ecrits de logique philosophique, Paris, Puf, 1989.
The Selected Letters of Bertrand Russell, edited by Nicholas Griffin, 2 vols., London, Allen Lane-The Penguin Press, 1992–2001.
Russell on Ethics: Selections from the Writings of Bertrand Russell, edited by Charles R. Pigden, London-New York, Routledge, 1999.
Russell on Religion: Selections from the Writings of Bertrand Russell, edited by Louis Greenspan and Stefan Andersson, London, Routledge, 1999.

Yours Faithfully, Bertrand Russell: A Lifelong Fight for Peace, Justice, and Truth in Letters to the Editor, edited by Ray Perkins, Chicago, Open Court, 2001.

Publications Co-authored by Bertrand Russell

Braithwaite R.B., Russell B., Waismann F., "Symposium: The Relevance of Psychology to Logic", in *Aristotelian Society, Supplementary Volume*, July 1938, vol. 17, no. 1, pp. 19–68.
Lawrence D.H., Russell B., *D.H. Lawrence's Letters to Bertrand Russell*, edited by Harry T. Moore, New York, Gotham Book Mart, 1948.
Russell B., Einstein A., "Russell-Einstein Manifesto", in *The New York Times*, 10 July, 1955, p. 25.
Russell B., MacColl H., "The Existential Import of Propositions", in *Mind*, July 1905, vol. 14, no. 55, pp. 398–402.
Russell B., Russell P. (eds.), *The Amberley Papers: The Letters and Diaries of Lord and Lady Amberley*, with Patricia Russell, 2 vols., London, Leonard & Virginia Woolf at the Hogarth Press, 1937.
Whitehead A.N., Russell B., *Principia Mathematica*, 3 vols., Cambridge, Cambridge University Press, 1910–1913.

Index

Abendroth W. 131
Acheson D. 97
Addams J. 21, 31, 79
Addison C. 96
Adenauer K. 110
Adler M. 13, 29
Agnelli A. 22
Agnelli G. 22, 23
Ahmed M. 143
Aiken L.W. 143
Alcaro M. 143
Ali T. 131
Alighieri D. 1
Allen C. 39, 55, 62, 63, 68
Alter T. 143
Amos M. 72, 73
Anderson C.A. 157
Anderson L. 124, 202
Andersson S. 202
Anellis I.H. 144
Angelini G. 8
Angell N. 17–21, 47, 48, 67, 72, 87, 111, 137, 138

Ansbro J.J. 30
Anta C.G. 2, 7, 14, 20, 24, 25, 70, 71
Arfé G. 13
Armstrong T. 31
Arnold L. 104
Arthur C.J. 11
Arthur R.T.W. 144
Asquith H.H. 39, 46, 52, 53, 133, 136
Atlee C. 84
Aybar M.A. 131
Ayer A.J. 45, 131, 144

Badesa C. 152
Baldwin J. 131
Baldwin L.V. 30
Baldwin S. 78, 80, 84
Baldwin T. 144
Bandyopadhyay P. 27
Banks E.C. 144
Barbusse H. 69, 78
Barlow M. 16
Barnes A.C. 144
Barr S. 29

Barrère J.-B. 19
Bartel W. 14
Baruch B. 97–100, 133, 134
Basso L. 131
Beauvoir (de) S. 131
Bebel A. 36
Behler E. 7
Belgion M. 144
Bell D.R. 144
Bell G. 96
Benedict XV (Pope) 64
Benmakhlouf A. 144
Bentham J. 18, 72
Bentivegna G. 145
Berger J. 124
Bergson H. 16
Berkeley G. 36
Besant A. 78
Beveridge W. 95
Bevin E. 60
Bille (de) T. 16
Billi M. 8
Birn D.S. 79
Bismarck (von) O. 8, 16
Black D. 40
Blackwell K. 41, 66, 144, 159
Blitz D. 144
Bobbio N. 2, 3, 5, 56, 88, 103, 111, 121, 132, 135, 138
Boersma D. 5, 57, 121, 138
Bolo P.
Bolsover P. 119
Bolt R. 124
Bondfield M. 68
Bone A.G. 106, 115, 117
Bonino G. 144
Bopp F. 110
Borgese G.A. 29
Bori P.C. 28
Born M. 109, 110
Bornet G. 144
Bosco A. 24
Bouglé C. 31
Boulton J.T. 51

Bradford D.E. 144
Bradie M.P. 144
Brailsford H.N. 91, 92
Braine J. 124
Braithwaite R.B. 203
Breck A.D. 150
Bredsdorff E. 87
Briand A. 23, 78, 79
Bricquir (Le) D. 31
Bridgman P.W. 109
Brink A. 144
Broad C.D. 45
Brock P. 27, 88
Brockway F. 39, 55, 62, 69, 72
Brooks V.W. 57
Brown S. 147
Buber M. 78
Buchele H. 30
Bulgakov V. 79
Bulganin N.A. 110, 112
Burgess M. 24
Burgio S. 145
Burhop E. 112
Burke T. 144
Butler N.M. 21
Butler R. 124
Buxton C.R. 32, 68
Byrd M. 145
Byrne P. 119

Cabiati A. 22, 23
Campbell Smith M. 6
Candlish S. 145
Canning G. 48
Cantor G. 37
Cappio J. 145
Cárdenas L. 131
Carey R. 44, 145
Carlyle T. 82
Carpenter E. 78
Carr B. 145
Carr H.W. 16, 61
Carson C. 30, 31
Carson E. 64

Carson S. 31
Castro F. 126, 127, 130
Castronovo V. 23
Cattaneo C. 8
Cavers D.F. 117
Cavour (Benso di) C. 8
Ceadel M. 17, 88, 94
Ce zong Z. 71
Chamberlain N. 67, 80, 88, 89, 92
Chatterjee M. 27
Chemello A. 31
Cheval R. 19
Chirico D. 16
Chisholm G.B. 117
Choate J.H. 9
Chomsky N. 145
Chou E. 128
Chow T.-T. 71
Churchill W. 80, 92, 93, 97, 104, 116
Clack R.J. 145
Clark C.H.D. 145
Clark P. 146
Clark R.W. 44, 102, 119, 128, 145
Clark W.D. 104
Clarke P. 84
Clausewitz (von) C. 105, 106, 111, 138
Clay A. 31
Claybourne A. 30
Clément C. 27
Clifford J. 39
Coates K. 60, 129, 145
Cobden R. 7, 19, 48, 138
Cocchiarella N. 145
Cole G.D.H. 11, 66
Collins J. 119, 123
Colombo A. 8
Colorni E. 24
Combesque M.-C. 30
Coniglione F. 145
Conway D.W. 15
Corry R. 155
Corsano A. 145
Cortright D. 4, 5, 133, 134, 138
Cosimo G. 145

Costelloe K. 145
Coty R. 110
Coudenhove-Kalergi R.N. 22
Coulton G.G. 17, 47
Cousins F. 123
Crankshaw E. 69, 145
Crawshay-Williams R. 145
Cripps M. 31
Cripps R.S. 84
Croddy S. 145
Culbertson E. 108, 112
Cumpa J. 144
Cunningham S. 145
Czernin O. 64

Dahms H.-J. 145
Dalton D. 27
Danysz M. 117
Darwin C. 9, 10
Dau P. 146
Davies C. 107
Davis A. 148
Davoren J.M. 149
Dawson J. 147
Decher F. 15
Dedijer V. 131
Dejnožka J. 146
Delavis L. 144
Deleury G. 30
Dellinger D. 131
Dematteis P.B. 146
Demopoulos W. 146
Demos R. 146
Denonn L.E. 36, 191, 197
Denton P.H. 146
Descotes M. 19
Despard C. 60
Devaux P. 146
Dewar L. 146
Dewey J. 43, 79, 146
Dickinson G.L. 58
Diem N.D. 128
Di Francesco M. 146
Dinerstein H. 105

Dodge D.L. 7
Doisy M. 19
Donati S. 146
Dorward A. 146
Doty P.M. 117
Douglas J. 60
Driver C. 123
Duchatelet B. 19
Duff P. 119
Dugdale B. 16
Duhamel G. 78
Dulles J.F. 105, 112, 118, 119
Duncan M. 146
Dungan M.E. 31
Durant W. 146
Dyason E.C. 102
Dyson M.E. 30

Eames E.R. 38, 146
Eastman M. 69, 147
Easwaran E. 27
Eaton C.S. 117
Eden A. 110, 112, 114, 116
Edwards P. 93, 195
Egner R.E. 36, 195, 197
Einaudi L. 22, 24
Einstein A. 20, 29, 43, 78, 79, 85, 86, 95, 98, 99, 109–112, 133, 134, 203
Eisenhower D.D. 104, 110, 112, 118
Eisler L. 147
Elkind L.D.C. 147
Elliot W. 107
Emundts D. 149
Engels F. 10, 11
Eros (Greek God of love) 26, 135
Esteves O. 147
Estrella M.A. 131
Evans R.J. 31
Everett E. 39

Falk A.E. 147
Falk R.A. 132
Faure E. 112

Feferman S. 147
Feibleman J.K. 147
Feinberg B. 75, 126, 128, 147, 202
Fenwik C.G. 9
Fernbach D. 11
Fiala A. 5
Fichte J. 82, 94
Finch E. 42
Fisher H.H. 13
Fitzgerald E. 147
Flathman R.E. 147
Flechtheim O.K. 14
Fleischmann R. 110
Forel A. 78, 79
Forster E.M. 51
Fosl P.S. 146
Foster J.S. 117
Foulkes P. 196
Fox M.A. 4, 5, 88, 89, 133
Fraley C. 202
Frangella F. 16
Freedman L. 105
Freeman E. 129, 199
Freeman M.A. 122
Frege G. 37
Frenz H. 103, 189
Freud A. 26
Freud S. 3, 26, 57, 58, 76, 77, 79, 135
Friedman M. 146
Fritz C.A. 147, 200
Fromkin D. 52
Frumkin A.N. 99
Fry R. 51
Fuhrmann A. 147

Gaitskell H. 114, 125
Galilei G. 123
Gallacher W. 60
Gallagher I.J. 16
Galtung J. 4, 5, 57, 121, 138
Ganapathy T.N. 147
Gandhi M.K. 19, 27, 28, 30, 31, 78, 93, 125, 134, 137
Gandon S. 147

Gangal S.C. 27
Garbett C. 96
Garciadiego A.R. 147
Garibaldi G. 8
Gastaldi V.P. 8
Genghis Khan (founder of the Mongol Empire) 26
George V (King of the United Kingdom) 80
George VI (King of the United Kingdom) 103
Gerassi J. 130
Gerlach W. 110
Germains V.W. 17
Giaquinto M. 147
Giaretta P. 147
Giesz L. 15
Gillouin R. 16
Glaiser B. 39
Glanzberg M. 159
Glock H.J. 153
Gobineau (de) A. 9, 10
Gödel K. 147
Goethe N.B. 147
Goldman E. 68
Gorky M. 19, 68
Gotlind E. 147
Gottschalk H. 147
Graham P.J. 147
Grandjean F. 16
Grant G. 148
Grattan-Guinness I. 148
Grau G.G. 15
Graubard S.R. 59
Grayling A.C. 148
Green J.L. 148
Green K. 148
Green M.B. 28
Green P. (Artifex) 63
Greenspan L. 148, 202
Greenwood E.B. 27
Grelling K. 148
Grey E. 46, 48, 50, 57, 133
Griffin N. 44, 62, 103, 148, 155, 202

Griffiths D.A. 148
Groff P.S. 15
Gromyko A.A. 97
Grossman H. 131
Grotius H. 117
Groves J. 156
Guérard A.L. 29
Guerlac S. 16
Guevara E. 130
Gustafson R.F. 27

Haaparanta L. 145, 152
Haberkamp G. 15
Haden-Guest L. 68
Hager P.J. 148
Hahn O. 110
Halbasch K. 148
Halliday F. 113
Hamilton A. 21, 22, 25, 122, 140
Hansen D.D. 30
Hardy G.H. 39, 148
Hare W. 149
Harris S. 47
Harrison B. 149
Harrison M. 68
Harrison R. 61, 66, 149
Harvey E. 47
Harwood L.D. 149
Haslam B. 72
Hatfield G. 149
Hattiangadi J.N. 149
Haxel O. 110
Hayhurst S. 149
Hazen A.P. 149
Hegel G.W.F. 6, 7, 36, 37, 94
Heisenberg W.K. 110
Hellman G. 149
Henderson A. 64, 65, 69
Hendley B.P. 149
Hercules (Roman hero) 19
Hernandez M. 131
Hess Gankin O. 13
Hesse H. 20
Hetherington W. 85

Hide Ø. 149
Hieke A. 153
Higgins P.A. 9
Hill C.O. 149
Hiller K. 78
Hillman T.A. 149
Hindenburg (von) P. 80
Hinderliter H. 149
Hintikka J. 145, 149
Hirohito (Emperor of Japan) 95
Hitaka K. 201
Hitler A. 23, 42, 80–83, 88, 92, 125
Hoare S. 72, 83, 96
Hobbes T. 21, 29, 74, 108, 112
Hobhouse L.T. 73
Hobson J.A. 12, 24
Hochberg H. 149
Hodgson D. 202
Høgsbjerg C. 60
Hookway C. 150
Hope V. 150
Horowitz I.L. 150
Hudson K. 119
Hugo V. 7, 8
Huizinga J. 81
Hull W.I. 9
Hume D. 36
Hutchins R.M. 29
Hylton P. 44, 150

Imaguire G. 150
Infeld L. 109
Inkpin A. 60
Innis H. 29
Ioffe A.F. 99
Ironside P. 150
Irvine A.D. 44, 150
Irvine W.B. 150
Isocrates (Greek Rhetorician) 1
Iyer R.N. 27

Jackson T.F. 30
Jacquette D. 148, 150
Jadacki J.J. 150
Jager R. 150
Jankélévitch V. 16
Järnefelt A. 79
Jay J. 21, 122, 130
Jesson G. 144
Jesus Christ 31
Jha A. 150
John A. 124
Johnson F. 60
Johnson K. 122
Johnston C. 150, 159
Joliot-Curie J.F. 102, 109, 120
Jones J.H. 17
Jorgensen L.M. 150
Judson L. 150
Julka K.L. 150
Jung D. 150

Kagawa T. 79
Kahler E. 29
Kallen H.M. 146
Kamenev L.B. 68
Kant I. 6, 21, 25, 33, 37, 122
Kapitza P. 114
Kaplan D. 150
Kasrils R. 75, 126, 128, 147, 202
Katz W.G. 29
Kellogg F. 23, 78, 79
Kemp G. 151
Kennedy J.F. 124, 126, 127, 134
Kennedy J.M. 15
Kennedy R.F. 126
Kennedy T.C. 151
Kerensky A. 59
Kerff W. 14
Keswani A.M. 125
Keynes J.M. 23, 51, 52, 73, 78, 80
Khrushchev N.S. 118, 119, 125–128, 134
Kimber C. 91

King M. 27
King M.L. 30, 31, 78, 137
Kinrade A.D. 151
Kirk J.A. 30
Kitchener R.F. 151
Kleene S. 147
Klein A. 151
Klembe E.D. 151
Klement K.C. 151
Kneale W.C. 151
Knight F.H. 151
Knight M.K. 151
Knox T.M. 7
Koehler C.J. 151
Kopfermann H. 110
Korhonen A. 151
Kovacs D. 151
Kripke S.A. 151
Kulas J. 149
Kuntz P.G. 151
Kuzin A. 117

Lacassagne A. 117
Lackey D. 100, 101, 151, 202
Ladd W. 7
Lademacher H. 13
Lagerlöf S. 79
Landini G. 44, 147, 151
Lang G. 98
Lansbury G. 59, 80, 84, 85
Lapointe S. 151, 154
Laschitza A. 14
Laski H.J. 73, 76
Lassalle F. 36
Latta R. 6
Laue (von) M. 110
Lawrence D.H. 51, 203
Lawrence T.J. 9
Le Roy E. 16
Lebens S. 44, 152
Lee H. 51
Lefebvre R. 69
Leggett H.W. 152

Leitgeb H. 153
Lenin V.I. 11–13, 66–68
Lessing D. 124
Levine J. 152
Levy A.R. 19
Lewis A.C. 148
Lewis J. 152
Lidman S. 131
Liebknecht K. 13, 14
Liebknecht W. 36
Lief A. 79
Lilienthal D. 97
Ling P. 30
Link G. 152
Linsky B. 44, 152, 161
Lipkind D. 152
Lippincott M. 108, 152
Litvinov M. 86
Lloyd George D. 52, 59–62, 64, 65, 80
Löbe P. 79
Locke J. 36
Lord Arnold 87
Lord Cecil 79, 87, 96
Lord Cherwell 96
Lord Derby 61
Lord Llewellin 96
Lord Lothian (Philip Kerr) 23, 24, 64
Lord Milner 59
Lord Pethick-Lawrence 96
Lord Shepherd 129
Lord Simon 120
Lord Strabolgi 96
Lowe-Porter H.T. 81
Lück U. 152
Lvov G. 59
Lynch M.P. 164
Lynn S. 31

MacBride F. 152
MacColl H. 203
MacDonald R. 47, 60, 69, 73, 74, 77, 80, 84
Machuca D. 147

Macmillan H. 112, 116, 124, 125
Madigan T. 152
Madison J. 21, 122, 140
Magnano G. 202
Magnano San Lio G. 145
Magnes J.L. 79
Mahler A.G. 130
Maier-Leibnitz H. 110
Makin G. 152
Makino T. 201
Malenkov G.M. 105
Mancosu P. 152
Mann T. 60, 79, 81
Manning W.T. 93
Mao Zedong 71, 110
Maracchia S. 152
Marinetti F.T. 16
Marjolin R. 152
Marrin A. 17
Marseille W. 99, 100
Marsh R.C. 194
Marshall C. 59, 62
Marshall E. 21
Martin G. 152
Martin K. 93
Martin W. 152
Martins A. 152
Marx K. 10, 11
Massingham H.J. 46
Mathien T. 158
Mattauch J. 110
Mattausch J. 119
Matteucci N. 2
May L. 4, 89
Mazzini G. 8, 82
McAllister G. 107–108
McGeeahan J.E. 93
McHenry L.B. 146
McIlwain C.H. 29
Mckenney J.L. 153
Mckeon M. 153
McLean A.C. 30
McLendon H.J. 153

McMichael A. 153
McTaggart J.E. 36
Merton T. 27
Meyer A.E. 81
Meyer K. 14
Miah S. 153
Miéville H.-L. 15
Migliaccio C. 16
Miliband R. 60, 123
Milkov N. 153
Mill J.S. 19, 36
Miller J.D.B. 17
Millington E. 98
Minnion J. 119
Miracchi S. 154
Molla S. 30
Molotov V. 112
Monk R. 44, 45, 51, 58, 96, 111, 120,
  153, 158
Monro D.H. 153
Monroe J. 22, 58
Montebello P. 15
Montefiore D. 60
Montesquieu (Secondat
  de) C.L. 18, 19
Monti M. 23
Moore G.E. 36, 37
Moore H.T. 203
Moorehead C. 44, 153
Morel E.D. 47, 69
Morgan M.L. 5
Morikawa K. 131
Mormann T. 153
Morrell O. 62
Morrell P. 47
Morris C.W. 153
Morris W.E. 153
Morrison S. 85
Mosley O. 80
Muehlmann R. 153
Mühlmann W.E. 3, 5, 57, 89, 133
Muirhead J.H. 172
Muller H.J. 109, 117

Mumford S. 153
Munitz M.K. 145
Muravyov M.N. 8
Murray G. 50, 55, 57, 79
Murry J.M. 85
Musacchio E. 201
Mussolini B. 23, 42, 83, 92
Myers O.F. 153

Nacci M. 153
Naess A. 27
Nagasawa Y. 143
Nagel E. 154
Nakhnikian G. 130, 154, 157
Napoleon III (Emperor of France) 8
Narskii I.S. 154
Nasim O.W. 154
Nasser G.A. 114
Nehru J. 128
Nelson M.T. 154
Nicholas II (Tsar of Russia) 8, 40
Nicod J. 154
Nietzsche F. 15, 82, 94
Nisbet B. 7
Northcliffe A.C.W. 52
Norton W. 88
Nuccetelli S. 155
Nuzzo A. 160

Oaklander L.N. 154
Oberdan T. 154
Ogawa I. 117
Ogbozo C.N. 154
Ogden S. 154
Oglesby C.P. 131
Oliphant M. 117
Ongley J. 44, 145
Orayen R. 154
Orilia F. 154
Ortega y Gasset J. 81
Osborne J. 124
Otto E. 16
Overskeid G. 154

Padia C. 154
Palazón Mayoral M.R. 154
Palmer A. 153
Paneth F.A. 110
Pankhurst S. 60
Parekh B.C. 27
Park J. 154
Parker R.A.C. 83
Parkin F. 119
Pasquino G. 2
Passy F. 8
Patterson W.A. 154
Patton L. 154
Pauli W.E. 110
Pauling L.C. 102, 109
Peach L.J. 31
Peano G. 37
Pears D.F. 154
Pearsall Smith A. 36
Pelham J. 155
Perkins R. 100, 101, 155, 203
Perry L.R. 155
Perry R.B. 49, 57
Perus J. 19
Peters F. 155
Phemister P. 147
Pickel B. 155
Pieper A. 15
Pigden C.R. 155, 202
Pinay A. 112
Pincock C. 151, 154
Pistone S. 22, 24
Pitt J. 155
Plato 71
Polignac (de) M. 5
Pollock F. 41
Pomogaeva E.F. 154
Ponsonby A. 79, 80, 87
Ponticelli L. 155
Potter M.K. 44, 155
Powell C.F. 109, 112, 117, 118
Pratt S.L. 155
Price H. 155
Prichard H.A. 155

Pritchard C. 119
Proops I. 155
Pujia R. 155
Pulkkinen J. 156
Purcell A.A. 68
Puri R.-S. 27
Pyne K. 104

Quidde L. 79
Quine W.V.O. 45, 156
Quinton A. 156

Rabinowitch E. 117, 118
Rádl E. 79
Radner M. 156
Ragaz L. 79
Ramana Murthi V.V. 130
Randle M. 124, 125
Ransome P. 91
Rawls J. 4, 5
Rawnsley D. 91
Read H.E. 124
Ready W.B. 156
Reck E.H. 149
Redfearn D. 27
Redfield R. 29
Reed B. 147
Reichel N. 15
Reinhardt L. 156
Reitan E. 4, 5
Rempel R.A. 46, 72, 165
Reves E. 95
Reynold (de) L.G. 17
Ribeiro H.J. 156
Riezler W. 110
Riverso E. 156
Riviere J. 26
Rizzacasa A. 156
Robbins L. 23, 24
Roberts G.W. 156
Robinson D. 156
Robles J.A. 156
Rodrigo P. 16
Rodriguez-Consuegra F.A. 156

Roland Holst H. 79
Rolf B. 156
Rolland R. 19–21, 70, 71, 79, 133
Roosevelt F.D. 92
Roosevelt P.R. 27
Roper H. 148
Rosenbaum S.P. 156
Rosenberg J.F. 156
Rosenbloom M. 97
Ross D. 156
Rossi E. 24, 25
Rossolillo F. 24
Rota Ghibaudi S. 156
Rotblat J. 109, 112, 117, 118
Rouilhan (de) P. 156
Rowntree J. 47
Royden M. 32
Rudolph L.I. 27
Rudolph S.H. 27
Ruja H. 66, 144, 156, 202
Russell C. 42
Russell D. 75, 171
Russell E. 114
Russell F. 36
Russell H. 156
Russell J. 35, 40, 61
Russell K. 40
Russell P. 203
Ruyssen T. 7
Ryan A. 104, 125, 157

Saarinen E. 157
Sainsbury R.M. 157
Saint-Laurent L. 110
Saint-Pierre (Castel de) C.I. 5, 6
Saint-Simon (de) C.-H. 8
Sakata S. 131
Samuel H. 96
Sandys D. 116
Santamaria Velasco F.O. 157
Santayana G. 157
Sartre J.-P. 30, 44, 130, 131, 135
Savage C.W. 157

Schaar (van der) M. 157
Schenk H. 31
Schiller F.C.S. 157
Schilpp P.A. 157, 185, 186
Schmid A.-F. 157
Schneewind J.B. 202
Schoenman R. 43, 123–125, 129–131, 157
Schott L.K. 31
Schram S.R. 71
Schucking W. 9
Schultz B. 157
Schumann H. 14
Schwarcz V. 157
Schweitzer A. 129
Schwerin A. 157
Scioscioli M. 8
Scott M. 43, 124, 125
Seay G. 155
Seckel A. 157
Sellon J.-J. 7
Selove W. 117
Semyonov N.N. 99
Senofonte C. 158
Sesmeyanov A.N. 112
Shapiro S. 146
Shaw G.B. 36, 76
Shaw J.L. 158
Shearn M. 158
Sheppard H.R.L. 85
Shosky J. 158
Shukla J. 158
Shute C. 158
Sibley M.Q. 3, 5, 57, 132
Siegbahn M. 110
Sierra Mejía H. 158
Silber J.R. 7
Sinclair U. 79
Singh A. 158
Sipriot P. 19
Skinner H. 68
Skobeltzyn D.V. 113, 117, 118
Slater J.G. 44, 70, 158
Slaw T. 68

Smart H.R. 158
Smillie R. 39
Smith A. 19
Smith H.M. 158
Smith J.F. 158
Snowden E. 68
Snowden P. 39, 60, 69, 80
Soames S. 158
Sofri G. 28
Sokolow J.A. 27
Spadolini G. 8
Spadoni C. 144
Spence P. 42
Spengler O. 17
Spiegelberg H. 158
Spinelli A. 24, 25
Spinoza B. 5, 41, 140
Spurrett D. 156
Stalin J. 42, 96, 98, 104
Stancati C. 16
Stapledon O. 158
Starr W.T. 19
Sterba J. 4, 89
Stevens G. 158
Stokes R.R. 116
Stol A. 158
Stone I.F. 159
Stone P. 152, 159
Strachey J. 26
Strachey L. 51
Strachey O. 159
Strassmann F. 110
Strauss F.-J. 110
Streit C.K. 91
Stroll A. 159
Strong C.A. 159
Stubbs J.O. 60
Sullivan P. 159
Sumares M. 159
Sutton E. 81
Swanwick H.M. 47
Swartz M. 47
Szilárd L. 117

Taft W.H. 58
Tagore R. 79
Tait K. 159
Tallon H.J. 159
Tamerlane (founder of the Timurid Empire) 27
Taubeneck S.A. 7
Tawney R.H. 76
Taylor G.G. 159
Taylor K. 31
Taylor R. 119
Tempini N. 159
Textor M. 152, 157
Thant (U) 128
Thibault O. 31
Thierry A. 8
Thirring H. 117
Thomas J.E. 159
Thomas M.H. 21
Thoreau H.D. 27
Tolstoy L. 2, 3, 19, 21, 25, 27, 52, 93, 133, 134
Tomonaga S. 117
Topchiev A.V. 117
Torlontano G. 8
Treitschke (von) H. 15, 16
Trejo W. 159
Trevelyan C. 47
Trevelyan R. 93
Trotsky L. 13, 66, 68, 78
Trotnow H. 14
Trucco A.M. 17
Tugnoli C. 159
Tugwell R.G. 29
Tully R.E. 159
Turcon S. 159
Turner B. 68
Turner J. 24

Unamuno (de) M. 79
Unna S. 159
Unruh (von) F. 79
Urbaniak R. 159

Urey H. 110
Urmson J.O. 159
Usborne H.C. 98, 107
Ushenko A. 160

Vaillant-Couturier P. 69
Van Patten J. 160
Vavilov S. 99
Vax L. 160
Vellacott J. 160
Vercillo F. 16
Verheggen C. 161
Vernant D. 160
Victoria (Queen of the United Kingdom) 35
Vuillemin J. 160

Wahl R. 160
Wainwright W. 106
Waismann F. 203
Walcher W. 110
Wallas G. 36
Wallhead R.C. 68
Wang H. 160
Warren G. 56
Waterlow S. 160
Watling J. 160
Watson J.B. 77
Webb B. 36
Webb S. 36, 76
Weber T. 27
Wedeking G.A. 150
Weiss B. 160
Weisskopf V. 117
Weizsäcker (von) C.F. 110
Wells H.G. 36, 79
Wenger A. 115
Wesker A. 124
Westphal K.R. 160
Wettstein H. 160
White S. 60
Whitehead A.N. 37, 160, 203
Whittemore R. 21

Wickham H. 160
Wielenberg E.J. 161
Williams R. 68
Willis K. 161
Wills R.W. 30
Wilmers A. 31
Wilson A.N. 27
Wilson H. 129
Wilson M. 161
Wilson T.W. 22, 56, 58, 65, 83
Wilson W.K. 161
Winchester I. 161
Winkler H.R. 80
Wirtz K. 110
Wishon D. 161
Wittgenstein L. 38, 39, 45
Wittner L.S. 102, 119
Wohlgemuth H. 14
Wolf L.O. 161
Wood A. 7, 44, 45, 161
Woodger J.H. 161
Woodhouse H. 161
Woolf L. 47, 51, 52, 91, 92

Woolf V. 51
Wright D.G. 158

Xenophon (Greek
 philosopher) 1

Yibao X. 161
Young N. 88
Yourgrau P. 161
Yourgrau W. 150
Yukawa H. 109, 117

Zach R. 152
Zajac M. 161
Zak G. 148
Zalabardo J.L. 150, 161
Zavadivker N. 161
Zhou L. 161
Zhou P. 117
Zijiang D. 161
Zouhar M. 161
Zürcher J.M. 162
Zweig S. 19, 79

Printed in Great Britain
by Amazon

f5b6b6d8-1a8b-4968-9b08-fa63cc5b0912R02